POPULAR AMERICAN COMPOSERS

FROM REVOLUTIONARY TIMES TO THE PRESENT

POPULAR AMERICAN COMPOSERS

FROM REVOLUTIONARY TIMES TO THE PRESENT

A Biographical and Critical Guide

Compiled and Edited by
DAVID EWEN

With an Index of Songs and Other Compositions

THE H. W. WILSON COMPANY
NEW YORK   1962

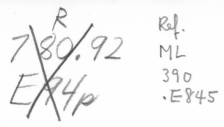

INTRODUCTION

Popular American Composers: From Revolutionary Times to the Present is a biographical guide (the first of its kind) to 130 of the foremost American popular composers of the past and present: ranging chronologically from William Billings (1746-1800) to André Previn (1929-   ) and alphabetically from Richard Adler to Victor Young. Approximately two thirds of the composers represented in this volume belong to the past; only one third are still alive.

The editor has attempted to make the representation of composers no longer living as comprehensive as possible. In many cases, biographical material on these men is hard to come by and up to now has been inaccessible to the average music lover seeking such information. It is hoped that this volume will fill a long-felt need in musical literature by providing material on past American popular composers whose biographies have not been readily available.

In the case of living popular composers, the editor has necessarily been selective. He has chosen those composers who in his opinion are of most interest to most people by virtue of their success, their productiveness, their contribution to our popular music. This group is not limited to composers from Tin Pan Alley, Broadway, and Hollywood. It includes also composers of art songs which have gained such widespread circulation that they are a part of our popular literature, and composers of instrumental or concert music of popular appeal.

For his material on living composers, the editor has in most cases gone to first-hand sources—the composers themselves. Of the fifty-four living composers found in this volume, forty-one were interviewed by the editor either in New York or in Hollywood; the others were asked for information by mail. To insure accuracy and authority, the editor dispatched to each living composer a first draft of his biography. Forty-five composers were kind enough to return the drafts with appropriate corrections and valuable interpolations and suggestions.

To supplement the biographical material a chronological list of composers and an index of songs and other compositions are included.

Some of the photographs in this volume came from the composers themselves; some were provided by ASCAP (the American Society of Composers, Authors and Publishers); and still others were found in the archives of the Music Division of the New York Public Library. The editor wishes to express his thanks for these courtesies.

David Ewen

Little Neck, New York

In the present printing the chronological list on pages 193-194 has been revised to include death dates of composers who have died since the first printing in 1962.

CONTENTS

POPULAR AMERICAN COMPOSERS

FROM REVOLUTIONARY TIMES TO THE PRESENT

Richard Adler *1921-*

RICHARD ADLER was born in New York City on August 3, 1921. Though he is the son of the eminent concert pianist and teacher Clarence Adler, he received no formal music instruction. As a matter of fact, he could neither play the piano nor read music when he first began writing songs. He received his academic education at the Columbia Grammar School, and at the University of North Carolina from which he was graduated in 1943. At North Carolina he took a course in playwriting with Paul Green.

After completing his college education, Adler served for three years in the South Pacific as an officer aboard a YP-PC boat. Upon leaving the armed forces, Adler found a job with the advertising department of the Celanese Corporation of America. He had already started to write songs, and in 1948 he decided to devote himself completely to songwriting, even though he had thus far been unsuccessful in marketing any of his compositions.

A decisive turn in his life came in 1950 when the well-known composer Frank Loesser introduced him to Jerold Ross. Ross was also a young, ambitious songwriter who had failed to interest either publishers or producers in his music. It was Loesser's idea that the two men might work together effectively. Adler and Ross at once responded favorably to each other, with the sympathy of two young men on common ground whose sights were fixed on the same goal. They formed a songwriting team—a somewhat unique arrangement since both of them wrote both words *and* music. For a while, in addition to writing songs, they earned a living writing special material for "Stop the Music" (a highly successful radio giveaway program of that period) and for such distinguished stage personalities as Jimmy Durante, Eddie Fisher, and Marlene Dietrich.

RICHARD ADLER

Soon Frank Loesser, who was head of his own publishing firm, began to issue some of their songs. The first to become a hit of major proportions was "Rags to Riches," which was represented on the "Hit Parade" over a period of several months and which sold over two million copies of sheet music and records. This song had been inspired by Eddie Fisher's career and a casual remark by Adler to Ross that Fisher had gone "from rags to riches." By 1954, Adler and Ross had written over 150 songs, among which were a few other major successes: "Teasin'," "The Newspaper Song," "The Strange Little Girl," "Now Hear This," "Even Now," "You're So Much a Part of Me," and "True Love Goes On and On." They also entered the Broadway theatre by contributing four songs to John Murray Anderson's *Almanac,* which opened on December 10, 1953.

Their *modus operandi,* which was unusual enough to deserve some explanation, consisted in working jointly on both the words and the music, each editing and revising what the other wrote. "It's impossible to say who does what and when," Adler once told an interviewer. "But we've got rules. If I come in with what I think is a beautiful idea, and he says, 'I don't like it,' I can scream, I can rave, but it's out. It obviates arguments. There has to be unanimity in our operation."

Their talent and success attracted the eminent stage director George Abbott, who was planning a musical comedy based on Richard Bissell's amusing novel *7½ Cents* about a strike in a Midwestern pajama factory. He contracted with Adler and Ross to write the complete score. Renamed *The Pajama Game,* the musical comedy opened on May 13, 1954, to become one of the outstanding box-office triumphs of the Broadway theatre, with a run of over a thousand performances. Briskly paced by George Abbott's direction, and enlivened by the performances of John Raitt and Carol Haney, *The Pajama Game* was, as Robert Coleman reported, "a deliriously daffy delight . . . a royal flush and a grand slam rolled into one."

The consistently fresh and lively score had two numbers that were hits of the first order: "Hey, There" and "Hernando's Hideaway." "Richard Adler and Jerry Ross," said Brooks Atkinson, "have written an exuberant score in any number of good American idioms without self-consciousness. . . . Mr. Adler and Mr. Ross wrote like musicians with a sense of humor."

Their second musical, also a formidable box-office success, was *Damn Yankees,* which opened on May 5, 1955. Another George Abbott production, it also enjoyed a run of more than a thousand performances. *Damn Yankees* was an adaptation of Douglass Wallop's novel *The Year the Yankees Lost the Pennant,* in which the baseball-loving hero makes a pact with the devil: he trades his soul so that his beloved Washington Senators may become a pennant-winning team, with himself as its outstanding star. With Ray Walston as the devil, Stephen Douglass as the baseball star, and Gwen Verdon as an irresistible witch, *Damn Yankees* was, as Brooks Atkinson reported, "as shiny as a new baseball," and proved to be "among the

healthy clouts of the campaign." The music of Adler and Ross was one of its strong points. "The music," said Mr. Atkinson further, "had the spirit and brass you'd expect to find out at the ball park." The standout numbers were "Heart" and "Whatever Lola Wants."

Both *The Pajama Game* and *Damn Yankees* became in time successful motion pictures—the former in 1957, starring Doris Day, with some of the principals of the original stage production; the latter, a year later, with Ray Walston, Gwen Verdon, and Tab Hunter.

With two solid stage successes in a row, and at least a dozen songs that were leaders in the field (they sold in excess of seven million records), Adler and Ross were recognized as the most talented songwriting team to emerge on the Broadway scene since World War II. Tragically, this flourishing partnership came to a sudden end. In November 1955 Jerold Ross died of chronic bronchiectasis before his thirtieth birthday.

Since Ross's death, Richard Adler has worked alone, writing lyrics as well as music. In 1958 his song "Everybody Loves a Lover" sold half a million records in its first six weeks. In 1958 he also wrote the words and music for two ambitious television musicals: *Little Women,* produced on October 16, and *The Gift of the Magi,* on December 9.

On January 3, 1958, Adler was married to Sally Ann Howes, the British star of stage and screen, who succeeded Julie Andrews in the leading feminine role in the New York production of *My Fair Lady.*

Richard Adler made his return to Broadway in the fall of 1961 with the music and lyrics to *Kwamina* (text by Robert Alan Aurthur). This musical, set in a West African colony, focuses on the relationship of an African and a white woman. "We were more interested," explains Adler, "in showing the conflicts between the old and new Africa than with a love affair. There's no physical manifestation of the friendship between the hero, who is an English-educated Negro, and Eve, the white African girl, because we're just showing one aspect of African society." Sally Ann Howes played the leading female role.

Adler is also a leading writer of advertising jingles. He has created the highly successful commercials for Newport and Kent cigarettes, among others.

ABOUT:
Green, Stanley. The World of Musical Comedy. New York Times Magazine, June 19, 1955.

Milton Ager 1893-

MILTON AGER was born into a middle-class family in Chicago, Illinois, on October 6, 1893, the sixth of nine children. Soon after the turn of the century, his sister bought a piano which Milton learned to play by a process of trial and error. His interest in music quickening, he began teaching himself to read and write music, encouraged by his mother, who was an amateur soprano. Ager's father, however, wanted him to prepare for some profession, and discouraged all this musical activity. But after grammar school and three years at McKinley High School, Milton Ager abandoned formal schooling in 1910.

His professional career in music began that year, when he worked as a pianist in local motion-picture houses playing illustrated songs during intermission. After that he found a job as a song plugger in Chicago and in the Southwest, and for a brief period he was accompanist for several performers on the Orpheum vaudeville circuit.

In 1913 he went to New York to advance his career in music. For a while he was employed as a staff pianist and song plugger, and subsequently as an arranger, for the publishing house of Waterson, Berlin and Snyder. During this period he collaborated with Pete Wendling in writing instrumental piano pieces which they sold outright to Waterson, Berlin and Snyder for $25 a composition. After leaving this publishing firm, Ager worked for the William Jerome Music Company. It was at this time that he wrote his first popular song, "Everything Is Peaches Down in Georgia," the melody produced in collaboration with George W. Meyer to lyrics by Grant Clarke. Al Jolson sang it at the Winter Garden in 1918, Leo Feist published it, and it became Ager's first hit.

During World War I, Ager served in the morale division of the army at Fort

MILTON AGER

Greenleaf, Georgia. Upon his return to civilian life, his first song was "Anything Is Nice If It Comes from Dixieland," once again written with George W. Meyer and Grant Clarke. This was followed immediately by two other moderately successful songs, both written with Cliff Hess to Howard Johnson's lyrics: "I'm in Heaven When I'm in My Mother's Arms" and "Freckles." Ager scored an even greater success with the song "Nobody's Baby" in 1921, written with Benny Davis and Lester Santly; this song was revived in 1939 for Judy Garland in the motion picture *Andy Hardy Meets a Debutante*.

Ager's first Broadway stage score was written in 1920 for the musical *What's in a Name*. One of the songs, "A Young Man's Fancy" (lyrics by Jack Yellen and John Murray Anderson), sold over a million records. Between 1922 and 1923 Ager wrote the music for two more Broadway shows, *Zig Zag* and *The Ted Lewis Frolic*, both failures. Meanwhile, in 1922, Ager helped found the song publishing house of Ager, Yellen and Bornstein. Among its earliest publications were two Ager hit songs with lyrics by Jack Yellen, "Lovin' Sam" and "Who Cares?" The latter was interpolated by Al Jolson in the Winter Garden extravaganza *Bombo*.

Between 1922 and 1930, Ager worked mainly with the lyricist Jack Yellen. Among their outstanding songs during this period were the following: "Mama Goes Where Papa Goes," "Bagdad," "Big Boy," "I Wonder What's Become of Sally," "Could I? I Certainly Could," "Ain't She Sweet?" "Crazy Words, Crazy Tune," and "Forgive Me," the last successfully revived in 1952. They also wrote songs for two important Broadway productions, *Rain or Shine* (1928) and John Murray Anderson's *Almanac* (1929).

A leading figure in Tin Pan Alley by the time the motion-picture screen had acquired sound, Ager was one of the first composers called out to Hollywood where, with his lyricist Jack Yellen, he began writing songs for motion pictures. Their first assignment was *Honky Tonk*, a film starring Sophie Tucker, in which five of their numbers appeared, including "I'm the Last of the Red Hot Mamas." For *The King of Jazz*, which featured Paul Whiteman and his orchestra, they wrote "Happy Feet," "A Bench in the Park," and "Song of the Dawn." For *Chasing Rainbows*, which starred Jack Benny, they created one of Ager's all-time favorites, "Happy Days Are Here Again." This song is unusual in that it was one of the earliest examples of a song with an extended chorus (fifty-six measures). One bandleader at the time remarked about its length: "Kill that tape-worm, it's too long!" Nevertheless, Ager stoutly refused to reduce his chorus to traditional length. In 1932 an alert song plugger succeeded in having the song played at the Democratic presidential convention in Chicago, after which it became the theme music for Franklin D. Roosevelt's campaigns. Since 1932, it has been played at virtually every presidential convention of the Democratic party.

In 1930, Yellen and Ager, after a decade of creating song successes as a team, had what Ager chooses to describe as a "Gilbert and Sullivan break-up." From then on, they went separate ways. Yellen sold his interest in Ager, Yellen and Bornstein, and Ager began writing melodies with other lyricists. Ager withdrew from the publishing business in 1944 when his firm was sold to the Advanced Music Corporation.

Since 1931, Ager's most important and successful songs have included: "You Can't Pull the Wool Over My Eyes" (with Charles Newman and Murray Mincher); "Auf Wiedersehen, My Dear," written in collaboration with Al Hoffman, Al Goodhart and Ed Nelson; "Roll Out of Bed with a Smile" (with Joe Young); "Trouble in Paradise," "If I Didn't Care," "In a Little Red Barn," and "Trust in Me," written in collaboration with Ned Wever and Jean Schwartz; "I Threw a Bean Bag at the Moon," and "Seein' Is Believin'" (lyrics by Stanley Adams); "Ten Pins in the Sky" (lyrics by Joe McCarthy), introduced by Judy Garland in the motion picture *Listen Darling;* "There's Rain in My Eyes," written with Joe McCarthy and Jean Schwartz; "Keep 'Em Smiling" (lyrics by Billy Rose); "This I Love Above All" (lyrics by the composer); "The Show Must Go On" (lyrics by Benny Davis); "Only a Moment Ago" (lyrics by Rose); "An Orchid for the Lady" (lyrics by Wever); and "Until You Said Goodbye," written with Benny Davis and Harry Akst.

Besides his prolific songwriting activity, Ager's achievements include numerous piano and band arrangements, as well as orchestrations, for other composers and publishers.

Fred Ahlert *1892-1953*

FRED E. AHLERT was born in New York City on September 19, 1892. Born with perfect pitch, he began to study the piano in his fourteenth year and made rapid progress. While attending Townsend Harris Hall High School, he turned to both the performance and the writing of popular music. For two summers he worked with Ben Bernie in an ice cream parlor at a salary of $7.00 a week.

After attending the City College of New York and completing his studies at Fordham Law School, he went to work in Tin Pan Alley. At the Waterson, Berlin and Snyder music publishing company, he made arrangements for the Irving Aaronson Commanders. He also wrote special material for several vaudeville performers (including the Avon Comedy Four, the Watson Sisters, and Fields and Seeley) and wrote arrangements for the Fred Waring Glee Club.

His first published composition was *Beets and Turnips,* an instrumental piece written

FRED AHLERT

ASCAP

with Cliff Hess and published in 1914. In 1920, Ahlert had his first song hit in "My Mammy's Arms" (lyrics by Sam Lewis and Joe Young). Between 1920 and 1928 several other highly successful songs appeared: "You Oughta See My Baby" (lyrics by Roy Turk); "I Gave You Up Just Before You Threw Me Down" (lyrics by Harry Ruby and Bert Kalmar); "Put Away a Little Ray of Golden Sunshine for a Rainy Day" (lyrics by Lewis and Young); "Maybe She'll Write," written with Ted Snyder (lyrics by Roy Turk); and "There's a Cradle in Caroline" (lyrics by Lewis and Young).

One of the outstanding song hits of Ahlert's career was "I'll Get By" (lyrics by Turk), published in 1928. In its own time it enjoyed sheet-music and record sales exceeding a million copies each. It was revived in 1944 and enjoyed a new success.

In 1929 Ahlert went to Hollywood for his first assignment, *Marianne*, starring Marion Davies in her first talking picture. Later he wrote songs for other screen productions, including *Navy Blues, Free and Easy, A Guy Named Joe,* and *Faithful in My Fashion.*

In 1937 Ahlert wrote the score for *The Riviera Follies,* a New York night club revue, and in 1940 for *It Happens on Ice,* the first Broadway ice revue, starring Sonja Henie. Meanwhile, from 1929 on, he pro-

duced a long string of song hits to Roy Turk's lyrics. Of special interest are "Mean to Me"; "Walkin' My Baby Back Home," written with Harry Richman, whose performances made it famous; "Where the Blue of the Night Meets the Gold of the Day," written with Bing Crosby and used as Crosby's theme song; "Why Dance?"; and "Love, You Funny Thing."

To Edgar Leslie's lyrics, Ahlert wrote: "Just a Little Home to the Old Folks"; "Lovely"; and "The Moon Was Yellow." To Joe Young's lyrics: "Sing an Old-Fashioned Song"; "Life Is a Song"; "I'm Gonna Sit Right Down and Write Myself a Letter," published in 1935 and revived more than twenty years later with phenomenal success by Billy Williams; "You Dropped Me Like a Red-Hot Penny"; "Take My Heart"; and "To a Sweet Pretty Thing."

In 1948 Ahlert succeeded Deems Taylor as president of ASCAP, holding this post until 1950. Ahlert died of a heart attack in New York City on October 20, 1953.

ABOUT:
Variety, July 31, 1940.

Louis Alter *1902-*

LOUIS ALTER has been as successful in the writing of popular instrumental compositions for orchestra as in the writing of songs. He was born in Haverhill, Massachusetts, on June 18, 1902. In his ninth year, while attending public school, he began to study the piano. At thirteen, he worked as a pianist in the local movie theatre, providing accompaniment to silent films; but instead of using the usual stereotyped repertory he would improvise his own mood music. As a student at Haverhill High School he led a jazz band that performed at school dances. After his graduation from high school, his family moved to Boston. There he attended the New England Conservatory, where he acquired a well-rounded background in the classics as a piano student of Stuart Mason.

Alter went to New York in 1924. The vaudeville star Nora Bayes hired him as her accompanist (a job previously held by George Gershwin), and for five years Alter toured with Bayes in America and Europe. During this time he occasionally wrote mate-

LOUIS ALTER

rial and played the piano for other famous performers, including Irene Bordoni, Helen Morgan, and Beatrice Lillie. When occasionally at liberty, he worked as song-arranger for the publishing houses of Shapiro, Bernstein and Irving Berlin; this experience, he feels, served him well when he entered the songwriting field.

Between 1925 and 1927 Alter had several songs published, including "To Be Loved," "I'm in Love with You," and his first hit, "Blue Shadows" (lyrics by Ray Klages), the last heard originally in the Earl Carroll *Vanities* of 1927. In 1928, inspired by the sights, sounds, and moods of New York City, he wrote a work that made him famous, *Manhattan Serenade*. It was originally published as a piano solo but was immediately adapted for orchestra and recorded by Paul Whiteman and his orchestra, whose rendition was largely responsible for the world-wide popularity of the composition. It has since become a standard in the repertory of symphonic jazz. In 1942 one of the themes became the basis for a vocal version with lyrics by Harold Adamson.

Alter wrote four other highly impressive and frequently played orchestral impressions of New York: *Manhattan Moonlight* (1930), *Manhattan Masquerade* (1932), *Metropolitan Nocturne* (1935), and *Side Street in Gotham* (1938). *Manhattan Moonlight* re-

ceived high honors in a national competition conducted by RCA Victor in 1930. *Metropolitan Nocturne* was the source of and inspiration for an RKO movie short which won a bronze medal at the International Film Festival in Venice in 1936. In 1953 Alter wrote another ambitious orchestral work, a suite entitled *Jewels from Cartier*, in ten movements, each movement a musical representation of a different gem.

In 1929 Alter went to Hollywood. His first songs for the screen were "Love Ain't Nothin' but the Blues" (lyrics by Joe Goodwin) in *Lord Byron of Broadway*, and "Got a Feelin' for You" (lyrics by Jo Trent) in *Hollywood Revue*. He has since written songs for about twenty-five motion pictures. Two of his screen songs were nominated for Academy awards: "A Melody from the Sky" (lyrics by Sidney D. Mitchell), written for *Trail of the Lonesome Pine* (1936) and "Dolores" (lyrics by Frank Loesser), written for *Las Vegas Nights* (1941).

Other successful screen songs were "Rainbow on the River" (lyrics by Paul Francis Webster), written for the film of the same name; "Twilight on the Trail" for *Trail of the Lonesome Pine*, and "You Turned the Tables on Me" for *Sing, Baby, Sing* (lyrics by Sidney Mitchell); "A Thousand Dreams of You" (lyrics by Webster) for *You Live Only Once;* and "Do You Know What It Means to Miss New Orleans?" (lyrics by Eddie de Lange) for *New Orleans*. "Twilight on the Trail" was a great favorite with President Franklin D. Roosevelt; the manuscript and a copy of the Bing Crosby recording can be found in the Roosevelt Memorial Library in Hyde Park, New York.

Louis Alter has also written songs for the Broadway stage: "My Kinda Love" (lyrics by Trent) for *Americana* (1928), a song soon made famous by Bing Crosby; "I'm One of God's Children Who Hasn't Got Wings" (lyrics by Oscar Hammerstein II) for *Ballyhoo* (1930); and "The Key to My Heart" (lyrics by Ira Gershwin) for *The Social Register*. Among other productions in which Alter songs were heard were *Sweet and Low* (1930), *Hold Your Horses*, which starred Joe Cook (1931), and *Casino Varieties* (1934).

Several other Alter songs deserve mention: "Sand in My Shoes," "Stranger in the City," "Overnight," "Nina Never Knew," and "Circus." The last, with lyrics by Bob Russell, was written in 1949 in honor of Alter's friend John Ringling North of the Ringling Brothers Circus.

In 1943 Alter appeared twice as soloist with the Los Angeles Philharmonic at the Hollywood Bowl in performances of his compositions. During World War II he served in the Air Force and was assigned to provide musical entertainment for cadets in training at twenty-six air bases of the Western Command. For his contributions he was honored with a special citation.

In 1960, with Paul Taubman, Alter wrote "New York, My New York" which is officially featured at New York's "Salute to Seasons" ceremonies in the spring and fall.

ABOUT:
Billboard, July 1, 1950.

Leroy Anderson *1908-*

L EROY ANDERSON, famous for his "concert music with a pop quality" (his own description), was born on June 29, 1908, in Cambridge, Massachusetts, of Swedish ancestry. His father was a Cambridge postal clerk, his mother organist of the Swedish Congregational Church. It was from his mother that he received his first music lessons at the organ. At eleven, he studied piano at the New England Conservatory. The following year he wrote his first composition, a minuet for string quartet. "My teacher saw it and gave me composition and harmony lessons for a year," he reveals. Later he studied the double bass with Gaston Dufresne and the organ with Henry Gideon. On several occasions when Gideon was ill, Anderson substituted for him at Temple Israel in Boston. Another musical activity was singing in choruses in outdoor performances of opera and oratorios.

While attending high school in Cambridge, Anderson wrote the school's graduation songs for three consecutive years. In 1925 he was admitted to Harvard, where he majored in music under Walter Raymond Spalding and Walter Piston among others. He was graduated in 1929, *magna cum laude,*

LEROY ANDERSON

and with a Phi Beta Kappa key. A year later, on an Elkan Naumberg Fellowship, he received his master's degree, also from Harvard.

His professional career in music began in 1929 when he was appointed choirmaster and organist of the East Congregational Church in Milton, Massachusetts. He remained there six years. During this period he was also a member of the music faculty of Radcliffe College for two years; director of the Harvard University Band—for which he made many arrangements—for four years; and a doctoral student of foreign languages while preparing to be a language teacher.

In 1935, with a thesis still to be written, he gave up language studies and engaged in free-lance activities as a conductor, composer, and arranger in Boston and New York. Appearing as a guest conductor of the Boston Pops Orchestra in a performance of his own arrangement of Harvard songs, he made a strong impression on the orchestra's regular conductor, Arthur Fiedler, who engaged Anderson as the permanent orchestrator of the Boston Pops Orchestra. During the next few years, Anderson made many transcriptions for symphony orchestra of popular songs, show tunes, and excerpts from ballet and opera, all performed by the Boston Pops Orchestra. He revealed a fine command of orchestration. and an exceptional gift for endowing popular music with a rich and varied palette of colors.

In 1937 Anderson wrote his first original composition for the Boston Pops Orchestra, *Jazz Pizzicato*. In this work there was already in evidence his remarkable gift for combining popular and symphonic elements without creating any contradiction in style.

Called by the Army in 1942, he was stationed in Iceland, where he served as a translator and liaison officer with the Iceland press and radio. Two years later he was transferred to Military Intelligence in Washington, D.C., where he was put in charge of the Scandinavian desk. After his discharge from the Army, with the rank of captain, he returned to his post as orchestrator for the Boston Pops Orchestra. He also resumed writing short orchestral semiclassical pieces which the Boston Pops Orchestra introduced successfully. Among them were *Fiddle-Faddle* and *The Syncopated Clock*. These were so well received that Anderson was engaged by Decca Records to conduct a fifty-piece orchestra in recordings of his compositions.

Subsequent compositions by Anderson made him one of America's most successful composers of semiclassical music. In many of these works he revealed not merely a skill in technique and a rich melodic gift, but also an engaging sense of humor and a flair for burlesque. He was particularly successful in creating programmatic and descriptive pieces that effectively borrow sounds and rhythms of the extramusical world, such as the ticking of a clock, the clicking of a typewriter, and the ringing of sleigh bells.

The following are Anderson's best known and more frequently performed compositions: *Belle of the Ball, Blue Tango, Bugler's Holiday, China Doll, A Christmas Festival, Horse and Buggy, The Irish Suite, The Penny Whistle Song, The Phantom Regiment, Pyramid Dance, Saraband, Serenata, Sleigh Ride, A Trumpeter's Lullaby, The Typewriter, The Waltzing Cat. Blue Tango* was one of Anderson's greatest commercial hits, selling over two million records and becoming the first strictly instrumental number to reach first place on the Hit Parade. *The Typewriter* was effectively used in 1959 in the motion picture *But Not For Me*, starring Clark Gable.

During the early part of the Korean conflict, Anderson was recalled to active duty. "They had no job for me," he says, "so I ran an officers' bar at Fort Bragg. Four months before I got out they put me back in Intelligence."

In 1958 Anderson wrote his first Broadway musical comedy score, *Goldilocks* (lyrics by Walter and Jean Kerr and Joan Ford). Anderson's score for this comedy about silent movies—it opened in New York on October 11, 1958—was praised as "charming" and "tuneful." The best numbers were "Shall I Take My Heart and Go?," "Save a Kiss," and "I Never Know When."

Anderson has appeared successfully as a conductor of major American orchestras and has made numerous recordings.

ABOUT:
Boston Sunday Post, May 19, 1952; Harvard Alumni Bulletin, November 8, 1952; Pathfinder, May 7, 1952; Music Journal, November 1954

Harry Archer *1888-1960*

HARRY ARCHER was born in Creston, Iowa, on February 21, 1888. During his boyhood, attending elementary and high school in Creston, he was taught music by his mother. He worked his way through Michigan Military School, playing the trombone in various theatre and popular orchestras. He later pursued advanced studies in music at Knox College in Galesburg, Illinois, and at Princeton University. In both places he contributed music to school productions.

After completing his study of music, he settled in Chicago where he organized and played in dance orchestras. (He was an adept performer on every brass instrument except the French horn.) In 1912 he wrote his first score for the Broadway stage, *Pearl Maiden*, which starred Jefferson DeAngelis. Later he contributed songs to various musical comedies and revues, finally achieving a success of the first magnitude with *Little Jesse James*, which opened in New York on August 15, 1923, and which ran for 453 performances. What is perhaps Archer's most famous song, "I Love You," was written for this score, as were "Suppose I'd Never Met You," "My Home Town in Kansas," and "From Broadway to Main Street" (lyrics by Harlan Thompson). *Little Jesse James* toured the United States with four road companies, was produced in London as *Lucky Break,* was seen on the Continent and in Scandinavia, and enjoyed an eight-month run in Australia.

Among the Broadway musicals for which Archer later wrote the music were *My Girl* (1924), *Paradise Alley* (1924), *Merry, Merry* (1925), and *Twinkle, Twinkle* (1926). From the first of these came "You and I" (lyrics by Harlan Thompson); from the second, the title number (lyrics by Howard Johnson); from *Merry, Merry,* "It Must Be Love (lyrics by Harlan Thompson).

Other successful Archer songs include "White Sails," "On a Desert Isle," "I Was Blue," "You Know and I Know," "Alone in My Dreams," "I'm Going to Dance with the Guy What Brung Me," "Rainbow," "Where the Golden Daffodils Grow," "Alone in My Dreams," and "The Sweetest Girl This Side of Heaven."

Harry Archer was married to the actress Ruth Gillette. During his last years he lived in retirement in New York City, on East 48th Street. He died in Doctors Hospital, New York, on April 23, 1960.

ABOUT:
Variety, April 27, 1960.

Harold Arlen *1905-*

HAROLD ARLEN was born Hyman Arluck in Buffalo, New York, on February 15, 1905. When he was seven he sang in the choir of the synagogue where his father was cantor. His mother encouraged him to take music lessons: she wanted him to become a music teacher so that he could select his own working hours and thus observe the Sabbath.

Harold soon revealed a fascination with popular music. "My big interest," he has said, "was in the jazz instrumentalists of the day. I even ran away from home once to hear the Memphis Five, a Dixieland group. They were my heroes." When he was fifteen he abandoned school and started earning his living by playing the piano in Buffalo cafés. Before long he organized his own ensemble, consisting of a piano, a violin, and a drum, which he called "The Snappy Trio." In time "The Snappy Trio" grew into a quintet, "The Southbound Shufflers," which performed on lake steamers. Later Arlen joined an eleven-

HAROLD ARLEN

man ensemble, "The Buffalodians." "I was the singer, pianist, and arranger," he has explained. "I could always improvise, and I loved to invent unconventional turns for the men in the band who couldn't do anything but follow the written melody. I wanted them to get off it and sound like somebody from New York."

Arlen wrote his first songs in 1924—"My Gal, My Pal" and "I Never Knew What Love Could Do." Neither one was published. "No one would ever have known from the early songs that I would have, could have, become a composer," Arlen says. His first published piece of music appeared in 1926, after he had moved to New York: a "blues fantasy" for piano, *Minor Gaff,* written in collaboration with Dick George.

After Arlen went to New York in 1925, his novel arrangements for jazz band interested members of the trade, particularly Arnold Johnson, then leader of the pit orchestra in the George White *Scandals* of 1928. Johnson hired Arlen as pianist, arranger, and vocalist; in that edition of the *Scandals,* Arlen could be heard singing in the pit during intermission.

Vincent Youmans became impressed with Arlen's talent and hired him as a singer for his musical *Great Day.* One day, Arlen was asked to substitute for an absent rehearsal pianist. During a break in that rehearsal, Arlen improvised a vamp on one of Youmans' songs. Will Marion Cooke, conductor of a Negro chorus appearing in *Great Day*, felt this vamp was good enough to stand on its own feet and urged Arlen to adapt it as a popular song. Ted Koehler wrote the lyrics and Ruth Etting sang it as "Get Happy" in the *9:15 Revue*, which had a brief Broadway run in 1930. George Gershwin, who had seen the out-of-town tryouts of this revue, came backstage to congratulate Arlen on having written an outstanding number.

Arlen now found employment with Remick's publishing house in Tin Pan Alley. A more important assignment came his way in 1930 when he was hired to write songs for the Cotton Club shows, then being produced in New York's Harlem. For eight of these revues, from 1930 to 1934, Arlen wrote some of the songs with which he first established his reputation as one of the foremost popular composers of his time and as an outstanding writer of songs in a Negro style and idiom. All were to Ted Koehler's lyrics. Among the best were "Between the Devil and the Deep Blue Sea," "I Love a Parade," "I've Got the World on a String," "Happy as the Day Is Long," "Ill Wind," "As Long as I Live," and, most important of all, "Stormy Weather." The last of these, now a classic in American popular music, was written for Cab Calloway, but Calloway did not actually introduce it. A recording made by Arlen himself became so popular that the song proved a substantial hit even before it was presented in the Cotton Club revue for which it had been written. In view of the immense popularity of the song, the producer of the revue encouraged Ethel Waters to emerge from retirement to sing it in his show.

While working for the Cotton Club, Arlen wrote other songs which found their way on to the Broadway stage. "Hittin' the Bottle" and "One Love" appeared in the Earl Carroll *Vanities* of 1930. In 1931 Arlen completed his first Broadway stage score, *You Said It*, starring Lyda Roberti. One of its songs, "Sweet and Hot" (lyrics by Jack Yellen), later became Lyda Roberti's signature. In 1932 Arlen contributed "I Got a Right to Sing the Blues" (lyrics by Koehler) to the Earl Carroll *Vanities*.

In addition to writing songs, Arlen made his first appearances on the New York stage in 1931-1932 when he joined Lou Holtz and Lyda Roberti in a long run at the Palace Theatre. About a year later, Arlen toured Loew's vaudeville circuit with a mixed chorus of sixteen voices in performances of his own songs.

In 1933 Arlen began writing music for the screen. During the next decade he wrote many of the songs for which he is now famous, songs memorable for their unusual construction, extended melodic lines, and expressive harmonies. One of the most significant of these is "Blues in the Night" (lyrics by Johnny Mercer). In 1941 Arlen was commissioned to write a score for a movie about an American jazz band, and he was instructed to write for it a major song in a blues idiom. "I went home," Arlen reveals, "and just thought about it for two days. After all, anybody can write a blues song. The hard thing is to write one that doesn't sound like every other blues song. Finally I decided to cast it in the traditional form of the early American blues—that is, three sections of twelve bars each, rather than in the conventional Tin Pan Alley song." When Arlen completed his song he played it for Jerome Kern, who listened silently, and then, without saying a word, went into another room and returned with a gift for Arlen, an ivory-handled cane once owned by Offenbach. The song was recorded before the picture was released and proved such a triumph that the Hollywood producers of the show decided to name the picture after the hit song.

Another of Arlen's early classics for the screen was "Over the Rainbow" (lyrics by E. Y. Harburg), one of several numbers written by Arlen for *The Wizard of Oz*, starring Judy Garland. This is the song that made Judy Garland a star of the first magnitude and the one with which she has been identified ever since. In 1939 the song received the Academy Award. In view of its formidable success it is interesting to note that on three different occasions MGM came to the decision to omit the song from the film, on the theory that "Over the Rainbow" was too sophisticated for the juvenile audience for which *The Wizard of Oz* had originally been slanted.

Many other remarkable Arlen songs came from motion pictures in the 1930's and early 1940's: "It's Only a Paper Moon" (lyrics by Billy Rose and E. Y. Harburg), written originally for a nonmusical Broadway play, *The Great Magoo,* but attaining popularity only after being interpolated in the movie *Take a Chance*; the title song of *Let's Fall in Love* (lyrics by Koehler); "That Old Black Magic" (lyrics by Mercer) for *Star-Spangled Rhythm*; "Happiness Is a Thing Called Joe" (lyrics by Harburg) for *Cabin in the Sky*; "Accentuate the Positive" (lyrics by Mercer) for *Here Come the Waves*; "This Time the Dream's on Me" (lyrics by Mercer) for *Blues in the Night*; and "My Shining Hour" and "One for My Baby" (lyrics by Mercer) for *The Sky's the Limit.*

Between 1934 and 1937 Arlen wrote the scores for two moderately successful Broadway musicals: *Life Begins at 8:40,* starring Ray Bolger and Bert Lahr, and *Hooray for What*, with Ed Wynn. Then, after an absence of more than seven years, Arlen returned to Broadway with *Bloomer Girl,* which began a run of 654 performances on October 5. This musical with a Civil War setting had as one of its principal characters Dolly Bloomer, the celebrated feminist, Temperance leader, and sponsor of bloomers as fitting apparel for women in place of hoop skirts. Arlen's best songs for the show—written to lyrics by Harburg—included "I Got a Song," "Evelina," and "T'morra, T'morra."

In 1946 Arlen wrote the music for *St. Louis Woman,* a Negro musical set in St. Louis at the end of the last century. Though it often had the artistic dignity of folk drama—and though it boasted several outstanding Arlen songs with lyrics by Johnny Mercer, including "A Woman's Prerogative," "Legalize My Name," "Come Rain or Come Shine," and "I Had Myself a True Love"—it was a box office failure. In 1954 Arlen was commissioned by Robert Breen to enlarge the scope and dimensions of *St. Louis Woman* by reworking it as an opera. Using the *St. Louis Woman* score as a base and supplementing it with several of his more famous songs from other productions, Arlen created a new full-length opera score. "The new material," wrote William K. Zinsser, "is

even more exhilarating than what was already there. It consists of dialogue set to music, but instead of emerging as recitative, it has spilled out in a variety of forms that are unfailingly melodic and often breathtaking in rhythm, even if they are nothing more than fragments or exhortations at the racetrack and gambling table, or street hawkers' calls. Sometimes they fall, perhaps only subconsciously, into traditional Negro forms—into spirituals, for instance, that sound plantation born."

Renamed *Free and Easy,* and greatly revised, the opera opened in Amsterdam, Holland, on December 22, 1959. An ambitious European tour, which was to have preceded an American opening, ended suddenly and unexpectedly in Paris early in February 1960. But prior to this, in 1957-1958, an orchestral suite from the score, *Blues Opera,* prepared by Samuel Matlowsky, had been introduced in New York by the New York Philharmonic under André Kostelanetz.

Other Broadway productions with Arlen's music have included two with Caribbean settings. The first was *The House of Flowers,* with book and lyrics by Truman Capote, which opened on December 30, 1954. The best songs, strongly spiced with West Indian flavor, included "Two Ladies in de Shade of de Banana Tree," "I Never Has Seen Now," and "Has I Let You Know." *Jamaica,* which arrived on Broadway on October 30, 1957, starred Lena Horne in her first Broadway appearance in a major role. Once more Arlen's songs, to lyrics by E. Y. Harburg, had a pronounced West Indian style; the leading numbers included "Take It Slow, Joe," "Cocoanut Sweet," "Little Biscuit," and "Incompatibility."

In 1959 Arlen wrote the music for *Saratoga,* a play adapted from the Edna Ferber novel *Saratoga Trunk* by Morton Da Costa. The lyrics were written by Johnny Mercer. *Saratoga* was not a critical or box office success and had a very short run.

Among Arlen's more recent scores for motion pictures were those for *A Star Is Born,* starring Judy Garland, and *The Country Girl,* with Bing Crosby. The songs for both films were written to lyrics by Ira Gershwin. "The Man That Got Away," from *A Star Is Born,* was nominated for an Academy Award in 1955.

In 1960 Arlen wrote two pieces for solo piano, *Ode* and *Bon-Bon*.

ABOUT:

Jablonski, Edward. Harold Arlen: Happy with the Blues.

Collier's, December 9, 1944; Harper's Magazine, May 1960; Hi-Fi Music at Home, April 1957; The Theatre, December 1959; Theatre Arts, October 1957.

Felix Arndt *1889-1918*

FELIX ARNDT was a pioneer in writing syncopated pieces for the piano, the most famous of which is *Nola*. Arndt was born in New York City on May 20, 1889. His mother, Countess Fevrier, was related to Napoleon III. After coming to the United States she had met and married Hugo Arndt, who was of German extraction.

Arndt was educated in the New York public schools and at Trinity School, where he was a choir boy and at times a junior organist at church services. He studied piano for several years at the New York Conservatory and also with private teachers, among whom Alexander Lambert was the most eminent. "As a pianist," wrote A. Walter Kramer in *Musical America*, "he was *sui generis*; his playing was marked by refinement even in ragtime . . . and he had as lovely a piano touch as I have known."

For several years Arndt wrote special material for vaudeville entertainers, including Nora Bayes and Jack Norworth, and Gus Edwards. Later he worked as a staff pianist for various music publishing establishments in New York. He also made over three thousand piano rolls of light classics for Duo-Art, Q.R.S., and others, as well as records for Victor. Some of these recordings and piano rolls were renditions of his own pieces.

As a composer, Arndt produced songs, intermezzos of the salon variety, dance tunes, ragtime versions of classical pieces, and original piano miniatures. Among his original works, in which syncopation and ragtime rhythms were skillfully exploited, were *Nola, Desecration, Marionette, Soup to Nuts, Toots, Clover Club,* and *Love in June*. Arndt wrote *Nola* in 1915 as a musical portrait of his sweetheart, Nola Locke, a gifted singer and pianist, to whom he presented this piece as an engagement gift ten months before their marriage. *Nola* was published in 1916 and later became the signature music of the noted bandleader Vincent Lopez. In 1958 Sunny Skylar wrote a set of lyrics for this melody.

Arndt's influence on serious composers of popular music of his day was far-reaching. In *A Journey to Greatness,* this writer has pointed out the influence of Arndt's piano pieces on the then young and still unknown George Gershwin. "Gershwin often visited Arndt at his studio in the Aeolian Building on 42nd Street and was a great admirer of his piano music, which the composer played to him by the hour. It was this contact with Arndt that possibly stimulated Gershwin to write *Rialto Ripples,* for piano. And it was also through Arndt that Gershwin came to make piano rolls in January 1916."

Although his professional activity was limited to popular music, Arndt was a serious musician with a profound admiration for the classics. He was an ardent admirer of the French school of Impressionism and the nationalist works of the Russian Five.

Arndt died of pneumonia at his summer bungalow at Harmon-on-Hudson on October 16, 1918.

ABOUT:

Musical America, October 26, 1918.

Ernest R. Ball *1878-1927*

ERNEST R. BALL, famed as one of America's best loved composers of Irish ballads and sometimes described as "the American Tosti," was born in Cleveland, Ohio, on July 21, 1878. Precocious in music, he was given comprehensive training at the Cleveland Conservatory. He was only thirteen when he himself started giving music lessons, and at fifteen he composed a march, his first piece of music.

Ball went to New York as a young man to advance his career in music. For six months he worked as a relief pianist at the Union Square Theatre. He then went to work as a demonstrator for the publishing house of Witmark in Tin Pan Alley. Ball remained in Witmark's employ for the rest of his life. In 1907 he signed a twenty-year contract as staff composer, a contract which was renewed for an additional ten years just before his death. Few other composers have ever been offered such long-term contracts by music publishers.

At Witmark, Ball was busily engaged not only in demonstrating songs but in composition. As he himself confessed, his "first serious effort was a flop." A little later, in 1904, he wrote "In the Shadow of the Pyramids" (lyrics by Cecil Mack). Though it was introduced on the stage by the dynamic May Irwin, it, too, failed to make an impression.

In 1905 Ball wrote his first hit, "Will You Love Me in December as You Do in May?," to lyrics by James J. Walker, the state senator who was later to become the dapper mayor of New York City. Ball recounted in the *American Magazine* how he came to write this hit: "One night in New York . . . I met State Senator James Walker. . . . He handed me some verses for a song. They were scribbled on a piece of paper. I read them over. . . . I put the bit of paper in my pocket and for the next two months carried the scribbled lines around with me. . . . Bit by bit, I worked out a tune that somehow seemed to fit and, finally, I wrote the music to the words. The result was 'Will You Love Me in December as You Do in May?' I awoke one morning to find that I had written a piece that was being sung from one end of the country to the other."

The success of this song led Ball to reevaluate his earlier efforts at composition. He recognized that this hit song had come from his heart, whereas his earlier songs had been synthetic. "Then and there I determined I would write honestly and sincerely of the things I knew about and that folks generally knew about and were interested in."

In this way Ball found his career as a composer of ballads. In 1906 he wrote "Love Me and the World Is Mine" to lyrics by Dave Reed. Though not too well received when introduced at the Proctor's Fifth Avenue Theatre, the ballad was soon popularized by Maude Lambert and Truly Shattuck, who helped it skyrocket to a million-copy sheet-music sale.

Between 1907 and 1910, Ball wrote the following successful ballads: "When the Birds in Georgia Sing of Tennessee" (lyrics by Arthur J. Lamb); "When Sweet Marie Was Sweet Sixteen" (lyrics by Raymond Moore); "As Long as the World Rolls On" (lyrics by George Graff, Jr.); "In the Gar-

ERNEST R. BALL

den of My Heart" (lyrics by Caro Roma); "All for Love of You" (lyrics by Dave Reed); and "My Heart Has Learned to Love You" (lyrics by Dave Reed).

In 1910 Ball wrote the first of his Irish classics, "Mother Machree," to lyrics by Rida Johnson Young and in collaboration with the actor-singer Chauncey Olcott, who introduced it on Broadway that year in *Barry of Ballymore,* a production in which four other Ball songs were heard. "Mother Machree" became basic in the repertory of many famous Irish tenors, including John McCormack, who built his early reputation as a singer of Irish ballads largely on this song. Two years later, Ball wrote another outstanding Irish ballad, "When Irish Eyes Are Smiling" (lyrics by Chauncey Olcott and George Graff, Jr.). It appeared in 1912 in the Broadway musical *Isle o' Dreams,* whose title song (lyrics by Rida Johnson Young), was another important Ball contribution.

Successful ballads, some of Irish interest, continued to pour richly from Ball's pen through the years. These are some of the most famous: "Till the Sands of the Desert Grow Cold" (lyrics by George Graff, Jr.); "A Little Bit of Heaven, Sure They Call It Ireland," "Ireland Is Ireland to Me," "That's How the Shannon Flows," "Goodbye, Good Luck, God Bless You," "Turn Back the Universe and Give Me Yesterday," "My Sunshine Jane," "Dear Little Boy of Mine," "Let the Rest of the World Go By," and "Out There in the Sunshine With You" (lyrics by J. Kevin Brennan); "She's the Daughter of Mother Machree" (lyrics by Jeff T. Nenarb); "To Have, To Hold, To Love" (lyrics by Darl MacBoyle); "You Planted a Rose in the Garden of Love" (lyrics by J. Will Callahan); "After the Roses Have Faded Away" (lyrics by Bessie Buchanan); "All the World Will Be Jealous of Me" (lyrics by Al Dubin), and "West of the Great Divide" (lyrics by George Whiting). Ball's last song, "Rose of Killarney" (lyrics by William Davidson), was written in 1927. It has been estimated that over the years sales of the sheet music of his ballads have totaled more than twenty-five million copies.

After 1905, Ball also enjoyed a successful career as a singer of his own ballads in leading vaudeville theatres. During his later appearances he was billed with Maude Lambert, his second wife. While appearing in Santa Ana, California, on May 3, 1927, he suffered a fatal heart attack in his dressing room. A half hour earlier he had presented on the stage a potpourri of his greatest song hits, as if in a final résumé of his life's achievement. When the news of his death reached John McCormack, the famous tenor said simply: "Ernie Ball is not dead. He will live forever in his songs."

ABOUT:
Gilbert, Douglas. Lost Chords; Witmark, Isidore. From Ragtime to Swingtime.

Irving Berlin 1888-

IRVING BERLIN was born Israel Baline in Temun, Russia, on May 11, 1888. He was the youngest of eight children. A pogrom in 1882, which the Balines escaped by hiding under a blanket in the fields outside the town, impelled them to leave Russia and come to the United States. Like so many other immigrants of that day, the family settled on the Lower East Side of New York City, where the father earned a meager livelihood supervising kosher meats in a market and filling in at times as a cantor or choirmaster in local synagogues. Four of the children helped support the family by working in sweatshops or selling newspapers.

During Israel's formative years, the city streets were his playground. He was a member of the Cherry Street gang; he swam with the other boys of the neighborhood in the East River at the foot of Cherry Street; he participated in all the street games. Soon after the death of his father, in 1896, he ran away from home, bringing his brief formal schooling to an end. He earned his keep on the Bowery by leading Blind Sol, a "busker," or singing beggar, through the streets and into cafés; occasionally he supplemented the performances of Blind Sol with his own renditions of current sentimental ballads. Before long, Israel found opportunities to sing at popular haunts near the Bowery, such as Callahan's and the Chatham. He was also hired by the publishing house of Harry Von Tilzer to plug songs at Tony Pastor's Music Hall in Union Square; one of the acts to which he was assigned was "The Three Keatons," whose youngest member, Buster, later became the famous comedian of the silent screen.

In 1906 Israel Baline was hired as a singing waiter at Pelham's Café in Chinatown. He worked from dusk to dawn, serving at tables, entertaining guests with renditions of popular songs and his own parodies of current lyrics, and cleaning up after the café was closed for the night. It was here that he received his first bit of newspaper publicity. The Café was often favored by slumming expeditions. One night it was visited by Prince Louis Battenberg and his party. After Berlin had sung his numbers, the Prince offered him a five-dollar tip, which he refused. The following day the incident was given dramatic treatment by Herbert Bayard Swope in a story written for a leading New York newspaper.

It was also at Pelham's Café that Berlin wrote his first song. In a rival café, two waiters had composed and successfully introduced an Italian ditty that was later published. Pelham's Café, making a bid for similar honors, commissioned its pianist, Nick (M. Nicholson), to write the music and recruited Berlin for the lyrics. Their song, "Marie from Sunny Italy," not only found favor with the clientele of the café but also was published (by Joseph W. Stern & Co. on May 8, 1907). It was on this occasion that young Baline assumed the name of Irving

Berlin. On the green-and-white cover of the sheet music, which displayed an illustration of a gondola and a picture of Lillian Russell, the name Irving Berlin stood out in bold print. For his part in the collaboration Berlin received a total royalty of thirty-seven cents.

Soon after the publication of his first lyric, Berlin left Pelham's Café and became a singing waiter at Jimmy Kelly's on Union Square. In 1908 he wrote, for the first time, the melody as well as the lyrics of a song— "Dorando." (Dorando was an Italian marathon runner then in the news.) At first Berlin created only the lyrics, which he tried to peddle to the firm of Ted Snyder. The manager assumed that Berlin also had a tune in mind and offered him $25 for both words and music. Rather than lose the sale, Berlin dictated a melody to an arranger. Another song with original music as well as lyrics was "The Best of Friends Must Part"; though written after "Dorando," it had been issued earlier that year by the Selig Music Corporation.

It was as a creator of lyrics to music by other men that Berlin first became successful. In 1909 "Sadie Salome, Go Home" (music by Edgar Leslie) sold over two hundred thousand copies. To music by Ted Stern Berlin wrote "Next to Your Mother, Who Do You Love?" in 1909, and, in 1910, "Call Me Up Some Rainy Afternoon" and "Kiss Me, My Honey, Kiss Me."

So popular had Berlin's lyrics become by 1910 that he was hired by the New York *Journal* to write several hundred verses. That year two of his lyrics, "That Beautiful Rag" and "Sweet Italian Love," written to Snyder's music, appeared in the revue *Up and Down Broadway*, which starred Eddie Foy and Emma Carus. One of Berlin's most successful lyrics, "My Wife's Gone to the Country" (written in collaboration with George Whiting and once again to Snyder's music), was published in 1913. It enjoyed a sheet music sale of almost half a million copies.

But Berlin was also writing original melodies to his own lyrics. "That Mesmerizing Mendelssohn Tune," a ragtime treatment of Mendelssohn's *Spring Song*, had a modest success in 1909. And in 1911 Berlin achieved his first gigantic success as composer-lyricist with "Alexander's Ragtime Band," a song that swept the country.

IRVING BERLIN   © Bachrach

Berlin had first written the song as a piano rag entitled *Alexander and His Clarinet*. When elected a member of the Friars Club in New York and invited to appear as a performer in its annual *Frolics*, Berlin rewrote his piano rag as a song with lyrics. Neither at the *Frolics* nor in the Broadway revue *The Merry Whirl*, in which it was soon heard again, did "Alexander's Ragtime Band" make much of an impression. It was Emma Carus who first made it famous. After she sang it in vaudeville in Chicago, a local newspaperman wrote: "If we were John D. Rockefeller or the Bank of England, we should engage the Coliseum and get together a sextet including Caruso. . . . After the sextet sang 'Alexander's Ragtime Band' about ten times we should, as a finale, have Sousa's Band march about the building tearing the melody to pieces with all kinds of variations."

"Alexander's Ragtime Band" spread across the country contagiously, infecting all who came into contact with it. It sold over a million copies of sheet music within a few months. Because of "Alexander," ragtime, though long in existence, became a national craze, and social dancing, till then restricted to the few, became a national pastime for the many.

Tin Pan Alley now began producing ragtime songs on an assembly-line basis. Some of the best were written by Berlin himself. In 1911 he published "That Mysterious Rag" (music written in collaboration with Ted Snyder), "Everybody's Doin' It," and "Ragtime Violin." In 1914 he signed a contract to write his first complete Broadway stage score for a "syncopated musical" entitled *Watch Your Step,* starring Vernon and Irene Castle. The show opened at the New Amsterdam Theatre on December 8, 1914. One of the most significant numbers was a ragtime tune, "Syncopated Walk," but also among the songs was an outstanding Berlin hit of that year, "Play a Simple Melody." "More than to any one else," wrote one critic, *"Watch Your Step* belongs to Irving Berlin. He is the young master of syncopation, the gifted and industrious writer of words and music for songs that have made him rich and envied. This is the first time that the author of 'Alexander's Ragtime Band' and the like has turned his attention to providing the music for an entire evening's entertainment. For it, he has written a score of his mad melodies, nearly all of them of the tickling sort, born to be caught up and whistled at every street corner, and warranted to set any roomful a-dancing."

In 1917 Berlin starred as "The Ragtime King" at the Hippodrome Theatre in London, where he introduced his new ragtime tune, "International Rag." When, after his performances, he asked his audiences which of his other ragtime songs they wanted to hear, they would shout the titles of practically every ragtime song ever written in the mistaken belief that Berlin had written them all.

From 1912 on, Berlin was to produce some of the most eloquent ballads in American popular music. The 1912 ballad "When I Lost You," was the first song to achieve a success almost equal to that of "Alexander's Ragtime Band." Unfortunately, this creative achievement, which reached new emotional depths, was motivated by a bitter personal tragedy: the sudden death of Berlin's wife, Dorothy Goetz Berlin, who died of typhoid fever contracted in Cuba on their honeymoon.

During World War I, Berlin served first as a private, then as a sergeant at Camp Upton, a temporary station for troops embarking for Europe. Convinced of the need for entertainment for these troops—and encouraged by the commanding general of the camp, who needed $35,000 for a new service center—Berlin prepared an all-soldier show, *Yip, Yip, Yaphank,* for which he wrote book, lyrics, and music. This musical, which opened at the Century Theatre in New York City on July 26, 1918, presented various aspects of a rookie's life at camp in song, comedy, sentiment, dance, and production numbers. Berlin's best songs were "Oh, How I Hate to Get Up in the Morning" and "Mandy." *Yip, Yip, Yaphank* eventually netted over $150,000 for the Camp Upton Service Center.

Upon his return to civilian life, Berlin began to expand his activities beyond songwriting. He formed his own publishing house, Irving Berlin, Inc.—an occasion that inspired an "Irving Berlin Week," celebrated throughout the country with performances of his songs in theatres and night clubs. He also embarked on a career as a vaudeville headliner, appearing in performances of his song hits in leading theatres. In 1921, with Sam H. Harris, he built a theatre of his own on 45th Street off Broadway and called it the Music Box. Here, from 1921 to 1924, he presented five editions of the lavish, star-studded *Music Box Revue.* Several of Berlin's song classics first heard in these productions were "Say It with Music," "Everybody Step," "Pack Up Your Sins," "Crinoline Days," "What'll I Do?" and "All Alone."

In 1925 Berlin met and fell in love with Ellin Mackay, the daughter and heiress of Clarence H. Mackay, head of Postal Telegraph. Mackay recruited his immense power and resources in an attempt to prevent their marriage and, when all other strategy failed, sent his daughter off to Europe for several months. During her absence Berlin wrote several of his most poignant love ballads, including "Always" and "Remember." When she returned to New York they were married secretly at City Hall on January 4, 1926, embarking immediately afterwards on a European honeymoon. When news of the marriage leaked out to the press, the newspapers gave much publicity to the romance which had so dramatically broken down social and religious barriers. The event even found its way into music in "When a Kid Who Came from the East Side Found a Sweet Society Rose" (lyrics by Al Dubin and music by Jimmy McHugh). Although Clarence H. Mackay disinherited his daughter and refused to communicate with her, even after the Berlins' first child was born, he later allowed a reconciliation to take place, and he remained sympathetic to his son-in-law.

In 1927 Berlin wrote a ballad, "The Song Is Ended," almost as if he had a prophetic glimpse of what awaited him: the uncreative years between 1929 and 1932. During this time he wrote little and seemed incapable of producing anything that either satisfied him or could win public approval. This period of sterility was made even more difficult by the depletion of his fortune during the economic crisis.

Then came a sudden change of fortune. In 1932 Rudy Vallee revived an old Berlin ballad, "Say It Isn't So," and helped make it a tremendous hit. Another old song, which Berlin had long considered too poor for publication, "How Deep Is the Ocean?" was issued in the same year and became a smash success. Still more important, Berlin returned to the Broadway stage with a substantial box-office hit, *Face the Music,* a musical comedy with book by Moss Hart which opened on February 17, 1932. In the songs "Soft Lights and Sweet Music" and "Let's Have Another Cup of Coffee," the master proved that he had not lost his touch. A year later, on September 30, 1933, *As Thousands Cheer* opened to become another box-office triumph. It was in this revue that Marilyn Miller and Clifton Webb introduced one of Berlin's most memorable songs, "Easter Parade." (Berlin had written this melody in 1917 to other lyrics, but as "Smile and Show Your Dimple" it had been a dismal failure.) Another outstanding song hit from *As Thousands Cheer* was "Heat Wave," in a torrid rendition by Ethel Waters.

After 1933 Berlin wrote songs for motion pictures as well. He was responsible for the scores for some of the most charming screen musicals of the thirties, including three which starred Ginger Rogers and Fred Astaire: *Top Hat, Follow the Fleet,* and *Carefree.* For *Top Hat* Berlin wrote "Cheek to Cheek," which earned him royalties of more than $250,000, besides the Academy Award. Berlin also wrote the music for *On the Avenue,* starring Dick Powell and Alice Faye; *Alexander's Ragtime Band,* a cavalcade of Berlin's hits with twenty-three old and three new songs; and *Second Fiddle,* with Sonja Henie

and Tyrone Power. Heard in these films were the following outstanding numbers: "The Piccolino" in *Top Hat;* "I've Got My Love to Keep Me Warm" in *On the Avenue;* "I Poured My Heart into a Song," in *Second Fiddle;* "I'm Putting All My Eggs in One Basket" and "Let Yourself Go" in *Follow the Fleet;* and "The Night Is Filled with Music" in *Carefree.*

In 1938, when the long shadow of fascism across Europe made the heritage of American freedom more precious than ever, Irving Berlin wrote "God Bless America." The melody was an old one he had written for *Yip, Yip, Yaphank* but never used; the lyrics were new. Written for and introduced by Kate Smith on her radio network program, "God Bless America" caught fire and in a short time became almost a second national anthem. It was played before each program in many of the country's motion picture theatres; it sold millions of copies of sheet music and records; it was used as a key song for both presidential conventions in 1940; it was honored by the National Committee of Music Appreciation in 1950; and in 1954 it brought Berlin a special gold medal, authorized by Congress and presented by President Eisenhower. Berlin refused to capitalize on his patriotism and allocated all his royalties (about $250,000) to the Boy Scouts, the Girl Scouts, and the Campfire Girls.

As international tensions mounted and finally erupted into war, Berlin became increasingly active as the nation's unofficial musical laureate. He wrote songs for various war funds including the Navy Relief, the March of Dimes, and the Red Cross, as well as for bond sales and arms production campaigns. Berlin's income from the sheet-music and record sales of these songs was contributed to war charities.

On May 28, 1940, a new Berlin musical comedy, *Louisiana Purchase,* appeared on Broadway. It starred William Gaxton, Victor Moore, Vera Zorina, and Irene Bordoni, and its main love song was "It's a Lovely Day, Tomorrow."

Soon after the attack on Pearl Harbor and the United States' subsequent declaration of war, Berlin was inspired to stage a new all-soldier show, as he had done in World War I. Upon receiving a reluctant go-ahead from the Pentagon, he went to live in the barracks of Camp Upton to gather firsthand experiences of army life in World War II. From these experiences he prepared book, lyrics, and music for *This Is the Army*. The all-soldier cast appeared at the Broadway Theatre for 113 performances beginning on July 4, 1942. A nation-wide tour followed. After touring all the combat areas of Europe, the Near East, and the Pacific, it was made into a motion picture. In time it earned over ten million dollars for United States Army Emergency Relief and another $350,000 for British relief agencies. For this monumental achievement Berlin was awarded the Medal of Merit by General George C. Marshall.

After the war, Berlin achieved the greatest Broadway stage success of his entire career with *Annie Get Your Gun*, in which Ethel Merman starred. Opening on May 16, 1946, it had an impressive run of over one thousand performances. One of Berlin's most varied and inventive scores, it included "They Say It's Wonderful" (the principal love song), "The Girl That I Marry," "Doin' What Comes Naturally," and "You Can't Get a Man with a Gun."

Berlin's later Broadway musicals were *Miss Liberty* (1949) and *Call Me Madam* (1950). Robert Sherwood wrote his only musical-comedy text for *Miss Liberty*; set in New York in 1885, the musical highlights the rivalry between James Gordon Bennett of the *Herald* and Joseph Pulitzer of the *World* and their respective efforts to raise money for the base of the Statue of Liberty. One of the songs was a poignant setting of Emma Lazarus' poem inscribed on the base of the Statue, "Give Me Your Tired, Your Poor." Two other musical numbers were of interest: "Let's Take an Old-Fashioned Walk" and "Paris Wakes Up and Smiles." *Call Me Madam* was a satire on Mrs. Perle Mesta, the American Ambassador to Luxembourg. One of its most stirring songs was "They Like Ike," of which effective use was made during Dwight D. Eisenhower's presidential campaign in 1952. Its main love song was "You're Just in Love."

After 1940 Berlin continued to write original scores for several important motion pictures. *Holiday Inn*, starring Bing Crosby and Fred Astaire, introduced Berlin's Yuletide classic "White Christmas," which won the Academy Award in 1942. Since then it has achieved the unprecedented sale of about twenty million records and four million copies of sheet music, and has acquired a status second only to that of "Silent Night, Holy Night" as America's favorite Christmas song. Among Berlin's subsequent motion pictures were *Blue Skies, Easter Parade, White Christmas*, and *There's No Business Like Show Business*. In each of these, old Berlin songs were combined with new ones. "Count Your Blessings" from *There's No Business Like Show Business* became a hit song of 1954. Berlin also wrote the title song for the nonmusical screen production *Sayonara*.

Irving Berlin's career in American popular music is probably without precedent. No one has accomplished as much as he, nor has anyone risen so high. For over half a century, he has been the top man in the industry in spite of changing song styles. "He is— really there is no other word which accounts for him — a genius," Alexander Woollcott once wrote. George Gershwin considered him an "American Franz Schubert" and to Jerome Kern "Berlin has no place in American music, he *is* American music." Yet Berlin can neither read nor write music. He can play the piano in only a single key (F-sharp) and has had a special device built into his piano that enables him to transpose any piece of music automatically to this favored key. Working more by instinct than technique, more by trial and error than from background or knowledge, he finds the creative process laborious. He usually writes his lyric first. He has been writing lyrics to his own melodies since 1908, and has achieved such mastery in this field that he must be numbered among the foremost lyricists of all time. Oscar Hammerstein II once said that he considered Berlin's line "all alone, by the telephone" one of the most perfect in any lyric he knew.

In 1958 Berlin selected among his own works his eight favorite musicals. They are: *Watch Your Step, Yip, Yip, Yaphank*, the Ziegfeld *Follies of 1919, The Music Box Revue of 1921, As Thousands Cheer, This Is the Army, Annie Get Your Gun*, and *Call Me Madam*. Of more than a thousand songs, his ten favorites are: "Alexander's Ragtime Band," "A Pretty Girl Is Like a Melody," "Always," "Blue Skies," "Easter Parade,"

"How Deep Is the Ocean?" "Oh, How I Hate to Get Up in the Morning," "White Christmas," "God Bless America," and "There's No Business Like Show Business."

ABOUT:
Ewen, David. The Story of Irving Berlin (a young people's biography); Woollcott, Alexander. The Story of Irving Berlin.
Coronet, September 1947; New York Times Magazine, May 9, 1948; New York Times Magazine, May 11, 1958; Saturday Evening Post, January 9, 1943; Theatre Arts, February 1958.

Leonard Bernstein *1918-*

L EONARD BERNSTEIN has successfully pursued several careers in music— as conductor, composer of serious music, composer of popular music, commentator, pianist, and author. Only his achievements in popular music will be surveyed here.

Bernstein was born in Lawrence, Massachusetts, on August 25, 1918. His early music instruction took place with piano teachers in Boston, and notably with Helen Coates and Heinrich Gebhard. From 1935 to 1939 he attended Harvard, where he studied music under Walter Piston, Arthur Tillman Merritt, and Edward Burlingame Hill, among others. He graduated *cum laude* in music in 1939, and went on to the Curtis Institute of Music for a year and a half as a pupil of Fritz Reiner in conducting and Isabelle Vengerova in piano. He also spent three summers at the Berkshire Music Center at Tanglewood in Lenox, Massachusetts, first as a student of, then an assistant conductor to, Serge Koussevitzky.

Bernstein became assistant conductor of the New York Philharmonic Orchestra in 1943. On November 14, 1943, he made his spectacular debut as a conductor. At a Sunday afternoon concert of the New York Philharmonic, he filled in at the last minute for the ailing Bruno Walter, and made such a brilliant impression that his concert was reported the next day on the front pages of the New York *Times* and *Herald Tribune* and discussed editorially in many newspapers. This marked the beginning of a rich and eventful career as a conductor which led him through the world of music to the podium of virtually every major symphony orchestra. In 1953 he became the first American-born conductor to direct performances at the his-

New York Philharmonic
LEONARD BERNSTEIN

toric La Scala opera house in Milan. In the fall of 1958 he became music director of the New York Philharmonic, the first American-born conductor ever to assume this post.

Bernstein first attracted attention as a serious composer with his initial attempt at writing symphonic music—the *Jeremiah Symphony,* which was introduced under his own direction in Pittsburgh in 1944 and which subsequently won the New York Music Critics Award as the best new American symphonic work of the season. Since then Bernstein has written a second symphony and various other serious compositions, including ballets and an opera.

His first ballet, *Fancy Free,* with which Jerome Robbins made his bow as choreographer, was introduced by the Ballet Theatre in New York in 1944. Bernstein's score made extensive use of jazz idioms and techniques as well as of melodies in a Tin Pan Alley style. *Fancy Free* thus represented Bernstein's first important attempt at writing popular music. This ballet and its score were also the germ of Bernstein's first musical comedy. The ballet text, which was based on an idea by Robbins, concerned the adventures of several sailors on shore leave in New York. This idea was extended into a musical comedy text by Betty Comden and Adolph Green. As *On the Town,* it opened in New York on December 28, 1944, and ran for more than a year. To Lewis Nichols it was one of "the freshest musicals to come to town in a long time," an ebullient, breezy production filled with the energy and bounce and irreverence of youth. In his score, Bernstein proved that though he had brought sophistication to his harmonic writing and orchestration, he was not afraid to write a catchy tune that lingered in the memory after a single hearing. The best of his songs included the sprightly "New York, New York" with which the play opened; the ballads "Lucky to Be Me" and "Lonely Town"; and two comic numbers, "I Get Carried Away" and "I Can Cook." Written in a more ambitious vein were his skillful and dramatically effective background music for the subway-ride fantasy and the two principal ballet sequences, "Miss Turnstiles" and "Gabey in the Playground of the Rich." In 1949 *On the Town* was made into an outstanding film musical starring Frank Sinatra and Gene Kelly. A year later the stage musical was revived in two off-Broadway productions.

Nine years after *On the Town* opened on Broadway, Bernstein scored another, even greater, Broadway success with *Wonderful Town,* a musical comedy adaptation of Ruth McKenney's *My Sister Eileen.* It opened on February 25, 1953, with Rosalind Russell in the leading role. The story recounts the adventures of Ruth, an ambitious young writer, and her sister Eileen, who have left Ohio to seek their fortune in New York. The experiences of these girls in Greenwich Village proved happy material for a farce which moved with breathless pace from beginning to end under George Abbott's confident direction. Bernstein's music again blended extraordinary craftsmanship and sophistication with a personal and winning lyricism of popular appeal. One of the favorite numbers in this score was "Ohio"; written as a parody of home-town songs, it became popular, ironically, as a serious ballad. Conscious satire and parody were also projected in "My Darlin' Eileen" (a take-off on Irish ballads), "Pass That Football," and "Story Vignettes," and a tender, sentimental mood was reflected in "A Quiet Girl" and "It's Love." A remarkable television presentation of *Wonderful Town,* again starring Rosalind Russell, was given on November 30, 1958.

Bernstein's popular writing gained spaciousness of design and variety and subtlety of expression in *Candide,* a musical comedy adaptation by Lillian Hellman of Voltaire's satire. It opened on December 1, 1956. *Candide* was a box office failure (it had only seventy-three performances) and Bernstein's inventive score passed unnoticed by the general public. But Brooks Atkinson observed in the New York *Times* that none of Bernstein's earlier theatre music had had "the joyous variety, humor and richness of this score."

On September 26, 1957, Bernstein was again represented on the Broadway stage with an artistic and box office triumph of the first magnitude—*West Side Story,* for which Arthur Laurents contributed the book and Jerome Robbins the choreography. Leaning heavily on ballet and music, the play retells the story of Shakespeare's *Romeo and Juliet* in the modern setting of New York, with two teen-age gangs as the factions embroiled in a bitter life-and-death struggle. The main plot involves a Puerto Rican girl, Maria, the sister of the leader of one of these gangs, and Tony, a member of the rival gang. As in Shakespeare's play, their love, doomed by the hatred of opposing groups, ends in tragedy. With so much of this story expressed through ballet and music, Bernstein was free to give his writing symphonic dimensions, to charge it with dramatic interest, and to color it with sensitive tone painting. At the same time, retaining his popular touch, he also composed songs—notably "I Feel Pretty," "Tonight," "Somewhere," and "Maria"—that soon became hits on records, radio, and television.

West Side Story remained for about two and a half years at the Winter Garden on Broadway and returned there after a nine-month road tour, on April 28, 1960, to begin a new Broadway run. During this time *West Side Story* also opened in London, on December 13, 1958, to receive an acclaim rarely bestowed on American musical productions. "It struck London," reported Cecil Wilson in the London *Daily Mail,* "like a flash of lightning set to music." Harold Conway in the *Daily Sketch* called it "a most dynamic, vital, electric musical." Early in 1961, *West Side Story* toured the Near East. A motion picture adaptation was released in the United States later that year.

This survey of Bernstein's achievements in popular music would not be complete without a word or two about his television activities as a commentator on many musical subjects. His discussions of "The World of Jazz" on October 16, 1955, and of "American Musical Comedy" on October 7, 1956, were engrossing, informative, and penetrating, as were his talks on Bach, Beethoven, and Mozart. The scripts of the talks on jazz and musical comedy were reprinted in Bernstein's book *The Joy of Music,* issued in 1959.

Bernstein is married to Felicia Montealegre, an actress of South American birth. They have two children and reside in a nine-room duplex apartment on 57th Street, New York, cater-corner to Carnegie Hall.

ABOUT:
Ewen, David. Leonard Bernstein (a biography for young people).
Holiday, October 1959; Life, January 7, 1957; The New Yorker, January 11 and 18, 1958; Saturday Evening Post, June 16, 1956; Time, February 4, 1957.

William Billings *1746-1800*

WILLIAM BILLINGS, creator of hymns and anthems, was America's first popular composer. He was born in Boston, Massachusetts, on October 7, 1746. Fate was not kind to him. He was born with a withered arm, legs of uneven length, and vision in only one eye. When he started to talk, he had a rasping voice that grew harsher as he grew older. Later in life, his outlandish dress and uncouth manner further helped to make him an eccentric and quixotic figure.

When Billings was fourteen, his father's death put an end to his formal schooling. By that time he had received a smattering of music instruction from a local choirmaster. He was now apprenticed to a tanner, but he spent much of his time at some sort of musical activity. He studied Tans'ur's *Musical Grammar* and memorized any published psalm book he could find. He also began to compose psalm tunes of his own, writing them down with chalk either on the walls of his tannery or on animal hides.

Before long, he abandoned the tanner's trade to devote himself completely to music; by doing so, he earned the distinction of becoming America's first professional musician.

What he lacked in personal address and deportment he made up for with his driving ambition, dynamic industry, and fearless pioneering spirit. In the ensuing years he taught singing and became the founder of America's first singing school; his singing class in Stoughton, Massachusetts, developed into the Stoughton Musical Society, our oldest musical organization. He also organized the first American church choir and was one of the first to introduce a cello in church music and to utilize a pitch pipe for church services.

As a composer of psalms, hymns, and "fuguing tunes," Billings injected into his music an entirely new vigor, freshness of idiom, and unorthodox technical approach. In the preface to his first collection of songs, *The New England Psalm Singer* (1770), he courageously expressed his independent artistic credo: "For my own part, I don't think myself confined to any Rules. . . . I think it is best for every composer to be his own learner. . . . Nature must lay the Foundation, Nature must give the thought." He subsequently published *The Singing Master's Assistant,* better known as *Billings' Best* (1776), *Music in Miniature* (1779), *The Psalm Singer's Amusement* (1781), *The Suffolk Harmony* (1786) and *The Continental Harmony* (1794).

In his effort to inject a new vitality and originality into American church music, Billings deliberately filled his psalms and fuguing tunes with harmonic and contrapuntal crudities. This so aroused some of his contemporaries that a few pranksters hung two cats by their tails on the signpost outside Billings' house, intending to suggest by means of the cats' cries the outlandish nature of Billings' brand of music. Billings' reply to this jest was to write an amusing and highly dissonant piece, *Jargon,* and to preface it with a "Manifesto to the Goddess of Discord." It was Billings who had the last laugh, for by 1790 there was hardly a psalm book in America that did not contain some of his tunes. And his techniques and style, unconventional and crude as they were, helped to free American psalm writing from its earlier stilted and formal techniques.

It was from these psalms that America's first popular songs emerged, inspired by the American Revolution. A friend of Samuel Adams and Paul Revere, Billings was a passionate advocate of the Revolution. Soon after the first shot was fired at Lexington, he adapted his psalm tunes as war songs with new lyrics. One of these was "Chester," America's first great war song and the most popular of the entire Revolution; it is now sometimes described as our "Marseillaise."

> Let tyrants shake their iron rod,
> And slav'ry clank her galling chains,
>   We'll fear them not,
>   We trust in God,
> New England's God forever reigns.

So ran the opening verse. The troops sang "Chester" lustily in the camps. There could be little doubt that this song was a powerful factor in maintaining morale among Revolutionary troops. Many of Billings' other psalms, adapted as war songs, spread through the colonies. "Retrospect," "Independence," and "Columbia" achieved great popularity, and "By the Waters of Babylon" became "Lamentation over Boston," with the colonists weeping "as they remembered Boston." A writer for the *Musical Reporter* commented: "Many of the New England soldiers who . . . were encamped in the Southern States, had his popular tunes by heart, and frequently amused themselves singing them in camp, to the delight of all those who heard them."

Despite his many contributions to American music in general and American popular music in particular, Billings died in extreme poverty in Boston on September 26, 1800. He was buried in an unmarked grave.

ABOUT:

Chase, Gilbert. America's Music; Goldberg, Isaac. Tin Pan Alley.

Hi-Fi Music at Home, October 5, 1958; Music Clubs Magazine, January 1953; Musical Quarterly, January 1939.

James A. Bland *1854-1911*

JAMES A. BLAND was born in Flushing, New York, on October 22, 1854. Soon after the birth of James, his father, one of the first Negroes to receive a college education, was appointed examiner in the United States Patent Office, the first Negro ever to hold that post.

After the family moved to Washington, D.C., James attended public school in that city. As a boy he enjoyed singing his own compositions to banjo accompaniment. For a while he served as a page in the House of Representatives and was often invited to entertain at parties at the homes of Washington notables and to perform for members of the Manhattan Club.

After his graduation from high school James enrolled at Howard University together with his father. James was interested in a general liberal arts education; his father wanted to study law. While attending the University, James continued with his avocation — composing and performing his own songs for social groups.

His overwhelming ambition, however, was to get on the stage. When he graduated from Howard University at nineteen he tried to join a minstrel troupe. But at that time minstrel shows preferred white performers impersonating Negroes to Negroes themselves. For a long time Bland suffered frustration and disappointment. But in 1875 he received his first job with an all-Negro minstrel troupe headed by Billy Kersands. For the next few years he toured the country with the Kersands troupe, with Callender's Original Georgia Minstrels (a troupe managed by the Frohman Brothers), and with several other companies. In these performances he introduced many of his own songs, always writing both lyrics and melodies. His first published songs were those by which he is most often remembered: "Carry Me Back to Old Virginny" and "Oh, Dem Golden Slippers," issued in 1878 and 1879 respectively. "In the Evening by the Moonlight" and "In the Morning by the Bright Light" were also issued in 1879, and a year later he wrote "Hand Me Down My Walking Stick" and "De Golden Wedding," both favorites with minstrel companies.

In 1881 Bland toured England with the Callender-Haverly minstrel show, another Negro company, opening at His Majesty's Theatre in London in July and scoring a substantial success with "Oh, Dem Golden Slippers." After touring England with the troupe for about two seasons, Bland decided to remain in that country, since there seemed no dearth of engagements. He became one of England's most celebrated Negro performers and was acclaimed "Prince of Negro songwriters." He gave command performances for Queen Victoria and the Prince of Wales.

JAMES A. BLAND

sesses copies of only thirty-eight. But the little that remains of Bland's life work that is recognized as authentic gives us good reason to rank him as a leading composer of minstrel show songs and popular Negro songs of his day. Besides those already mentioned, the following Bland songs are noteworthy: "Tapioca," "Close Dem Windows," "Pretty Little Carolina Rose," "Listen to the Silver Trumpets," "Christmas Dinner," "Way Up Yonder," "Travelling Back to Alabam'," and "Gabriel's Band."

ABOUT:
Daly, John Jay. A Song in His Heart; Haywood, Charles. The Outstanding Songs of James A. Bland.
Music Journal, November-December 1947; Virginia Cavalcade, Spring 1952.

His annual income was more than $10,000, a not inconsiderable figure for that period. But he was careless about his money and when his popularity finally waned he was penniless.

In 1901 he managed to make his way back to the United States, where he was saved from outright starvation by a friend in Washington, D.C., who provided him with an unimportant desk job. Bland then drifted on from Washington to Philadelphia, where he spent the last few years of his life in appalling poverty. He died there on May 5, 1911. No newspaper carried a notice of his death. He was buried in an unmarked grave in a secluded corner of a Negro cemetery in Merion, Pennsylvania.

In 1939, through the efforts of ASCAP, his grave was finally located and landscaped, and a headstone was erected to identify it. In 1940 the Virginia Legislature designated "Carry Me Back to Old Virginny" as the song of the state.

An inscription on the headstone over Bland's grave states that he wrote six hundred songs. It is impossible to say how many he really wrote, since most were not copyrighted and many were expropriated by minstrel show performers who introduced them as their own creations. Only fifty-three songs by Bland are listed in the Library of Congress in Washington, and the Library pos-

Jerry Bock *1928-*

JERRY BOCK was born in New Haven, Connecticut, on November 23, 1928. His father was a salesman. Jerry spent the first two years of his life in the Bronx and Brooklyn, New York, and his boyhood in Flushing, Queens, where he attended Flushing High School. He began to take piano lessons at the age of nine, studying with Mrs. Rodwin, who had been a pupil of Ernest Hutcheson, and other teachers. "I was an erratic piano student with an insatiable desire to start the new piece and no drive whatsoever to practice it," he says. He preferred "noodling some thoughts of my own and got great joy out of improvising all sorts of things." In his last year at high school he wrote the score for an amateur show produced to raise money for a new Navy hospital ship. By the time he completed high school he had stopped taking piano lessons and was "hands deep in informal piano study, improvising, playing at parties, and writing songs."

As editor of the high school newspaper he aspired toward a career in journalism. With this in mind he went out to the University of Wisconsin in Madison, intending to specialize in the study of journalism or advertising. But upon reaching Madison, he impulsively decided to apply instead to its School of Music. Other aspirants came to the audition prepared to play the classics, but Bock, having no such abilities, performed a

JERRY BOCK

series of his own variations on army bugle calls, each variation in the style of some famous composer, and concluded the performance with a jazz improvisation. He was accepted by the School on the condition that he study music as a complete beginner. He took courses in harmony, counterpoint, theory, and violin, as well as in the liberal arts. "I still infinitely preferred accompanying some singer at a party or playing for various college functions or writing music apart from my studies rather than buckle down to my courses," he recalls. In his third year he wrote the music for an original college musical which toured several midwestern cities.

He left Wisconsin in 1949 and went to New York. There, in 1950, he married Patti Faggen, a girl he had met at the University. A successful audition for Max Liebman, then producing television shows, led to the writing of songs (to lyrics by Larry Holofcener) for Liebman's "Admiral Broadway Revue" and later for his "Your Show of Shows," starring Sid Caesar and Imogene Coca. He worked three years for Liebman. During the summer months of 1950, 1951, and 1953, he wrote songs for the weekly musicals produced at Camp Tamiment, an adult camp in Pennsylvania directed by Monroe B. Hack.

In 1952 the growing reluctance on the part of television producers to use original songs for their musical shows made it neces-sary for Bock and Holofcener to earn their living by writing continuity, dialogue, and special material for several television programs, including those of Kate Smith and Mel Torme. In 1955 they wrote four songs as background music for *Wonders of Manhattan,* a movie travelogue of New York that received honorable mention at the Cannes Festival in 1956. They also contributed three numbers to a Broadway musical, *Catch a Star.* Two of these, a comic madrigal, "The Story of Alice," and a ballad, "Fly Little Heart," were praised by the critics.

Bock played his songs one day for the composer Jule Styne, who recognized their merit and commissioned him to provide the entire score (to Holofcener's lyrics, with the collaborative assistance of George Weiss) for a musical he was co-producing with George Gilbert and Lester Osterman, Jr. The show was *Mr. Wonderful.* The production gave the star, Sammy Davis, Jr., ample opportunity to display his special gifts and perform his famous night club routines. *Mr. Wonderful* opened on March 22, 1956, and ran about a year; it could have extended its run indefinitely but for the fact that Davis had to leave the show to fulfill other commitments. Bock's first important song hits were heard in this production: the title number and "Too Close for Comfort."

While working on *Mr. Wonderful,* Bock and Holofcener wrote three numbers for a musical starring Tallulah Bankhead, *The Ziegfeld Follies,* which opened out of town and collapsed before reaching Broadway. Then, with Sheldon Harnick as his lyricist, Bock wrote the score for *The Body Beautiful,* a show that ran on Broadway for only two months early in 1958. "In my most objective mood," he says, "I still feel that the show and the score deserved a longer life."

Though *The Body Beautiful* was a failure, it did not prove a total loss for Bock. Robert E. Griffith and Harold S. Prince commissioned him and Harnick to provide the music for a musical they were planning at the time. The play was *Fiorello!;* it arrived quietly and unobtrusively in New York on November 23, 1959, to receive a thunderous acclaim from the critics. With book by Jerome Weidman and George Abbott, *Fiorello!* was built around the colorful personality and provocative political career of New York's fiery little mayor, Fiorello La Guardia, tracing his life from a humble law practice in Greenwich Village to his election in 1932 as New York's Fusion party Mayor. "As put on . . . last evening," wrote Brooks Atkinson, "it recaptures a fabulous political firebrand and a breezy period in the life of New York. . . . Jerry Bock has set it to a bouncy score that has a satiric line as well as a wonderful waltz of the period." The satiric line was found in two numbers, "Little Tin Box" and "Politics and Poker." The "wonderful waltz" was "'Til Tomorrow," a nostalgic hesitation waltz that is heard in the first act during a tenement-party scene. Bock's outstanding ballad was "When Did I Fall in Love?"

Fiorello! captured the three major theatrical awards conferred each season: the New York Drama Critics Circle Award and the Antoinette Perry Award (the latter shared with *The Sound of Music* by Rodgers and Hammerstein) for the best musical of the season, and the Pulitzer Prize in drama. (Only two other musicals—*Of Thee I Sing!* in 1932 and *South Pacific* in 1950—had received the Pulitzer Prize in drama.) A national company of *Fiorello!* toured the United States for over a year, and a London company was formed in 1962.

The authors of *Fiorello!* (Jerome Weidman and George Abbott, librettists, and Sheldon Harnick, lyricist) joined Bock in describing still another colorful chapter from New York's past in *Tenderloin.* This was a musical comedy based on a novel by Samuel Hopkins Adams which opened on October 17, 1960. "Tenderloin" was a disreputable New York neighborhood during the Gay Nineties. A crusading clergyman (enacted by Maurice Evans in his first musical-comedy appearance) uses it as his battleground in his fight against sin. "The songwriters," said Howard Taubman, in the New York *Times,* "have not let the new effort down. They have supplied material that has color and flavor in its own right and that makes possible some sprightly production numbers. Sheldon Harnick's lyrics and Jerry Bock's music are the best excuse for *Tenderloin.*" A satirical note is sounded in songs like "What's in It for You?" and "How the Money Changes Hands"; "My Miss Mary" and "Tommy, Tommy" are in a more lyrical and sentimental vein.

In 1961 Bock was assigned to write thirty-one children's songs for "Sing Something Special," the Board of Education radio show over WNYE, New York City.

The Bocks live in New Rochelle, New York, with their son and daughter.

ABOUT:
Green, Stanley. The World of Musical Comedy.

Carrie Jacobs Bond *1862-1946*

ALTHOUGH the songs of Carrie Jacobs Bond are art songs rather than Tin Pan Alley compositions, they have achieved such wide distribution and success that they deserve consideration as popular music. Carrie Jacobs Bond was born Carrie Jacobs in Janesville, Wisconsin, on August 11, 1862. She came from a musical family, and one of her distant relatives was John Howard Payne, who wrote the words for "Home, Sweet Home." As a small child she played piano by ear. She started to take formal lessons at the age of nine and afterwards made numerous appearances as a child prodigy.

When she was twelve, her father died and she went to live with her grandfather. Her adolescence was devoted not only to music but also to painting and design, in both of which she demonstrated unusual aptitude; for a while she seriously considered making art her life work. At eighteen she was married for the first time, but this marriage soon ended in divorce. She was remarried in 1887, to Dr. Frank L. Bond, a physician from her home town.

A few years after their marriage, Dr. Bond lost all his money in an investment in the mining town of Iron River, Michigan. This was the first of a series of misfortunes: the poverty that haunted them after they moved to Chicago with their small son; a fall on an icy sidewalk, which seriously injured Mrs. Bond; and finally, in 1895, the sudden death of Dr. Bond, which left his family completely penniless. Although she was an invalid, Mrs. Bond was compelled to rely on her own resources to support herself and her son. At first she supported herself by renting rooms, painting china, and taking in sewing. Then she decided to put to profit an activity which had been merely a diversion —songwriting. Publishers at first considered

CARRIE JACOBS BOND

was on the verge of bankruptcy when an old friend, Walter Gale, helped her out by purchasing a small interest in her firm. Now the house started to prosper as her songs began to sell in carload lots. Her greatest triumph, in 1909, was "The End of a Perfect Day," a ballad that was catapulted to national fame after it was sung by David Bispham as an encore at a New York recital. More than five million copies of the ballad were sold within a few years; it was heard at weddings and funerals, in barrooms and churches, and in soldiers' camps. From the royalties of this one song Carrie Jacobs Bond was able to buy a spacious home in southern California where she lived in semiretirement for the last twelve years of her life.

During the administrations of Theodore Roosevelt and Warren G. Harding she gave concerts at the White House. She also gave vocal concerts in army camps during World War I. She received several awards for achievement in music and, in 1941, was singled out by the Federation of Music Clubs as one of the outstanding American women in the field of music.

She died in Hollywood, California, on December 28, 1946, and was buried in the Fairlawn Memorial Court of Honor. She was the second person to receive such an honor, the first having been the sculptor Gutzon Borglum.

Besides the songs already mentioned, her greatest successes include "God Remembers When the World Forgets," "Life's Garden," "A Little Bit o' Honey," "I've Done My Work," "His Lullaby," "Roses Are in Bloom," and "A Little Pink Rose."

Carrie Jacobs Bond was the author of an autobiography, three volumes of animal stories, and a book of poems and philosophic comments entitled *The End of the Road.*

ABOUT:
Bond, Carrie Jacobs. The Roads to Melody.
Music of the West, January 1947; Pacific Coast Musician, November 2, 1946.

her efforts too serious for popular taste. One of them, however, suggested that she try her hand at children's songs, and a children's song—"Is Dolly Dead?"—was, in fact, her first published work. But she also continued to write songs for adults and was able to sell a few of these outright for about twenty-five dollars each.

She soon realized, however, that if she was to support herself by her compositions she would have to publish them herself. To raise the money for a publishing venture, she gave a song recital at Steinway Hall, New York City, appearing in a dress made out of an old lace curtain. Having handled the promotion and ticket sale herself, she was able to realize a profit of several hundred dollars; and with an additional fifteen hundred dollars borrowed from a neighborhood druggist she set up a publishing firm in a hall bedroom, calling it "The Bond Shop." She issued her songs (usually to her own lyrics), designed the title covers, and plugged them at concerts. Her first book was *Seven Songs*; it included "I Love You Truly" and "Just a-Wearyin' for You," the latter to Frank Stanton's lyrics. The modest success of this publication led her to issue each of these songs separately, "Just a-Wearyin' For You" in 1901 and "I Love You Truly" five years later.

But it was some time before her publishing venture proved profitable. In fact, she

David Braham *1838-1905*

DAVID BRAHAM, whose most successful songs were written for the popular stage burlesques of Harrigan and Hart, was born in London in 1838. As a boy he studied the harp until one day, while trying to board a stagecoach with his harp, he became so exasperated with his futile attempts to handle its bulk that he decided to master a more manageable instrument. He studied and became adept at the violin, appearing in several concerts. When he was eighteen he went to New York, where he found a job as violinist in the orchestra of Tony Moore's Minstrels. During the next few years he played the violin in the pit orchestra of most of New York's leading theatres. He also led a military band. In 1865 he was appointed music director at Tony Pastor's Theatre and in 1868 he assumed the post of conductor for the Lingard company in New York.

Braham first achieved recognition as a song composer in the early 1870's with tunes and ballads modeled after English music hall songs. Some of these songs were written as special material for performers like Annie Yeamans, then a child star, James McKee, and Major Tom Thumb; they included "The Bootblack," "The Sailing on the Lake" and "Over the Hill to the Poorhouse."

In 1873 Braham wrote the music for "The Mulligan Guard," which was introduced by Ed Harrigan (who had written the lyrics) and his partner, Tony Hart, in a vaudeville sketch at the Academy of Music in Chicago on July 15, 1873. "The Mulligan Guard" lampooned popular organizations of the day that made a fetish of appearing in uniform; the sketch and song made such a mockery of the practice that the fad soon died out.

During the next few years Harrigan and Hart continued to write their own vaudeville burlesques, for which Braham wrote such songs as "The Skidmore Guard" and "Patrick's Day Parade" in 1874, and "Sweet Mary Ann" and "The Skidmore Fancy Ball" in 1879. These were also written to Harrigan's lyrics.

The success of *The Mulligan Guard* and other one-act burlesques in a similar vein encouraged Harrigan and Hart to embark on a whole series of full-length Mulligan productions which presented a cross-section of the life and characters of a big city. The first important hit in the series was *The Mulligan Guard's Ball*, introduced at the Theatre Comique in New York City on January 13, 1879. It was so popular that other Mulligan shows followed, including *The Mulligan*

Guard's Picnic, The Mulligan Guard's Chowder, The Mulligan Guard's Christmas, The Mulligan Guard's Nominee, and others. These burlesques described the everyday activities of ordinary people in a metropolis and were outstanding for their subtle racial characterizations. The Harrigan and Hart burlesques became a vogue in the American theatre, lasting for almost a decade. David Braham wrote the music, to Harrigan's lyrics, for all of these productions. Many of these songs became outstandingly popular, notably the following: "The Babies on Our Block" and "The Skidmore Fancy Ball" from *The Mulligan Guard's Ball* (1879); "The Horseshoe from the Door" from *The Mulligan Guard's Chowder* (1879); "The Pitcher of Beer" from *The Mulligan Guard's Christmas* (1879); "Locked Out After Nine" from *The Mulligan Guard's Picnic* (1880); "The Skidmore Masquerade" and "The Mulligan Braves" from *The Mulligan Guard's Nominee* (1880); "The Full Moon Union" from *The Mulligan Guard's Surprise* (1880); "Paddy Duffy's Cart" from *Squatter's Sovereignty* (1882); "I Never Drank Behind the Bar" from *McSorley's Inflation* (1883); and "My Dad's Dinner Pail" from *Cordelia's Aspirations* (1883).

During this period Braham also wrote songs for other lyricists, songs not intended for the Harrigan and Hart burlesques. To C. L. Stout's lyrics he wrote "The Eagle," "Emancipation Day," and "Eily Machree," the last popularized by the minstrel George Coes. To lyrics by George Cooper he wrote "To Rest Let Him Gently Be Laid"; and, to Hartley Neville's lyrics, "Sway the Cot Gently for Baby's Asleep."

The partnership of Harrigan and Hart was terminated by personal dissensions and bitter disagreements between the partners. After 1885 Harrigan and Hart went their separate ways in the theatre, and Braham continued to write songs for Ed Harrigan's plays. In 1885 "When Poverty's Tears Ebb and Flow" and "Sweetest Love" were featured in *Old Lavender*. Later Harrigan productions featured some of the best and most successful songs of Braham's career: the popular waltz "Maggie Murphy's Home," "The Jolly Commodore," and "Taking in the Town" from *Reilly and the 400* (1890); "Danny by My Side," "The Last of the

Hogans," and "Take a Day Off, Mary Ann" from *The Last of the Hogans* (1891); "They Never Tell All They Know" from the *The Woolen Stocking* (1893); and "The Pride of the London Stage" from Harrigan's last production, *The Merry Malones* (1896). One of these songs—"Danny by My Side"— was sung by Al Smith at the fiftieth-anniversary ceremonies of the Brooklyn Bridge in 1933.

David Braham married Ed Harrigan's sixteen-year-old daughter, Annie, in 1876. He died in New York on April 11, 1905, six years before his lyricist Harrigan.

ABOUT:
Kahn, E. J. The Merry Partners.
American Mercury, February 1929.

Shelton Brooks *1886-*

SHELTON BROOKS was born in Amesburg, Ontario, Canada, on May 4, 1886. He received his first instruction in music with lessons on the family pipe organ, playing at the keyboard while his older brother pumped away at the bellows. While he was still a boy, his family moved to Detroit, where Shelton appeared as a musical prodigy. His professional career as a pianist also began in Detroit with performances in cafés. Shelton eventually became famous as a Negro entertainer with a special gift for mimicry; Bert Williams, whom he imitated in his act, was one of his many admirers.

In 1910 Shelton Brooks wrote the song that first made him famous as a composer, a song that has never lost its popularity. It was "Some of These Days," written to his own lyrics and published by Will Rossiter in Chicago. The inspiration for this song came to Brooks in a restaurant where he overheard the phrase "some of these days" in a conversation. The song, introduced by Brooks in vaudeville, helped to launch Sophie Tucker on her career as a "red-hot mama" when she sang it for the first time at the White City Park in Chicago. Since then the song has served as her theme music; in fact, she used it for the title of her autobiography. The song sold several million copies of sheet music and records.

Brooks also wrote words and music for another equally famous song, the ragtime classic "The Darktown Strutters' Ball," published in 1917. A social gathering which Brooks attended at the San Francisco Exposition was his inspiration for this tune. It was publicly introduced by the Original Dixieland Jazz Band soon after its publication.

Between 1911 and the outbreak of World War I, Brooks produced other successful songs, all written to his own lyrics. These included: "There'll Come a Time," "Jean," "All Night Long," "Walkin' the Dog," "You Ain't Talkin' to Me," and "Honey Gal." The last two were made popular by Al Jolson at the Winter Garden.

For many years after 1910, Shelton Brooks was a headliner on the vaudeville circuit. He was also Florence Mills's co-star in the *Negro Plantation Revue,* produced on Broadway in 1922.

ABOUT:
Variety, July 31, 1940.

Nacio Herb Brown *1896-*

NACIO HERB BROWN was born in Deming, New Mexico, on February 22, 1896. His father was the local sheriff. While attending public school in Deming, Nacio studied piano with his mother, a trained musician, and later took violin lessons from a local teacher. When he was eight Nacio was taken to Los Angeles, where his father became a deputy sheriff. After attending Los Angeles public schools and graduating from the Musical Arts High School, Brown entered the University of California to study business administration. He stayed there less than a year, however, and left the University to work for a year as piano accompanist for Alice Doll on her vaudeville circuit. Then he opened a tailor shop in Hollywood, establishing a flourishing business that catered mainly to movie stars. In 1920 he began to invest his profits in Beverly Hills real estate. After the boom in land values in Beverly Hills during the next few years had made him wealthy, he gave up tailoring for a career in real estate.

During these years music remained his favorite avocation. In 1920, with King Zany, he wrote his first song, "Coral Sea," which Paul Whiteman and his orchestra helped make popular at the Alexandria Hotel in Los Angeles. The next year he wrote

"When Buddha Smiles" (lyrics by Arthur Freed), and in 1926 an instrumental piece, *Doll Dance,* was interpolated into Carter De Haven's *Music Box Revue* in Los Angeles.

In 1928 Irving Thalberg, head of production at MGM, persuaded Brown to write the music for his first all-talking, all-singing musical, *Broadway Melody.* With Freed as his lyricist, Brown wrote his first two song hits, the title song and "The Wedding of the Painted Doll." In 1929 *Broadway Melody* won the Academy Award; it was the first musical film to win that distinction. Brown now took a temporary leave of absence from his real estate business and continued to write songs for motion pictures in collaboration with Freed. For the *Hollywood Revue* he created "You Were Meant for Me"; for *The Pagan,* "The Pagan Love Song"; for *Lord Byron of Broadway,* "Should I?" and "The Woman in the Show"; and for *Untamed,* "The Chant of the Jungle."

Reassured about his talent and success as a composer, Brown decided to retire permanently from the business world in order to concentrate on composition. Unfortunately, this was a period when a reaction had set in against musical films. Although Brown managed to have one of his songs, "Temptation," interpolated into *A Woman Commands,* the opportunities for composers in Hollywood were scarce, and in 1932 Brown went to New York. There, in collaboration with Richard A. Whiting and the lyricist Buddy De Sylva, he contributed several important songs to the Broadway musical *Take a Chance,* which starred Ethel Merman. Among these were "You're an Old Smoothie" and "Eadie Was a Lady."

In 1933 Brown returned to Hollywood, resuming his partnership with Arthur Freed. From then on he assumed a dominant position among composers for the screen. During the ensuing fifteen years he wrote songs for more than thirty films. Some of these songs were among the greatest successes to emerge from the motion picture capital. To lyrics by Arthur Freed he wrote "We'll Make Hay While the Sun Shines" for *Going Hollywood;* "Love Songs of the Nile" for *The Barbarian;* "All I Do Is Dream of You" for *Sadie McKee;* "You Are My Lucky Star" and "Broadway Rhythm" for *Broadway Melody of 1936;* "Alone" for *A Night*

NACIO HERB BROWN   ASCAP

at the *Opera;* and "Would You?" for *San Francisco.* He also wrote, to Gus Kahn's lyrics, "You Stepped Out of a Dream" for *The Ziegfeld Girl;* and, to lyrics by Edward Heyman and Earl Brent, "If I Steal a Kiss," "Senorita," "Love Is Where You Find It," and "What's Wrong with Me?" for *The Kissing Bandit.*

In 1935 Brown wrote a successful instrumental composition, *American Bolero,* which exploited rhythms and melodies that were influential in American popular music: the primitive rhythms of African drums; the sensual lyricism of Latin American folk songs; the exotic atmosphere of Oriental music; the lilting three-quarter time of the Viennese waltz; and the intriguing rhythmic clicking of castanets of Spanish dances.

On February 23, 1960, the town of Deming honored Nacio Herb Brown by naming a city park after him. The dedication ceremonies were headed by Governor John Burroughs of New Mexico.

Hoagy Carmichael *1899-*

HOAGLAND CARMICHAEL was born in Bloomington, Indiana, on November 22, 1899. His mother was a pianist in the local motion picture theatre. Hoagy first realized that he was musical when, as a young boy, he found himself reproducing correctly

HOAGY CARMICHAEL

on the piano the tones from the nearby Indiana University tower bells. "The Dunn Meadows Demons lost an incompetent sixty-pound third baseman that day," he says. "Baseball was gone. The piano had me." Without taking a single lesson he soon acquired considerable proficiency in playing popular tunes.

When he was sixteen, his family moved to Indianapolis. Carmichael left high school in his freshman year to work at various jobs, including one as a cement mixer on a twelve-hour night shift. He spent his days at the piano, either at his own home or with a Negro pianist, Reggie Duval, who gave him valuable pointers on playing ragtime.

In 1919 Carmichael returned to Bloomington to complete his long-interrupted education. He graduated from high school in 1922 and entered Indiana University to study law, supporting himself during this time by playing piano in jazz bands (some of which he helped organize) and performing at resorts, university dances, and private parties. He also started to write music and succeeded in publishing a work called *Riverboat Shuffle* in 1924, an instrumental piece recorded by the Wolverines, one of Chicago's leading jazz groups, which included Bix Beiderbecke. A year later he wrote "Washboard Blues" to lyrics by Fred Callahan. This song was soon made popular through a recording by Paul Whiteman and his orchestra.

After receiving his law degree in 1926, Carmichael settled down in Florida to practice his profession. However, hearing a new recording of "Washboard Blues" by Red Nichols and his men convinced him that his future lay in music rather than law. He now returned to Bloomington, where he collaborated with the Paul Whiteman orchestra in a new recording of "Washboard Blues." This was the first time that his now famous rasping singing voice was preserved on records. He also found assignments to play piano for jazz orchestras led by Jean Goldkette and Don Redman and to serve as a demonstrator for several Tin Pan Alley firms.

One evening, in 1927, he was sitting on the so-called "spooning wall" of Indiana University, recalling a girl he had once loved and lost, when a melody suddenly came to him. He went over to the nearby "Book Nook," which boasted an old, battered piano, and wrote the first version of what was ultimately to become his classic song—"Stardust." But it was a long time before "Stardust" became popular. In its first version it was a piano rag, introduced by the Don Redman orchestra without attracting attention. Later, Jimmy Dale, an arranger, suggested that the piece be played in a slower tempo and a more sentimental style. Isham Jones first presented it in this new adaptation, and Emile Seidel recorded it with the composer at the piano. During the playback Carmichael felt for the first time that this song might become a huge success. "This melody was bigger than I," he recalls in his autobiography. "It didn't seem to be a part of me. Maybe I hadn't written it at all. It didn't sound familiar, even. . . . To lay my claims, I wanted to shout back at it, 'Maybe I didn't write you, but I found you!' "

In 1928 Carmichael's publisher, Irving Mills, prevailed on him to have a lyric written for a sweet version of this melody, a job that fell to Mitchell Parish, with whom Carmichael had already collaborated. Now many popular singers and bands started to feature "Stardust" with increasing success. Walter Winchell heaped praises on the song in his column. A 1935 recording by Artie Shaw sold two million copies and finally established the song as a major hit. Since then, "Stardust" has become one of the greatest American all-time song successes. It has been recorded almost five hundred times in forty-six different arrangements; the lyrics have been translated into about forty languages; and it is perhaps the only song ever recorded on both sides of the same disc, one side featuring an arrangement by Tommy Dorsey and the other an arrangement by Benny Goodman.

Long before "Stardust" established his reputation as a composer, Carmichael went to New York where he supported himself by working at several nonmusical jobs while writing songs. In 1930 he wrote "Georgia on My Mind" (lyrics by Stuart Gorrell) and "Rockin' Chair" (to his own lyrics); in 1931, "Lazy River" (lyrics by Sidney Arodin), revived seventeen years later in the motion picture *The Best Years of Our Lives;* in 1932, "Lazybones," with which he began a words-and-music partnership with the lyricist Johnny Mercer that yielded a veritable harvest of hits through the years; and in 1934, "Judy" (lyrics by Sammy Lerner). "Little Old Lady" (lyrics by Stanley Adams) was a high spot of the Broadway revue *The Show Is On* in 1937.

In 1936 Carmichael started to write songs for motion pictures, beginning with "Moonburn" (lyrics by Edward Heyman). In the next few years some of Carmichael's most important songs were written for motion pictures. Two of these were to lyrics by Frank Loesser: "Small Fry," sung by Bing Crosby in *Sing You Sinners,* and "Two Sleepy People," introduced by Bob Hope in *Thanks for the Memory.* Among Carmichael's later songs for the screen were "The Old Music Master" (lyrics by Johnny Mercer) for *True to Life;* "Doctor, Lawyer, Indian Chief" (lyrics by Paul Francis Webster) for *Stork Club;* "Memphis in June" (lyrics by Webster) for *Johnny Angel;* and "Ol' Buttermilk Sky" (lyrics by Jack Brooks) for *Canyon Passage.* He received the Academy Award in 1951 for "In the Cool, Cool, Cool of the Evening" (lyrics by Mercer), written for *Here Comes the Groom.*

In 1940, with Mercer as his lyricist, Carmichael wrote the songs for the Broadway musical *Walk with Music,* starring Kitty Carlisle and Mitzi Green. In 1945 he entered upon another fruitful career, as a motion-picture actor, when he appeared as Crickett,

the pianist in a Martinique honky-tonk, in *To Have and Have Not.* He developed an informal acting style of his own, while introducing some of his own songs, including "Hong Kong Blues" and "How Little We Know" (lyrics by Mercer). Carmichael has since been seen quite often in motion pictures and has been a frequent performer on radio and television, as the star of his own show and also in guest spots.

Other successful songs by Carmichael include "The Nearness of You" (lyrics by Ned Washington), "The Lamplighter's Serenade" (lyrics by Webster), and (to his own lyrics) "Ivy."

ABOUT:

Carmichael, Hoagy. The Stardust Road.
Metronome, January 1947; Newsweek, June 4, 1945; Songwriter's Review, January 1948.

Harry Carroll 1892-

HARRY CARROLL was born in Atlantic City, New Jersey, on November 28, 1892. Mainly self-taught in music, he began to earn his living while attending grade school by playing the piano in local movie theatres. After graduating from high school he went to New York where he found work as an arranger in Tin Pan Alley. At night he played the piano in a trio at the Garden Café on 7th Avenue and 50th Street. In 1912 he was placed under contract to the Shuberts to provide songs for some of their productions. "On the Mississippi," which he wrote with Arthur Fields to lyrics by Ballard MacDonald, appeared in *The Whirl of Society* (1912) and became his first hit. Within the next three years his songs were heard in *Dancing Abroad* (1914), *The Passing Show of 1914,* and *Maid in America* (1915).

During this time he also wrote hit songs not intended for the stage. In 1913 he wrote three tunes to MacDonald's lyrics: "There's a Girl in the Heart of Maryland," "The Trail of the Lonesome Pine" and "It Takes a Little Rain with the Sunshine to Make the World Go Round." Later products of this collaboration were "Tip-Top Tipperary Mary," "Down in Bom-Bombay," and "She Is the Sunshine of Virginia"; and another noteworthy song, this to Harold Atteridge's lyrics, was "By the Beautiful Sea."

HARRY CARROLL   ASCAP

In 1918 Carroll wrote songs to lyrics by Joseph McCarthy for a Broadway musical which he himself produced, *Oh, Look!* It is in this score that we find the greatest song success of Carroll's career, "I'm Always Chasing Rainbows," its main melody lifted unabashedly from Chopin's Fantaisie-Impromptu in C-sharp minor. This song sold over a million copies of sheet music in 1918 and was successfully revived in 1945 in the motion picture *The Dolly Sisters.* In 1919 Carroll wrote the songs (to lyrics by Atteridge) for a Broadway musical, *The Little Blue Devil,* which starred Lillian Lorraine.

For many years Harry Carroll was a headliner in vaudeville, first in an act in which he co-starred with his wife, Anna Wheaton, and later in a lavish stage production. After the decline of vaudeville, Harry Carroll appeared as a "single" in leading night clubs, singing his own song hits. From 1914 to 1917 Carroll was the director of ASCAP.

Ivan Caryll *1861-1921*

IVAN CARYLL was born Felix Tilken in Liége, Belgium, in 1861. He received a thorough education in serious music, first with private teachers, next at the Liége Conservatory, and last with Eugene Ysaÿe and Camille Saint-Saëns. He made his debut as a composer for the stage in Paris, and later went to London, where he established permanent residence and became principal conductor of the Gaiety Theatre, a center for musical productions in England. For a while he wrote incidental music for several plays produced in London; then he made adaptations of French farces for the English stage. One of these adaptations, *La Cigale,* appeared in an American version that starred Lillian Russell. This was the first time that Caryll's music was performed in the United States.

Caryll began his career as a composer of operettas with *Little Christopher Columbus,* which was produced in London in 1893, and in New York a year later with additional music by Gustave Kerker. From then until 1910 he ranked as one of England's most prolific and successful composers of musicals. Some of these musicals were written in collaboration with Lionel Monckton. Some were brought to New York, notably *The Girl from Paris* (1897), *The Runaway Girl* (1898), *The Girl from Kay's* (1903), *The Earl and the Girl* (1905), and *The Orchid* (1907). These shows made him famous on Broadway years before he emigrated to the United States.

Ivan Caryll moved to the United States in 1911 and remained there for the rest of his life, acquiring American citizenship. Writing music for the Broadway stage, he now achieved some of the greatest successes of his career. On March 13, 1911, *The Pink Lady,* adapted from a French farce, arrived at the New Amsterdam Theatre with Alice Dovey in the title role. *The Pink Lady* was one of the most successful operettas of the time. The popularity of this show made pink the 1911 color vogue in women's clothes; and its two best numbers, the waltzes "My Beautiful Lady" and "The Kiss Waltz" (lyrics by Harry Morton), are still remembered. In 1912 Caryll wrote the music for *Oh, Oh, Delphine,* which opened on September 30, and in 1914 for *Chin-Chin,* an oriental fantasy which appeared on October 20 with David Montgomery and Fred Stone in the leading roles. The first show featured the title number (lyrics by Morton) and "Venus Waltz"; the second "Goodbye, Girls, I'm Through" (lyrics by John Golden), "Love Moon," and "Violet." The last two were written to lyrics by Anne Caldwell and James O'Dea.

Courtesy of The New York Public Library,
Joseph Muller Collection, Music Division

IVAN CARYLL

After 1917 some of Caryll's most important operettas were *Jack O'Lantern* (1917), which starred Fred Stone and featured the numbers "Wait Till the Cows Come Home" and "Come and Have a Swing with Me" (lyrics by Caldwell); *The Girl Behind the Gun* (1918), which included "There's a Light in Your Eyes" and "There's Life in the Old Dog Yet," with lyrics by P. G. Wodehouse; and *The Canary* (1918), also written in collaboration with Wodehouse. He wrote his last operetta, *Tip Top*, in 1920.

Caryll died in New York City on November 28, 1921. His music, as described in an obituary in the New York *Herald*, "combined freshness and lightness with careful workmanship, a knowledge of his medium . . . uncommon among musical-comedy composers . . . [of his time], that enabled him to turn out musical hits of enduring merit."

ABOUT:
Smith, Cecil. Musical Comedy in America.
Musical America, December 10, 1921.

George M. Cohan *1878-1942*

GEORGE MICHAEL COHAN was successful as a serious actor, song-and-dance man, playwright, song composer, lyricist, and producer. But it is his career in popular music that will be dealt with here. He was born in Providence, Rhode Island, on July 3, 1878. (Cohan himself believed he was born on July 4 and many biographies carry that date; but July 3 appears on his birth certificate.) He was the last of three children; the first died in infancy, and the second, Josephine, was born two years before George. His parents, Jeremiah and Helen Cohan, were vaudevillians who toured the circuit. Continuously on the move, they stayed in shabby boarding houses and lived out of battered valises. The Cohan children shared this nomadic existence, often sleeping in musty dressing rooms while their parents performed on the stage.

As a child George received a smattering of public school education and some lessons on the violin. But the theatre was, for the most part, his elementary school, high school, and college. He made his first stage appearance while still an infant, as a human prop in one of the vaudeville sketches enacted by his parents. At nine he became an official member of the act by speaking a few lines in a sketch entitled "The Two Barneys," first performed in Haverstraw, New York. A year later Josephine joined, and the act from then on was billed as "The Four Cohans." George's performances included buck-and-wing dances, a bootblack specialty, and some sentimental recitations. At eleven he started to write material for the act, and at thirteen he contributed some of the songs, writing lyrics and music.

His songwriting career took an important leap forward in 1894, when "Why Did Nellie Leave Home?" was purchased by Witmark for $25 and published. In 1895 May Irwin bought one of his songs, "Hot Tamale Alley," and featured it in her vaudeville act. In 1897 he had a minor success, "The Warmest Baby in the Bunch," and in 1898 a major one, "I Guess I'll Have to Telegraph My Baby."

Isidore Witmark writes in his autobiography, *From Ragtime to Swingtime*, that the young George M. Cohan, like the mature performer of later years, was brash, self-assured, and cocky, a "self-opinioned youngster with implicit faith in his gifts. . . . When he was not arguing with theatre folk, he was tramping the streets of New York with unrecognized masterpieces under his arm. He was no more afraid of publishers than he was of managers. . . . Everybody in those days

GEORGE M. COHAN

was swell-headed to Georgie, except the ardent, impatient boy who made the ready diagnosis. He would pass the Witmark offices and call the brothers 'big stiffs'—to himself. 'Just goes to show how smart those babies in there are, publishing all that bum material written by a lot of hams, and here am I, the best song writer, walking right by their door with four or five big sure hits under my arm.' "

As "The Four Cohans" began to achieve the status of headliners, earning a weekly salary of $1,000, George took increasing control of virtually every department of their act. He wrote the songs and sketches, assumed a starring role, and managed the business affairs. With seemingly limitless energy, he also wrote songs and sketches for other vaudevillians, selling his material outright for a small cash price.

In 1899 Cohan married the popular singing comedienne Ethel Levey, who joined "The Four Cohans." George now began to feel that he had gone as far as he could in vaudeville, that he must now conquer a new world —the Broadway musical comedy stage. He proceeded cautiously in this direction, at first writing only musicals based on his vaudeville sketches. *The Governor's Son* was produced in 1901 and *Running for Office* in 1903. Both were failures.

His first major success on the Broadway legitimate stage was also his first original musical comedy. For it he wrote book, music, and lyrics. *Little Johnny Jones* opened on Broadway on November 7, 1904, with Cohan in the leading role as an American jockey in England—a character suggested by a well-known jockey of the time, Tod Sloan. Cohan introduced two of his songs which became favorites: "The Yankee Doodle Boy" and "Give My Regards to Broadway." When *Little Johnny Jones* first appeared on Broadway it was poorly reviewed, and the public was unresponsive. But after Cohan took the show on an extended tour and subjected it to elaborate revision, it revisited Broadway, remaining for almost four months. This run placed it in the solid hit class.

On January 1, 1906, *Forty-Five Minutes from Broadway*—for which Cohan again wrote book, lyrics, and music—opened at the New Amsterdam. Fay Templeton starred in it, and Victor Moore appeared in a supporting role, achieving his first important success as a comedian in the musical theatre. This time Cohan left it to other performers to introduce songs like the homespun, sentimental "Mary's a Grand Old Name" and "So Long Mary," which became resounding hits. But he did star in this show when it was revived on Broadway in 1912; and he did have a part— the title role—in another of his plays which opened in 1906 for a successful Broadway run: *George Washington, Jr.* It was in this play that Cohan introduced the routine which he made famous and with which he afterwards identified himself—marching up and down the stage with an American flag as he sang a rousing patriotic tribute to the colors. In *George Washington, Jr.*, this routine was performed to the song "You're a Grand Old Flag." Curiously, the song created a small scandal when it was first introduced. Its original title, "You're a Grand Old Rag," was strongly opposed by several patriotic societies that objected to the American flag's being referred to as a rag. Cohan bowed to the judgment of his critics and changed the offending word.

Before the decade was over Cohan had several other successful musicals to his credit: *The Talk of the Town* (1907), *Fifty Miles from Boston* (1908), *The Yankee Prince* (1908), *The American Idea* (1908), and *The Man Who Owns Broadway* (1909). The best songs in these plays were "I Want You," "Under Any Old Flag at All," and "When a

Fellow's on the Level with a Girl That's on the Square" from *The Talk of the Town;* "Come on Down Town" *(The Yankee Prince);* and "There's Something About a Uniform" *(The Man Who Owns Broadway).*

Meanwhile two important developments had taken place in his life. In 1907 his divorce from Ethel Levey brought their personal and professional association to an end. Later that year he married Agnes Nolan. Earlier, in 1904, he had gone into partnership with Sam H. Harris. Their producing firm, which presented many Broadway plays (some by Cohan), became one of the most successful in the country and in 1911 had six hits on Broadway and a controlling interest in seven theatres. (There was also a family relationship between Cohan and Harris; Cohan's second wife, Agnes, was Harris's sister-in-law.)

From 1910 to 1917 Cohan wrote the music for four more musicals—*The Little Millionaire* (1911), *Hello Broadway* (1914), and two editions of the *Cohan Revue* (1916 and 1917). But he distinguished himself even more by the pleasing and amiable nonmusical stage comedies *Get Rich Quick Wallingford* (1910), *Broadway Jones* (1913), and *Seven Keys to Baldpate* (1913), which won him recognition as one of America's foremost contemporary playwrights.

Cohan's popular songs, like his plays, could be called sentimental, trite, and cliché-ridden. But he did inject into them a fresh viewpoint and an individual personality—an American viewpoint that was idiomatic and colloquial and that proved a bracing tonic at a time when the American theatre was flooded with operettas and lilting three-quarter-time music that aped the Viennese style.

His greatest single success as a popular composer, however, was not written for a play but was inspired by America's entry into the maelstrom of World War I. "I read those war headlines," he said, "and I got to thinking and humming to myself—and for a minute I thought I was going to dance. I was all finished with both the chorus and the verse by the time I got to town, and I also had a title." The title was "Over There," a song that became one of America's greatest and most popular martial tunes. After its New York introduction at the Hippodrome Theatre by Charles King in the fall of 1917, "Over

There" was made into a nation-wide hit by Nora Bayes. It sold over two million copies of sheet music and a million records. President Woodrow Wilson described it as "a genuine inspiration to all American manhood," and, a quarter of a century later, Congress authorized President Franklin Delano Roosevelt to present Cohan with a Congressional Medal of Honor for this war classic.

In 1919 Cohan was seriously affected, both as a producer and as a playwright, when Actors' Equity called a strike in order to gain recognition as a bargaining agent for its members. When he saw many of his old friends and colleagues (including some whom he had generously helped to advance their careers) lining up on the side of Equity, Cohan took it as a personal affront and did everything he could to defeat Equity. The strike won despite his efforts, and Cohan, as a result, lost some of his old zest and enthusiasm for the theatre: he broke up the successful producing firm of Cohan and Harris, withdrew his membership from the Friars and Lambs Clubs, and spoke of retiring permanently. For a while he traveled and rested. In the end, however, the lure of the stage proved irresistible and he returned with several plays, musical and nonmusical: *The Song and Dance Man* (1923), *The Merry Malones* (1927), and, in 1929, *The Tavern,* a revival of a 1920 play. His last musical comedy was *Billie* (1928). These were not successful, and Cohan's failure to win audiences added to his pent-up bitterness. "It's getting to be too much for me, kid," he told a friend. "I guess people don't understand me any more, and I don't understand them."

In 1932 he went to Hollywood to star in *The Phantom President.* This experience proved even more harrowing than his Broadway failures. Directors tried to teach him how to act, how to sing, and even how to do his famous flag routine. Producers did not give him the homage he felt was his due. He returned from Hollywood vowing never again to appear in films. "If I had my choice between Hollywood and Atlanta," he remarked bitterly, "I'd take Leavenworth."

But soon afterwards Cohan made a comeback. On Broadway, two acting appearances brought him accolades from critics and public. In 1933 he starred in Eugene O'Neill's comedy *Ah, Wilderness!* and in 1937 he appeared as President Roosevelt in the Rodgers and Hart musical *I'd Rather Be Right*. In Hollywood, his fabulous career was dramatized in 1942 in *Yankee Doodle Dandy,* with James Cagney impersonating Cohan in an Academy Award-winning performance.

In 1940 Cohan made his last attempt to recapture Broadway with an original play, *The Return of the Vagabond.* It closed after seven performances. "They don't want me no more," he told a friend.

In 1942, while recovering from an abdominal operation, Cohan paid his last visit to Broadway. Insisting that his nurse accompany him on a taxi ride around Broadway, he cruised up and down from Union Square to Times Square, almost as if reviewing his career. Then he stopped off for a few minutes at the Hollywood Theatre to watch a scene from *Yankee Doodle Dandy.* He never revisited Broadway. When he died in New York on November 5, 1942, President Roosevelt wired, "A beloved figure is lost to our national life." The writer and producer Gene Buck, a former president of ASCAP, called him "the greatest single figure the American theatre ever produced."

Cohan left behind a record of achievement unique in the American theatre. All but eight of his sixty-four years had been spent on the stage. He had written 40 plays, collaborated in the writing of 40 others, and shared in the production of about 150 more. He had made thousands of appearances as an actor. And he had written over 500 songs, including some that ranked as the greatest hits of their time.

ABOUT:
Morehouse, Ward. George M. Cohan: Prince of the American Theater.
Music Journal, January 1958.

Con Conrad *1891-1938*

CON CONRAD was born Conrad K. Dober on the Lower East Side of New York on June 18, 1891. He resisted formal schooling. He entered public school reluctantly and, for a short time, attended a military academy, working at the same time to help support his family. He worked as a page in a Wall Street brokerage house, as a program boy at the Grand Opera House, and as an usher in local movie theatres. He had been playing the piano from childhood on, though here, too, he resisted systematic training. When he was sixteen he left high school and made his bow as a professional musician, working as a pianist in a theatre on 125th Street. He soon graduated from the pit to the stage itself, working first as an accompanist to various vaudeville performers. Later he became a performer on the Keith vaudeville circuit as well as in vaudeville theatres and revues in London. Then in 1912 he entered a new field of activity, songwriting. His first published work was "Down in Dear Old New Orleans" (lyrics by Joe Young), a song interpolated into the Ziegfeld *Follies* of 1912. In 1913 he became the producer of the Broadway musical *The Honeymoon Express,* which starred the young and unknown Al Jolson.

Conrad's career as a composer did not begin in earnest until after he had formed a publishing partnership with Henry Waterson and had started to write musical numbers for his own firm. His first successful songs were "Oh, Frenchy!" (lyrics by Sam Ehrlich) in 1918, and, two years later, "Palesteena," written in collaboration with J. Russel Robinson. In 1920 he also produced a formidable hit song, "Margie" (lyrics by Benny Davis), also written with Robinson. Conrad proceeded to turn out popular songs in rapid succession: "Ma, He's Making Eyes at Me" (lyrics by Sidney Clare), introduced on Broadway in the *Midnight Rounders* (1921); "Barney Google" (made successful by Olsen and Johnson), "You've Got to See Your Mama Ev'ry Night," and "Come On, Spark Plug!" to lyrics by Billy Rose; "Memory Lane," written with Larry Spier to Buddy De Sylva's lyrics; and "Lonesome and Sorry" to lyrics by Benny Davis. During this period his songs were also featured more frequently in Broadway stage productions. In 1921 four of his songs were heard in *Bombo,* a show starring Al Jolson. From 1924 to 1926 he wrote either the complete scores or most of the scores for such varied stage attractions as *Moonlight* (1924), *Mercenary Mary* (1925), *The Comic Supplement* (1925), *Kitty's Kisses* (1926), and *Americana* (1926).

When the motion picture industry began to produce sound movies, Con Conrad was one of the first Broadway composers lured to Hollywood. His initial assignment, in 1929, was to write five songs for one of the first screen revues, *The Fox Movietone Follies*; the best of these was "Walking With Susie" (lyrics by Sidney Mitchell). During the next few years he continued to write for motion pictures, producing hits like "A Needle in a Haystack" (for *The Gay Divorcee)*, and "Midnight in Paris" and the title number for *Here's to Romance*, all to lyrics by Herb Magidson. In 1934 he became the first composer to win an Academy Award for a song: this honor went to "The Continental" from *The Gay Divorcee* (lyrics by Magidson).

While working in Hollywood, Conrad wrote some successful independent numbers in collaboration with other composers. With Archie Gottler he wrote "Sing a Little Love Song" (lyrics by Mitchell); with Clarence Gaiskill, "Prisoner of Love" (lyrics by Leo Robin); and with Russ Columbo, "You Call It Madness but I Call It Love" (lyrics by Gladys Du Bois and Paul Gregory).

Conrad's first wife was the celebrated Broadway actress Francine Larrimore. In the late 1920's he lost his fortune financing a number of musical productions and went into bankruptcy in 1928. He died in Van Nuys, California, on September 28, 1938.

ABOUT:
Musical America, October 10, 1938; Music Trades, October 1938; Pacific Coast Musician, October 1, 1938.

J. Fred Coots *1897-*

J. FRED COOTS was born in Brooklyn, New York, on May 2, 1897. He studied piano with his mother while attending grade school. At the age of sixteen he left high school to work as a clerk for a Wall Street bank. One day, in 1914, while listening to a song plugger play a current hit in a nearby music shop, he suddenly decided to look for a career in popular music. He became a song plugger for the New York branch of McKinley Music Company, a Chicago firm. In 1917 his first song was published; it was "Mister Ford, You've Got the Right Idea" (lyrics by Ray Sherwood), inspired by Henry Ford's announcement that he was sending a "peace ship" to Europe to try to end World War I. Though he earned for this maiden effort only five dollars, which he shared with his lyricist, Coots felt he

was on his way as a songwriter. During the next few years he wrote special song material for several vaudeville headliners, including Sophie Tucker and Van and Schenk.

He saved enough money to enter the Friars Club, where he met Eddie Dowling, who was planning to produce the Broadway musical *Sally, Irene and Mary.* Dowling hoped to get some famous composer for its score but was finally persuaded by Coots to take a chance on him. *Sally, Irene and Mary,* starring Eddie Dowling and Edna Morn, opened on September 4, 1922, to run for almost two years. Coots' reputation as a composer was established with such appealing numbers as "I Wonder Why," "Do You Remember the Days?," "Jimmie," and "Time Will Tell" (lyrics by Raymond Klages). Coots now signed a contract with the Shuberts to write music for many of their musical productions. During the next decade his songs were heard in two editions of *Artists and Models, June Days* (1925), *Gay Paree* (1925), *The Merry World* (1926), *A Night in Paris* (1926), *White Lights* (1927), and *Sons o' Guns* (1920). For *Sons o' Guns*— which was, incidentally, his farewell to the stage—he wrote two highly acclaimed numbers: "Why?" and "Cross Your Fingers" (lyrics by Benny Davis and Arthur Swanstorm).

Coots did not confine his talent exclusively to the theatre. He also wrote songs for night

J. FRED COOTS

clubs and motion pictures, as well as individual numbers not intended for specific productions. His most important songs included: "Doin' the Raccoon" (lyrics by Klages); "I Still Get a Thrill Thinking of You" (lyrics by Benny Davis); "Love Letters in the Sand" (lyrics by Nick Kenny), successfully revived by Pat Boone a quarter of a century later; "Two Tickets to Georgia" (lyrics by Joe Young and Charles Tobias); "For All We Know" (lyrics by Sam M. Lewis); "Santa Claus Is Coming to Town" (lyrics by Haven Gillespie); "Beautiful Lady in Blue" (lyrics by Lewis); "This Time It's Love" (lyrics by Lewis); "You Go to My Head" (lyrics by Gillespie); and "Precious Little Thing Called Love" (lyrics by Lou Davis). The last was introduced in the motion picture *The Shopworn Angel* and sold over two million copies of sheet music.

In the 1920's Coots was a successful performer on the vaudeville stage, and more recently he has made many appearances in night clubs. He is credited with having discovered Jimmy Durante, whom he found in the Alamo, a Harlem night club, and whom he persuaded to turn to comedy with Eddie Jackson and Lou Clayton.

Between 1936 and 1939 Coots, with Benny Davis as his lyricist, wrote the score for three editions of the Cotton Club Revue starring Cab Calloway. Among their songs were "The Boogie-Woogie," "Copper Colored Gal," "The Harlem Bolero," and "I'm at the Mercy of Love." In 1952 Coots tried his hand at writing another kind of song—"kiddie songs." The first, "Me and My Teddy Bear," launched singer Rosemary Clooney on her way to stardom in records and on television. "Who'll Tie the Bell on the Old Cat's Tail?," "Little Johnny Chickadee," "When the Teddy Bears Go Marching on Parade," "Little Sally One-Shoe," and "Ozzie the Ostrich" are other "kiddie songs" recorded by Rosemary Clooney.

Besides writing over three thousand songs (seven hundred of which have been published), Coots has distinguished himself on the lecture platform. In a program entitled "Melodies and Memories," he made over two hundred lecture appearances over a five-year period.

About:
Music Business, February 1947.

H. P. Danks *1834-1903*

HART PEASE DANKS was born in New Haven, Connecticut, on April 6, 1834. His father was a builder. When he was eight, Hart moved with his family to Saratoga Springs, New York. There he studied music with Dr. L. E. Whiting and served as a boy chorister. After his family resettled in Chicago, Hart helped out for several years in his father's building enterprise. At nineteen he entered the trade of carpentry, but soon abandoned it for a career in music. He started as a choir leader, bass singer, conductor of several music societies, and composer. His first composition was a hymn, "Lake Street," which later appeared in William Bradbury's *Jubilee Collection.* In 1856 he published two songs, "Anna Lee" and "The Old Lane," for which he wrote words and music. He went to New York in 1864 and supported himself by performing as a bass singer and directing various musical groups while he continued to write songs. In 1870 he produced a major success, a sentimental ballad, "Don't Be Angry With Me, Darling."

One day, while reading a Wisconsin farm journal, Danks came across a poem written by the editor of the journal, Eben E. Rexford. The poem so impressed him that he wrote to Rexford, offering three dollars for permission to use it as a song lyric. Rexford apparently was so pleased at finding an admirer that he sent Danks an entire batch of poems. One of these was called "Silver Threads Among the Gold."

In 1872—a year in which he wrote about forty songs and his first operetta, *Pauline*—Danks set to music, as a loving, sentimental tribute to his wife, the poem "Silver Threads Among the Gold." "Silver Threads Among the Gold," published in 1873, soon became one of the most famous of American sentimental ballads. It sold over two million copies of sheet music before the end of the century. In 1902 it was revived in vaudeville by the minstrel Richard José, a member of the Primrose and West Minstrels, and it became, once again, an outstanding commercial success. Its sale, which rose to a million copies, was the largest a revived number had ever achieved. Unfortunately, Danks had sold this song outright for a pittance and never profited from its fabulous sale. Ironi-

H. P. DANKS

cally, too, Danks and his wife were separated a year after the song was written.

"Silver Threads Among the Gold" is the only song Danks wrote that is still remembered. But he wrote many others, popular and religious, which were successful in their time. He published over thirteen hundred individual numbers; in 1881 he completed a second operetta, *Conquered by Kindness;* and in 1892 he published a volume of hymns, *Superior Anthems for Church Choirs.* His mose celebrated hymn was "Not Ashamed of Christ," published in 1883. Among his most famous secular songs were "Allie Darling," and "Little Bright Eyes, Will You Miss Me?" both to lyrics by W. J. D. Rutledge.

Danks died in poverty in a dismal rooming house in Philadelphia, on November 20, 1903. The last words he committed to paper were: "It's hard to die alone."

ABOUT:
Spaeth, Sigmund. A History of Popular Music in America.

Reginald De Koven *1859-1920*

HENRY LOUIS REGINALD DE KOVEN was born in Middletown, Connecticut, on April 3, 1859. His father was a clergyman. When Reginald was eleven, his family moved to England, and he at-tended school there, graduating from St. John's College, Oxford, in 1879. Having made the decision to engage in a professional career in music, he went to Europe to study intensively under Lebert and Pruckner in Germany, Vannucini in Italy, von Suppé and Genée in Vienna, and Delibes in France.

In 1882 De Koven returned to the United States and settled in Chicago, where, after working for several years as a bank teller and as a clerk in a brokerage house, he fell in love with and married Anna Farwell, the daughter of a prominent Chicago businessman. Later, De Koven entered the business world as the proprietor of a large dry-goods establishment. His great success in this endeavor and in his speculations in Texas real estate enabled him not only to live in a grand style but also to turn exclusively to musical activity. He now divided his efforts between criticism and composition. As a music critic he worked first, in 1889, for the Chicago *Evening Post,* then, from 1895 to 1897, for *Harper's Weekly,* and from 1898 to 1900—and again from 1907 to 1912—for the New York *World.*

De Koven first distinguished himself as a composer in the field of comic opera, which drew his interest as a result of his friendship with the librettist H. B. Smith. The two collaborated on a work modeled after Gilbert and Sullivan's *The Mikado.* Entitled *The Begum,* it was set in India, and it starred De Wolf Hopper. After opening in Philadelphia on November 17, 1888, it went to New York four days later.

The Begum was a failure, as was a second opera, *Don Quixote,* in 1889. At last, however, De Koven and Smith achieved not only a major success but a work generally considered to be the most important operetta (or comic opera) written in America before Victor Herbert. With a cast including Eugene Cowles and Jessie Bartlett Davis, *Robin Hood* opened in Boston on June 9, 1890, and in New York on September 28, 1891.

Robin Hood was the comic opera in which De Koven's most memorable song, "Oh, Promise Me," was first heard. Now a classic, it is most often performed at weddings. "Oh, Promise Me" (lyrics by Clement Scott) was not written for *Robin Hood* but was originally published as an independent

Courtesy of The New York Public Library, Music Division
REGINALD DE KOVEN

number in 1889 by Schirmer. During the rehearsals of *Robin Hood* a need was felt for an additional song, and De Koven suggested using "Oh, Promise Me." Nobody in the cast, however, seemed interested in the song until Jessie Bartlett Davis, who was cast as Alan-a-Dale, happened to be humming the melody in her dressing room one day. The producer heard her and said, "If you sing that song as you are now doing, in a lower key, it will make your reputation."

"Oh, Promise Me" is, of course, the song for which *Robin Hood* will always be remembered, and its popularity is the reason behind the occasional revivals of this comic opera. But the score also contained other delightful melodies—evidence that in De Koven America had produced its first important composer of comic operas. These songs included "The Tailor's Song," "The Armorer's Song," and "Brown October Ale."

For two decades De Koven and Smith continued to write operettas. None are revived today, and few are remembered. But in their day many were popular favorites: *The Knickerbockers* (1892); *Rob Roy* (1894); *The Highwayman* (1897), probably De Koven's best score next to *Robin Hood; The Little Duchess* (1901); *Maid Marian* (1902); *The Golden Butterfly* (1908); and *Her Little Highness* (1913). De Koven's

most famous songs were "My Home Is Where the Heather Blooms" and "Dearest of My Heart" from *Rob Roy;* and "Do You Remember Love?" and "Moonlight Song" from *The Highwayman.*

De Koven also achieved recognition as a composer of two American operas. *The Canterbury Pilgrims,* a setting for a poetical drama by Percy Mackaye, was produced by the Metropolitan Opera in 1917. *Rip Van Winkle* was introduced in Chicago three years after that. De Koven also wrote an orchestral suite, a piano sonata, and about four hundred art songs and incidental compositions.

De Koven died in Chicago on January 15, 1920. For many years before his death he lived in a mansion at 1025 Park Avenue in New York. For two decades—until the building was demolished—his bedroom and study were left unchanged by his widow as a memorial to him.

ABOUT:
De Koven, Anna. A Musician and His Wife; Goldberg, Isaac. Tin Pan Alley; Howard, John Tasker. Our American Music; Paris, Leonard Allen. Men of Melodies.

Peter De Rose *1900-1953*

PETER DE ROSE was born on New York's Lower East Side on March 10, 1900. He was one of nine children. An older sister began to give him piano lessons when he was twelve; but after his fourth lesson he refused to study and learned to play by ear. His attempts at composition began when he was thirteen. After attending New York public schools and graduating from De Witt Clinton High School, he found a job in the stock room at Schirmer's music publishing establishment. During this period he wrote, in 1920, his first song, "When You're Gone I Won't Forget" (lyrics by Ivan Reid), which he sold outright to Haviland for $25.00. The song sold almost a million copies of sheet music. Although De Rose did not profit directly from this immense sale, the success of his song enabled him to get a desirable position with G. Ricordi, the music publishing house. One of the employees there was the Negro composer and singer Harry Burleigh, who encouraged De Rose in his creative work.

For sixteen years, from 1923 to 1939, Peter De Rose was featured with May Singhi Breen on a program on the NBC network; the two were billed as "The Sweethearts of the Air." (May Singhi Breen later became De Rose's wife.) De Rose played the piano and his partner the ukulele; both sang popular tunes of the day. Many of De Rose's great song hits were first introduced on this program. In 1926 he scored a major success with "Muddy Water," written in collaboration with Harry Richman to lyrics by Jo' Trent. During the next seven years he wrote "I Just Roll Along, Havin' My Ups and Downs" (lyrics by Jo' Trent); "Walking with My Sweetness Down Among the Sugar Cane" (lyrics by Charles Tobias and Sidney Clare); "When Your Hair Has Turned to Silver" and "One More Kiss Then Goodbye" (lyrics by Tobias); "Wagon Wheels" (lyrics by Billy Hill), introduced in *The New Ziegfeld Follies* (1934); "Have You Ever Been Lonely" and "There's a Home in Wyoming" (lyrics by Hill); and "Song of the Blacksmith" (lyrics by Al Stillman).

Peter De Rose's greatest song, and the one for which he will probably best be remembered, is "Deep Purple." He wrote it as a piano composition in 1933. A year later it was transcribed for orchestra in a version introduced by Paul Whiteman and his orchestra on May 10, 1934. It did not become a hit until 1939, when it was reintroduced with lyrics by Mitchell Parish as a sentimental ballad. Since then it has been one of the classics of American popular music. Babe Ruth loved the song so deeply that De Rose performed it as a kind of birthday ritual during the last ten years of the home-run king's life.

After 1939 De Rose's songs further established him as one of America's most gifted popular composers. Among them were "The Lamp Is Low," adapted from Maurice Ravel's *Pavane pour une Infante Défunte* and written in collaboration with Bert Shefter to Parish's lyrics; "All I Need Is You" (lyrics by Benny Davis and Parish); "Who Do You Know in Heaven?" (lyrics by Stillman); "Lilacs in the Rain" (lyrics by Parish); "Twenty-Four Hours of Sunshine," "The Breeze Is My Sweetheart," and "No Range

PETER DE ROSE   ASCAP

to Ride No More" (lyrics by Carl Sigman); and "Autumn Serenade" (lyrics by Sammy Gallop.

De Rose's "As Years Go By" (lyrics by Charles Tobias), based on Brahms's *Hungarian Dance No. 4,* was the only popular song used in the motion-picture biography of Robert Schumann, *Song of Love.* De Rose also contributed other songs to motion pictures: "Song of the Seabees" (lyrics by Sam M. Lewis) for *The Fighting Seabees* and the title song (lyrics by Stillman) for *Harvey.*

Peter De Rose died in New York City on April 24, 1953. The sixth anniversary of his death was commemorated on April 24, 1959, with ceremonies sponsored by the Manhattan borough president at Times Square. For the occasion, Times Square was temporarily renamed Peter De Rose Memorial Square.

ABOUT:
International Musician, October 1948; Variety, July 31, 1949.

Walter Donaldson *1893-1947*

WALTER DONALDSON was born in Brooklyn, New York, on February 15, 1893. His parents were musical. Though he did not receive formal training in music, he wrote school songs and music for school productions. When he graduated from high

ASCAP
WALTER DONALDSON

during which he wrote many of the song hits that brought him to the top in his profession. In 1920 "My Mammy" (lyrics by Sam M. Lewis and Joe Young) was introduced in vaudeville by Bill Frawley; and soon afterwards Al Jolson, in *Sinbad,* won such acclaim with his performance of the song that he made it part of his basic repertoire. It was mainly because of this song and Jolson's famous rendition of it that all interpreters of songs about mothers became known as "mammy singers."

In 1922 Walter Donaldson began a successful collaboration with the lyricist Gus Kahn, a partnership which lasted for several years. In 1922 they wrote "My Buddy" and "Carolina in the Morning," the latter interpolated into the Broadway production *The Passing Show of 1922.* Later successes included "Beside a Babbling Brook," "Yes, Sir, That's My Baby," "That Certain Party," "My Sweetie Turned Me Down," "Isn't She the Sweetest Thing?," "For My Sweetheart," and the songs for the Ziegfeld production *Whoopee,* which starred Eddie Cantor. *Whoopee,* adapted by William Anthony McGuire from Owen Davis's Broadway comedy *The Nervous Wreck,* ran for more than a year after its opening on December 4, 1928. For this musical Donaldson and Kahn wrote two songs which Eddie Cantor introduced and with which he has since been identified: "Makin' Whoopee" and "My Baby Just Cares for Me." Another successful song in this production was "Love Me or Leave Me," introduced by Ruth Etting. (A quarter of a century later, the song title was used as the name of a screen biography of Ruth Etting.) The film adaptation of *Whoopee* starred Eddie Cantor in his first major role in talking pictures.

During this period Donaldson worked with several other lyricists. With Lew Brown he wrote "Seven or Eleven"; with Edgar Leslie, "On the 'Gin, 'Gin, 'Ginny Shore" and "Kansas City Kitty"; with Cliff Friend, "Let It Rain! Let It Pour!"; with Billy Rose, "In the Middle of the Night"; with Howard Johnson, "Georgia"; and with George Whiting, one of his greatest ballads, "My Blue Heaven." He also wrote several songs, with Ballard MacDonald as his lyricist, for the Broadway musical *Sweetheart Time* (1926).

school, he went to work in a brokerage house on Wall Street. He soon found employment in Tin Pan Alley as a demonstration pianist but lost this job when he was discovered writing songs during business hours. In 1915 his first song, "Back Home in Tennessee" (lyrics by William Jerome), was published; an immediate hit, it later was often associated musically with the state of Tennessee. Donaldson published two other songs that year: "You'd Never Know the Old Home-Town of Mine" (lyrics by Howard Johnson) and "We'll Have a Jubilee in My Old Kentucky Home" (lyrics by Coleman Goetz).

During World War I, Donaldson worked for eighteen months as an entertainer at Camp Upton, New York. In 1919 he wrote two humorous hits inspired by the war, to lyrics by Sam M. Lewis and Joe Young: "Don't Cry, Frenchy" and "How Ya Gonna Keep 'Em Down on the Farm?" During the war years he also wrote "The Daughter of Rosie O'Grady" to lyrics by Monty C. Brice and two songs to lyrics by Lewis and Young, "You're a Million Miles from Nowhere" and "I'll Be Happy When the Preacher Makes You Mine."

After the war Donaldson became a member of the newly organized firm of Irving Berlin, Inc., with which he remained for more than a decade. This was the period

Donaldson also wrote his own lyrics for some of his songs: "My Best Girl," "Sam, the Old Accordion Man," "At Sundown," "Just Like a Melody out of the Sky," "You're Driving Me Crazy," "Little White Lies," "You Didn't Have to Tell Me," and "An Evening in Carolina."

Almost as soon as motion pictures began to use sound, Donaldson went to Hollywood to write songs for the screen. Two of his former hits, "At Sundown" and "Sam, the Old Accordion Man" were used in the film *Glorifying the American Girl* in 1929, one of the first Paramount sound movies. Other Donaldson songs written for screen musicals were "Did I Remember?" for *Suzi*, and "You" and "It's Been So Long" for *The Great Ziegfeld*. These were written to Harold Adamson's lyrics. Donaldson also contributed several songs to the film versions of *Panama Hattie* and *Follow the Boys*.

When Donaldson resigned from the Irving Berlin Music Corporation in 1928, he helped to found his own publishing house (Donaldson, Douglas and Gumble) of which he was president for many years. Ill health compelled him to withdraw from all activities in 1946, and he died in Santa Monica, California, on July 15, 1947.

ABOUT:
Musical Opinion, September 1947.

Paul Dresser *1857-1906*

PAUL DRESSER was born Paul Dreiser in Terre Haute, Indiana, on April 21, 1857. He was the older brother of the novelist Theodore Dreiser. Their father was a deeply religious man who wished Paul to be a priest. But Paul's interest lay only in music —in playing the piano and guitar and singing songs. When he was sixteen he ran away from home and joined a medicine show that marketed a "wizard oil." It was on this occasion that he changed his name to Dresser. A year later he performed with a troupe on one-night stands; then he joined a stock company in which he was billed as "the sensational comique." He spent his free time writing songs, and his first published effort, "Wide Wings," was issued by a small firm in Evansville, Indiana. Soon afterward the *Paul Dresser Songster* appeared in Chicago.

In 1885 he joined the Billy Rice Minstrels, working as a blackface end-man and writing some songs for the shows. It was for this company that he wrote, in 1886, his first hit, a sentimental ballad, "The Letter That Never Came," which is said to have been inspired by a frustrated love affair. He wrote his own lyrics for this song, as he did for all his later compositions. Some of the songs that followed were "I Believe It for My Mother Told Me So" and "The Outcast Unknown" in 1887; "The Convict and the Bird" in 1888; and, in 1889, "I Can't Believe Her Faithless." By the turn of the new decade, especially after the publication of "The Pardon Came Too Late," Dresser had solidly established his reputation as one of the foremost writers of sentimental ballads.

Dresser was an extraordinarily · prolific songwriter, and he earned a fortune from the compositions that seemed to flow inexhaustibly from his pen. A lavish spender, he lived in the grand style, courting women, entertaining friends, residing at Gilsey House or the Marlborough Hotel in Chicago, affecting the expansive, generous air of a born cavalier. His half-million-dollar fortune slipped through his fingers.

His songs were great favorites in the 1890's, an era that glorified the sentimental ballad. Between 1890 and 1895 he wrote "Take a Seat, Old Lady," "Ev'ry Year," "We Were Sweethearts for Many Years," "Jean," "I Was Looking for My Boy," "I Wonder If She'll Ever Come Back to Me," "I Wish That You Were Here Tonight," "He Fought for a Cause He Thought Was Right," "He Brought Home Another," and, most popular of all, "Just Tell Them That You Saw Me," the last based on a factual story of a woman ruined by an unwise love affair. Theodore Dreiser recalled that when his brother first sang this ballad to him "tears stood in his [Paul Dresser's] eyes and he wiped them away." The song attained phenomenal popularity not only through its fabulous sheet music sale and its frequent renditions on the stage but also through song slides. The phrase "just tell them that you saw me" became a popular remark of the day.

Some of Dresser's most important songs between 1895 and 1900 were "A Dream of My Boyhood Days," "You're Goin' Far

PAUL DRESSER

Away, Lad," "Don't Tell Her That You Love Her," "Wish You Were Here Tonight," "If You See My Sweetheart," "Come Tell Me What's Your Answer," "Every Night There's a Light," "The Old Flame Flickers, I Wonder Why," "The Path That Leads the Other Way," "The Curse of the Dreamer," and, perhaps the most celebrated song of his entire career, "On the Banks of the Wabash."

"The Curse of the Dreamer" was inspired by Dresser's unhappy marriage with May Howard, a burlesque queen. When they parted bitterly he wrote the song and called it "The Curse," filling it with anger and hatred. Soon afterward, however, he withdrew the song from publication, rewrote it with a happy ending, and entitled it "The Curse of the Dreamer."

Dresser wrote "On the Banks of the Wabash" in 1899; it has since become the official song of the state of Indiana. Theodore Dreiser has claimed credit for suggesting to his brother a song about the Wabash and giving him some ideas for the lyrics. Dresser, however, seems not to have mentioned this. Max Hoffman, an orchestrator for Witmark, has described the evening when Dresser wrote the melody and the lyric: "I went to his room at the Auditorium Hotel [in Chicago]. . . . Paul was mulling over a melody . . . practically in finished form. But he did not have the words. So he had me play the full chorus over and over again at least for two or three hours, while he was writing down the words, changing a line here and a phrase there until the lyric suited him. . . . I have always felt that Paul got the idea from glancing out of the window now and again as he wrote and seeing the lights glimmering on Lake Michigan. . . . The song was published precisely as I arranged it. . . . During the whole evening we spent together, Paul made no mention of anyone's having helped him with the song."

After 1900 Dresser wrote "I'd Still Believe You True," "I Just Want to Go Back and Start the Whole Thing Over," "Where Are the Friends of Other Days?" "She Went to the City," "Way Down in Old Indiana," "When I'm Away from You, Dear," and "The Day That Grew Colder." He also wrote many patriotic songs and—during the Spanish-American conflict—war songs. Of the last, "The Blue and the Gray" was especially popular.

In 1901 Dresser entered into partnership with his publishers Howley and Haviland; the new firm was now called Howley, Haviland and Dresser. But by 1903 Dresser's creativity seemed exhausted and, more unfortunately, his publishing house went bankrupt. Having squandered his money, Dresser had no private funds to rely on, and his many friends, who had formerly accepted his generosity, now avoided him. In the face of this adversity Dresser shriveled, broken in spirit and health.

He did write one more hit—the outstanding "My Gal Sal." Convinced that he would regain his lost wealth and position with this one song, he published it at his own expense in 1905. But he had lost the money and influence necessary to promote it properly and he did not live to witness its triumph. On January 30, 1906, in abject poverty and obscurity, he died of a heart attack at the home of a sister in Brooklyn, New York. As he had foreseen, "My Gal Sal" sold several million copies of sheet music and realized a fortune. In 1942 this song provided the title for a screen biography in which Victor Mature played the part of Paul Dresser.

About:

Dreiser, Theodore, editor. The Songs of Paul Dresser; Gilbert, Douglas. Lost Chords; Spaeth, Sigmund. A History of Popular Music in America; Thompson, David. Songs That My Mother Used to Sing.

Vernon Duke *1903-*

VERNON DUKE was born Vladimir Dukelsky in Pskov, northern Russia, on October 10, 1903. Although born in Russia, he is only one quarter Russian in origin. His mother's father, Alexis Kopylov, general manager of the Count Bobrinsky sugar refineries, married a Miss von Koestel, who was half Viennese and half Spanish. On his father's side, the composer is half Lithuanian, half Georgian; his paternal grandfather was general administrator under the Grand Duke Michael, the lord lieutenant of the Caucasus. His paternal grandmother was born Princess Daria Toumanov.

Vladimir's parents loved music but had no professional musical background. After studying piano with private teachers, Vladimir, instead of preparing for the diplomatic career planned for him, insisted on becoming a composer and enrolled at the Conservatory in Kiev, the city where the family had settled after the death of Vladimir's father in 1913. The boy studied with Reinhold Glière, Serge Prokofiev's teacher; Prokofiev, thirteen years older than Dukelsky, became the young composer's closest friend and chief supporter.

With the outbreak of the February Revolution, the Dukelskys escaped to Odessa. In 1920 they went on by ship to Constantinople. It was a harrowing voyage, on a ship with a drunken captain and a broken compass. The combination almost had disastrous consequences, but two American sailors aboard the ship succeeded in guiding it safely to its destination.

In Constantinople, Dukelsky continued to compose, and completed several works, including a ballet. He also helped to support his family by arranging concerts for a club run for refugees by the Y.M.C.A. There he came across some sheet music of American popular songs. One of these was George Gershwin's "Swanee," and it awakened an enthusiasm for Gershwin and American popular music that persisted while he wrote serious music. Eventually, it led him to extend his efforts to popular music.

In 1921 Dukelsky arrived in the United States. He gained an introduction to Gershwin, who proved helpful and encouraging, advising him to try his hand at popular music and suggesting that he assume the anglicized name of "Vernon Duke." For many years

VERNON DUKE

Duke reserved his original Russian name for his concert output and used the anglicized one for his popular efforts. But in the closing paragraph of his autobiography, *Passport to Paris*, published in 1955, Duke stated that he would use the name Vernon Duke for all his music.

During his first years in the United States, Duke supported himself with several poorly paid positions, writing music for a magician's act, playing the piano in a restaurant, conducting a burlesque theatre orchestra, and writing music for a night-club show. Meanwhile he composed an excellent piano concerto and a concert overture for orchestra.

In 1924 Duke went to Paris, where he met Serge Diaghilev, impresario of the Ballet Russe. Diaghilev, impressed by Duke's piano concerto, commissioned him to write the music for a ballet, *Zephyr et Flore*. This ballet was introduced in Monte Carlo in 1925 and performed in Paris, London, Berlin, and Barcelona. Another important acquaintance in Paris was Serge Koussevitzky, the renowned conductor. As head of his own publishing house in Paris, Koussevitzky accepted several of Duke's major works for publication; as a conductor in Paris and Boston, he helped to introduce Duke's most important works for orchestra, including the first two symphonies, various concertos, and several shorter orchestral works.

In 1925 Duke left for London. There, for a fee of 250 pounds, he was commissioned by Charles Cochran to write the score for a stage musical. The show was never produced. But in 1926 a Viennese operetta, *Yvonne*, was introduced in London at Daly's Theatre; it included six interpolations by Duke—his first music for the popular theatre. Duke also wrote the score for an Edgar Wallace musical thriller, *The Yellow Mask*, which had a seven-month run in London.

In 1929 he returned to the United States. For a while he wrote background music for the Paramount film studios in Astoria, Long Island, as well as songs for Broadway musical productions. Two songs were heard in the third edition of the *Garrick Gaieties* (1930): "I'm Only Human After All" (lyrics by E. Y. Harburg and Ira Gershwin)—his first success, and "Too, Too Divine" (lyrics by Harburg). Other songs were "Talkative Toes" (lyrics by Howard Dietz) in *Three's a Crowd* (1930); "Muchacha" (lyrics by Harburg) in *Shoot the Works* (1931); "Let Me Match My Private Life with Yours" (lyrics by Harburg) in *Americana* (1932); and "Autumn in New York" (lyrics by the composer) in *Thumbs Up* (1934).

Meanwhile, in 1932, Duke wrote his first full score for a Broadway production, *Walk a Little Faster,* a revue starring Beatrice Lillie and Clark and McCullough. Duke's score, written to Harburg's lyrics, included a song that has remained a favorite, "April in Paris." " 'April in Paris,' " wrote Isaac Goldberg in a letter to Duke, "is one of the finest musical compositions that ever graced an American production. If I had my way, I'd make the study of it compulsory in all harmony courses." Curiously, the song went unnoticed at first. It languished for several years until it was revived in night clubs and on a Liberty record by Marian Chase, a popular society chanteuse.

During the next few years Duke wrote the scores for two editions of the Ziegfeld *Follies* and most of the music for *The Show Is On* (1934, 1935, 1936). The *Follies* of 1934 included three outstanding Duke songs: "What Is There to Say?" "I Like the Likes of You," and "Suddenly" (lyrics by Harburg.) The *Follies* of 1935 featured "I Can't Get Started with You" (lyrics by Ira Gershwin). In

The Show Is On the best song was a number entitled "Now" (lyrics by Ted Fetter).

In 1937 Duke was invited to Hollywood by Samuel Goldwyn to complete the score of the *Goldwyn Follies,* left unfinished because of George Gershwin's tragic death. For this film Duke wrote two ballets choreographed by Georges Balanchine. He also wrote a song, "Spring Again" (lyrics by Ira Gershwin), and supplied verses for three Gershwin tunes.

Vernon Duke's most important Broadway musical thus far is *Cabin in the Sky,* a Negro fantasy with book by Lynn Root and lyrics by John La Touche. Its première took place in New York on October 25, 1940. This musical had the simplicity and poignancy of true folklore, and it was further enriched by the splendid choreography of Georges Balanchine, the dance interpretation of Katherine Dunham (in her first Broadway appearance), and the performances of Ethel Waters, Rex Ingram, and Todd Duncan. This stage show is one of the finest Duke has written. Its best songs were the title number; "Taking a Chance on Love" (lyrics by La Touche and Fetter), with which Ethel Waters stopped the show every night; "Honey in the Honeycomb"; and "Love Me Tomorrow."

During World War II, Duke served in the United States Coast Guard. He wrote the music for *Tars and Spars,* the United States Coast Guard revue starring the then unknown Sid Caesar.

Duke's Broadway musicals since 1940 have included *Banjo Eyes* (1941), starring Eddie Cantor; *Sadie Thompson* (1944), a musical adaptation of Somerset Maugham's *Rain;* and *Two's Company* (1952), a revue starring Bette Davis. In 1957 Duke also wrote the background music and two songs (to his own lyrics) for Jean Anouilh's *Time Remembered,* which starred Helen Hayes. He has also composed the ballets *Public Gardens* (1935); *Washerwoman's Ball* (1946), Duke's greatest success in this genre; *Emperor Norton* (1957), written for the San Francisco Ballet; and *Lady Blue* (1961), written for Roland Petit.

In 1957, Vernon Duke was married to Kay McCracken, a young Montana concert singer who had studied with Lotte Lehmann. They live in Pacific Palisades, California. In addition to composing, Duke has been director of the Society for Forgotten Music, a division of Contemporary Records devoted to unearthing forgotten compositions in serious music.

ABOUT:
Duke, Vernon. Passport to Paris.
Christian Science Monitor, August 21, 1943.

Gus Edwards 1879-1945

GUS EDWARDS was born Gus Simon in Hohensalza, Germany, on August 18, 1879. His family came to the United States in 1887 and settled in the Williamsburg section of Brooklyn, New York. Gus worked in his uncle's cigar store during the day, and each evening he would haunt the theatres of Brooklyn and Manhattan in search of a job as a boy soprano. For a while he worked as a song plugger at Tony Pastor's, the Bowery Theatre, and Koster and Bial's. This involved rising from his balcony seat to repeat songs that stars like Emma Carus, Lottie Gilson, and Maggie Cline had just performed. He found other engagements as a singer in saloons, on ferry boats, at lodge halls, and between bouts at athletic clubs. He also sold sheet music in theatre lobbies.

In 1896, while appearing at Johnny Palmer's Gaiety Saloon in Brooklyn, he caught the interest of James Hyde, a vaudeville booking agent, who arranged for Edwards to tour the vaudeville circuit with four other boys in an act known as "The Newsboy Quintet." It was in this act that Edwards introduced, in 1898, his first original song, "All I Want Is My Black Baby Back" (lyrics by Tom Daly). Unable to write music at the time, Edwards had Charles Previn write down the notes for him. May Irwin helped to make this song a moderate success.

During the Spanish-American War, Edwards entertained American soldiers at Camp Black. There he met the young lyricist Will Cobb, with whom he established a songwriting partnership—nicknamed "Words and Music" —that continued for many years, yielding many hits. They wrote their first songs, "I Couldn't Stand to See My Baby Lose" and "The Singer and the Song," in 1899, and their first major hit, "I Can't Tell Why I Love You, But I Do," a year later. (The latter number was revived in 1944 in the film *The Belle of the Yukon*.) During the next

GUS EDWARDS   ASCAP

few years their reputation as songwriters was established with "I'll Be with You When the Roses Bloom Again," "Way Down Yonder in the Cornfield," "In Zanzibar" (introduced in the Broadway musical *The Medal and the Maid*), "Could You Be True to Eyes of Blue," "Goodbye, Little Girl, Goodbye," and "If a Girl Like You Loved a Boy Like Me."

Three of Edwards' outstanding song hits of 1905 were written to words by another lyricist, Vincent Bryan. These songs were "He's Me Pal," "Tammany," and "In My Merry Oldsmobile." "Tammany" was written for a party held by the National Democratic Club of New York in 1905. Gus Edwards was master of ceremonies, and a half hour before the formal program began he wrote this song, apparently inspired by some Indian songs he had heard at the Club that day. "Tammany" was a hit at the party and was soon interpolated into the Broadway musical *Fantana*, where it was introduced by Lee Harrison. It later became the official song of New York's Tammany Hall.

In 1905 Gus Edwards established his own publishing firm in Tin Pan Alley. In 1906, again with Will Cobb, he wrote "I Just Can't Make My Eyes Behave," popularized by Anna Held in *The Parisian Model*. In 1907 they published what is undoubtedly their greatest song success, "School Days," which sold over three million copies of sheet music.

"School Days" was written for a vaude-ville revue called *School Boys and Girls* which Edwards wrote, directed, and starred in. The revue featured Edwards as a teacher in a schoolroom filled with youngsters who were dancers, singers, and mimics. This act was so successful that for the next two decades Edwards created and starred in sim-ilar revues, of his own creation, each with new material and new youngsters. For his acts Edwards scoured the country in quest of fresh talent. So intensive was his search that it gave rise to the popular saying "Pull your kids in, here comes Gus Edwards." With an uncanny gift for sniffing out potential talent, Edwards presented a remarkable succession of young, unknown performers who later became leading stage personalities: Eddie Cantor, George Jessel, Groucho Marx, Lila Lee, Eddie Buzzell, George Price, the Duncan Sisters, and many others. For these acts, Gus Edwards wrote some of his greatest songs, including "Sunbonnet Sue" and "If I Was a Millionaire," written to lyrics by Cobb; and, to Edward Madden's lyrics, "By the Light of the Silvery Moon" (introduced by Georgie Price) and "Jimmy Valentine."

In addition to writing songs for his own vaudeville sketches, Gus Edwards also wrote music for the Broadway stage: notably for two editions of the *Ziegfeld Follies* (the first edition of the *Follies*, in 1907, and another in 1910), and for the Weber and Fields extrava-ganza *Hip, Hip Hooray* (1907).

In 1928 Edwards retired temporarily from the Broadway scene to work for Hollywood. He wrote and directed several shorts, wrote several songs to Joe Goodwin's lyrics for the *Hollywood Revue of 1929*, and appeared in several full-length films, including *The Songwriter's Revue* and *The Doll Shop*. In the early 1930's he returned to vaudeville, heading a new group of unknown youngsters that included the three Lane sisters (Pris-cilla, Rosemary, and Lola) and Ray Bolger.

Gus Edwards went into retirement in 1939. A year later his screen biography, *The Star Maker*, starring Bing Crosby, was pro-duced by Paramount. During the last six years of his life Edwards was in poor health. He died in Los Angeles on November 7, 1945.

ABOUT:

Gilbert, Douglas. American Vaudeville: Its Life and Times; Witmark, Isidore. From Ragtime to Swingtime.

New York Times Magazine, March 23, 1941.

Duke Ellington *1899-*

DUKE ELLINGTON was born Edward Kennedy Ellington in Washington, D.C., on April 29, 1899. His father was a butler who later became a blueprint tracer at the Navy Yard. After graduating from Arm-strong High School, Duke received a scholar-ship to the Pratt Institute in Brooklyn for the study of art. But a temporary job as a soda jerk changed these plans. Ellington never entered Pratt because the ice cream parlor in which he worked had a piano.

Ellington had begun to study piano when he was seven, and had soon shown an ex-ceptional gift for improvisation. Now he started to play the piano in the ice cream parlor, delighting the clients with his jazz performances, especially those imitating the flamboyant style of Luckey Roberts. One of the clients arranged for Ellington to join a jazz band in 1916, and Ellington's career received further stimulus in 1918, when he organized a small jazz band of his own and began to fill engagements in and near Wash-ington.

When he was twenty-three, he went to New York, where he played the piano first with Wilbur Sweatman's jazz band, then with Elmer Snowden's band at Barron's in Harlem, and finally with his own five-piece group at the Hollywood, a Harlem night club later renamed the Kentucky Club. Ell-ington's ragtime performances and the im-provisational style of his band attracted a great deal of interest. Particularly impressed with Ellington's music was the publisher Irving Mills, who placed the young man under an exclusive contract. Mills enabled Ellington to enlarge his band to twelve per-formers, arranged for a recording contract, and found a booking for him at the Cotton Club. This engagement at the Cotton Club began on December 4, 1927, and during their five-year stay, Ellington and his orchestra became famous. "We came in with a new style," says Ellington. "Our playing was stark and wild and tense. . . . We tried new effects. One of our trombones turned up one night with an ordinary kitchen pot for a sliphorn. It sounded good. We let him keep it, until we could get him a handsome gadget that gave him the same effects. We put the Negro feeling and spirit in our music."

The performances of Duke Ellington and his orchestra represented some of the best jazz heard in New York; jazz *aficionados* from all parts of the city were drawn to the Cotton Club. Ellington's records now began to sell in enormous numbers. He made successful radio appearances. In 1929 he starred in his first Broadway show, George Gershwin's *Show Girl*, produced by Ziegfeld. A year later he appeared in his first motion picture, *Check and Double Check*. His first triumphant tour of Europe followed in 1933, with a command performance at Buckingham Palace. In the next few years he rose to a leading position in the world of jazz. *Swing Magazine*, in 1940, chose seventeen of his records among the twenty-eight best of the year, and two years later *Down Beat* elected him leading man in jazz in a nation-wide poll. Ellington also took first place in the *Down Beat* polls of 1944, 1946, and 1948.

Duke Ellington celebrated his twentieth anniversary as a jazz musician on January 21, 1943, with an appearance at Carnegie Hall in New York. At that concert he introduced an extended composition of his own in the jazz idiom, *Black, Brown and Beige*, a "tone poem parallel to the history of the Negro in America." This was Ellington's first appearance at Carnegie Hall, but not his only excursion into the realm of serious music. He was one of the first jazz men to give an exhibition of his style and idiom at a serious music appreciation course, at New York University, and to give a concert of jazz music at an institution of higher learning, Colgate University.

Besides having distinguished himself as a jazz pianist, orchestrator, and conductor, Ellington has become one of America's most successful composers of popular songs and compositions in the jazz style. The first tune he wrote was a ragtime instrumental number, *The Soda Fountain Rag*, composed in 1923. In 1927 he wrote a successful popular song, "The Blues I Love to Sing" (lyrics by Bob Miley), and two excellent instrumental numbers that have since become Ellington standards: *East St. Louis Toodle-oo* (his radio theme music) and *Black and Tan Fantasy* (which was the inspiration for a motion picture short). Between 1928 and 1934 he produced several songs for which he earned nation-wide recognition: "The Mooche"

DUKE ELLINGTON

(lyrics by Irving Mills); "It Don't Mean a Thing If It Ain't Got That Swing" (lyrics by Mills); "Sophisticated Lady" (originally an instrumental composition, but later provided with lyrics by Mills and Mitchell Parish); "Mood Indigo" (lyrics by Mills and Albany Bigard); "Solitude" (lyrics by Mills and Eddie De Lange); "In a Sentimental Mood" (lyrics by the composer); "Caravan" (lyrics by Mills); "I Let a Song Go Out of My Heart" (lyrics by Mills and Harry Nemo); "I Got It Bad and That Ain't Good" (lyrics by Paul Webster); "Don't Get Around Much Anymore" (lyrics by Bob Russell); "Do Nothin' Till You Hear from Me" (lyrics by Russell); "Just Squeeze Me" (lyrics by Lee Gaines); and "Indigo Echoes" (lyrics by Mills).

In addition to popular songs, Ellington has written many orchestral works of varying lengths which successfully exploit the colorations, instrumentations, blues harmonies, and other techniques and idioms of jazz. The best of his shorter works are *Black Beauty, Creole Rhapsody, Rockin' in Rhythm, Transbluency, On a Turquoise Cloud, Reminiscing in Tempo, Daybreak Express, Rude Interlude, Stompy Jones, Blue Harlem,* and *Blue Rambler*. His more ambitious instrumental compositions include *Black, Brown and Beige;* the *Liberian Suite*, written in 1947 on a commission from the Liberian government to commemorate its one hundredth anniversary as a republic; *New World a-Comin'*; *Perfume Suite*; *Deep South Suite*; *Harlem*, performed for the first time at an Ellington concert given at the Metropolitan Opera House in 1951; *Blutopia*; *Blue Bells of Harlem*; *Tattooed Bride*; *Night Creature*, introduced in 1955 at Carnegie Hall by Ellington and his orchestra; and *Such Sweet Thunder*, a Shakespearean suite.

Ellington has written scores for several Broadway stage productions, including *Jump for Joy* (1941) and *Beggar's Holiday* (1946), the latter a modernized version of *The Beggar's Opera*, with book and lyrics by John La Touche. He has also written music for motion pictures — for example, the background music for *Anatomy of a Murder* in 1959, and *Paris Blues* in 1961.

ABOUT:

Breston, Denis. Mood Indigo; Gammond, Peter, editor. Duke Ellington: His Life and Music; Trazegnies, Jean de. Duke Ellington; Ulanov, Barry. Duke Ellington.

Down Beat, November 5, 1952; International Musician, December 1949; Metronome, September 1953.

Dan Emmett *1815-1904*

DANIEL DECATUR EMMETT was born in Mount Vernon, Ohio, on October 29, 1815. While a boy he helped out in his father's blacksmith shop and also learned to play the violin. Impelled by an urge to see the world, Emmett enlisted in the army while still under age and became a piper in the band. The disclosure of his age and his father's objections to his enlistment brought this adventure to an early end; but several months later Dan ran away again and joined the Spalding and Rogers circus as a drummer. Of greater importance was his stay with Thomas ("Daddy") Rice's minstrel troupe, in which he sang and played the banjo. Rice's Negro routines made a deep impression on the young Emmett, and they were the inspiration for his first Negro songs, which he began to write about 1839, and which he introduced as a member of the Rice company.

In 1843 Emmett founded the Virginia Minstrels. After trying out their act in a New York billiard parlor, the minstrels made their debut at the Chatham Square Theatre on February 17, 1843, and scored a huge success. This company was one of the pioneers in establishing the routines and ritual of the minstrel show: the blue swallow-tail coat, striped calico shirt, and white pantaloon costume; the walk-arounds; the exchange of banter; the Negro songs and dances. So successful were the performances of Dan Emmett's Virginia Minstrels that competitive troupes mushroomed everywhere. The minstrel show became the most popular form of stage entertainment in the immediate pre-Civil War era.

In the 1840's Emmett took his troupe to England. After a short period of success, the English public lost interest, the box office receipts dwindled, and the troupe was left stranded. Emmett finally acquired enough money to make his way back to America, where he joined the Dan Bryant Minstrels.

Dan Emmett wrote many songs (words and music) throughout his career for his appearances in minstrel shows. In 1843, the year he organized the Virginia Minstrels, he published "My Old Aunt Sally" and "Old Dan Tucker." The latter was his first hit, and it soon became a staple in minstrel show entertainment everywhere. Its hero was a ne'er-do-well always getting into trouble and continually being warned to "get out de way." So immediate and far-reaching was the popularity of this song that only one year after its publication it was parodied by New York farmers in their revolt against feudal conditions perpetuated from the period of Dutch and English rule. A few years later "Old Dan Tucker," with still another set of lyrics, was used by the Abolitionists. The song is still heard at square dances.

Other Emmett songs written for and made popular in minstrel shows before the Civil War were "Jordan Is a Hard Road to Travel"; "The Blue-Tail Fly" (better known today as "Jimmie Crack Corn"); "The Boatman's Dance"; "Walk Along John"; and his most famous and memorable song, the great Civil War classic, "Dixie."

Though it became famous as a war song, "Dixie" (first called "Dixie Land") was originally written as a walk-around for a minstrel show. Emmett has left a record of how he came to write it: "One Saturday night, in 1859, as I was leaving Bryant's Theatre where I was playing, Bryant called after me. 'I want a walk-around for Monday, Dan.' The next day it rained and I stayed indoors. At first when I went at the song I couldn't get anything. But a line, 'I wish I was in Dixie,' kept repeating itself in my mind, and I finally took it for my start. The rest wasn't long in coming. And that's the whole story of how 'Dixie' was written. It made a hit at once, and before the end of the week everybody in New York was whistling it."

"Dixie" was introduced by Bryant's Minstrels in New York on April 4, 1859 and was so successful that other minstrel troupes took it over. One burlesque production entitled *Pocahontas* featured the song as a march for zouaves on its tour of the South. The publication of the lyrics on a broadside was a sell-out, as was the song itself when issued by a New Orleans publisher; and the melody was soon heard throughout the country, often with improvised lyrics. Unfortunately, Emmett, who had sold his song outright for five hundred dollars, was unable to capitalize on his success.

Despite the fact that Emmett was a northerner and that the song was born in the North, "Dixie" was appropriated by the South. It was first used for political purposes as a campaign song against Lincoln during the 1860 presidential campaign. As soon as war broke out, "Dixie" became the Confederacy's major war song. General George Pickett ordered it to be played during the historic charge at Gettysburg. After the surrender of the South at Appomattox, President Lincoln requested a band outside the White House to play "Dixie" for him, asserting that since the North had conquered the southern army it had also conquered "Dixie." This identification of "Dixie" with the southern cause subjected Emmett, the unwitting composer, to considerable abuse and criticism on the part of the northern press. In an attempt to silence his critics, he wrote new war lyrics espousing the northern cause for his melody.

In 1878 Emmett retired to his native town, Mount Vernon, Ohio. He supported himself by appearing occasionally in traveling musical shows, featured as the composer of "Dixie," and by raising chickens on his farm. These modest earnings were supple-

DAN EMMETT

mented by a small pension from the Actors Fund.

At eighty, Emmett was still making stage appearances—with Al. G. Field's Minstrels. "Uncle Daniel was not in his best voice," Field recalled, "but every time he appeared before the footlights to sing 'Dixie' the audience went wild." Emmett died in Mount Vernon, Ohio, on June 28, 1904, and was buried in Mount View Cemetery. His life story was dramatized in 1943 in the motion picture *Dixie,* which starred Bing Crosby as the composer.

ABOUT:
Galbreath, C. B. Daniel Decatur Emmett; Paskman, Dailey and Spaeth, Sigmund. Gentlemen, Be Seated!; Street, James H. Look Away! A Dixie Notebook; Wintermute, H. O. Daniel Decatur Emmett; Wittke, Carl. Tambo and Bones, a History of the American Minstrel Stage.
Musical Quarterly, January 1949.

Ludwig Englander *1859-1914*

LUDWIG ENGLANDER was one of the most prolific composers for the Broadway stage in the first decade of the twentieth century; yet biographical information about him is meager. Born in Vienna in 1859, he received his academic education at the University of Vienna and his musical training with private teachers in that city. For a short time he studied under Jacques Offenbach. In 1882 he came to the United

States, settling in New York, where he became conductor at the Thalia Theatre. He soon began to write music for operettas, but his first few ventures were failures. In 1894 he wrote the score for *The Passing Show,* a successful production at the Casino Theatre; this musical (not to be confused with *The Passing Show* series later put on annually by the Shuberts) marked the birth of the revue.

In 1896 Englander started to write operettas to Harry B. Smith's texts and lyrics. The collaboration resulted in two productions that year: *The Caliph* and *Half a King.* It was with Smith that Englander achieved his most remarkable stage successes. The first was *The Rounders,* produced in 1899, which included the delightful numbers "What's the Use of Anything?" and "The Same Old Story." In 1900 Englander and Smith had three operettas on Broadway: *The Cadet Girl, The Casino Girl,* and *The Belle of Bohemia.* The last two starred Sam Bernard, a popular Broadway comedian, and were outstanding hits. In *The Casino Girl* the title number, "New York," and "Slave Dealer's Song" were noteworthy; and *The Belle of Bohemia* featured "He Was a Married Man" and "When Shall I Find Him?"

The Strollers (1901) was an American adaptation of a German operetta for which Englander and Smith wrote such intriguing numbers as "Gossip Chorus" and "A Lesson in Flirtation." This show was followed in 1903 by *The Jewel of Asia* and *The Office Boy;* in 1904 by *A Madcap Princess,* an adaptation of Charles Major's best-selling romance, *When Knighthood Was in Flower;* and, from 1905 to 1907, by *The White Cat, The Rich Mr. Hoggenheimer,* and *Miss Innocence,* the last of which starred Anna Held. *The Rich Mr. Hoggenheimer* included some of Englander's best songs: "This World Is a Toy Shop" and "Don't You Want a Paper, Dearie?"

Occasionally, Englander worked with other librettists and lyricists. In 1901 his collaborator on *The New Yorkers* was Glen MacDonough; in 1902, on *Sally in Our Alley,* George V. Hobart; in 1904, on *The Two Roses* (an operetta adaptation of Oliver Goldsmith's *She Stoops to Conquer*), Stanislaus Stange; and in 1907, on *The Gay White Way,* Sydney Rosenfeld and J. Clarence Harvey.

After the production of *Miss Innocence,* most of Englander's shows were box office failures. His last musical, *Mlle. Moselle* (book and lyrics by Edward A. Paulton), produced in 1914, had a run of only nine performances. Englander died in Far Rockaway, New York, on September 13, 1914.

ABOUT:
Metronome, October 1914.

Sammy Fain *1902-*

SAMMY FAIN, the son of a prominent cantor and a first cousin of the famous stage comedians Willie and Eugene Howard, was born in New York City on June 17, 1902. When he was still a boy, his family moved to the Catskill Mountains in upstate New York. Sammy taught himself to play piano and write music; while attending high school, he started to compose songs which he even tried —unsuccessfully—to sell in Tin Pan Alley. After graduating from high school, he returned to New York City and found employment as a staff pianist for the publisher Jack Mills. He later appeared in vaudeville with Artie Dunn, in an act entitled "Fain and Dunn," and gave performances over the radio. In 1925 he published his first hit song, "Nobody Knows What a Red-Headed Mama Can Do" (lyrics by Irving Mills and Al Dubin).

SAMMY FAIN

In 1927 Sammy Fain formed one of his most productive partnerships when he met Irving Kahal, a young lyricist who had been appearing in vaudeville sketches written and produced by Gus Edwards. Fain and Kahal began to collaborate, and almost immediately they achieved an outstanding hit, "Let a Smile Be Your Umbrella" (lyrics by Kahal and Francis Wheeler). Their collaboration lasted for seventeen years, until Kahal's death in 1942. During that period they wrote many songs, Kahal often working on his lyrics with other writers. The most successful were "There's Something About a Rose" (lyrics by Kahal and Wheeler); "Wedding Bells Are Breaking Up That Old Gang of Mine" (lyrics by Kahal and Willie Raskin); "When I Take My Sugar to Tea" (lyrics by Kahal and Pierre Norman); and "I Can Dream, Can't I?" Fain contributed songs to two important Broadway musicals: *Hellzapoppin* (lyrics by Charles Tobias), the burlesque extravaganza starring Olsen and Johnson that started a run of more than 1,400 performances in 1938; and its successor, *Sons o' Fun* (1940), for which he wrote "Happy in Love" (lyrics by Jack Yellen).

After 1930 Fain and Kahal wrote songs for many motion pictures. Some of the most outstanding were "By a Waterfall" for *Footlight Parade;* "I'll Be Seeing You," written in 1938 and used with great success in the 1943 film of the same title; and "You Brought a New Kind of Love to Me" (lyrics by Kahal and Norman), which was made famous by Maurice Chevalier in *The Big Pond.* Fain's music was subsequently featured in films released by virtually every studio, including the Walt Disney productions of *Peter Pan* and *Alice in Wonderland.*

Since Kahal's death, Fain's most important lyricist has been Paul Francis Webster. Fain and Webster received Academy Awards twice: in 1953 for "Secret Love" from *Calamity Jane,* and in 1955 for "Love Is a Many-Splendored Thing" from the picture of the same title. The latter song earned Fain two awards at Italian and French music festivals. Two other songs were nominated for Academy Awards in 1959: the title song for *A Certain Smile,* and "A Very Precious Love" from *Marjorie Morningstar,* which achieved the motion picture industry's "Laurel Awards." "April Love," a motion

picture title song, was one of their 1957 hits and an Academy Award nomination. In 1958 they wrote the complete score for the movie *Mardi Gras,* two of whose songs deserve special mention: "Loyalty" and "I'll Remember Tonight." In 1961 they wrote the title theme song for *Tender Is the Night.*

In 1959 Fain and Webster wrote the songs for *A Diamond for Carla,* an original musical comedy produced for television. In 1960 they contributed the score for a Broadway musical with an Indian setting: *Christine* (book by Pearl S. Buck and Charles K. Peck, Jr.), based on Hilda Wernher's book *My Indian Family.*

There are several other lyricists with whom Fain has collaborated successfully. With Lew Brown he achieved an outstanding hit in "That Old Feeling," first heard in the motion picture *Vogues of 1938* and nominated for an Academy Award; and with Bob Hilliard he wrote "Dear Hearts and Gentle People," a memorable hit song of 1949.

ABOUT:

Billboard, August 18, 1958; Music Business, January 1947; Saturday Review, June 26, 1954; Time, January 23, 1950.

Fred Fisher *1875-1942*

FRED FISHER was born in Cologne, Germany, on September 30, 1875. He had an adventurous, even picaresque, boyhood and adolescence. At thirteen he ran away from home and joined the German navy. A few years later he joined the French Foreign Legion. In 1900 he came to the United States, settling in Chicago, where a saloon musician taught him to play the piano. In 1904 Fisher first attempted to write popular music. A year later he founded his own publishing house, and in 1906 he composed his first major success, "If the Man in the Moon Were a Coon" (written to his own lyrics), a song that sold over three million copies of sheet music.

During the next fifteen years Fisher wrote many solid hits. In 1910 he published "Any Little Girl That's a Nice Little Girl" (lyrics by Thomas J. Gray) and "Come, Josephine, in My Flying Machine" (lyrics by Alfred Bryan); and, in 1913, "Peg o' My Heart" (lyrics by Bryan), inspired by the

ASCAP
FRED FISHER

Harley Manners Broadway stage play that starred Laurette Taylor. (A modest hit in 1913, it returned in 1947 to score a far greater success, gaining top rating on the Hit Parade.) In 1914 Al Jolson helped to popularize "Who Paid the Rent for Mrs. Rip Van Winkle When Rip Van Winkle Went Away?" (lyrics by Bryan), a year which also saw the publication of "There's a Little Spark of Love Still Burning" (lyrics by Joe McCarthy). In 1916 Fisher contributed to the repertory of Irish tenors the ballad "Ireland Must Be Heaven for My Mother Came from There" (lyrics by McCarthy and Howard Johnson). Other songs of that year included two to Grant Clarke's lyrics: "You Can't Get Along with 'Em or Without 'Em" and "There's a Little Bit of Bad in Every Good Little Girl." Two outstanding comedy numbers were written in the years 1917 and 1918: "They Go Wild, Simply Wild, Over Me" (lyrics by McCarthy) and "Oui, Oui, Marie" (lyrics by Bryan and McCarthy). The latter inspired a comedy sketch starring Bobby Clark in the Broadway revue *Star and Garter* (1942), and was revived in 1948 for the Betty Grable motion picture *When My Baby Smiles at Me.* Another song from the World War I era was "Lorraine, My Beautiful Alsace Lorraine" (lyrics by Bryan).

Fisher's greatest success came in 1919 with "Dardanella." This song started out as a piano rag number by Johnny S. Black. Later Fisher, in collaboration with Felix Bernard, adapted it into a popular song which sold over six million records and over two million copies of sheet music. The main appeal of "Dardanella" lay in its recurring bass rhythm, a technique later frequently used in boogie-woogie music. Fisher considered this technique so strongly as his and Bernard's personal invention that when Jerome Kern used a similar device in his song, "Ka-lu-a," Fisher rushed to the law courts to sue him for plagiarism. Fisher was awarded damages of two hundred and fifty dollars.

After writing the words and music for "Daddy, You've Been a Mother to Me," "When the Honeymoon Was Over," and "Chicago" (1920 to 1922), Fisher went out to Hollywood. For a while he wrote background music for silent film productions. After the emergence of talking pictures he had several songs interpolated into the *Hollywood Revue of 1929,* and a year later into *Their Own Desire,* which starred Norma Shearer. "Whispering Grass," which he wrote in collaboration with his daughter early in World War II, became the Number One song on the BBC Hit Parade in England in 1941.

During the last years of his life, Fisher was afflicted with an incurable disease to which he succumbed on January 14, 1942, in New York City.

ABOUT:
Metronome, February 1942; Newsweek, January 26, 1942.

Stephen Foster *1826-1864*

STEPHEN COLLINS FOSTER was born in Lawrenceville, near Pittsburgh, Pennsylvania, on July 4, 1826. Though as a child he showed unusual enthusiasm and talent for music, he received no formal training. He learned by himself to play the flute and he soon wrote several pieces for that instrument. His main musical influence at the time was the songs of the Negro: the religious chants he heard in a Negro church to which he was taken by a household servant when he was seven, and immediately thereafter, the popular songs and dances of blackface performers.

For his academic schooling he was sent to the Athens Academy at Tioga Point, Pennsylvania. It was there, on April 1, 1841, that his first piece of music was performed, *Tioga Waltz*. From the Athens Academy, Foster was sent to Jefferson College at Canonsburg. His complete lack of interest in his studies—combined with an uncontrolled inclination to spend his time playing the flute, writing music, and day dreaming—impelled him to leave college after he had been there only several days. At this point his academic education came to an end.

Foster now devoted himself to music completely. In 1844, Foster had his first song published, "Open Thy Lattice, Love," with lyrics by George F. Morris. Foster wrote several other songs for a biweekly gathering of young men at his home. One was "Old Uncle Ned," in the style of the minstrel show tunes towards which he was partial, and at the same time in the sentimental vein of his later songs about Negroes. Another was "Oh, Susanna!," still one of his most popular efforts. A third was "Lou'siana Belle."

In or about 1846 his parents prevailed upon him to accept a job as bookkeeper in his brother's commission house in Cincinnati. There he interested a publisher in his songs. "Lou'siana Belle" was issued in 1847; "Old Uncle Ned" and "Oh, Susanna!" in 1848. For the first two he received no payment whatsoever, while for "Oh, Susanna!" he received one hundred dollars. It is the last of these songs that first brought him fame. After being introduced in an ice-cream parlor in Pittsburgh on September 11, 1847, "Oh, Susanna!" was soon heard extensively in minstrel shows. By 1849 it was adopted with improvised lyrics by the forty-niners en route to California gold.

His career as bookkeeper was short-lived. In 1848 he settled in Pittsburgh, determined to pursue his career as songwriter more actively. He found an important ally in the blackface minstrel Ed Christy, who bought Foster's songs (which he often palmed off as his own compositions) and introduced them in his minstrel shows. A second important development in Foster's career also came at this time: a contract from the New York publishing house of Firth, Pond & Company, by which he received a royalty on

Courtesy of The New York Public Library,
Joseph Muller Collection, Music Division

STEPHEN FOSTER

his songs rather than an outright payment. In 1850 "Camptown Races" was published, and immediately became a minstrel show favorite. In 1851 came "Old Folks at Home" (or "Swanee River"). Ed Christy paid Foster fifteen dollars for the privilege of introducing the song and for being allowed to put his own name on the sheet music as its composer; but all royalties from the sale of the sheet music were Foster's.

The selection of Swanee River as the geographical setting for his most famous song was more or less the result of chance. Foster had intended to wax sentimental over the Pedee River, but decided that this name was not sufficiently euphonious for a song. He went to a Florida map to seek out another river and came upon "Suwanee" which he contracted to "Swanee."

As introduced by Ed Christy, "Old Folks at Home" became such an instantaneous success that the *Musical World* of 1852 reported that the "publishers keep two presses running on it, and sometimes three; yet they cannot supply the demand." Within six months, Foster earned a royalty of fifteen hundred dollars, a considerable figure for that period. This success finally convinced him of the folly of permitting Ed Christy to pass as the composer of his songs. "I find that by my efforts I have done a great deal to build up a taste for Ethiopian songs among refined people," he wrote Christy. "Therefore I have concluded to reinstate my name on my songs and to pursue the Ethiopian business without fear or shame and lend all my energies to making the business live, at the same time that I will wish to establish my name as the best Ethiopian writer." In line with his ambition to become the leading writer of "Ethiopian songs," he wrote "Massa's in de Cold, Cold Ground" in 1852, and "My Old Kentucky Home" in 1853, both successfully introduced by the Ed Christy Minstrels. In less than a year each of these achieved a sale of over fifty thousand copies of sheet music and his royalties from the two songs alone exceeded two thousand dollars.

Now convinced that he could make a comfortable living from his music, Foster married Jane Denny McDowell on July 22, 1850. She was the "Jeanie" who later was the inspiration for his beautiful ballad "Jeanie with the Light Brown Hair." They were opposites in every way. Where Foster was the dreamer, Jane was practical to a fault. A devout Methodist, she objected to his drinking habits and to his associations with theatre people. She did not even have much use for his music, feeling he should devote himself to some other more respectable and more remunerative endeavor.

Despite an unhappy home life, Foster continued to produce numerous songs, all of them rich in emotion and fresh in lyricism: in 1853, "Old Dog Tray"; in 1854, "Willie, We Have Missed You," "Hard Times Come Again No More," "Ellen Bayne," and "Jeanie with the Light Brown Hair"; in 1855, "Come Where My Love Lies Dreaming"; in 1856, "Gentle Annie." In 1860 he wrote one of his last Negro songs, and one of his best, "Old Black Joe." Afterwards he produced many sentimental ballads, including the famous "Beautiful Dreamer," and the less familiar "Poor Drooping Maiden" and "Under the Willow She's Sleeping." During the Civil War he composed several martial tunes, the best being "We Are Coming, Father Abraham" and "We've a Million in the Field."

In 1860 Foster went with his wife and daughter to New York, where he was continually faced with frustration and despair. He was no longer able to find a market for his songs and was forced to produce pot-boilers to keep from starvation. He found he was forgotten by the public and avoided by his publishers. He lived in a miserable room on the Bowery, often without the price of the next meal. After his family left him to return to Pittsburgh, his moral and physical disintegration became complete. Now more than ever he sought refuge in alcohol, and for periods was in an inebriated stupor. One day, while washing himself, he fainted at the basin. He lay bleeding on the floor until he was discovered by the chambermaid. He was taken to Bellevue Hospital, where he died on January 13, 1864. In the pocket of his frayed suit were found three pennies and a slip of paper on which he had scribbled what he probably intended as the title of a new song, "dear friends and gentle hearts."

"This was the great tragedy of his life: his utter incapacity to exploit his genius as it deserved," this editor has written. "Ingenuous, impractical, maladjusted to his environment, given to dreams and fancies that carried him away from reality, he was usually incapable of looking after himself. He wasted his life as well as his genius. He was of that imperial race of born melodists which, across the Atlantic, had embraced Schubert, Schumann, Robert Franz, and Hugo Wolf. Beautiful melodies came to him as naturally as breathing. When he was inspired he was able to fill the formal patterns of the popular song with a tenderness of expression, a freshness of idiom, and a refinement and aristocracy of style that carried him to greatness. His world was a limited one, but it was his own, and in it he was lord and master. He was one of the first of America's great composers of song."

Two motion picture biographies of Stephen Foster have been produced in Hollywood. The first, released in 1939, was *Swanee River*, starring Al Jolson and Don Ameche, and featuring eight Foster songs; the other was *I Dream of Jeanie* (1952), with a cast including Ray Middleton and Muriel Lawrence, and a score of seven Foster songs and three more derived from Foster melodies.

Several American composers have created interesting symphonic works based on Foster's songs. They include Robert Russell Bennett (*Commemoration Symphony: Ste-*

phen Foster); Lucien Caillet (*Fantasia and Fugue on Oh, Susanna!*); Mario Castelnuovo-Tedesco (*Humoresques on Foster Themes*); Arcady Dubensky (*Stephen Foster Suite*); Morton Gould (*Foster Gallery*); and Alan Shulman (*Oh, Susanna!*).

ABOUT:
Howard, John Tasker. Stephen Foster, America's Troubadour; Howard, John Tasker, editor. A Treasury of Stephen Foster; Milligan, Harold Vincent. Stephen Collins Foster; Morneweck, Evelyn Foster. Chronicles of Stephen Foster's Family; Walter, Raymond. Stephen Foster, Youth's Golden Dream.

Anatole Friedland *1888-1938*

ANATOLE FRIEDLAND was born in St. Petersburg, Russia, on March 21, 1888. He received much of his academic training in private schools in St. Petersburg, and all of his musical training at the Moscow Conservatory. As a young man he came to the United States and pursued the study of architecture at Columbia University. As a student there he wrote music for several varsity shows. After completing his studies at Columbia he went to work for an architect at sixteen dollars a week.

Vitally interested in American popular music, Friedland spent his leisure hours writing songs. In 1911 he collaborated with Malvin Franklin in writing the score for *The Wife Hunters,* a Broadway musical starring Emma Carus and Lew Fields. Some of his songs impressed the Shuberts, who engaged him to compose the music for some of their productions at the Winter Garden. During the next few years, Friedland contributed material for *The Passing Show,* and in 1912, with Harold Atteridge as his lyricist, he wrote all the songs for *Broadway to Paris,* a Broadway revue with Gertrude Hoffman, Louise Dresser, and Irene Bordoni.

Just before World War I, Friedland began writing music to the lyrics of L. Wolfe Gilbert, with whom he achieved his outstanding song successes. Together they created such noteworthy hits as "My Sweet Adair," "Lily of the Valley," "My Little Dream Girl," "I Love You, That's the One Thing I Know," and "My Own Iona." Another hit— "Are You from Heaven?"—was the first song issued by their own publishing firm, which operated successfully for a few years.

A disastrous deal with a five-and-ten-cent store, which had ordered five million copies of a song called "Afghanistan" and then reneged because of the failure of the song to catch on, spelled doom for the firm.

Among Friedland's other songs are "My Little Persian Rose," "Shades of Night," "Singapore," "Out of the Cradle," "Who Believed in You?" and "The Greatest Enemy of Love."

For many years, Anatole Friedland was a headliner in vaudeville: sometimes in an act with L. Wolfe Gilbert; sometimes in a solo act in which he sang his leading hits at the piano; sometimes as the star of miniature or elaborately mounted revues. During the Prohibition era, Friedland also operated the Club Anatole, a successful night club on West 44th Street, New York City. And in the early 1930's he produced tabloid versions of famous Broadway musicals which toured motion picture and vaudeville theatres. Many stars of stage and screen, including Barbara Stanwyck, the De Marcos, and Mae Clark, received their first recognition in some of Friedland's night club and vaudeville productions.

After the amputation of a leg in the spring of 1936, Friedland lived in retirement at the Ritz-Carlton Hotel in Atlantic City, New Jersey, where he died on July 24, 1938.

ABOUT:
Gilbert, L. Wolfe. Without Rhyme or Reason.

Rudolf Friml *1879-*

RUDOLF FRIML was born in Prague, Czechoslovakia, on December 7, 1879. He was the son of a humble baker who loved music passionately and who gave creditable performances on the zither and the accordion. Rudolf started to study the piano early in life. He was only ten when his first composition was published, *Barcarolle,* for the piano. When he was fourteen, his friends and relatives contributed money to pay for his musical education. He took the entrance examinations for the Prague Conservatory, then directed by Dvořák, and was placed in the third year; thus he completed a six-year course of study in only three.

After his graduation from the Conservatory, Friml was engaged by a fellow Conservatory student, the violinist Jan Kubelik,

RUDOLF FRIML

to appear with him in concert performances throughout Europe. Friml was Kubelik's assisting artist for about a decade, a period in which Kubelik achieved recognition as one of Europe's most brilliant virtuosos.

The American producer Daniel Frohman signed a contract with Kubelik for an eighty-concert tour of the United States in 1901. Just then Kubelik's accompanist became indisposed and the violinist prevailed upon Friml to assume that role. Friml served as Kubelik's accompanist not only during the American tour, but on subsequent European tours and during a return visit to the United States in 1906.

In 1906 Friml decided to stay in the United States for good and pursue his own career as pianist and composer. He had already made his American debut on November 17, 1904, with a concert at Carnegie Hall that included the première of his own Concerto in B-flat. In the fall of 1906, Friml repeated his performance of that concerto with the New York Symphony Society. He soon thereafter appeared with other orchestras and in recitals. He also did a great deal of composing—mainly songs, piano pieces, and other instrumental numbers, all of serious. intent. Some of these were published.

Chance brought him into the Broadway musical theatre, and to popular music. Victor Herbert was planning to write an operetta

for Emma Trentini, who had recently been triumphant in his *Naughty Marietta.* But during the run of *Naughty Marietta* a misunderstanding between Herbert and Trentini resulted in considerable bitterness and ill will. When Herbert announced he was no longer interested in writing an operetta for Trentini, Rudolf Schirmer and Max Dreyfus, prominent publishers, induced Arthur Hammerstein, who was planning to produce the Trentini operetta, to take a chance on the then unknown Friml. The two publishers felt that Friml had the lyric inventiveness, the musicianship, and the popular touch to create a successful operetta score.

The operetta for which Friml was engaged to write the music was *The Firefly,* opening in New York on December 2, 1912. Friml's score was filled with melodic delights in a continental style; and Emma Trentini gave a winning performance as Nina, an Italian street singer who goes through much of the play disguised as a boy, but who eventually becomes a famous prima donna. Friml's best numbers were "Sympathy," "Giannina Mia," "Love Is Like a Firefly," "The Dawn of Love" and "When a Maid Comes Knocking at Your Heart," a few of which are still almost as popular today as they were in 1912. All the lyrics—as well as the operetta text—were by Otto Harbach.

During the next decade Friml wrote many scores for Broadway musicals. The most successful were *High Jinks* (1913), *Katinka* (1915), *You're in Love* (1917), *Sometime* (1918), and *Tumble Inn* (1919). Some of the delightful songs to come from these productions were "The Bubble" and "Something Seems Tingle-Ingleing" (lyrics by Harbach) from *High Jinks,* and the title number and "Keep on Smiling" from *Sometime* (lyrics by Rida Johnson Young).

Nevertheless it was not until 1924 that Friml wrote another score as rich and varied as that for *The Firefly. Rose Marie,* with book and lyrics by Otto Harbach and Oscar Hammerstein II, was set in the Canadian Rockies (it was the only successful operetta ever to use this setting) and had for some of its characters members of the Royal Canadian Mounted Police. Opening on September 2, 1924, it had the longest Broadway run of any Friml musical (550 performances), besides four road companies. Friml's tuneful score was undoubtedly one of the reasons for such a resounding success—"the most entrancing music it has long been our privilege to hear," as Charles Belmont-Davis reported in the New York *Tribune.* Two songs from this operetta are among Friml's most famous, the title song and "Indian Love Call." But "Totem Tom Tom" and "The Door of My Dreams" are also distinguished and popular; Robert Benchley, writing in the old *Life* magazine, called the former "one of the most effective chorus numbers we have seen."

After *Rose Marie,* Friml's greatest box office successes came with *The Vagabond King* and *The Three Musketeers.* The first, which opened on September 21, 1925, was a romantic operetta about François Villon, the fifteenth century French vagabond poet; the book and lyrics by Brian Hooker and W. H. Post were based on J. H. McCarthy's successful romance, *If I Were King.* From this bountiful score came the stirring "Song of the Vagabonds," and such unforgettable lyrical episodes as "Some Day," "Only a Rose" and "Huguette Waltz." *The Three Musketeers*—which came to Broadway on March 13, 1928—was William Anthony McGuire's adaptation of the celebrated romance of Alexandre Dumas, with lyrics by Clifford Grey and P. G. Wodehouse. The most memorable musical numbers from this operetta were "All for One," "With Red Wine," "Heart of Mine" and "Ma Belle."

Friml's last two musicals for Broadway were failures. One was a play with a Hawaiian setting, *Luana* (1930), and the other was *Anina* (1934).

After 1934 Friml concentrated his activity on the motion picture screen. He set up permanent residence in Hollywood and during the next decade and a half helped to adapt some of his successful operettas for the screen besides writing some original scores for several pictures, including *Music for Madame* and *Northwest Outpost.* He has, however, produced little that has become popular, and nothing to rival his formidable stage successes of the earlier decades. A single exception is a delightful number called "The Donkey Serenade" which he wrote with Herbert Stothart to lyrics by Chet Forrest and Bob White for the motion picture adap-

tation of *The Firefly,* released in 1937, and without which no subsequent stage revival of the operetta seems complete.

Friml was in his heyday at a time when operettas modeled after European patterns were in vogue in the United States. As he told an interviewer in the 1930's: "I like books with charm to them. And charm suggests old things—the finest being things that were done long ago. I like a full-blooded libretto with a luscious melody, rousing choruses, and romantic passion." On another occasion he remarked sadly: "I can't write music unless there are romance, glamour and heroes." The changing Broadway theatre in which the make-believe world of the operetta made way for realism, vivid characterizations and integration of music and text made Friml and his lilting tunes somewhat of an anachronism.

Friml now lives in semiretirement in Hollywood. In 1952 he married his secretary, Kay Ling, a Chinese-American. He has paid many visits to the Orient, in which he has had a lifelong interest, and has made sound recordings of native music and motion pictures of native dances. He has also written several concert works in a Chinese idiom.

ABOUT:

Ewen, David. Complete Book of the American Musical Theater; Smith, Cecil. Musical Comedy in America.

Music Business, April 1946.

Percy Gaunt *1852-1896*

PERCY GAUNT'S songs are identified with Charles H. Hoyt's farces and burlesques on contemporary themes which, in the closing decades of the nineteenth century, rivaled in popularity the burlesques of Harrigan and Hart. Gaunt was born in Philadelphia in 1852. Little is known of his childhood and youth. He served his apprenticeship as the music director of Barry and Fay, a theatrical troupe touring the country. In 1883 he was appointed Charles H. Hoyt's music director. The first production with which he was associated was *A Bunch of Keys,* produced that year at the San Francisco Opera House. In the next decade Gaunt was not only the music director of, but also one of the principal composers for, the following Hoyt farces: *A Parlor Match,*

A Brass Monkey, A Rag Baby, A Hole in the Ground, A Tin Soldier, A Midnight Belle (in which Maude Adams made her stage debut), *A Trip to Chinatown, A Runaway Colt, A Contented Woman* (a satire on the woman suffrage movement), *A Texas Steer,* and *A Black Sheep.*

The most successful of these Hoyt burlesques was *A Trip to Chinatown,* which toured the country for about a year before arriving at the Madison Square Theatre in New York on August 7, 1893, to begin the longest run of any stage production in the history of the New York theatre up to that time (650 performances). The music was mainly by Gaunt, though there were some numbers by other composers interpolated during the run of the play, such as Charles K. Harris' "After the Ball." Three of Gaunt's songs from this production were also fabulous successes: "The Bowery" (to this day one of the favorite numbers about New York), "Reuben, Reuben," and "Push dem Clouds Away," all of them to Gaunt's own lyrics. The three songs sold so many copies of sheet music that Gaunt earned over forty thousand dollars in royalties within a year or so. Indeed, *A Trip to Chinatown* proved to be the first American musical to provide through the sale of sheet music a rich source of revenue.

In 1893 Gaunt wrote still another highly successful song, "Love Me Little, Love Me Long," once again to his own lyrics. By 1894 Gaunt was sufficiently wealthy to indulge himself in the dream of his life—to write an opera. Ill health, however, not only frustrated his plan but also depleted his financial resources, and in 1895 a benefit for him was run by his friends. Now once again in need of a job, Gaunt was reengaged by Hoyt, but he was too sick ever to begin the new assignment. He died in Palenville, New York, on September 5, 1896. In reporting his death, the New York *Dramatic Mirror* remarked upon this coincidence: while the funeral services were taking place, outside in the street a lonely organ grinder was playing "Push dem Clouds Away."

ABOUT:
Musical Times (London), September 5, 1896.

George Gershwin *1898-1937*

GEORGE GERSHWIN was born Jacob Gershvin in Brooklyn, New York, on September 26, 1898, the second of four children. Eight months after George's birth, the Gershwins moved to the Lower East Side of New York where, with minor exceptions, they remained for about two decades. George's father was a middle-class businessman who through the years was involved in varied endeavors. Since he liked living near his place of business, the Gershwins were continually moving. Before 1917 they occupied twenty-eight different apartments.

It was on New York's Lower East Side that George Gershwin spent his childhood and boyhood days. As far back as memory could trace, none of the Gershwins had been musical; and in his early boyhood George gave little indication of being an exception. He enjoyed playing the games of the city streets, mostly punch ball, street hockey, "cat," and roller skating. At school he repeatedly got into trouble for misbehaving or failing to do homework.

Several episodes, however, proved that a love for music was latent in him. He was about six when he heard Anton Rubinstein's *Melody in F* on an automatic piano in a penny arcade. "The peculiar jumps in the music held me rooted," he later recalled. "To this day, I can't hear the tune without picturing myself outside that arcade." At about the same time, while roller skating in Harlem, he happened to hear Jim Europe's jazz music outside Baron Wilkins' club. From then on he kept returning to the place to sit for hours on the sidewalk outside the club listening to the sound of blues, rags, and spirituals. When he was ten, while playing ball outside school, he heard the strains of Dvořák's *Humoresque* played on the violin by one of his schoolmates. This music made such an impression on him that he went out of his way to befriend the performer, a young musician named Maxie Rosenzweig, who subsequently became famous as a violin virtuoso under the name of Max Rosen. It was through Maxie that George learned for the first time about the world of good music; it was because of Maxie that George started by himself to try to learn to play the piano at the home of one of his friends. George even tried writing music. When he showed one of these pieces to Maxie, the latter said firmly: "You haven't got it in you to be a musician, George. Take my word for it, *I* know."

The Gershwin family acquired a piano in 1910. George started piano lessons at once, first with several local teachers, and beginning in 1912 with Charles Hambitzer. Hambitzer, a splendid musician, had a profound influence on the boy's musical development. He introduced him not only to the classics but also to the works of the moderns; he made him conscious of harmony, theory, and instrumentation; he encouraged him to go to concerts; he helped develop his piano technique. Hambitzer appears to have been well aware of George's talent. He wrote his sister: "I have a new pupil who will make a mark in music if anybody else will. The boy is a genius, without a doubt; he's crazy about music and can't wait until it's time to take his lessons."

But though Hambitzer was able to inflame his pupil with his own passion for the great composers and their music, he was not successful in discouraging the boy from enjoying popular music. Popular music was a passion with the young Gershwin; even then he seemed to sense that this was the field which he would some day cultivate fully. In 1913 he wrote his first real piece of music. It was a popular song called "Since I Found You" (never published). In 1914 he appeared as pianist at an entertainment sponsored by a literary club; his performance consisted of a tango of his own. Gershwin was an ardent propagandist for the songs of Irving Berlin and ragtime. Again and again he tried to convince Hambitzer that there was artistic validity in popular American idioms; that an American composer could well profit by exploiting those idioms; that it would be highly fruitful for a composer to bring the fullest resources of the rhythm, harmony, counterpoint, and melody of serious music to the popular song.

Certain that his destiny lay with popular rather than serious music, Gershwin soon found a job in Tin Pan Alley, as staff pianist and song plugger for Remick at fifteen dollars a week. He was only fifteen at the time, the youngest employee in the Alley. He now learned the song business from the inside.

GEORGE GERSHWIN

He became acquainted with the great men of the Alley who produced hits, composers like Jerome Kern and Irving Berlin. His serious approach to popular music is illustrated by the fact that in 1915 he became a pupil of Edward Kilenyi in harmony, theory, and orchestration.

By 1916 he had entered the professional ranks as a songwriter. "When You Want 'Em You Can't Get 'Em" was published by Harry Von Tilzer that year. Another Gershwin song, "The Making of a Girl," was the first of his to be heard in the Broadway theatre, in *The Passing Show of 1916*.

His talent was beginning to attract notice. Harry Ruby, then a song plugger, remarked of Gershwin's piano playing at that time: "It was far and beyond better than [that] of any of us. As I look back upon it I can say it was a completely different musical world from ours, and we did not completely understand it at the time, though we all reacted to it instinctively." Irving Caesar, the lyricist, said: "I had never before heard such playing of popular music."

After more than two years at Remick's, Gershwin left Tin Pan Alley to find greater scope for his talents. He became a rehearsal pianist for *Miss 1917*, a musical by Jerome Kern and Victor Herbert, and his remarkable piano playing and improvisations made Kern sit up and take notice. "This young man,"

Kern said, "is going places." Gershwin also continued to write songs, several of them to lyrics by Irving Caesar. Two of these were introduced by Vivienne Segal at a concert at the Century Theatre in 1917: "You-oo Just You" and "There's More to a Kiss than X-X-X." One day, he applied to Irving Berlin for a job as arranger and musical secretary. "The job is yours," Berlin told him, "but I hope you won't take it. You are too talented to be anybody's arranger. You are meant for big things."

Gershwin soon found a job in which his creative talent could find proper encouragement, at the publishing house of Harms headed by Max Dreyfus. He was paid thirty-five dollars a week merely to write songs and submit them to Dreyfus; he had no other duties, nor any set hours. Through Dreyfus' influence Gershwin found rapid advancement in his professional career. In 1918 he was assigned to write the music for a revue, *Half Past Eight*, which died before reaching New York. Some of his other songs were interpolated into various important productions, including *Ladies First*, starring Nora Bayes, and *Hitchy-Koo*.

The year 1919 brought Gershwin his first successes. A song, "Swanee," with lyrics by Irving Caesar, was carried to great heights in sheet music and record sales by Al Jolson, who interpolated it into his Winter Garden extravaganza *Sinbad*. (No later song by Gershwin equaled the commercial triumph of "Swanee.") And Gershwin's first musical comedy, *La, La, Lucille*, appeared on Broadway on May 26, 1919; its best song was "Nobody But You," with lyrics by Buddy De Sylva.

Between 1920 and 1924 Gershwin wrote the complete scores for five annual editions of the George White *Scandals*. It was in songs for these productions that he first revealed a remarkable technical skill and originality in the use of rhythm, changing meters, and modulations—a skill that led Beryl Rubinstein, a famous concert pianist and teacher, to describe Gershwin as "a great composer" with "the spark of musical genius." Among the songs were "I'll Build a Stairway to Paradise" (lyrics by De Sylva and Ira Gershwin) and "Somebody Loves Me" (lyrics by De Sylva and Ballard MacDonald). For the 1922 edition Gershwin

also made his first experiment in using jazz idioms in an artistic manner by writing (to a libretto by De Sylva) a one-act Negro opera, originally entitled *Blue Monday* but later renamed *135th Street*. *Blue Monday* was kept in a single performance—on opening night; George White deleted it from the revue because he felt it was too somber. But the work later enjoyed successful performances in Carnegie Hall and in 1953 was televised on the "Omnibus" program.

One of those strongly impressed by the new vistas opened up by *Blue Monday* was Paul Whiteman, the orchestra leader who conducted the opera in the *Scandals*. Whiteman was planning a concert of American music at Aeolian Hall, New York, and for this event he urged Gershwin to write an extended serious work for orchestra in a jazz idiom. The composition Gershwin finally produced for Whiteman was the *Rhapsody in Blue*, introduced on February 12, 1924. It was an overwhelming success, eliciting an ovation that lasted several minutes. The next day several critics called it one of the most significant works in twentieth century music. There were several dissenting voices —notably those of Lawrence Gilman and Pitts Sanborn—but nonetheless *Rhapsody in Blue* immediately established itself as "the foremost serious effort by an American composer," as one critic described it. It was performed extensively in Europe and America; it was transcribed for every possible instrument or combination of instruments; it was the inspiration for several ballets; its initial recording by Paul Whiteman was a best seller; it was sold to the movies. The *Rhapsody in Blue* made Gershwin a wealthy man, as well as a composer who had won the admiration of the entire music world.

Gershwin maintained his position as one of America's most significant creative musical figures with a succession of serious compositions in which popular American styles and idioms were skillfully combined with the forms, techniques, and resources of serious music. On December 3, 1925 he introduced his *Piano Concerto in F* at Carnegie Hall with the New York Symphony Society, Walter Damrosch conducting. In 1926 he completed five jazz piano preludes, three of which became popular after they were published and recorded. His tone poem, *An American in*

Paris, was first performed by the New York Philharmonic under Damrosch on December 13, 1928; the *Second Rhapsody,* by the Boston Symphony under Koussevitzky on January 29, 1932. After that came the *Cuban Overture* (1932), the *Variations on I Got Rhythm* for piano and orchestra (1934), and the folk opera *Porgy and Bess,* which had its world première in Boston on September 30, 1935, and its New York opening on October 10. Though originally a box office failure, and the object of a considerable amount of disparaging criticism, *Porgy and Bess* has become one of the most widely performed and highly acclaimed operas of our times. Between 1952 and 1955 it was performed by an American Negro company throughout Western Europe, the Near East, the Soviet Union and other countries behind the Iron Curtain, and Latin America. In 1959 a motion picture adaptation was produced by Samuel Goldwyn.

As a popular composer, Gershwin continued writing scores for the Broadway stage and the Hollywood screen, productions studded with some of the most remarkable songs produced in the 1920's and 1930's, many of which are now popular classics. In 1924 he wrote the music for *Lady Be Good,* starring Fred and Adele Astaire. This score included the delightful title number, "Fascinating Rhythm" and "So Am I." It was for this production that Gershwin originally wrote one of his most famous songs, "The Man I Love," but it was deleted from the play during the Philadelphia tryouts. Several years later, an attempt was made to include "The Man I Love" in *Strike Up the Band* and once again it was removed. It never appeared in any Broadway musical, but in time it won the admiration of music lovers in London and New York.

In *Lady Be Good,* George Gershwin found a distinguished and permanent collaborator in his brother, Ira, who, from that time on, provided brilliant lyrics for Gershwin's music. On several occasions before *Lady Be Good* they had worked together; their first song was "The Real American Folk Song" which Nora Bayes had introduced in *Ladies First* in 1918. *Lady Be Good,* however, was the first musical comedy for which Ira Gershwin wrote all the lyrics to his brother's melodies.

Tip Toes, in 1925, had several remarkable numbers in "That Certain Feeling," "Sweet and Low Down" and "Looking for a Boy." In the same year Gershwin also wrote the music for a romantic operetta with a Russian setting, *A Song of the Flame,* a production that failed. But in 1926 *Oh Kay!,* starring Gertrude Lawrence and Victor Moore, was a major hit; here the best songs included the haunting ballad "Someone to Watch Over Me," the dynamically charged number "Clap Yo' Hands," and the piquant and charming "Do, Do, Do" and "Maybe." *Oh Kay!* enjoyed a successful off-Broadway revival in 1960.

After 1926 George and Ira Gershwin wrote songs for such successful Broadway musicals as *Funny Face* (1927), starring Fred and Adele Astaire; *Strike Up the Band* (1930), a stinging satire on war and international politics with a strongly acid text by George S. Kaufman and Morrie Ryskind; *Girl Crazy* (1930), in which Ethel Merman made her sensational debut in the musical theatre; and *Of Thee I Sing* (1931), a satire on politics in Washington which became the first musical comedy to win the Pulitzer Prize in drama. These productions proved a veritable cornucopia of musical riches. The cream of the crop were " 'S Wonderful" from *Funny Face;* the title song and "Soon" from *Strike Up The Band;* "Sam and Delilah," "I Got Rhythm," "Embraceable You," and "But Not for Me" from *Girl Crazy;* the title song, "Wintergreen for President," and "Love Is Sweeping the Country" from *Of Thee I Sing.*

Of Thee I Sing was Gershwin's last Broadway success. His next two musicals were failures. One was *Let 'Em Eat Cake* (1933), a sequel to *Of Thee I Sing* which included the song "Mine." The other was *Pardon My English* (1933). His last musical production on Broadway was the opera *Porgy and Bess,* in 1935.

After 1935 Gershwin wrote exclusively for motion pictures. George and Ira Gershwin had first worked in Hollywood in 1931, when they wrote the score for *Delicious.* They returned to the movie capital in 1936, and remained. In 1937 came *Damsel in Distress* and *Shall We Dance,* both starring Fred Astaire; and, in 1938, the *Goldwyn Follies.* Among the most important songs from these screen productions were "Foggy Day in London Town" and "Nice Work If You Can Get It" from *Damsel in Distress;* "Let's Call the Whole Thing Off" and "They Can't Take That Away from Me" from *Shall We Dance*; and "Love Walked In" and "Our Love Is Here to Stay" from the *Goldwyn Follies.*

While working on the *Goldwyn Follies,* Gershwin suffered a physical collapse. On July 9, 1937, he was taken to the Cedars of Lebanon Hospital for a brain operation. Examination revealed a cystic degeneration of a tumor on a part of the brain that could not be touched. He died in the hospital on the morning of July 11, 1937.

After Gershwin's death several important motion pictures were produced with his music. One was his screen biography, *Rhapsody in Blue,* distributed in 1945, with Robert Alda playing the composer. In 1947 *The Shocking Miss Pilgrim* was produced with a score prepared by Kay Swift from manuscripts left behind by Gershwin; one of the songs, "For You, For Me, For Evermore" proved a find. Three years later, *An American in Paris,* starring Gene Kelly, was filmed with several Gershwin favorites and with the tone poem that gave the film its title used as the background music for an elaborate dance sequence. *An American in Paris* received the Academy Award in 1951 as the best motion picture of the year.

ABOUT:
Ewen, David. A Journey to Greatness: The Life and Music of George Gershwin; Gershwin, Ira. Lyrics on Several Occasions; Goldberg, Isaac. George Gershwin; Jablonski, Edward and Stewart, Lawrence D. The Gershwin Years.

Edwin Franko Goldman *1878-1956*

EDWIN FRANKO GOLDMAN, distinguished bandleader and composer of march music, was born in Louisville, Kentucky, on January 1, 1878. He came from a family of prominent musicians. Two of his uncles—Sam and Nahan Franko—were famous as violinists, conductors and founders of very notable musical organizations in New York. His cousin was Gustav Hollander, composer of German operettas and director of the renowned Stern Conservatory in Berlin. His mother had been a child prodigy pianist.

When Edwin was eight, the family moved to New York. Here his musical education took place. At first he studied the cornet with private teachers. Later he attended the National Conservatory, then directed by Dvořák, and completed his training on the cornet with Jules Levey. When he was seventeen, he joined the orchestra of the Metropolitan Opera, its youngest member. He held this post for about a decade after which, for several years, he taught the cornet.

In 1911 Goldman founded and conducted his first band. He continued to conduct band concerts for the next few years. In 1918 he helped raise a public subscription to pay for free band concerts on the grounds of Columbia University; it was there that the celebrated Goldman Band came into existence. In 1922 the Goldman Band started to give free concerts in New York's Central Park; from 1924 these concerts were financed by the Guggenheim family.

During the next three decades Goldman led his band in free concerts in Central Park and Brooklyn, and elsewhere on tour. He created a remarkable ensemble which performed the popular and semiclassical repertory and with it an extensive library of symphonic music adapted for band. Many outstanding modern composers wrote works expressly for the Goldman Band. Goldman also initiated an annual event known as the "Music Memory Contest," in which prizes were offered to those getting the highest scores.

Goldman wrote over a hundred marches, many of which he helped make outstandingly popular. His most famous marches were *On the Mall, Children's March* (an adaptation of famous children's songs), *Central Park, On the Farm, Young America, Emblem of Freedom, On the Campus, On Parade, Sunapee,* and *Indian March.* By virtue of this music, as well as of his remarkable career as conductor, Edwin Franko Goldman was universally acknowledged as the successor to John Philip Sousa as America's "march king." In 1933 Goldman succeeded Sousa as honorary life president of the American Bandmasters Association, which he had helped to organize in 1929, and whose president he was from then until 1933.

Besides his marches, Goldman also wrote several popular songs, though none of these

EDWIN FRANKO GOLDMAN

achieved the popularity of his instrumental compositions. Among these songs were "The Love I Have for You," "Why?" "In the Twilight," "My Heaven of Love," and "In the Springtime."

For his many achievements in the field of band music, Goldman was the recipient of over a hundred medals, besides numerous other honors. He was made Officier de l'Instruction Publique in 1929; Cavaliere of the Order of the Crown in 1931; and a member of the Order of the White Lion in 1936. He was the author of several books of instruction on band instruments and two books on bands. He died in New York City on February 21, 1956. He was succeeded as conductor of the Goldman Band by his son, Richard Franko Goldman, who for many years previously had been his assistant conductor.

ABOUT:
Goldman, Edwin Franko. Facing the Music.

Jay Gorney 1896-

JAY GORNEY was born in Bialystok, Russia, on December 12, 1896. The Gorney family fled in the wake of a pogrom in 1906, came to the United States, and settled in Detroit, where the boy started taking piano lessons. While attending Cass Technical High School he organized and led the

school orchestra. On weekends, he played piano in a local movie theatre. In addition to providing a little money, his experience accompanying silent pictures led him into the art of improvisation and original composition, which made the silent movies come to life.

Aspiring to a career in law, Gorney attended the University of Michigan, from which he was graduated with degrees in the arts and in law (A.B. and LL.B.). While at the University he studied harmony, counterpoint, and orchestration with Professor Earl V. Moore, head of the University's School of Music. He then organized and led a jazz band which played at college functions. For one year he practiced law in Michigan. Then, realizing that music meant more to him than law, he gave up practice for good, went to New York, and for a while worked in Tin Pan Alley.

He was soon writing popular songs. One, "I've Been Wanting You," appeared in the Broadway revue *The Dancing Girl* (1923). In 1924 he placed three songs in the *Greenwich Village Follies*, and wrote the complete score for *Top Hole*. He also wrote complete scores for *Merry-Go-Round* (1927), *The Sketch Book* (1929), the Earl Carroll *Vanities* (1930) and *Americana* (1932). Other songs were introduced in the Ziegfeld *Follies of 1931* and *Shoot the Works* (1931). "Like Me Less, Love Me More" and "Kinda Cute" came out of *The Sketch Book*, and "I Came to Life" and "One Love" from the *Vanities;* all were written to E. Y. Harburg's lyrics. From *Americana* emerged Gorney's greatest song hit up to that time, "Brother, Can You Spare a Dime?" (lyrics by Harburg), a number that soon became the classic theme song for the years of the Depression.

In 1929 and 1930 Gorney worked for the Paramount studios in New York as composer and musical adviser. During this period he wrote "What Makes My Baby Blue?" and "When I'm Housekeeping with You" (lyrics by Howard Dietz) for the movie *The Battle of the Sexes*, starring Gertrude Lawrence. He also wrote "Just a Melody for a Memory" and "It Can't Go on Like This" (lyrics by Harburg) for *Roadhouse Nights,* starring Helen Morgan, and

JAY GORNEY

"What Wouldn't I Do for That Man" (lyrics by Harburg) for *Glorifying the American Girl*.

In 1931 Gorney became a member of the editorial board of Paramount Pictures as adviser on musical motion pictures. Two years after that he went to work in the movie capital at the Fox Studios, where he is credited with the discovery of Shirley Temple, having suggested her for a starring role in her first important picture, *Stand Up and Cheer*. Among Gorney's best songs for motion pictures in the 1930's were "Ah, But Is It Love?" and the title number of *Moonlight and Pretzels* (lyrics by Harburg); "Baby, Take a Bow" (lyrics by Lew Brown) from *Stand Up and Cheer*; and "You're My Thrill" (lyrics by Sidney Clare) from *Jimmy and Sallie*. Other songs of this period included "Forbidden Lips" from *Springtime for Henry*, "Love at Last" from *Romance in the Rain*, and "Song of a Dreamer" from *Marie Galante*, all with lyrics by Don Hartman; and "It's Home" from *Marie Galante* (lyrics by Jack Yellen).

In 1942 and 1943 Gorney served as a producer for Columbia Pictures. There he also wrote the scores for *Hey, Rookie, The Gay Senorita*, and *The Heat's On*.

Gorney's greatest stage success came with *Meet the People*, an intimate, topical revue which originated in Hollywood, where it re-mained a year, had a short run in several other major American cities, then opened on Broadway on December 25, 1940, for a successful stay. After that it played for two years on the road. This score contained such lyrical items as "A Fellow and a Girl," "The Stars Remain," "In Chichicastenango," "No Lookin' Back," and several songs in a witty or satirical vein, including "Let's Steal a Tune from Offenbach," "It's the Same Old South," and "The Bill of Rights." The lyrics were by Henry Myers and Edward Eliscu. There were two later editions of *Meet the People* in Hollywood in 1943 and 1944; because of the war these productions were unable to tour the country.

During World War II Gorney wrote songs and sketches for broadcasts and films for the armed forces. After the war, his songs were heard on Broadway in two musicals, *Heaven on Earth* (1948) and *Touch and Go* (1949). The leading musical numbers from the first production were "You're the First Cup of Coffee in the Morning," and "So Near and Yet So Far"; those from the second musical included "Wish Me Luck," "Funny Old, Little Old World," and the satirical finale, "Great Dane a-Comin'." *Touch and Go* was produced successfully in London, where it stayed a year.

In 1948 Gorney and his wife Sondra were invited to create a musical play department at the Dramatic Workshop of the New School for Social Research in New York. They conducted it successfully for three years, and during that time produced five student musicals. In 1952 they joined the faculty of the American Theatre Wing professional training program where they produced an original student musical, *On the Wing*, in 1954. During this period, Gorney was also a writer-composer-producer for CBS-TV. He has frequently given lectures on the musical theatre for various educational organizations, and has written musical spectaculars for television presentations. With Henry Myers as his collaborator, he has written and had published two children's musical fantasies, *The Geografoof* and *Kris Kringle Rides Again*.

Gorney adapted the music of Jacques Offenbach for the 1961 Broadway musical *The Happiest Girl in the World* (lyrics by E. Y. Harburg). In 1961 Gorney also wrote a

series of original musicals (lyrics by John
W. Bloch) for NBC-TV, entitled *Frontiers
of Faith.*

Morton Gould *1913-*

MORTON GOULD

MORTON GOULD, though essentially a
composer of serious concert music, has
written a great number of lighter works that
have won popular favor. Besides his major
orchestral compositions, he has written for
symphonic bands, stage, screen and ballet.

He was born in Richmond Hill, New
York, on December 10, 1913. A musical
prodigy, he played piano and composed at an
early age, publishing his first opus (a waltz
for the piano) when he was only six. In his
eighth year he received a scholarship to the
Institute of Musical Arts. Subsequently, most
of his piano studies were with the late
Abby Whiteside; he also studied composition
and theory with Dr. Vincent Jones of New
York University.

Following the completion of his music
studies, Gould earned his living in theatre,
vaudeville, and radio as solo pianist and member of a two-piano team. In the early 1930's
he was a staff pianist at Radio City Music
Hall and the National Broadcasting Company.
In 1934 Gould began a long and fruitful
association with radio as conductor of an
orchestra for the WOR Mutual network.
From that time, he was sponsored on the
Columbia Broadcasting network in a series
of musical programs. These programs featured his orchestral settings of popular music
as well as original works. His fresh and
musically inventive performances, combined
with his skillful transcriptions, made him a
radio and recording favorite.

Gould's early concert works usually combined the jazz and popular element with the
classical style. His *Second Symphonette* is
one of the early examples; the second movement of the work, "Pavanne," has become a
popular standard. The *Latin-American Symphonette* is another example of his fusion of
the popular and formalistic.

On January 2, 1936, Stokowski introduced Gould's *Chorale and Fugue in Jazz* for
piano and orchestra. Since that time, Gould
has written many works with a purpose
similar to that of the works mentioned above:
to bring the structural dimensions and tech-

nical resources of serious music to American
popular idioms. The *Cowboy Rhapsody*
(1944) gives symphonic treatment to such
famous cowboy melodies as "Home on the
Range" and "Old Paint." *Foster Gallery*
(1941) offers a similar treatment of several
of Foster's best loved melodies. In *Interplay*
—a ballet with choreography by Jerome
Robbins, introduced in New York in 1945—
effective use is made of the blues; and there
is a jazz Scherzo in Gould's *Symphony No. 3*
(1947). In addition, he has written brilliant
orchestral adaptations of such famous American tunes as "When Johnny Comes Marching
Home" (in *American Salute*).

Gould has written music for two Broadway musical comedies. The first was "Billion
Dollar Baby" in 1945, with book and lyrics
by Adolph Green and Betty Comden. Among
the songs were "Bad Timing," "I Got a One
Track Mind," and "I'm Sure of Your Love,"
and among the instrumental ballet numbers,
Charleston.

In 1950 he wrote for the Theatre Guild a
musical comedy adaptation of *The Pursuit of
Happiness* called *Arms and the Girl!* Dorothy Fields was the lyricist; among the songs
were "That's My Fella," "There Must Be
Somethin' Better than Love," and "You
Kissed Me."

Gould wrote the music for and appeared
in the motion picture *Delightfully Dangerous.*
The lyrics were by Edward Heyman; among

the songs was "Through Your Eyes to Your Heart." He also composed the background scores for *Cinerama Holiday* and *Windjammer* and for several television programs.

A great deal of Gould's music is used by school and college bands and ensembles, for which he has written many works in both short and extended forms.

ABOUT:
Howard, John Tasker. Our American Music.
Musical America, December 25, 1943.

Johnny Green 1908-

JOHN W. GREEN, known professionally as Johnny Green, was born in New York City on October 10, 1908. His father, a builder and banker, hoped to direct his son to his own professions. Johnny attended the Horace Mann School and the New York Military Academy, and in 1928 was graduated from Harvard. He then worked for a brief period as a clerk in a Wall Street bond house before deciding to devote himself to music, the one interest that absorbed him from boyhood on.

As a college student, he had a song published—"Coquette," written in collaboration with Carmen Lombardo to Gus Kahn's lyrics. Two important songs in 1930 helped establish Green's career as a songwriter. One was "I'm Yours" (lyrics by E. Y. Harburg), featured in the motion picture *Leave It to Lester*. The other was a song which to this day remains Green's most famous, "Body and Soul" (lyrics by Edward Heyman and Robert Sour), introduced in the smart, intimate Broadway revue *Three's a Crowd*. Actually, "Body and Soul" was an international hit before it came to Broadway. Green had written it as special material for Gertrude Lawrence, whose accompanist Green was at that time. She took the unpublished manuscript to England, sang it over the BBC, and made it so popular that in a short time it was published in England and played there by many leading popular orchestras. It was then that Max Gordon, producer of *Three's a Crowd*, bought it for his revue.

Green's most substantial song hits during the next few years included "Out of No-

JOHNNY GREEN

where" and "I Cover the Waterfront" (lyrics by Heyman) and "I Wanna Be Loved" (lyrics by Heyman and Billy Rose). These and some later Green songs were recorded in the best-selling album entitled "The Johnny Ever-Greens." Green also wrote some popular music in a more ambitious form than the song. One of these compositions was *Night Club: Six Impressions*, for three pianos and orchestra, commissioned by Paul Whiteman for his orchestra. It was subsequently performed at the Lewisohn Stadium, by the BBC Orchestra in London, and by the CBS Symphony under André Kostelanetz and Bernard Herrman.

Between 1930 and 1933 Green worked as a composer, conductor, and arranger at the Paramount studios in Astoria, Long Island. During this period he also made numerous appearances in Paramount theatres throughout the country as a featured conductor and master of ceremonies. From 1933 to 1940 he toured the country with his own dance band. At this time he started to perform over the radio as conductor or host on numerous coast-to-coast programs, including the Jack Benny program, the Packard Hour with Fred Astaire, and for two years the Philip Morris program.

From 1949 to 1958 Green was the general music director and executive in charge of music at the MGM studios in Hollywood. He was associated either as musical director or conductor (or both) with many outstandingly successful screen musicals, including *An American in Paris* (which won Academy Awards not only as the best picture of the year but also for Green's scoring); *Rhapsody; The Great Caruso; Brigadoon; Meet Me in Las Vegas* (for which he wrote an ambitious musical sequence, *Frankie and Johnny*, as a ballet for Cyd Charisse); and *High Society.* He was also conductor for and composer of the score of the Elizabeth Taylor film *Raintree County*, from which two successful songs emerged, "The Song of Raintree County" and "Never Till Now." Green adapted some of the music from this motion picture score into a symphonic suite that has been performed by several leading American orchestras, *Raintree County: Three Themes for Symphony Orchestra.* For his contributions to motion picture music, Green was nine times a nominee for Academy Awards, and three times a recipient.

On four occasions, between 1945 and 1957, Green was the musical director and conductor of the Academy Award ceremonies in Hollywood. When these ceremonies were first televised in 1953, he produced and directed the entire show. He was also the first important composer to be commissioned to write a special score for TV film, the Desilu production of *Bernadette.* Since April 1958 he has been the producer of several important television "specials," including *Music U.S.A.* in 1958 and *A Diamond for Carla* in 1959.

Green has distinguished himself as a conductor of symphony orchestras. For several seasons, beginning with 1958, he has served as music director and permanent conductor of the Promenade Concerts of the Los Angeles Philharmonic. He has also appeared as guest conductor of many other important American symphony orchestras.

Green's wife is the former Bonnie (Bunny) Waters, the swimming champion.

ABOUT:
Down Beat, September 19, 1957.

Ferde Grofé *1892-*

FERDE GROFÉ was born Ferdinand Rudolph von Grofé in New York City on March 27, 1892. His father was an actor and baritone, his mother an excellent cellist and teacher. When Ferde was still a child, his family moved to Los Angeles, where he received his first music instruction from his mother while he attended Los Angeles public schools. When he was seven he went with his mother to Germany, where for three years she attended the Leipzig Conservatory. Back in Los Angeles, Grofé started writing his first pieces of music in 1906, all of them for the piano, and some in a ragtime style. His ambition was to become a musician, but his parents wanted him to study either law or architecture. Family pressure, combined with the fact that his mother remarried soon after the death of his father, led the boy to run away from home. For three years he supported himself in various occupations, including those of bookbinder, newsboy, elevator operator, usher, truck driver, lithographer, and steel worker. But all the while he continued to study music.

In 1908 he began taking on random assignments as pianist or violinist at conventions and lodge dances, and as pianist for a dancing master with whom he toured California. In 1909 he joined the viola section of the Los Angeles Symphony with which he remained on and off for about a decade. Also in 1909 he received his first commission to write a piece of music, *The Elks Grand Reunion March,* for a convention in Los Angeles; this was his first published work.

While with the Los Angeles Symphony, Grofé made numerous appearances with jazz orchestras. He soon formed a jazz outfit of his own for which he wrote all the arrangements. These arrangements, combined with Grofé's brilliant improvisations, brought lovers of jazz to night spots in Los Angeles and San Francisco where the Grofé ensemble played. One of these jazz devotees was Paul Whiteman, whose high opinion of Grofé's talent led him to engage Grofé as pianist and arranger for his own orchestra. This was late in 1919. Grofé remained with the Whiteman Orchestra for the next dozen years; it was due largely Grofé's fresh and vital or-

FERDE GROFÉ

chestrations that the Paul Whiteman Orchestra was acclaimed throughout the world of music and in every possible medium. Grofé's very first arrangement for Whiteman, "Whispering," sold more than a million and a half records. That of George Gershwin's *Rhapsody in Blue*, for its première in 1924, helped make popular music history.

Grofé emerged as a composer of serious musical works in a popular style with *Broadway at Night* in 1924. Success came a year later with the *Mississippi Suite*, written for the Paul Whiteman Orchestra, which introduced it at Carnegie Hall. The *Mississippi Suite* is in four movements, the first of which ("Father of the Waters") pays tribute to the river itself. The remaining movements are entitled "Huckleberry Finn," "Old Creole Days" and "Mardi Gras," the last of these the most popular section of the entire work, and one of the composer's own particular favorites.

Grofé's most famous composition, the *Grand Canyon Suite*, was written in 1931 and was introduced by the Paul Whiteman Orchestra in Chicago on November 22 of the same year. Here the composer offers a tonal picture of one of America's natural wonders in five movements: "Sunrise," "The Painted Desert," "On the Trail," "Sunset," and "Cloudburst." The third movement is par-

ticularly famous, having been used for many years as the radio signature for the Philip Morris program.

Grofé has been outstandingly successful in introducing popular American idioms into the spacious forms of serious music while utilizing the fullest resources of harmony and orchestration. Among his other orchestral works are *Three Shades of Blue, Theme and Variations on Noises from a Garage, Death Valley Suite, Metropolis, Tabloid Suite* (in which the sound of typewriters is simulated), *Hollywood Suite* (a score calling for the shouts of directors and the banging of carpenters on a set), *Killarney-Irish Fantasy, Kentucky Derby, New England Suite, Atlantic Crossing, Gettysburg Address, San Francisco Suite, Hudson River Suite, Valley of the Sun, Valley of Enchantment, Aviation Suite*, and *Concerto in D*, for piano and orchestra.

Grofé has also produced musical scores for industry. In this category belong *Symphony in Steel* (written for the American Rolling Mill Company) and *Wheels* (for Henry Ford). He has also contributed music for motion pictures, including *Time Out of Mind, The Return of Jesse James*, and *Minstrel Man*. (The last was a documentary for which Grofé received an Academy Award.) In 1960 Grofé was commissioned by the New York State Power Authority to write a symphonic work celebrating the opening of the Niagara Power Project at Niagara Falls: the *Niagara Suite*. In 1961 Grofé was commissioned by Robert Moses to write an orchestral suite for the New York World's Fair of 1964. Grofé has also produced orchestrations for the musical stage; written the scores for two ballets, *Hollywood Ballet* (in which the great and near great of Hollywood are portrayed) and *Café Society;* and published a number of chamber music works, including *Table d'Hôte*, for flute, violin, and piano.

After leaving the Paul Whiteman Orchestra in 1932, Grofé formed his own ensemble with which he appeared for many years in public concerts and on many major sponsored radio programs. He has also appeared as a guest conductor of several important American symphony orchestras. Since 1954 he has appeared in concerts of two-piano music with his wife, Anne.

Between 1939 and 1942 Grofé taught orchestration at the Juilliard School of Music in New York.

ABOUT:

Ewen, David. American Composers Today.

International Musician, August 1953; Musical Courier, January 15, 1956; New Yorker, May 25, 1940; Time, May 9, 1960.

David W. Guion 1892-

DAVID WENDELL DE FENTRESSE GUION was born in Ballinger, Texas, on December 15, 1892. He is of French Huguenot descent. His grandfather, John I. Guion, had been governor of Mississippi; his father, also John I. Guion, was an influential Texas judge; his mother was a gifted pianist and singer.

David received his first music instruction from his mother when he was six. Soon after that formal training began with local teachers. When he was twelve, he earned six dollars a week playing the piano nightly in an open-air motion picture theatre. While holding this job he wrote his first piece of music, *Million Dollar Mystery Rag*, named after a movie serial then playing in his theatre. This was followed by the *Texas Fox Trot*, which was reproduced on phonograph records and player-piano rolls.

After completing his academic education at the Whipple Academy in Jacksonville, Illinois, and the Polytechnic College in Fort Worth, Texas, Guion spent three years in Europe for advanced music study, principally the piano with Leopold Godowsky in Vienna. From 1915 to 1917 Guion was director of the School of Music at the Daniel Baker College in Texas. During the next decade he held various posts as a teacher of piano in Texas colleges and music schools, and from 1925 to 1928 he was a faculty member of the Chicago Musical College.

America's folk music played a significant role in Guion's musical development. As a boy he was raised on cowboy ballads, Negro spirituals, western folk tunes, and square dances. As a composer Guion has used all such idioms successfully, besides achieving renown for his felicitous transcriptions of various American folk songs. One of his earliest compositions was a set of spirituals arranged for voice and piano. His arrangements of

DAVID W. GUION

other spirituals and Negro songs, deservedly famous, include "Swing Low, Sweet Chariot," "Nobody Knows de Trouble I've Seen," "Short'nin' Bread," and "De Ol' Ark's a-Moverin'."

Guion is perhaps most celebrated for his arrangements of western folk songs, and most especially for "Home on the Range," which became so famous in his version that he is sometimes falsely credited as being its author. (Several different composers and lyricists have claimed authorship of "Home on the Range.") But there can be little doubt that it was through David Guion's arrangement, published in 1930, that "Home on the Range" first became famous. It became extremely popular over the radio and was said to have been the favorite song of President Franklin D. Roosevelt and Will Rogers.

Other successful transcriptions of western tunes by Guion include the "Arkansas Traveler," "Oh, Bury Me Not on the Lone Prairie," "Turkey in the Straw," and "Carry Me Home to the Lone Prairie."

Guion has written several large works for orchestra which combine folk tunes with original material. These include the *Prairie Suite, Mother Goose Suite, Alley Tunes* (in which is found his very popular "The Harmonica Player"), and *Texas*. A symphonic suite comprising fourteen sections and scored for solo voices and orchestra,

Texas received its world première in Houston on February 5, 1952, with Efrem Kurtz conducting the Houston Symphony. Guion also rote the scores for two ballets, *Western Ballet* and *Shingandi*, the latter a primitive African ballet based on African intervals (major third and minor second).

In the early 1930's Guion produced and starred in a cowboy production featuring his own music at the Roxy Theatre in New York. After that Guion was associated with radio. For sixty-four weeks he performed over NBC and WOR radio networks on his own program; one of the distinguishing features of these broadcasts was the extensive use of actual sounds, yells, and hoofbeats to dramatize the proceedings. In 1936 Guion appeared in an all-Guion program at Carnegie Hall, and in the same year he wrote "My Cowboy Love Song" for the Texas Centennial. In 1950, between January 29 and February 4, a David Guion Week was celebrated throughout Texas, sponsored by the Texas Federation of Music Clubs.

In 1958 the National Federation of Music Clubs named Guion second only to Stephen Foster as America's most significant composer of music in the folk vein. In March 1960, at the invitation of the dean of the College of Fine Arts at the University of Texas, Guion presented over a hundred of his original manuscripts for a permanent Guion Collection.

ABOUT:

Howard, John Tasker. Our American Music; Spaeth, Sigmund. A History of Popular Music in America.

Albert Hague *1920-*

ALBERT HAGUE was born in Berlin, Germany, on October 13, 1920. He began to study the piano when he was five, and composition a year after that. Between 1935 and 1937 he studied piano and composition with Arthur Perleberg. In 1938 he received a one-year scholarship for the Santa Cecilia Academy in Rome, as a pupil of Dante Alderighi. In 1939 he came to the United States, where he attended the College of Music of the University of Cincinnati, again on a scholarship. There he studied composition with Sidney Durst, and piano with Quincy Bass. Following his graduation in 1942, he served

ALBERT HAGUE

for two and a half years in the United States Air Force.

Hague went to New York in 1946 to pursue actively his career as a popular composer. His first full-length musical comedy was *Reluctant Lady* (book and lyrics by Maurice Valency), produced by Canada Lee in Cleveland, Ohio; its leading lady, Renee Orin, subsequently became Hague's wife. One of the numbers from this show, "One Is a Lonely Number," later became Hague's first song heard on the Broadway stage, in *Dance Me a Song* in 1950. Hague, meanwhile, had made his bow in the New York theatre with incidental music for *The Madwoman of Chaillot*, in 1948. After that he wrote background music for a motion picture short, *Coney Island, U.S.A.*, which won first prizes at both the Edinburgh and Venice Festivals in 1951, and which was introduced in New York in 1952. In 1953 he wrote all the music for *The Mercer Girls*, a television production on the Hallmark Hall of Fame program; he also created the piano arrangements for the *Burl Ives Song Book*, published the same year. In 1954 he wrote the incidental music for Robert Anderson's Broadway play *All Summer Long*.

His first song success was "Wait for Me, Darling," which Georgia Gibbs helped to make famous in the United States, and which also achieved considerable popularity in England. This was followed by his first full-length Broadway musical production, *Plain and Fancy,* which began a run of 461 performances on January 27, 1955. The story by Joseph Stein and William Glickman was set among the Amish inhabitants of Lancaster County, Pennsylvania, and touched upon the strict but colorful speech, dress, and morality of this sect. Hague's score (lyrics by Arnold B. Horwitt) boasted a substantial hit in "Young and Foolish," and included two other excellent numbers in "Plain We Live" and "It Wonders Me," in which a picture of Amish people is graphically portrayed in lyrics and music.

Hague followed the success of *Plain and Fancy* with another substantial Broadway hit, *Redhead,* starring Gwen Verdon, which opened on February 5, 1959. The opulent score, with lyrics by Dorothy Fields, included such winning numbers as "Look Who's in Love," "Just for Once," "I Feel Merely Marvelous" and "My Girl Is Just Enough Woman for Me."

Two Hague songs were included by Carl Sandburg in the *New American Songbag* in 1950: "Telephone Book" and "Tell Irene Hello" (lyrics by Waring Cuney).

W. C. Handy *1873-1958*

WILLIAM CHRISTOPHER HANDY, sometimes described as "the father of the blues," was born in Florence, Alabama, on November 16, 1873. Both his grandfather and his father were ministers. The latter considered a musical career as sacrilegious and did what he could to discourage the boy's natural bent for music. "I'd rather see you in a hearse than have you become a musician," William's father once told him. Nevertheless, the boy managed to purchase a trumpet for a dollar from a circus musician and to learn to play it. Before long he was playing with a brass band, and soon after that with a touring minstrel show.

Despite his ambition to become a musician, Handy was educated as a teacher. In 1892 he was graduated from the Teachers Agricultural and Mechanical College in Huntsville, Alabama. He was a teacher only for a short time. After that he supported himself by working in a foundry while further pursuing various musical activities. In 1893 he played the cornet at the Chicago

W. C. HANDY   ASCAP

World's Fair. Three years after that he found a permanent job with Mahara's Minstrels as cornetist, arranger, and performer; eventually he became the leader of the band. From 1900 to 1902 he taught music at the Teachers Agricultural and Mechanical College, and in 1903 he organized the first of several bands, with which he gave concerts of popular music throughout the South for a quarter of a century.

Two events helped shape his musical destiny. One day, at a deserted railroad station, he happened to hear a Negro sing a lament which, for the first time, made him fully conscious of the power and beauty of Negro folk songs. Another time, while visiting Cleveland, Mississippi, he heard several local colored musicians perform Negro folk and jazz tunes. "That night," he confessed, "a composer was born, an American composer. Those country black boys had taught me something that could not possibly have been gained from books, something that would, however, cause books to be written."

These two experiences led Handy to try writing songs in the style of Negro folk music. Thus he came upon the "blues." It cannot be said that Handy invented this song form which had long existed as the "sorrow music" of the lower strata of Negro society. But he was responsible for making it popular, for carrying it into commercial popular music.

In discussing the style and technique he adopted for his own compositions, Handy has thrown illumination on the methods adopted by all blues composers: "The primitive southern Negro as he sang was sure to bear down on the third and seventh tone of the scale, slurring between major and minor. Whether in the cotton field of the Delta or on the levee up St. Louis way, it was always the same. Till then, however, I had never heard this slur used by a more sophisticated Negro, or by any white man. I tried to convey this effect . . . by introducing flat thirds and sevenths (now called blue notes) into my song, although its prevailing key was major, and I carried this device into my melody as well. . . . This was a distinct departure, but as it turned out, it touched the spot. In the folk blues the singer fills up occasional gaps with words like 'Oh, Lawdy,' or 'Oh, Baby,' and the like. This meant that in writing a melody to be sung in the blues manner, one would have to provide gaps or waits. In my composition I decided to embellish the piano and orchestral score at these points. This kind of business is called a 'break' . . . and 'breaks' became a fertile source of the orchestral improvisation, which became the essence of jazz. . . . I used a plagal cadence to give 'spiritual' effects in the harmony. Altogether I aimed to use all that is characteristic of the Negro from Africa to Alabama."

Handy wrote his first blues in 1909. It was called "The Memphis Blues," and it was written to further the mayoralty campaign of Edward H. Crump, then running on a reform ticket in Memphis, Tennessee. In an effort to gain the support of the Negroes of Beale Street for his candidate, Handy wrote a campaign song in the style of the folk music so familiar to his people; he called his song "Mr. Crump." It became so popular in Memphis that after Crump had been elected, Handy decided to publish it at his own expense. He now called it "The Memphis Blues," and issued it as a piano composition. This was the first blues ever published. A New York publisher bought out all the rights for fifty dollars and issued it in New York with lyrics by George A. Norton. It became a huge success.

Disappointed that he had failed to capitalize financially on the immense popularity of "The Memphis Blues," Handy decided to write another song in the same style for more judicious exploitation. As he sought a suitable theme for a new blues, he wrote in his autobiography, "a flood of memories" filled his mind. "First there was the picture I had of myself, unshaven, wanting even a decent meal, and standing before the lighted saloon in St. Louis without a shirt under my frayed coat. There was also from that same period a curious and dramatic little fragment that till now seemed to have little or no importance. While occupied with my own memories during the sojourn, I had seen a woman whose pain seemed even greater. She had tried to take the edge off her grief by heavy drinking, but it hadn't worked. Stumbling along the poorly lighted street, she muttered as she walked, 'My man's got a heart like a rock cast in the sea.' . . . By the time I had finished all this heavy thinking and remembering, I figured it was time to get something down on paper, so I wrote 'I hate to see de evenin' sun go down.' If you ever had to sleep on the cobbles down by the river in St. Louis, you'll understand the complaint."

Thus Handy wrote his masterpiece, "The St. Louis Blues." Despite the fortunes of "The Memphis Blues," Handy's new blues failed to find a single interested publisher. Handy was finally obliged to form a publishing organization of his own, in partnership with Harry Pace, and in 1914 "The St. Louis Blues" was published. After Handy had transferred his company to New York, the song began to catch on—especially after Victor had issued a highly successful recording, after Sophie Tucker had sung it in vaudeville, and after Gilda Gray had introduced it in revues. Before several more years had gone by, every known recording and piano-roll company had issued the song. In time it sold more records than any other single piece of music, popular or serious. It was the inspiration for a full-length movie and a movie short and was used as the title for several more films after that. The sale of sheet music and records remained so healthy through the years that even towards the end of his life Handy was receiving an annual royalty of about twenty-five thousand dollars.

"The St. Louis Blues" is one of the enduring classics in American popular music. It has been performed in every possible arrangement and on every conceivable instrument or combination of instruments. When Prime Minister Ramsay MacDonald of England first visited the United States, Nathaniel Shilkret played "The St. Louis Blues" for him, as a distinctive American composition. Queen Elizabeth of England (mother of Elizabeth II) chose it as one of her favorite musical numbers. When Prince George of England and Princess Marina of Greece were married, the royal pair danced to its strains. When Ethiopia was invaded by Italy, "The St. Louis Blues" became the battle hymn for the beleaguered African country.

Handy continued writing successful blues after 1914. The best were "The Beale Street Blues," "The John Henry Blues," "The Harlem Blues," "The Joe Turner Blues" and "Careless Love." Besides the blues, Handy wrote several effective marches (*Hail to the Spirit of Freedom, The Big Stick Blues March* and *Go Down Moses March*) and some orchestral music (*Blue-Destiny Symphony* and *Afro-American Hymn*).

Named after Handy were several theatres and schools, a swimming pool, a foundation for the blind, and a public park in Memphis. At the New York World's Fair in 1939 he was named one of America's greatest contributors to world culture. On his sixty-fifth birthday he received an eloquent tribute at Carnegie Hall. His life story was dramatized in *St. Louis Blues*, released in 1958, with Nat "King" Cole playing the role of the composer.

During the last years of his life, Handy was totally blind. He managed, nevertheless, to play the trumpet on several occasions, to perform over radio and television, and to help conduct the affairs of his publishing house. He edited several volumes, including *Negro Spirituals and Songs* (1926), *Book of Negro Spirituals* .(1938), *Negro Music and Musicians* (1944), and *A Treasury of the Blues* (1949). A few years before his death, in 1954, he married his secretary, Irma Louise Logan; this was his second marriage. He died in New York City on March 28, 1958.

ABOUT:

Handy, W. C. Father of the Blues; Handy, W. C. editor. A Treasury of the Blues; Stearns, Marshall. The Story of Jazz.

Music Journal, November 1950; Record Changer, May 1952.

Ben Harney *1872-1938*

BENJAMIN ROBERTSON HARNEY, a pioneer in the writing of piano rags, was born in or about 1872. Little is known about his birth or early life. He first became interested in ragtime when he served as piano accompanist to a Negro performer touring in vaudeville. After that Harney played rags in saloons in Kansas City and St. Louis. In the early 1890's Harney toured the Midwest and West as ragtime pianist, one of his successful routines being the ragging of the major scale. In 1895 he became a member of a minstrel show act in which he did stickdance specialties and sang songs of his own composition. As a writer of popular songs—lyrics as well as music—he scored his first hit with "Mister Johnson Turn Me Loose," published in 1895, an early example of ragtime song. May Irwin sang it with dynamic effect in the musical *Courted in Court.* During the same year Harney wrote a second ragtime hit song in "You've Been a Good Old Wagon, But You've Done Broke Down."

Harney arrived in New York in the mid-1890's and became a star at Tony Pastor's Music Hall, where his piano rags became the rage. He is credited with being one of the first to introduce and popularize ragtime in New York; he was also probably the first white man to put down ragtime effects on paper. In his vaudeville act he not only performed and sang his ragtime music, but he also had the assistance of a Negro singer named Strap Hill, probably one of the first "stooges" in vaudeville. Strap Hill would sit in the audience where he would sing a shout. Harney would repeat the shout on the stage imitating Strap Hill, after which the latter would mount the stage and continue his ragtime performance in collaboration with Harney.

Isidore Witmark described Harney's ragtime singing as follows: "He had the huskiest voice most people had ever heard in a human being, and this quality made his voice just right for ragtime singing. It had queer breaks in it that affected the words as well as the music. Broadly speaking, he might even be called the first of the crooners. He would sustain certain notes for special effect to extravagant, breathtaking lengths; others he would break in a way that he alone could manage."

In 1897 the house of Witmark issued Harney's *Ragtime Instructor*, described as "the only work published giving full instructions on how to play ragtime music on the piano." In it Harney emphasized that ragtime was not a style of composition but a style of performance, that any piece of music could be ragged by putting the accent on the off beat, thus syncopating the tune. Harney tried to prove this thesis by offering ragtime versions of such semiclassics as Mendelssohn's *Spring Song*, Rubinstein's *Melody in F*, Mascagni's "Intermezzo" from *Cavalleria Rusticana*. These are probably among the earliest examples in American popular music of jazzing or ragging the classics.

Besides these ragtime pieces, Harney wrote many ragtime songs. The most successful were "I Love My Little Honey," "The Cakewalk in the Sky" (one of the first examples of lyrics being written in a ragtime style to conform to the rhythm of the melody), "If You Got Any Sense You'll Go," "Tell It to Me" and "The Black Man's Kissing Bug."

Harney's last appearance in vaudeville took place in 1923 in California. He died of a heart attack in Philadelphia on February 28, 1938.

ABOUT:

Gilbert, Douglas. Lost Chords; Goldberg, Isaac. Tin Pan Alley; Witmark, Isidore. From Ragtime to Swingtime.

Charles K. Harris *1867-1930*

CHARLES KASSELL HARRIS was born in Poughkeepsie, New York, on May 1, 1867. He spent his boyhood in Milwaukee, where he became so interested in minstrel shows that he fashioned a banjo from an empty oyster can and some strands of wire and learned to play popular minstrel show tunes. Soon afterwards, a vaudeville entertainer presented him with an authentic banjo. He acquired such proficiency that he was able to get engagements in small variety theatres and clubs in Milwaukee, accompanying himself in the performance of popular tunes; he also began giving banjo lessons to young

From AFTER THE BALL, copyright renewed 1953 by James J. Geller; by permission of the copyright owner

CHARLES K. HARRIS

pupils. In his sixteenth year he started to learn to play the piano, once again without a teacher.

One day, while attending a performance of *The Skating Rink* starring Nat Goodwin, he became convinced he could writing a skating song suitable for that production. Somehow he managed to gain access to Goodwin and to persuade him to interpolate his "Since Maggie Learned to Skate" into that musical. This official debut as a composer encouraged Harris to write other numbers for specific performers and productions. Here, as later, he was his own lyricist. Among these early Harris songs were "Creep, Baby, Creep," "Let's Kiss and Make Up," and "Thou Art Ever in My Thoughts."

From these first fruits Harris earned almost nothing, since in his eagerness to get his songs performed he allowed performers to use them without payment. He became convinced that the only way he could make a living as a songwriter was by publishing his songs himself. When he was eighteen he opened a one-room office on Grand Avenue in Milwaukee; outside his office he hung a shingle reading: "Charles K. Harris, Banjoist and Songwriter, Songs Written to Order."

His firm, as well as his career as a composer of popular ballads, were both solidly established on the foundation of a single hit, "After the Ball," the first popular song to sell several million copies of sheet music. His inspiration for this ballad came from an actual incident witnessed at a dance in Chicago. Harris happened to notice a young couple quarrel and go their separate ways. Suddenly a thought came to him: "Many a heart is aching after the ball." He knew at once that he had come upon a felicitous subject for a sentimental ballad. After returning to Milwaukee he wrote both lyrics and music of "After the Ball," designating it a "song story." The story concerned an old man who explains to his niece the reason why he never married: He had seen his sweetheart kiss a strange man at a ball. Only many years later did he learn that the stranger was his sweetheart's brother.

The first performance of "After the Ball" took place in a variety theatre in Milwaukee in 1892; the performer was Sam Doctor. The song was then a failure, mainly because midway in the ballad the singer forgot his lyrics. Soon after that "After the Ball" was interpolated into a performance of *A Trip to Chinatown* by one of the stars of that production, J. Aldrich Libby. He brought down the house. "For a full minute," Harris recalled in his autobiography, "the audience remained quiet, and then broke loose with applause. . . . The entire audience arose and, standing, applauded wildly for five minutes." One repercussion of this success was an unprecedented order for 75,000 copies of sheet music by a Boston music shop, the first of many other large orders that brought the total sale of the sheet music to five million within a few years. At the Chicago World's Fair of 1893, John Philip Sousa included it on his program; it received such acclaim that for many years Sousa played it at each of his concerts.

Though Harris was a prolific song writer, he managed to create only three other substantial song hits after that. The first was "Break the News to Mother," which in its original version dealt with the death of a young fireman. In 1897 Harris revised his lyric, changing the fireman to a soldier; the ballad thus gained timeliness during the Spanish-American War. In 1901, Harris published "Hello Central, Give Me Heaven," one of the first examples of telephone songs and

of a song whose lyric begins with "hello." In 1903 Harris published a popular waltz, "Always in the Way."

Other Harris songs included the following: "There'll Come a Time," "Better than Gold," "I've Just Come to Say Goodbye," " 'Mid the Green Fields of Virginia," "One Night in June," "I've a Longing in My Heart for You, Louise," "For Old Time's Sake," "Would You Care?," "The Best Things in Life," and "Nobody Knows, Nobody Cares."

Harris wrote several scenarios for silent movies and a few stage plays including *The Barker* and *The Luckiest Man in the World*. He died in New York City on December 22, 1930.

ABOUT:
Harris, Charles K. After the Ball: Forty Years of Melody; Spaeth, Sigmund. Read 'Em and Weep. Music Trades, April 1947.

Will S. Hays 1837-1907

WILLIAM SHAKESPEARE HAYS was one of the most prolific composers of popular songs in the latter half of the nineteenth century. He was born in July 1837 in Louisville, Kentucky, a city where he spent most of his life. He had little musical or academic education to speak of. His main occupation was that of staff writer for the Louisville *Courier-Journal*, but at one time in his life he was a riverman, and during the Civil War he commanded a river transport on the Mississippi. He began songwriting in or about 1856 with "Little Ones at Home" and "I'm Looking for Him." His first published song appeared in 1862— "Evangeline," the lyrics based on Longfellow's poem. In that year he also realized his first major success as a composer with a war song called "Drummer Boy of Shiloh" which had such popular appeal that it was heard with equal frequency in the camps of both Union and Confederate armies. Here, as in all his other songs, Hays was his own lyricist.

After the Civil War, songwriting was Hays' main activity. In 1866 he created three songs, each of which sold over a quarter of a million copies of sheet music: "Write Me a Letter Home," "We Parted by the River Side," and "Nora O'Nea." In 1871 he had four solid hits to his credit in "The Little Old Log Cabin in the Lane," "Susan Jane,"

"Mollie Darling" (probably his most popular song of all), and "Number Twenty Nine" (written to celebrate the success of the Thatcher Perkins locomotive on the Louisville and Nashville Railroad). Among his subsequent song hits were "Oh, Give Me a Home in the South," "Take This Letter to Your Mother," "Out in the Snow," "Angels Meet Me at the Cross Roads," and "Nellie Brown." All of these were ballads, but beginning in 1877 Hays also succeeded in writing several significant numbers in Negro dialect, the best of which were "Early in de Mornin'," "Roll Out, Heave Dat Cotton," and "Walk in de Middle of de Road," the last often erroneously classified as a Negro spiritual.

Hays is believed to have written over three hundred songs whose combined sheet music sale exceeded twenty million copies. He died in Louisville, Kentucky, in July 1907.

ABOUT:
Spaeth, Sigmund. A History of Popular Music in America.

Ray Henderson 1896-

RAY HENDERSON was born in Buffalo, New York, on December 1, 1896. Both his parents were musical. His father was an excellent amateur flautist, violinist, and pianist. Ray demonstrated his musical precocity by performing on the organ and singing in the choir of the local Episcopal church and making his first efforts at serious composition. While receiving a comprehensive training with private teachers, he helped support himself by playing with dance bands and serving as accompanist for several local singers.

When he decided to concentrate on popular music, he went to New York and found a job as song plugger for Leo Feist in Tin Pan Alley. This assignment lasted only a few weeks. He was then hired as staff pianist and arranger by the publishing house of Fred Fisher, and after that in a similar capacity by Shapiro-Bernstein. Louis Bernstein, of the latter firm, became personally interested in him and did what he could to advance Henderson's career. Bernstein found for him various jobs as an accompanist in vaudeville—for several dance teams, for a

violinist named Annette, and for Lew Brice. Bernstein also arranged for Henderson to write music to the lyrics of a young but already highly experienced lyricist, Lew Brown. Their first hit song, "Georgette," was published in 1922 and was heard in the *Greenwich Village Follies* the same year.

Encouraged by the reception given this song, Henderson started to write industriously. "That Old Gang of Mine" (lyrics by Billy Rose and Mort Dixon), was a resounding hit in 1923, the year in which he also wrote "Annabelle" (lyrics by Brown). In 1924, once again with Rose and Dixon, he produced "Follow the Swallow." A year later a number of songs were outstanding commercial successes: "Alabamy Bound" (lyrics by Bud Green and Buddy De Sylva), which sold over a million copies of sheet music; "Bye, Bye, Blackbird" (lyrics by Dixon); "Five Foot Two, Eyes of Blue" and "I'm Sitting on Top of the World," both to lyrics by Sam Lewis and Joe Young.

In 1925 a song partnership was formed by Henderson with Buddy De Sylva and Lew Brown and soon came to be known in the music world as De Sylva, Brown, and Henderson. It was a working arrangement as unique as it was fruitful. While Henderson concentrated on the music and De Sylva and Brown on the words, each member did not hesitate to provide the others with valuable ideas and suggestions, so that each of their songs became a collaborative effort in every sense of the word.

Between 1925 and 1928 De Sylva, Brown, and Henderson wrote the songs for three editions of the George White *Scandals*. It was for these productions that they created their first important songs as a team: "The Birth of the Blues," "Black Bottom," "Lucky Day," and "The Girl Is You." During this period they also wrote several other distinguished songs, independent of any stage productions, among them "It All Depends on You," "Broken Hearted," "Just a Memory," and "Together."

In 1927—a year in which there was no edition of the George White *Scandals*—De Sylva, Brown and Henderson wrote the score for their first Broadway musical comedy, *Good News*, a spirited production with a small college as its setting. *Good News* enjoyed a run of 551 performances after its opening on September 6, 1927. This gay musical was alive with a rah-rah college spirit, which also infected songs like "Varsity Drag," "Just Imagine," "Lucky in Love" and the title number. The most popular song to come out of this musical comedy, however, was "The Best Things in Life Are Free."

De Sylva, Brown, and Henderson wrote the scores for three more highly successful Broadway musicals. *Hold Everything,* in which Bert Lahr became a musical comedy star for the first time, had its première on October 10, 1928. *Follow Through,* described in the program as a "musical slice of country life," opened on January 9, 1929. And *Flying High,* a comedy about airmail pilots starring Bert Lahr, appeared on March 3, 1930. The most significant songs to emerge from these productions were "You're the Cream in My Coffee" and "Don't Hold Everything" from *Hold Everything;* "Button Up Your Overcoat," "You Are My Lucky Star," and "I Want to Be Bad" from *Follow Through;* and "Without Love," "Thank Your Father," and "Wasn't It Beautiful While It Lasted?" from *Flying High.*

In 1928 De Sylva, Brown, and Henderson began writing songs for the screen. For *The Singing Fool,* an early Al Jolson talking picture triumph, they wrote an all-time Jolson favorite, "Sonny Boy." In 1929 they wrote the score for *Sunny Side Up,* a charming musical starring Janet Gaynor and Charles Farrell, which featured "Keep Your Sunny Side Up," "If I Had a Talking Picture of You," and "I'm a Dreamer, Aren't We All?" They also wrote songs for *Say It with Songs* starring Al Jolson; *Follow the Leader,* with Ed Wynn, based on their unsuccessful musical comedy of 1927, *Manhattan Mary;* and *Just Imagine.*

The collaboration of De Sylva, Brown, and Henderson ended after 1930. De Sylva remained in Hollywood for a while to become a successful producer, after which he returned to the Broadway theatre to produce several significant musicals, for some of which he also provided the texts; he died in Hollywood in 1950. Brown continued to provide lyrics for Henderson's music, songs heard in the George White *Scandals* of 1931 and 1935, *Hot Cha* (1932), *Strike Me Pink* (1933) with Jimmy Durante, and *Say When* (1934)

RAY HENDERSON

with Bob Hope and Harry Richman. Their most successful numbers were heard in the 1931 *Scandals*: "Life Is Just a Bowl of Cherries," "The Thrill Is Gone," "My Song," and "This Is the Missus." After 1935 Henderson worked with several other lyricists in writing songs for several motion pictures, including *Curly Top* with Shirley Temple and *George White's Scandals.* (Lew Brown died in New York in 1958.)

In 1956 the songwriting history of De Sylva, Brown and Henderson was dramatized for motion pictures in *The Best Things in Life Are Free,* in which Henderson was portrayed by Dan Dailey.

ABOUT:
Ewen, David. Complete Book of the American Musical Theater.

Victor Herbert *1859-1924*

VICTOR HERBERT was born in Dublin, Ireland, on February 1, 1859. When Victor was three years old his father died. He and his mother went to live for five years at Seven Oaks (a town twenty miles from London) with his maternal grandfather, Samuel Lover, author of *Handy Andy.* Lover was a dilettante who was well cultivated in the arts. Victor's boyhood was spent in a highly cultured environment.

ASCAP

VICTOR HERBERT

When Victor was seven, he began taking piano lessons with his mother, a well-trained performer. His talent for music was in evidence so early that his grandfather insisted the boy be taken to Germany for comprehensive training. In 1867 mother and son went to a German village on Lake Constance, where the mother soon met and married a physician, Carl Schmid. The Schmids, and Victor with them, settled in Stuttgart; there the boy received a comprehensive academic and musical education, the latter at the city Conservatory, where for six years he specialized in the cello. Additional cello study took place with Bernhard Cossmann in Baden-Baden. "My lessons," Herbert later recalled, "were no fifteen-minute affairs, and then away at something else. I was under the constant eye of my master, and I could not help making rapid progress."

His cello study completed, Victor Herbert spent four years playing in various orchestras in Germany and Austria, some of them small-town groups and some important symphony orchestras conducted by such world-renowned musicians as Brahms, Liszt, Saint-Saëns and Anton Rubinstein. As a member of the Stuttgart Royal Orchestra, Herbert came under the influence of its conductor, Max Seyfritz, who not only gave the younger man lessons in composition and orchestration, but also encouraged him to begin

serious composition. Herbert's first two major works were a suite and a concerto, both of them for cello and orchestra, and both introduced by the Stuttgart Orchestra under Seyfritz (with the composer as soloist) in 1883 and 1885 respectively.

By that time the young Irish-born and English-raised musician had become a typical Teuton. For the remainder of his life he was to remain partial to German music, culture, food, and beer. Tall and strikingly handsome, he was what the Germans would describe as a *Feinschmecker*—a man most fastidious about dress, manners, appearance, food, and good living. Women fell in love with him. He became engaged to Theresa Foerster, prima donna of the Stuttgart Opera, who received occasional coaching from him. When Theresa Foerster was offered a contract by the Metropolitan Opera in New York, she accepted on the condition that Herbert be employed as a member of the opera house orchestra so that he could accompany her to the United States.

Victor Herbert and Theresa Foerster were married on August 14, 1886. Soon after that they set sail for their new, and henceforth permanent, home. Mme. Foerster made a successful American debut at the Metropolitan Opera on November 8, 1886, in the title role of Karl Goldmark's *The Queen of Sheba.*

Soon after arriving in the United States, Victor Herbert applied for American citizenship. He never again set foot on either Irish or German soil, and except for a single hurried visit to England never even left America. His identification with American music became complete. For many years he played the cello in leading American orchestras, including the Theodore Thomas Orchestra and the New York Philharmonic. From 1889 to 1891 he was associate conductor of the Worcester Festival in Massachusetts, and from then on made frequent appearances as conductor with leading orchestras and at major festivals. In 1893 he succeeded P. S. Gilmore as leader of the famous 22nd Regiment Band, and from 1898 to 1904 he was principal conductor of the Pittsburgh Symphony. And from 1904 on he led the Victor Herbert Orchestra. He also wrote music, often with a strong American flavor—works like the *American Fantasia,* based on patriotic anthems; the orchestra suite *Pan Americana;*

and the opera *Natoma,* which was introduced in Philadelphia in 1911.

Despite his varied and significant achievements as a conductor, Victor Herbert became most famous for his compositions. And despite the numerous ambitious works created for the concert and operatic stage, Herbert is most famous for his music for the popular theatre.

Herbert's earliest operetta was *La Vivandière,* written in 1893 for Lillian Russell, but it was never produced and the score is lost. His debut as a composer of operettas took place in 1894 with *Prince Ananias* (book by Francis Neilson, who later distinguished himself as a political writer). This operetta had been commissioned by a Boston light opera company, which introduced it. *Prince Ananias* was a failure, but the operetta that followed was a major success: *The Wizard of the Nile,* first presented in New York on November 2, 1895, with Frank Daniels starring as Kibosh, a Persian magician. The most important musical number was the waltz, "Star Light, Star Bright," while other highlights included "My Angeline" and "In Dreamland." A phrase used by Kibosh throughout the play—"Am I a wiz?"—became a popular expression of the day.

Herbert's next operetta was *The Serenade,* first given in New York on March 16, 1897; it presented Alice Nielsen in her first starring role. The serenade after which this musical was named—and which recurs throughout the production like a *Leitmotiv*—is "I Love Thee, I Adore Thee," first heard as the second half of a duet. After that the song is heard again in many different forms: as a monks' chant, a song of brigands, a parody on grand opera, a parrot's call, and finally as a sentimental love song.

Having established herself in *The Serenade* as an outstanding star of the musical stage, Alice Nielsen enjoyed the privilege of having Herbert write a new operetta especially for her, *The Fortune Teller,* produced on September 26, 1898. Nielsen was here cast as Irma, a ballet student in love with a hussar captain. The Hungarian setting stimulated Herbert to write music with a strong Hungarian flavor: the hussar chorus in the first act and "Gypsy Jan." But the big song of the show was a sentimental serenade in Herbert's identifiable manner, "Gypsy Love Song," sometimes also known as "Slumber On, My Little Gypsy Sweetheart." This is one of Herbert's best loved melodies.

There were three Herbert operettas on the boards in 1899: *Cyrano de Bergerac, The Singing Girl,* and *The Ameer.* He was now one of the most successful and sought-after composers on Broadway. Rupert Hughes said of him that year: "The music of Victor Herbert dignifies the American stage. It reaches the highest level of European comic opera. Then, too, it is learnedly humorous. He sprinkles his scores with Attic salt."

In the first decade of the new century, Herbert continued to maintain this preeminent position among Broadway composers. His most successful operettas of that period were *It Happened in Nordland, Babes in Toyland, Mlle. Modiste, The Red Mill,* and *Naughty Marietta.*

Babes in Toyland, which opened on October 13, 1903, was an unashamed attempt to capitalize on the success of a current extravaganza, *The Wizard of Oz. Babes in Toyland* presented characters from fairy tales and children's stories in numerous elaborately staged scenes, including one in Toyland. For this delightful fantasy Herbert created such musical delights as the "March of the Toys"; "Toyland"; a children's choral number called "I Can't Do the Sum"; and a song, "Rock-a-bye Baby," in which the composer indulged his flair for parody by imitating the styles of several famous composers. *Babes in Toyland* was given a spectacular television production in the winter of 1960.

It Happened in Nordland, which opened on December 5, 1904, starred Marie Cahill as an American ambassadress to a mythical kingdom (thereby anticipating Irving Berlin's *Call Me Madam* by almost half a century). This score boasted a delightful waltz in "A Knot of Blue"; a sophisticated piece, "Absinthe Frappé"; and a now familiar instrumental number, "Al Fresco," which opened the second act.

In *Mlle. Modiste,* on December 25, 1905, Fritzi Scheff of the Metropolitan Opera became an operetta star—and largely by virtue of singing one of Herbert's best known waltzes, "Kiss Me Again." It is interesting to point out that the composer originally planned this number not as a suave and lilting love waltz but as a parody. For the first act of *Mlle. Modiste* he wrote a humorous episode called "If I Were on the Stage" in which Fifi, the heroine who aspires to be a prima donna, tries to prove her talent by singing various types of songs, including a gavotte, a polonaise, a waltz, and so forth. For his caricature of a waltz, Herbert reached into his trunk for a composition he had written two years earlier and discarded. But the first-night audience liked the waltz so well, and made its enthusiasm so strongly felt, that new verses were immediately written for it, and the song now became featured in the operetta as a sentimental number. Besides "Kiss Me Again," Herbert's music for *Mlle. Modiste* included an excellent march, "The Mascot of the Troop," and a humorous ditty, "I Want What I Want When I Want It."

The Red Mill, which opened on September 24, 1906, was set in Holland. Fred Stone and David Montgomery starred in the amusing roles of Con Kidder and Kid Conner, two Americans who help bring about the marriage of the heroine, Gretchen, to the man she loves, but who manage to get involved in all kinds of merry escapades. Among the musical riches of this score are "The Isle of Our Dreams," "Moonbeams," and "Every Day Is Ladies' Day with Me." When *The Red Mill* was revived on Broadway in 1945 with a modernized text, it had an impressive run of 531 performances.

The score for *Naughty Marietta*—an operetta first produced on November 7, 1910 —was perhaps Herbert's most opulent, including as it did "Ah, Sweet Mystery of Life," "I'm Falling in Love with Someone," "Italian Street Song," and " 'Neath the Southern Moon." This was the production in which Emma Trentini (like Fritzi Scheff a graduate of grand opera) became a queen of operetta. She was cast as the eighteenth century noblewoman Marietta, come from Naples to New Orleans to escape an undesirable marriage; in New Orleans she finds her true love in Captain Dick Warrington.

In the remarkable outpouring of song to be found in his best operettas—those of the period ending in 1910—Herbert proved himself to be a born melodist capable of producing a fresh and pliant melody as easily as he breathed. But he was much more than just a fashioner of pretty tunes. He had a sound feeling for interesting harmonies; he was a supremely gifted orchestrator; and he was amazingly versatile in his feelings and moods. It is possible to overestimate him, and many have done so. It is hardly likely that he was an "Irish Wagner," as James Gibbons Huneker once described him, nor was he "America's greatest composer" as Gene Buck said. But he was a distinguished composer—with limitations. He was no innovator; he was perhaps too ready to accept any stage text, however trite or stylized, that was presented to him; he wrote too much, and a great deal of his writing reveals haste and lack of discrimination. But at his best he succeeded in writing songs whose seductive charm and popular appeal never fade. To this day they have remained as inviting and as lovable as they were half a century ago. "My idea of heaven," Andrew Carnegie once said, "is to be able to sit and listen to the music of Victor Herbert all I want to."

Though Herbert remained productive until the end of his life, and though his songs continued to be heard on the Broadway stage in many operettas and revues, he went more or less into an artistic decline after *Naughty Marietta.* His most significant operetta after 1910 was *Sweethearts*, opening on September 8, 1913, for which he wrote the notable waltz "Sweethearts" and "The Angelus." (*Sweethearts,* starring Bobby Clark, was revived on Broadway in 1947 with a modernized book.) *Eileen,* in 1917, had a remarkable song in "Thine Alone"—probably Herbert's greatest song success since "Ah, Sweet Mystery of Life." But *Eileen* was a dismal failure and so were other operettas and musicals with Victor Herbert scores, including *Orange Blossoms* (1922), for which he wrote "A Kiss in the Dark." The truth was that his day had ended with World War I. He belonged to the age of the waltz, and his music was the voice of a placid and sentimental era that came to an end in 1917. In the more febrile postwar era of ragtime and jazz, his music sounded almost like an anachronism. As he himself once lamented: "My day is over. They are forgetting poor old Herbert."

Before 1900 most of the lyrics for Herbert's songs were written by Harry B. Smith. Glen MacDonough was Herbert's lyricist for *Babes in Toyland* and *It Happened in Nordland;* Henry Blossom for *Mlle. Modiste, The*

Red Mill, and *Eileen;* Harry B. Smith once again for *Sweethearts;* and Buddy De Sylva for *Orange Blossoms.*

Besides writing music for operettas, Herbert also contributed special numbers to the Ziegfeld *Follies* between 1918 and 1923, usually to Gene Buck's lyrics. He was working on some music for the Ziegfeld *Follies* of 1924 when he suddenly collapsed in his doctor's office on May 26, 1924, and died of a heart attack. After his death, a bust of him (by Edmund T. Quinn) was placed in the Central Park Mall. He was subsequently honored by the United States government with his likeness on a three-cent stamp and his name on a Victory Ship. His life story was dramatized in the motion picture *The Great Victor Herbert,* released in 1939. Many of his most famous operettas enjoyed numerous revivals throughout the country and were adapted for the screen. Victor Herbert may have died thinking of himself as a "has-been" but he had actually become a classic in the American musical theatre.

A genial, jovial, happy-go-lucky man who had an enormous capacity for enjoying life, Herbert was not one to seek a fight. But on those rare occasions when he was summoned to battle he could be a veritable gladiator. On one occasion the editor of *Musical Courier* commented in 1901 that "everything Herbert wrote is copied." Herbert brought suit against the magazine and won a judgment of fifteen thousand dollars (reduced to five thousand dollars on appeal).

A second bitter legal fight involving Herbert came a decade later. In 1913, while dining at Shanley's Restaurant in New York, he heard the orchestra play some of his music. It then occurred to him how unjust it was for a restaurant to make use of the music of a living composer without making some compensation to him. Herbert instituted suit against Shanley's, and the legal battle went on for four years through all the levels of the American courts. In 1917 the United States Supreme Court finally ruled in favor of Herbert. It was because of this suit that Herbert decided to gather several of America's leading composers, lyricists, and publishers to help form an organization to protect and promote their financial interests, an organization which became the eventually powerful American Society of Composers, Authors and Publishers (ASCAP).

ABOUT:
Kaye, Joseph. *Victor Herbert;* Waters, Edward N. *Victor Herbert: A Life in Music.*
Hi-Fi Review, February 1959; Musical America, October 11, 1913.

John Hill Hewitt *1801-1890*

JOHN HILL HEWITT, one of the earliest American-born composers of popular ballads, was born in New York City on July 11, 1801. He was the oldest son of James Hewitt, who distinguished himself in early American music as a violinist, organist, impresario, publisher, and composer of ballad operas, songs, and piano music. John was eleven when his family moved to Boston, where he was educated in the public schools. He was then apprenticed to a sign painter, but he found this work so distasteful that he ran away from home and supported himself by working in a commission house. In 1818 he was back in New York City and soon after that was appointed to the Military Academy at West Point where he studied music with the leader of the Academy Band.

Hewitt left West Point in 1822 without graduating, and became a member of a theatrical company organized by his father. When this troupe went into bankruptcy in Augusta, Georgia, Hewitt stayed on in that city as a teacher of music. In 1825 he settled in Greenville, South Carolina, where he founded and edited *The Republican.* Upon the death of his father, in 1827, he went back to Boston, and one year after that established permanent residence in Baltimore. For many years he was engaged in editing various journals and magazines, including the Baltimore *Clipper,* of which he was part owner. As the editor of *The Visitor,* he sponsored a literary contest in which he entered one of his own poems under a pseudonym. That poem received first prize, winning over a contribution submitted by Edgar Allan Poe ("The Coliseum").

After selling his interest in the Baltimore *Clipper* in 1840, Hewitt went to Washington, D.C., as editor of *The Capitol.* For nine years after that he was a music teacher at the Chesapeake Female College in Hampton, Virginia.

JOHN HILL HEWITT

Among Hewitt's later ballads were "The Knight of the Raven Black Plume," "Take Me Home Where the Sweet Magnolia Blooms," "Our Native Land," and "The Mountain Bugle." During the Civil War he wrote "All Quiet Along the Potomac" (lyrics by Lamar Fontaine). Hewitt dedicated this number "to the unknown dead of the present revolution." It proved such a popular war song that it was sung enthusiastically both in the North and in the South. After the war, Hewitt wrote "Carry Me Back to the Sweet Sunny South," an expression of his nostalgia for the South. Besides his songs, Hewitt wrote several oratorios, cantatas, and ballad operas.

ABOUT:
Dictionary of American Biography; Harwell, Richard B. Confederate Music; Hewitt, John Hill. Shadows on the Wall.
Musical Quarterly, January 1931.

When the Civil War broke out, he became a drillmaster for Confederate recruits in Richmond, Virginia. After that he edited the *Evening Mirror* in Savannah.

With the end of the Civil War, Hewitt taught music in various southern cities, finally returning to Baltimore in 1870. He died in Baltimore on October 7, 1890. As John Tasker Howard wrote: "He became one of the characters of the city, and when he died at the age of eighty-nine, Baltimore felt that it had lost one of its links with the past. He had seen Fulton's first steamboat on the Hudson, he was present when the first despatch was sent over Morse's telegraph line between Baltimore and Washington, and he was a passenger on the first train of cars that pulled out of Baltimore by locomotive."

Hewitt wrote over three hundred ballads, usually creating both the lyrics and the music. His first published song was an outstanding success: "The Minstrel's Return from the War," written in Greenville in 1825 and published two years later by his brother. Apparently his brother thought so little of the song that he did not bother to take out a copyright. But as Hewitt wrote: "It was eagerly taken up by the public and established my reputation as a ballad composer. It was sung all over the world—and my brother, not securing the copyright, told me that he missed making at least ten thousand dollars."

Billy Hill 1899-1940

BILLY HILL, who became famous for his cowboy songs, was born William Joseph Hill in Boston, Massachusetts, on July 14, 1899. He attended the Boston public schools, and the New England Conservatory as a violin student. When he was seventeen he went West. For the next few years he suffered extreme hardship and poverty trying to earn a living. His jobs were menial; he punched cattle in Montana, worked in the mines of Death Valley, and washed dishes in roadhouses. When he finally returned to music it was to organize and play in a jazz band that performed in a Chinese restaurant in Salt Lake City.

Billy Hill wrote his first song, "Rock-a-Bye Your Baby Blues" (lyrics by Larry Yoell), in 1927. In 1929 he wrote "They Cut Down the Old Pine Tree" to his own lyrics. He sold both songs outright for a few dollars. Meanwhile he continued to lead and play in his own jazz band throughout the West until 1930, when he went to New York. Unable to make his way in music there, he worked for two years as a doorman of a Fifth Avenue apartment house, his salary hardly enough to sustain himself and his family. He lived in a cold-water flat in Greenwich Village; often the gas was shut off because he could not pay his bill, and just as often the kitchen would be bare of food for days at a time. A loan of several hundred dollars from Gene Buck, president of ASCAP, sustained him for a while during this lean period.

Hill first became successful in 1933 with a cowboy song for which he wrote both music and lyrics—"The Last Roundup." He had written the song two years earlier and would have sold out his rights for a pittance to defray an overdue bill for twenty-five dollars if the loan from Gene Buck had not enabled him to take a chance on the royalties. As it turned out, he earned a fortune from the sale of sheet music and records. "The Last Roundup" was introduced by Joe Morrison at the New York Paramount Theatre, and it attracted immediate interest. It was frequently heard on the Hit Parade that year. A year later "Wagon Wheels," a song by Peter De Rose for which he wrote the lyrics, was published and successfully introduced in the Ziegfeld *Follies*. These two songs brought Billy Hill's financial problems to an end. He left his doorman's job, moved into a spacious apartment on 57th Street, and devoted himself exclusively to writing songs —sometimes only lyrics, but most often both lyrics and music.

Other successful songs by Hill included "The Old Spinning Wheel," "Lights Out," "Empty Saddles" (featured in the 1936 Bing Crosby movie *Rhythm on the Range*), "In the Chapel in the Moonlight," "There's a Cabin in the Pines," "There's a Home in Wyoming," and "Call of the Canyon." He also wrote the lyrics to songs by Peter De Rose: "Have You Ever Been Lonely?," "Down the Old Oregon Trail," "In a Mission by the Sea" and "On a Little Street in Singapore." "Call of the Canyon" was his last published song.

Hill died in New York City on December 24, 1940.

ABOUT:
Etude, February 1941.

Louis Hirsch *1887-1924*

L OUIS ACHILLE HIRSCH was born in New York City on November 28, 1887. While attending New York City elementary and high schools and the City College of New York, he studied the piano, first by himself and later with private teachers. During

LOUIS HIRSCH   ASCAP

his senior year in college he took a few months off to go to Europe to study the piano with Rafael Joseffy at the Stern Conservatory in Berlin. At that time his ambition was to become a concert pianist. But soon after returning to the United States in 1906 he decided to direct his energies into more practical channels. He went to work as a staff pianist for the publishing house of Gus Edwards in Tin Pan Alley and soon afterwards took a similar position with Shapiro-Bernstein.

Besides making piano arrangements for these firms, Hirsch also started to write music of his own. His first important assignment was the music for Lew Dockstader's Minstrels. Between 1907 and 1909 Hirsch's songs were interpolated into several important Broadway musical productions, including *The Gay White Way, Miss Innocence* (which starred Anna Held), and *The Girl and the Wizard*. In 1910 Hirsch completed his first musical comedy score, *He Came from Milwaukee;* and one year after that he wrote the score for the *Revue of Revues* in which Gaby Deslys made her American debut.

With *Vera Violetta* (1911), Hirsch achieved his first important stage success. This was an extravaganza adapted from the German and made up of spectacular scenes and production numbers. It was also the musical in which Al Jolson became a star and in which Gaby Deslys scored a sensation singing Hirsch's "The Gaby Glide" (lyrics by Harry Pilcer)—a song that made effective use of blues harmonies and ragtime rhythm. Other successful Hirsch songs from the production, to lyrics by Harold Atteridge, were "Come Dance with Me" and "When You Hear Love's Hello."

In 1912 the Shuberts engaged Hirsch to write music for their Broadway productions. That year Hirsch wrote the music for *The Whirl of Society*, which starred Al Jolson, and for the first edition of *The Passing Show*. The latter featured two notable Hirsch songs (lyrics by Atteridge), "Always Together" and "The Wedding Glide."

The following year Hirsch parted company with the Shuberts and left New York to work in England. At the outbreak of World War I, he returned to the United States, and was now engaged by Florenz Ziegfeld to write music for the *Follies*. Hirsch's music, usually written to Gene Buck's lyrics, was prominently featured in the *Follies* of 1915, 1916, 1918, and 1922. His songs included such outstanding numbers as "Hello, Frisco, Hello" and "Hold Me in Your Loving Arms" in 1915; "Beautiful Island of Girls" in 1916; "Garden of Your Dreams," "When I'm Looking at You," and "Any Old Time at All" in 1918; and, in 1922, " 'Neath the South Sea Moon" and "My Rambler Rose" in collaboration with Dave Stamper, and "Some Sweet Day" and "Hello, Hello, Hello."

During this period Hirsch also collaborated with Otto Harbach in writing for several important musical comedies. *Going Up* in 1917 had "Tickle Toe," "If You Look in Her Eyes," and the title song. For *Mary*, in 1920, Hirsch wrote the greatest song success of his career, "Love Nest." It has since become a standard and was for many years the theme song for the Burns and Allen radio and television series. The *O'Brien Girl* (1921) included "Learn to Smile."

In 1922 and 1923 Hirsch wrote the music to Irving Caesar's lyrics for two editions of *The Greenwich Village Follies*. The most notable songs in these revues were "A Kiss from a Red-Headed Miss" and "Sixty Sec-

onds Every Minute I Dream of You" (1922) and "Just a Bit of Heaven in Your Smile" (1923).

Louis Hirsch died of pneumonia in New York City on May 13, 1924.

ABOUT:
Ewen, David. Complete Book of the American Musical Theater.

Karl Hoschna *1877-1911*

KARL HOSCHNA was born in Kuschwarda, Bohemia, on August 16, 1877. He attended the Vienna Conservatory on a scholarship, specializing in the oboe. After graduating with honors he played the oboe for several years in the Austrian army band.

He came to the United States in 1896 and for the first two years played the oboe in Victor Herbert's orchestra. During this period he became obsessed with the groundless fear that the vibrations from the oboe's double reed would affect his mind. Determined to give up playing the oboe, he wrote to Witmark, the Tin Pan Alley publisher, begging for any job, however menial. Witmark hired him at first as a copyist, but within a short time Hoschna assumed more important duties, writing arrangements and serving as Isidore Witmark's assistant in the selection of songs for publication.

In 1902 Hoschna met and became a friend of Otto Hauerbach (later Otto Harbach), a young advertising executive with the ambition to write lyrics and texts for the musical stage. They worked together on a musical, *The Daughter of the Desert*, which they revised several times during the next few years. Although they received several options on this play it was never produced. In 1905 they did reach Broadway with another show, *The Belle of the West*. This musical, however, was a failure, and two more failures followed before the operetta *The Three Twins* opened successfully on June 15, 1908. *The Three Twins* starred Bessie McCoy in her first stage triumph; she proved such a success singing "Yama Yama Man" (lyrics to this song by Collin Davis) that she was described from then on as the "Yama Yama Girl." Another outstanding hit in this operetta was "Cuddle Up a Little Closer." It is interesting to note

KARL HOSCHNA

that neither of these songs had originally been planned for this production. "Cuddle Up a Little Closer" had been written by Hoschna and Harbach for a vaudeville sketch a few years earlier; and "Yama Yama Man" was written while the operetta was already in rehearsal and interpolated during the Chicago tryouts.

In 1909 Hoschna and Harbach wrote the title song for the operetta *Bright Eyes,* and, in 1910, "Doctor Tinkle Tinker" for *The Girl of My Dreams.* But their major production of 1910 was *Madame Sherry.* This musical, which opened on August 30, was an adaptation of a French vaudeville farce. Its outstanding numbers were "Every Little Movement," the seductive waltz "Girl of My Dreams," and "The Birth of Passion." So distinctive was this music that the editor of *Theatre Magazine* called it "the best native score since *Mlle. Modiste.*"

In 1912 Hoschna, working with the lyricist Hapgood Burt, wrote the music for *Wall Street Girl.* It was in this production that Blanche Ring became a Broadway star. One of her best numbers was a song called "I Want a Regular Man."

Wall Street Girl was produced on April 15, 1912, but Hoschna did not live to attend the première. He died prematurely on De-

cember 23, 1911, at the age of thirty-four, at the height of his success.

ABOUT:
Witmark, Isidore. From Ragtime to Swingtime. Musical America, January 1912; New York Dramatic Mirror, January 3, 1912.

Joseph E. Howard *1867-1961*

JOSEPH E. HOWARD was born in New York City on February 12, 1867. His father was a saloon keeper on Mulberry Street on New York's Lower East Side, and it was in a back room of that saloon that Joseph was born. When he was eight Howard ran away from home and found a temporary haven in a Catholic orphanage. He then escaped from the orphanage on a freight train bound for St. Louis, where he sang ballads in saloons and billiard parlors and sold newspapers. When he was eleven he made his debut as a vaudeville entertainer in St. Louis, billed as "Master Joseph, Boy Soprano." Next he became a member of a traveling stock company, appearing as Little Eva in *Uncle Tom's Cabin.* When this company was stranded in St. Joseph, Missouri, Howard continued his travels, earning his living by singing in dance halls and saloons and appearing with various minstrel troupes in Dodge City, Tombstone, Virginia City, and Denver. While in Denver he eloped with a young dancer, but the marriage was annulled by the girl's parents twenty-four hours after the ceremony. This was the first of nine marriages.

When he was seventeen Howard organized a song-and-dance team with Ida Emerson, whom he later married. They performed in small vaudeville theatres throughout the Midwest and the West. In 1895 they came to Chicago, starring at the Olympic Theatre; then they made successful appearances at Tony Pastor's Music Hall in New York.

In 1897 Howard wrote his first song, "On the Boulevard." Two years later, in collaboration with his wife, he wrote and published his first hit, "Hello, My Baby," which sold over a million copies of sheet music. During the next six years he wrote other successful numbers: "On a Saturday Night" (lyrics by Andrew J. Sterling) in

JOSEPH E. HOWARD

1902; and "Goodbye, My Lady Love," to his own lyrics, in 1904.

Between 1905 and 1915 Howard wrote the music for twenty musical productions staged in Chicago. Many had books and lyrics by Will M. Hough and Frank R. Adams. The first was *The Isle of Bong Bong* in 1905, the last *In and Out* (book and lyrics by Collin Davis and Howard Swope) in 1915. The many songs which Howard produced for these musicals included some of the outstanding hits of the day. The most famous were "How'd You Like to Be the Umpire" in *The Umpire* (1905); "What's the Use of Dreaming?" in *The District Leader* (1906); "Oh, Gee, Be Sweet to Me, Kid" in *The Girl Question* (1907); "Blow the Smoke Away" in *The Time, the Place and the Girl* (1907) ; and "Honeymoon Trail," the title song of the 1908 musical.

The song most often attributed to Howard, and with which he achieved his greatest triumph, "I Wonder Who's Kissing Her Now" (lyrics by Will M. Hough and Frank R. Adams), has turned out to be somebody else's creation. For many years, Howard maintained the fiction that he, and he alone, had written it—that overhearing a remark of a college student in Chicago had given him the idea for it. He introduced the song in one of his Chicago shows, *The Prince of Tonight*, in 1909. From there it went on to

become one of the smash song hits of the decade, selling over three million copies of sheet music. It was this song above all others which was always requested of the composer whenever he made a public appearance. It was this song that provided the title for Howard's 1947 screen biography, which starred June Haver, Martha Scott, and Mark Stevens. It had also been heard previously in 1929 in the motion-picture adaptation of Howard's 1907 musical comedy, *The Time, the Place and the Girl.*

Yet not Howard, but Harold Orlob, was the composer of this well-loved melody. Orlob was working for Howard in 1909 and as his employee he wrote the melody to be introduced in Howard's musical comedy. As was common practice at the time, the copyright and ownership of the song passed to Howard.

Orlob made no effort to claim authorship of the song until 1947 when the motion-picture biography of Howard was released. He then went to court to have himself declared the composer, but he refused to claim any damages. A compromise was reached out of court ; Orlob and Howard were acknowledged as co-composers, but no financial restitution was made to Orlob.

After the depression of 1930 Howard toured extensively in vaudeville, night clubs and stage productions. He also presented his hit songs on the radio.

During World War II, Howard ran a successful restaurant in New York, the Club Zanzibar. He also appeared as the master of ceremonies on a coast-to-coast radio program, "The Gay Nineties." After the war he went into retirement at Fort Lauderdale, Florida, from which he emerged at infrequent intervals to make spot appearances on radio, on television, and in benefit stage performances.

He died of a heart attack on May 19, 1961, while appearing at the Opera House in Chicago in a benefit performance. He had just finished singing "Let Me Call You Sweetheart," the audience joining him in the refrain. Taking a curtain call at center stage, he blew a kiss, and suddenly collapsed. The curtain was dropped and Howard was taken into the wings where, a few minutes later, a physician pronounced him dead.

ABOUT:

Howard, Joseph E. Gay Nineties Troubadour.

Raymond Hubbell *1879-1954*

RAYMOND HUBBELL was born in Urbana, Ohio, on June 1, 1879. After attending public school in Urbana, he went to Chicago to study harmony and counterpoint. His professional career as a musician began when he organized and led a dance orchestra in Chicago. After that he worked as arranger and staff pianist for the publishing firm of Charles K. Harris. His bow as a composer for the stage took place in 1902 in Chicago with *Chow Chow*, which had a year's run before coming to New York under a new title, *The Runaways*. This production subsequently went on the road for five years. The most appealing musical numbers were "If I Were a Bright Little Star" and "A Kiss for Each Day in the Week" (lyrics by Addison Burkhardt).

Hubbell's next successful Broadway musical was *Fantana*, produced on January 14, 1905, in which Jefferson de Angelis starred as a valet who assumes the identity of a Japanese minister. Hubbell wrote two delightful humorous ditties for his star: "That's Art" and "What Would Mrs. Grundy Say?" while his more lyrical vein was tapped in "My Word" and "The Farewell Waltz," all written to lyrics by Robert B. Smith.

Mexicana in 1906 and *A Knight for a Day* in 1907 were also box office successes. For the latter operetta, Hubbell wrote "Life Is a See-Saw" and "Little Girl Blue," again to Smith's lyrics.

Between 1911 and 1917 Hubbell was active as a composer for the Ziegfeld *Follies* of 1911, 1912, 1913, and 1917. In the 1911 *Follies* Bessie McCoy scored a major success with "Take Care, Little Girl." This song and "My Beautiful Lady," both to lyrics by George V. Hobart, were among this edition's best musical numbers. To the 1912 edition Hubbell contributed "Romantic Girl," and "The Broadway Glide" (lyrics by Smith); and in the 1917 edition, Hubbell's best songs were "Beautiful Garden of Girls," "Just You and Me," and a ragtime number, "Chu Chin Chow" (lyrics by Hobart and Gene Buck).

Between 1915 and 1922 Hubbell wrote the music for several extravaganzas produced at the Hippodrome Theatre in New York. The first was *Hip-Hip Hooray* (1915) and

ASCAP

RAYMOND HUBBELL

the last *Better Times* (1922). It was for a Hippodrome extravaganza that Hubbell wrote the most successful song of his career: "Poor Butterfly" (lyrics by John Golden), introduced by a Japanese soprano in *The Big Show* (1916). Other important Hubbell songs in these extravaganzas were "The Ladder of Roses" from *Hip-Hip Hooray* (1915), "Hello, I've Been Looking for You" from *The Big Show* (1916), and "Melodyland" from *Cheer Up* (1917).

Besides working for Ziegfeld and the Hippodrome, Hubbell also wrote the scores for numerous Broadway musical comedies. The most important of these were *The Jolly Bachelors* (1910), starring Nora Bayes; *The Bachelor Belles* (1910); *The Man from Cook's* (1912); *A Winsome Widow* (1912), an adaptation of Charles Hoyt's *A Trip to Chinatown; The Kiss Burglar* (1918); *The Elusive Lady* (1922), starring Julian Eltinge; *Yours Truly* (1927), with Irene Dunne and Leon Errol; and *The Girl from Cook's* (1927).

Hubbell's last Broadway musical was *Three Cheers* in 1928, in which Will Rogers and Dorothy Stone starred. After that he went into complete retirement in Miami, Florida, where he died on December 13, 1954.

ABOUT:
Music Business, April 1946.

Victor Jacobi *1883-1921*

VICTOR JACOBI was born in Budapest, Hungary, on October 22, 1883. He received his musical training in his native city and embarked upon a career as a composer of operettas. The first of these, *The Proud Princess,* was produced in Budapest when Jacobi was twenty-nine. During the next few years Jacobi wrote several more operettas for theatrical production. These included *The Brave Hussar, Yes or No, The Rose and the Thorn, The Queen's Gown,* and *Johnny.*

Before the outbreak of World War I in Europe, Jacobi came to the United States and established his permanent residence in New York. His first Broadway production was *The Marriage Market,* in 1913. This was a German musical adapted for the American stage by Gladys Ungar, starring Donald Brian as an American cowboy at a San Francisco marriage mart. To lyrics by Adrian Ross and Arthur Anderson, Jacobi wrote several catchy tunes, including "Love of Mine," "The Golden Day of Love," "Come Nestle in My Arms," and "All the Girls Love a Sailor Man." *The Marriage Market* proved successful not only on Broadway but also in London and helped to establish Jacobi's reputation in America.

Sibyl (book and lyrics by Harry Graham and Harry B. Smith) was also a resounding box office success. This 1916 production starred Julia Sanderson and Donald Brian. Among Jacobi's best songs were "Sibyl," "When Cupid Calls," and "Love May Be a Mystery." A year later Jacobi wrote the score for *Rambler Rose* (another show starring Julia Sanderson) in which were introduced "Just a Little Bit of Love," "I Know Now," and "One Look, One Word" (lyrics by Smith).

On the strength of these successes, Jacobi was engaged by Charles Dillingham to collaborate with the renowned violin virtuoso Fritz Kreisler in writing the music for *Apple Blossoms* (book and lyrics by William Le Baron), an operetta based on Dumas' *A Marriage of Convenience. Apple Blossoms* opened on October 7, 1919, with a cast that included John Charles Thomas, Wilda Bennett, and Fred and Adele Astaire. The New York *American* described it as an operetta "of supreme elegance and old-time musical dignity." Kreisler provided half the score. Jacobi's half included "Little Girls, Goodbye," and "You Are Free."

In 1920 Jacobi wrote the music for *The Half Moon.* Among its songs was "Deep in Your Eyes" (lyrics by William Le Baron). After this production opened, Jacobi went to Europe to attend the London première of *Sibyl.* While there he completed the score for a new operetta, *The Love Letter,* adapted by William Le Baron from Ferenc Molnar's *The Phantom Rival,* which opened in New York in 1921, starring John Charles Thomas. This was Jacobi's last production. He suffered a heart attack late in 1921, and after a brief illness died at the Lenox Hill Hospital in New York on December 10, 1921.

Isham Jones *1894-1956*

ISHAM JONES, eminent both as a jazz band leader and as a composer of popular songs, was born in Coalton, Ohio, on January 31, 1894. While attending public school he studied piano and saxophone. In 1915 he went to Chicago for advanced music study. At the age of twenty he formed a jazz band that played at dances and other social functions in Michigan. During the next few years he played saxophone with various dance

ISHAM JONES

orchestras as well as with his own ensemble. Success as a jazz band leader came in Chicago, first at the Golden Mill, next at the Rainbow Gardens (which he had helped to open) and last for six years at the College Inn. After leaving the Chicago night clubs he toured the United States and Europe with his band.

In 1919 Isham Jones published his first song, "Meet Me in Bubble Land" (lyrics by Caspar Nathan and Joe Manne). Three years later he wrote his first hit song, "On the Alamo" (lyrics by Gilbert Keyes and Joe Lyons). Other hits followed in rapid succession, most of them written to Gus Kahn's lyrics. These included "Swingin' Down the Lane," "It Had to Be You," "I'll See You in My Dreams," "Indiana Moon" (lyrics by Benny Davis), "Spain," and "The One I Love Belongs to Somebody Else." During the thirties and forties Isham Jones's leading songs were "There Is No Greater Love" (lyrics by Marty Symes), "My Best to You" (lyrics by Gene Willadsen) and "How Many Tears Must Fall."

Earlier, in the twenties, Isham Jones had also been responsible for helping to make Hoagy Carmichael's "Stardust" a success; he was the first to introduce this American classic by performing it as a piano solo in its original ragtime version.

Late in the thirties Jones retired as a band leader to live in semiseclusion on a ranch in Colorado. He died in Hollywood, California, on October 19, 1956.

Scott Joplin *1868-1919*

SCOTT JOPLIN, the Negro jazz pianist and composer of the first published piano rags, was born in Texarkana, Texas, on November 24, 1868. Having musical parents, he was soon taught to play piano. He completed his piano studies with Louis Chauvin, who gave him his first lessons in ragtime. After his musical education was completed, Joplin worked as a pianist in several St. Louis cafés, and as an orchestra leader at the Chicago World's Fair in 1893. In 1896 he settled in Sedalia, Missouri, where he found employment as a performer of rags in various cafés. One evening, at the Maple Leaf Club, he was discovered by John Scott, a local publisher, who offered to publish some of his rag pieces.

Original Rag, published by Scott in 1899, was the first piece of piano rag music ever issued in printed form. It was followed the same year by what is still recognized as Joplin's masterpiece, *The Maple Leaf Rag.* After that Joplin wrote more than fifty piano rags. The most famous are *Sunflower Rag, Paragon Rag, Wall Street Rag, Pineapple Rag, Country Club Rag, Gladiolus Rag, Magnetic Rag,* and *Sugar Cane Rag.*

Joplin also wrote a primer in ragtime performance and a composition called *The School of Ragtime.* He composed a ragtime opera, *A Guest of Honor,* which was produced in St. Louis in 1903. A second opera, *Tremonisha,* was performed in Harlem in 1911.

Scott Joplin died in New York City on April 4, 1919.

Gustave A. Kerker *1857-1923*

GUSTAVE A. KERKER was born in Herford, Westphalia, Germany, on February 28, 1857. Both his parents were musical. He started to study at the age of seven. When he was ten his family immigrated to the United States, settling in Louisville, Kentucky, where the boy continued his music study with private teachers. He then earned his living by directing orchestras in various theatres.

At twenty-two he wrote the music for his first musical, *The Cadets,* an operetta that toured the South for about four months. It made a deep impression on the producer Edward E. Rice, who arranged for Kerker to go to New York to serve as conductor at the Casino Theatre, which featured operettas and musical comedies. In 1888 Kerker made his Broadway bow as a composer with *The Pearl of Pekin.* One year later he became successful with *Castles in the Air,* in which De Wolf Hopper appeared in his first starring role. Kerker's best songs were the title number, "What in the World Could Compare to This?" and "Is It a Dream?" to lyrics by Charles A. Byrne.

During the next twelve years, seventeen Kerker operettas were performed in New York, most of them at the Casino Theatre. The best were *In Gay New York* (1896), with two outstanding Kerker numbers—the title song and "It's Forty Miles from Schenectady

GUSTAVE A. KERKER

ASCAP

to Troy" (lyrics by Hugh Morton); *The Belle of New York* (1897), in which Edna May became an overnight star as a Salvation Army lass, singing "I'm the Belle of New York," "They All Follow Me," and "Teach Me How to Kiss" (lyrics by Morton); *The Whirl of the Town* (1897), whose hit song was "The Good Old Days" (lyrics by Morton); *The Telephone Girl* (1898), which included "Little Birdies Learning How to Fly" (lyrics by Morton); *A Chinese Honeymoon* (1902), for which Kerker wrote "À la Girl" and the title song to George Dance's lyrics; and *The Social Whirl* (1908), whose score included "You're Just the Girl I'm Looking For" and "Old Man Manhattan" (lyrics by Joseph Herbert).

Another one of his operettas, *The American Beauty* (1897), was written expressly for Lillian Russell, whose orchestra was conducted by Kerker during most of her New York appearances apart from operettas and musical comedies.

A number of Kerker's songs from other operettas deserve mention. They include "Golly, Charlie!" (lyrics by Morton) from *Yankee Doodle Dandy* (1898); "Cynthia Jane" (lyrics by Harry B. Smith) from *The Blonde in Black* (1903); "Loud Let the Bugles Sound" (lyrics by Frederic Ranken) from *Winsome Winnie* (1903); and "It's

Nice to Have a Sweetheart" (lyrics by R. H. Burnside) from *The Tourists* (1906).

Gustave Kerker died in New York City on June 29, 1923.

ABOUT:

Ewen, David. Complete Book of the American Musical Theater; Lee, Amy Freeman. A Critic's Notebook.

Jerome Kern *1885-1945*

JEROME DAVID KERN was born in New York City on January 27, 1885, the youngest of nine children of whom only three boys survived. His father was president of a company responsible for sprinkling water on city streets; he also dealt in real estate. Jerome's mother was a fine amateur pianist. She gave him his first piano lessons when he was only five. Jerome continued to study the piano while attending grade school. He also started to attend performances of Broadway musical productions and instantly became a passionate fan of the musical stage.

In 1895 Kern's family moved to Newark, New Jersey, where his father acquired control of a merchandising house. At Barringer High School Jerome often played piano and organ at school assemblies and wrote music for school productions; his teachers referred to him as "the little genius."

Upon graduating from high school in June 1902, Kern hoped to pursue his musical education more intensively. His father preferred to have him enter the business world, but a disastrous business deal convinced him almost immediately that the boy belonged in music and not in commerce. Sent to a New York factory to buy two pianos, the young Kern was so completely entranced by the salesmanship and hospitality of the factory owner that he bought not two but two hundred pianos, a deal that almost ruined his father's business. (His father finally managed to extricate himself from this difficulty by devising an installment plan by means of which he disposed of the pianos.)

In the fall of 1902 Kern entered the New York College of Music to study under Alexander Lambert, Albert von Doenhoff, Paolo Gallico, and Austen Pearce. During this period he also entered the field of popular music with a piano piece named *At the Casino*, which was published by the Lyceum Company on September 5, 1902.

Leaving college after his first year, Kern spent a year in Europe, studying music and absorbing musical influences. In London he found a job with the American producer Charles Frohman, who was putting on musicals in England. Kern's job was to write fillers to be used in the early part of each Frohman production—songs that were never noticed, since both audience and critics habitually arrived late at the theatre. The first song Kern wrote in London was "My Little Canoe," which Billie Burke sang in *The School Girl* in 1903. In London Kern also started a collaboration with P. G. Wodehouse, then a young and unknown writer. To Wodehouse's lyrics Kern produced an outstanding hit in the topical song "Mr. Chamberlain," which Seymour Hicks sang in *The Beauty of the Bath*. The "Mr. Chamberlain" of this song was a famous political leader of the time and the father of Neville Chamberlain, who later became Prime Minister.

Kern returned to the United States in 1904 and found employment in Tin Pan Alley. He also started to write songs for the Broadway stage. In 1904 he adapted the music of an English operetta, *Mr. Wix of Wickham,* bringing such invention to his harmonic writing and orchestration that the critic Alan Dale was led to inquire: "Who is this Jerome Kern whose music towers above the average primitive hurdy-gurdy accomplishments of the present-day musical comedy?" In the next eight years over one hundred Kern songs were interpolated into about thirty Broadway musicals. Kern's greatest success was "How'd You Like to Spoon with Me?" (lyrics by Edward Laska), introduced by Georgia Caine and Victor Morley in *The Earl and the Girl* (1905).

On October 25, 1910, Kern was married in England to a young English girl, Eva Leale, whom he brought back to the United States. He now began to make rapid strides in the American theatre. In 1911 he wrote the music for *La Belle Paree,* an extravaganza with which the Winter Garden in New York opened and in which Al Jolson made his Broadway stage debut. In 1912 he first became associated with Florenz Ziegfeld when the song "Call Me Flo" was interpolated into the Ziegfeld production *A Winsome Widow.* That year he also wrote his first, but un-

George Gershwin

JEROME KERN

successful, complete original score for the Broadway stage—*The Red Petticoat.* But in 1914 he achieved a great Broadway success with *The Girl from Utah,* an adaptation of an English operetta. For this play Kern wrote eight songs. One was a delightful rhythmic number, "Why Don't They Dance the Polka Anymore?"; another was a tender piece, "I'd Like to Wander with Alice in Wonderland"; a third was an unqualified masterpiece, the first of the songs for which Kern will always be remembered, "They Didn't Believe Me" (lyrics by Herbert Reynolds). Victor Herbert, hearing these songs, said: "This man will inherit my mantle."

Between 1915 and 1918 Kern wrote the music for several shows which helped to revolutionize the American musical theatre—the "Princess Theatre Shows," named after the theatre in which they were produced. Necessity happened to be the mother of this invention. Elizabeth Marbury, the part owner of a small and intimate New York house, the Princess Theatre, had difficulty finding plays that could be produced economically, and thought of creating intimate little musicals with modest casts, sets, orchestra, and chorus, and no stars at all. She asked Kern to be the composer, and he in turn brought Guy Bolton into the picture as librettist and lyricist. The first Princess Theatre Show was *Nobody Home* (1915), an adaptation of an

English operetta. *Nobody Home* boasted two delightful Kern songs, "The Magic Melody" and "You Know and I Know."

Nobody Home did well enough at the box office and in newspaper reviews to encourage Elizabeth Marbury to continue along the same lines. Later that year the Princess Theatre presented *Very Good, Eddie,* an American musical comedy with book by Guy Bolton and Philip Bartholomae and lyrics by Schuyler Green. This was a smart and sophisticated production, with such an intimate quality that one critic called it "parlor entertainment." Song, lyric, and humor grew naturally out of the situation and action; setting and character were thoroughly American. Kern's music added to this charm and gaiety with such winning selections as "Nodding Roses" and "Babes in the Wood." *Very Good, Eddie* had a run of 341 performances.

An even more substantial box office success was achieved in 1917 with *Oh, Boy!* which ran for 463 performances. *Oh, Boy!* (book by Bolton and lyrics by Wodehouse) was a delightful comedy of amatory errors in a college town atmosphere. Its outstanding song was "Till the Clouds Roll By," a title borrowed many years later for Kern's motion picture biography.

The last of the Kern Princess Theatre Shows was *Oh, Lady, Lady!* (1918), again with book by Bolton and lyrics by Wodehouse. Three charming Kern songs were found here: "Before I Met You," "You Found Me, I Found You," and the title song.

Between the productions of *Oh, Boy!* and *Oh, Lady, Lady!* the team of Kern, Bolton, and Wodehouse created a musical comedy of more ambitious proportions, more formal in approach and concept than the Princess Theatre Shows. This was *Leave It to Jane* (1917), based on George Ade's play *The College Widow.* "The Siren's Song," the title number, and the comedy tune "Cleopatterer" were its principal songs. *Leave It to Jane* enjoyed a highly successful revival in an off-Broadway production which opened in 1959 and embarked on a national tour in 1961.

In the first six years of the 1920's Kern's leading musical comedies were *Sally* (1920) and *Sunny* (1925), both of them lavishly produced and both starring Marilyn Miller. In *Sally* Marilyn Miller sang "Look for the Silver Lining" (lyrics by Clifford Grey); in *Sunny* her principal song was "Who?" (lyrics by Oscar Hammerstein II). Other successful Kern musicals of this period were *Good Morning, Dearie* (1921), which included "Ka-lu-a" (lyrics by Anne Caldwell); and *Stepping Stones* (1923) and *Criss Cross* (1926), both of which starred Fred Stone and his wife and daughter.

In 1927 Jerome Kern made stage history with *Show Boat,* now a classic of the American musical theatre. It was Kern's idea to adapt into a musical comedy, to text and lyrics by Oscar Hammerstein II, Edna Ferber's novel of life on a Mississippi show boat in the nineteenth century. Edna Ferber was skeptical about the possibilities of her novel for the musical stage because she was thinking in terms of the traditional musical theatre with its set and pat routines, chorus girls, synthetic humor, and stereotyped characters and situations. But Kern had in mind a new kind of theatre that would scrupulously avoid clichés and accepted procedures in realizing authentic backgrounds and characterizations, a logical story line, and dramatic truth. He was thinking in terms of a musical play rather than a musical comedy, one in which every element of the production would spring naturally from the situations, and in which the music would enhance dialogue and lyrics in projecting the plot.

Show Boat arrived in New York on December 27, 1927, in a sumptuous production by Florenz Ziegfeld. Among the principals in that cast were Helen Morgan, Norma Terris, and Howard Marsh. The audience and critics were enchanted. *"Show Boat,"* wrote Alan Dale prophetically, "is going to have a wonderful sail—no storms—no adverse winds—nothing to keep it from making port —goodness knows when." *Show Boat* remained in New York for 572 performances, then toured the country. Since then it has been frequently revived in all parts of the country, and has had three motion picture adaptations. In 1954 it received what was perhaps the highest accolade of all by being included for the first time in the regular repertory of an opera company—the New York City Opera.

Kern's score for *Show Boat* was the most inventive and varied of his career, which is perhaps why *Show Boat* never fails to cast a spell on audiences everywhere. "Only Make Believe," "Can't Help Lovin' That Man," and "Why Do I Love You?" are some of its major musical numbers. "Ol' Man River," is often classified as folk music— music, as Edna Ferber once wrote, that would "outlast Jerome Kern's day and mine."

Although the above-mentioned songs were composed with Hammerstein as lyricist, the verses for one ballad, "Bill," were written by P. G. Wodehouse. "Bill" had originally been written in 1918 for the Princess Theatre Show *Oh, Lady, Lady!* but had been discarded. Nine years later, when Kern auditioned Helen Morgan for the role of Julie in *Show Boat,* he knew that the ballad had finally found the singer who could do it justice, and a place was found for it in the play.

Kern utilized the basic melodic material of *Show Boat* for a major symphonic work entitled *Scenario* which was introduced on October 23, 1941, by the Cleveland Orchestra, with Artur Rodzinski conducting. A few months later Kern wrote a second symphonic composition, commissioned by André Kostelanetz: *Mark Twain: A Portrait for Orchestra.* Its world première took place in Cincinnati, with Kostelanetz conducting the Cincinnati Symphony.

After creating *Show Boat* Kern continued to write musicals in which the stress lay on integration of songs and text and in which some of the stereotypes of traditional musical comedy were abandoned. For *The Cat and the Fiddle,* in 1931, Kern wrote, to Otto Harbach's lyrics, "The Night Was Made for Love" and "She Didn't Say Yes." For *Music in the Air,* in 1932, he wrote "I've Told Ev'ry Little Star" and "The Song Is You" (lyrics by Hammerstein). In both musicals Kern's style and scope went beyond those of the popular song. For *Cat and the Fiddle* he wrote a fugue; for *Music in the Air* he produced several numbers with the characteristics of German folk songs and beer-hall tunes.

But Kern did not abandon the more formal musical theatre. *Sweet Adeline* (1929), with book and lyrics by Oscar Hammerstein II, was a musical romance of the nineties. In it Helen Morgan introduced "Why Was I Born?" and "Here Am I." *Roberta* (1933), adapted by Otto Harbach from a novel by Alice Duer Miller, was something of a fashion parade set in a Paris dress shop. In this play Tamara sang a song that has become one of Kern's most celebrated—"Smoke Gets in Your Eyes," the highlight of a score that also included "The Touch of Your Hand" and "Yesterdays" (lyrics by Harbach). "Smoke Gets in Your Eyes" was revived in 1958 by the Platters with such success that their recording sold over two million discs; at this time Bob Hope, who had appeared in the original production, revived *Roberta* for television.

Kern's last musical for Broadway was *Very Warm for May* (1939). Although a box office disaster, it had one great claim to distinction, "All the Things You Are" (lyrics by Hammerstein), one of Kern's most beautiful and popular songs.

After 1939 Kern devoted himself exclusively to motion pictures. He settled in Hollywood and built a palatial home in Beverly Hills. During the next six years he wrote original music for several delightful screen musicals. Among these were *I Dream Too Much,* starring Lily Pons; *Swingtime* with Fred Astaire and Ginger Rogers; *High, Wide and Handsome* and *Joy of Living,* with Irene Dunne; *When You're in Love,* with Grace Moore; *You Were Never Lovelier* and *Cover Girl,* with Rita Hayworth; *Can't Help Singing,* with Deanna Durbin; and *Centennial Summer.* Some of the outstanding songs in these productions were the title song and "Jockey on the Carousel" (lyrics by Dorothy Fields) in *I Dream Too Much;* "The Way You Look Tonight" (lyrics by Fields) in *Swingtime,* winner of the Academy Award in 1936; "Folks Who Live on the Hill" (lyrics by Hammerstein) in *High, Wide and Handsome;* "Dearly Beloved" (lyrics by Johnny Mercer) in *You Were Never Lovelier;* "Long Ago and Far Away" (lyrics by Ira Gershwin) in *Cover Girl;* and "All Through the Day" (lyrics by Hammerstein) and "In Love in Vain" (lyrics by Leo Robin) in *Centennial Summer.*

What is probably the most important single song by Kern during his Hollywood period was not specifically intended for a motion picture. It was "The Last Time I Saw Paris," written to lyrics by Oscar Hammerstein II, soon after the occupation of Paris by the Nazis during World War II. It was at Hammerstein's request that Kern set the lyric to music. Thus "The Last Time I Saw Paris" is unique among Kern's thousand songs in being the only one not written for either a stage or a screen production and the only one in which the lyric preceded the melody. Hildegarde, Noël Coward, and Sophie Tucker popularized the song in night clubs, and a Hildegarde recording supervised by Kern himself further advanced its success. It was finally interpolated into the motion picture *Lady Be Good*, and it received the Academy Award in 1941.

In November 1945 Kern went East to assist in a revival of *Show Boat*. He suffered a heart attack on Park Avenue and 57th Street on November 4, and died on November 11, at Doctors Hospital. "Genius is surely not too extravagant a word for him," said an editorial in the New York *Herald Tribune*.

Shortly after his death Kern's screen biography, *Till the Clouds Roll By*, which had been in preparation while Kern was still alive, was released. Robert Walker played the part of the composer.

Robert Russell Bennett wrote two symphonic works based on Kern's songs. One was the tone poem *Symphonic Study*, based on the following songs in their chronological sequence: "They Didn't Believe Me," "Babes in the Wood," "The Siren's Song," "Left All Alone Again Blues," "Who?," "Ol' Man River," "Smoke Gets in Your Eyes," and "All the Things You Are." The other was *Variations on a Theme by Jerome Kern*, the theme taken from "Once in a Blue Moon" in *Stepping Stones*.

ABOUT:

Ewen, David. The World of Jerome Kern; Hammerstein, Oscar II, editor. The Jerome Kern Song Book.

Look, January 23, 1945; Saturday Review, November 12, 1955.

Robert A. King *1862-1932*

ROBERT A. ("BOBO") KING was born Robert Keiser in New York City on September 20, 1862. He was only six when he started to take piano lessons, and he continued these studies for ten years while attending public school. As a boy he worked at Ditson's music store. He then found employment with the publishing house of Leo Feist in Tin Pan Alley. He was soon en-

gaged in writing popular songs, achieving his first hit in 1903 with "Anona," the melody in a pseudo-Indian style.

In 1918 King was engaged by Shapiro-Bernstein on a guarantee basis to write four songs a month. Under this arrangement King forthwith produced two impressive hits. One was the song by which he is still remembered, the waltz "Beautiful Ohio," with lyrics by Ballard Smith, published in 1918; it achieved a sheet music sale of five million copies and earned for King a royalty of more than sixty thousand dollars. The other, composed in 1919 to his own lyrics, was "Dreamy Alabama," which he published under the pseudonym "Mary Earl."

King was a prolific composer; but he issued so many songs under pen names (usually feminine), and others anonymously, that it is impossible to estimate his over-all output. The following, however, are some of his best songs: "Hawaiian Smiles," "Beautiful Hawaii," "Isle of Paradise," "In Old Manila," "Apple Blossoms," "I Ain't Nobody's Darling," "Why Did I Kiss That Girl?," "Just Like a Rainbow," "Ain't My Baby Grand?," "I Scream, You Scream," and "Moonlight on the Colorado." Some of these songs were written to King's own lyrics, some to lyrics by Elmer Hughes, Billy Moll, and others.

During World War I King wrote a few stirring war songs; among these were "When the Boys Come Home" and "Lafayette, We Hear You Calling." King also composed concert and salon music, including ballades, waltzes, marches, gavottes, and polkas. He died in New York City on April 13, 1932.

ABOUT:

Gilbert, Douglas. Lost Chords.

Manuel Klein *1876-1919*

MANUEL KLEIN was born in London on December 6, 1876. Three of his brothers distinguished themselves in the cultural life of England. Herman Klein became famous as a music critic; Charles achieved note as a playwright; and Alfred was a well-known actor.

Manuel was directed to music study at an early age, receiving intensive training with private teachers in London in his boyhood.

MANUEL KLEIN

In the early 1900's he came to the United States where he made his permanent home. Soon after his arrival he wrote the score for his first Broadway production, *Mr. Pickwick*, for which his brother prepared the text and Grant Stewart the lyrics; it was produced in 1903 with De Wolf Hopper in the leading male role.

Gus Edwards—the distinguished songwriter, publisher, and vaudevillian—became interested in him and used his influence to gain for Klein the musical direction of the Hippodrome Theatre in New York, which housed spectacles and extravaganzas. Besides conducting the Hippodrome Theatre orchestra, Manuel Klein began to write the music for these lavish productions. The series began with *A Society Circus*, which opened on December 13, 1905. Between 1906 and 1914, Klein's music was heard in the following Hippodrome extravaganzas: *Pioneer Days* (1906), *The Auto Race* (1907), *Sporting Days* (1908), *A Trip to Japan* (1909), *The International Cup and the Ballet of Niagara* (1910), *Around the World* (1911), *Under Many Flags* (1912), *America* (1913), and *The Wars of the World* (1914).

Among his most successful songs for these productions (for which he wrote both lyrics and music) were "Moon Dear" in *A Society Circus;* "Meet Me When the Lanterns Glow" in *A Trip to Japan;* "Sweet-heart" and "Home Is Where the Heart Is" in *Under Many Flags;* "In Siam" in *The Wars of the World;* and "Love Is Like a Rainbow" in *The International Cup and the Ballet of Niagara.*

While writing for the Hippodrome Theatre, Manuel Klein also wrote music for several musical comedies starring De Wolf Hopper; among them were *The Man from Now* (1906), *The Pied Piper* (1908), and *Hop o' My Thumb* (1913).

In 1915 Klein became embroiled in a disagreeable quarrel with J. J. Shubert, producer of the Hippodrome extravaganzas. Shubert sent to the Hippodrome for some trumpets and drums needed at the Winter Garden, but Klein turned down this request because he needed them for his own orchestra. In the ensuing exchange of heated words and denunciations, Klein submitted his resignation as music director of the Hippodrome. It was accepted. This episode so antagonized the entire Hippodrome company that Shubert was ultimately compelled to sell his interests in these productions to Charles Dillingham.

After returning to London in 1915 Klein became conductor of the Gaiety Theatre. He died in London on June 1, 1919.

Burton Lane *1912-*

BURTON LANE was born in New York City on February 2, 1912. His father was a successful real estate dealer. Burton attended New York public schools and, for a short period, the Dwight School for Concentration. He also studied piano with Simon Bucharoff. When Burton was fifteen his ability to compose music came to the attention of Harold Stern, music director for the Shuberts. Stern arranged to have J. J. Shubert listen to Lane's music, and their meeting resulted in Shubert's commissioning Lane to write the score for an edition of the *Greenwich Village Follies*. Unfortunately, the illness of one of the principals prevented that edition from materializing, and none of Lane's songs was heard or ever published. However, two songs he had written for the High School of Commerce were published at this time.

While attending the High School of Commerce, Lane was hired as a staff composer at

BURTON LANE

Remick's, a Tin Pan Alley publishing house. He now wrote songs continuously, receiving encouragement and advice from some of Tin Pan Alley's successful composers, including George Gershwin. After Lane left Remick's, Howard Dietz, the lyricist, wrote lyrics to two of Lane's melodies for the Broadway revue *Three's a Crowd* (1930): "Forget All Your Books" and "Out in the Open Air." In 1931 "Say the Word" (lyrics by Harold Adamson) appeared in *The Third Little Show;* and in the same year, Lane wrote, to Adamson's lyrics, most of the score for the ninth edition of the Earl Carroll *Vanities,* including "Have a Heart," "Heigh-Ho, the Gang's All Here," and "Love Came into My Heart."

The Depression brought Lane's career on Broadway to a sudden standstill. He managed to get a number of songs published, two of which became quite popular: "Look Who's Here" and "Tony's Wife" (lyrics by Adamson). But beyond this he made no headway.

In 1933 Lane and Adamson were signed by the Irving Berlin publishing house and sent to Hollywood for six weeks to see if they could make a go of it. Lane ended up staying twenty-one years. During the next few years he worked as a composer for various studios, writing songs for about thirty pictures. The most successful were "Every-

thing I Have Is Yours" (lyrics by Adamson) from *Dancing Lady,* which starred Joan Crawford, Clark Gable, and Fred Astaire; "Swing High, Swing Low" (lyrics by Ralph Freed) from the picture of the same name; "Stop! You're Breaking My Heart" (lyrics by Ted Koehler) from *Artists and Models;* "Moments Like This" and "How'dja Like to Love Me" (lyrics by Frank Loesser) from *College Swing;* "The Lady's in Love with You" (lyrics by Loesser) from *Some Like It Hot;* "I Hear Music" (lyrics by Loesser) from *Dancing on a Dime.*

Lane's first complete score for the Broadway stage was written in 1940. *Hold On to Your Hats,* the musical in which Al Jolson made his last Broadway stage appearance, represented a milestone in Lane's career, for it brought him together with the lyricist E. Y. Harburg, with whom he was destined to do some of his finest music writing. In *Hold On to Your Hats,* Lane's best numbers were delivered by Jolson with his customary verve: "Walkin' Along Mindin' My Business," "There's a Great Day Coming Mañana," "The World Is in My Arms," and "Would You Be So Kindly?"

Between 1940 and 1944 Lane contributed songs to various motion pictures: "How About You?" (lyrics by Ralph Freed) for *Babes on Broadway* starring Mickey Rooney and Judy Garland—a song that had a highly successful revival a decade and a half later; "I'll Take Tallulah" for *Ship Ahoy;* and "It's Smart to Be People." The last two were written to Harburg's lyrics.

In 1944 Lane returned to Broadway with the score for the Olsen and Johnson extravaganza *Laughing Room Only.* One of the songs for this play was the greatest commercial success he had enjoyed up to then, "Feudin' and Fightin'" (lyrics by Al Dubin and Burton Lane), though this song did not become popular until a few years after the show closed, when it was revived by Dorothy Shay on the Bing Crosby radio program.

Lane's most successful stage success was achieved in 1947 with *Finian's Rainbow* (lyrics by Harburg). This delightful little Irish fantasy involved a leprechaun, a deaf-mute who made herself understood through dancing, and two visitors to the southern part of the United States from a mythical Irish town. Yet this text, for all its recourse to

Irish lore, was vibrantly contemporary, vitally concerned with social and racial problems in the South, filled with laughing allusions to the poll tax, anti-Negro legislation, share-cropping, and social injustice. The fantasy and the romance of the play were neatly caught in two of the production's hit songs, "How Are Things in Glocca Morra?" and "Look to the Rainbow." Mockery, satire, and laughter were found in "When the Idle Poor Become the Idle Rich," "The Begat," "Something Sort of Grandish," and "When I'm Not Near the Girl I Love," for which Harburg wrote some of the most brilliant and scintillating lyrics of his career.

Finian's Rainbow was revived on Broadway for the first time in 1955. It returned to New York for a brief two-week run at the New York City Center on April 27, 1960. It received such an enthusiastic response from audience and critics that it was brought back to Broadway on May 23.

Since writing *Finian's Rainbow*, Lane has been working for motion pictures. In 1951, with Alan Jay Lerner as his lyricist, he contributed excellent scores for *Royal Wedding*, starring Fred Astaire and Jane Powell, and for *Huckleberry Finn*.

In 1957 Lane was elected president of the American Guild of Authors and Composers, and he held this office for several years.

ABOUT:
Green, Stanley. The World of Musical Comedy.

Jay Livingston *1915-*

JAY HAROLD LIVINGSTON was born in McDonald, Pennsylvania, on March 28, 1915. He studied piano with Harry Archer in Pittsburgh, and while attending the University of Pennsylvania was a pupil in composition and orchestration of Harl McDonald. As a university student he organized and played in a dance orchestra that performed at college functions; he also played in other bands at various social functions and on cruises that covered a good part of the world. Another member of these bands was Raymond B. Evans, Livingston's fellow student at the university. Evans soon became Livingston's lyricist, and it was as a song-writing team that Livingston and Evans became famous.

JAY LIVINGSTON

After leaving college in 1937 Livingston spent six years in New York as a pianist and vocal arranger. During this period he wrote his first hit song with Ray Evans, "G'bye Now." In 1939 he wrote the score for the motion picture *The Cat and the Canary*, for which he received an Academy Award. One year later, with Evans as his collaborator, he wrote special material and songs for Olsen and Johnson, some of which were featured in the Broadway extravaganza *Sons o' Fun* (1940).

During World War II Livingston served in the armed forces. He and Ray Evans went to Hollywood in 1944 and signed a contract with Paramount Pictures; they remained ten years and wrote songs for over one hundred motion pictures.

In 1946 their song "To Each His Own," from the motion picture of that name starring Olivia de Haviland, became one of their greatest commercial successes, selling over three million records and about a million copies of sheet music. In 1948 they received an Academy Award for their song "Buttons and Bows," which had been introduced in *The Paleface*, starring Bob Hope. They received two more Academy Awards after that: in 1951 for "Mona Lisa" *(Captain Carey of the U.S.A.);* and in 1957 for "Whatever Will Be, Will Be" (Qué Será"), *(The Man Who Knew Too Much).*

Some of their other successful songs for the screen are the title number for *Copper Canyon;* "Marshmallow Moon" *(Aaron Slick from Punkin Crick);* "My Own True Love" (title song); "The Song of Surrender" (title song); "Paramount Don't Want Me Blues" from *Sunset Boulevard,* which starred Gloria Swanson; "Bonne Nuit, Good Night" *(Here Comes the Groom).*

After 1955 Livingston and Evans worked as free-lancers in Hollywood. Since that time they have written the title song of *Tammy,* which was introduced and made famous by Debbie Reynolds and nominated for an Academy Award in 1958; and "Almost in Your Arms" *(Houseboat),* nominated for an Academy Award in 1959.

In addition to their songs, Livingston and Evans also wrote the scores for *The Lemon Drop Kid* with Bob Hope, *My Friend Irma, Dream Girl,* and *Isn't It Romantic?*

They made their bow in the Broadway theatre with *Oh, Captain.* This musical comedy, which opened on January 4, 1958, was an adaptation of the successful motion picture *The Captain's Paradise,* which had starred Alec Guinness. It featured "Give It All You Got," "Femininity," and "Montmartre in the Morning."

Early in 1959 Livingston and Evans wrote the score for *No Man Can Tame Me,* a musical production written directly for television.

Livingston and Evans returned to the Broadway stage in the fall of 1961 with *Let It Ride!* This was a musical-comedy adaptation of the successful Broadway play *Three Men on a Horse,* by John Cecil Holm and George Abbott. In the musical, Sam Levene returned to play the role of Patsy the horseplayer which he had created in the original non-musical production. George Gobel was starred as Erwin, the greeting-card poet with a knack for picking winners in horse races. "Jay Livingston and Ray Evans," reported Henry T. Murdock, "have written frail but appealing little tunes."

Frank Loesser 1910-

FRANK LOESSER, composer and lyricist, was born in New York City on June 29, 1910. His father was a piano teacher who had come to the United States from his native Germany in the 1880's; his brother, Arthur, became a distinguished piano virtuoso and teacher. Despite his family background, however, Frank received no musical training. He taught himself to play both piano and harmonica, in time acquiring facility in performing popular tunes. What he later learned about harmony and theory came mainly from experimentation and trial and error.

He attended the local public schools, the Speyer and Townsend Harris Hall high schools and, for one year, the City College of New York. Concluding that he was no scholar, Loesser decided to enter the world of commerce. He held one job after another —as an office boy in a wholesale jewelry house, waiter and pianist at a Berkshire mountain resort, reporter for a small New Rochelle newspaper, press agent, knit goods editor of the *Women's Wear Daily,* process server for almost one hundred lawyers at the same time, and inspector testing foods for a chain of restaurants. "In those times," he remarks, "I had a rendezvous with failure every day."

One day he was asked to write verses about the guests attending a Lions Club dinner. The couplets he wrote were amateurish and silly; one of them ran "Secretary Albert Vincent, Read the Minutes, Right This Instant." But they delighted the members of the Lions Club who showered him with enthusiastic praise. This encouraged him to write more verses, and then lyrics for popular songs. "Armful of You" was sold to a vaudevillian for fifteen dollars. In time he submitted some of his best lyrics to Leo Feist, who engaged him for fifty dollars a week. The year he was employed there, Loesser contributed the words to many songs, most to the music of Joseph Brandfron, but none were considered good enough for publication. When Feist finally did publish one of his efforts it was only after he had left the firm in 1931. The song was "In Love with the Memory of You," with music by a young composer named William Schuman. Later in life Schuman became one of America's most distinguished composers of concert music, and, as president of the Juilliard School of Music, an outstanding music educator.

In 1934 Loesser wrote the lyrics for "I Wish I Were Twins" (music by Joseph

Meyer and Eddie De Lange). In 1936, with Irving Actman as his composer, he wrote most of the lyrics for the revue *The Illustrators Show,* which ran for four days at the 48th Street Theatre. "Someone from Universal Pictures came to see the show on its last (rainy) night and was drunk enough to offer Actman and me a Universal contract," Loesser recalls. From there he went to Paramount, where he remained several years, writing lyrics to the music of some of Hollywood's most eminent composers, and for some of the screen's most important musicals. He wrote, to Hoagy Carmichael's music, "Small Fry" for the Bing Crosby musical *Sing You Sinners,* and "Two Sleepy People" for the Bob Hope comedy *Thanks for the Memory;* with Joseph J. Lilley, "Jingle, Jangle, Jingle" for *Forest Rangers;* and with Frederick Hollander, "See What the Boys in the Back Room Will Have," which Marlene Dietrich introduced in *Destry Rides Again.* He also wrote lyrics to music by Jimmy McHugh, Jule Styne, and Arthur Schwartz, among others. Thus Loesser became an accomplished lyricist before he started to write music.

His first attempt at composition was motivated by the outbreak of World War II. Immediately after Pearl Harbor, he wrote the words and music of "Praise the Lord and Pass the Ammunition." He had originally planned to write only the lyric; but, as was habitual with him, he prepared a dummy melody for his lyrics in order to test whether his words could be sung easily. This melody proved so fresh in style and so direct in emotional appeal that his friends insisted upon his issuing it with the words. "Praise the Lord and Pass the Ammunition" was the first major song hit of World War II, selling over two million records and one million copies of sheet music.

Another important World War II song for which Loesser wrote the words and music was "Rodger Young," also in the folk song style of "Praise the Lord." This ballad was written at the request of Infantry officials who wanted a song glorifying the exploits of an infantryman. Loesser chose Rodger Young, a twenty-five-year-old soldier who had sacrificed his own life in the Solomons by attacking a Japanese pillbox in order to save the lives of his comrades.

FRANK LOESSER

Loesser wrote still other war songs. As a private first class in the Special Services division his duty was to write soldier shows and package and distribute them to army camps. In this capacity he wrote songs for various branches of the service; one of these, "What Do You Do in the Infantry?," became an official song of the Infantry.

After World War II Loesser went back to Hollywood and rapidly became one of its most successful composers. For most of his songs for the screen he wrote both music and lyrics. The best of these were "Tallahassee" *(Varsity Girl);* "I Wish I Didn't Love You So" *(The Perils of Pauline);* "Now That I Need You" *(Red, Hot and Blue);* and a song that won a 1949 Academy Award, "Baby, It's Cold Outside" *(Neptune's Daughter).* In 1952 he composed an outstanding score for *Hans Christian Andersen,* in which Danny Kaye starred; one of its songs, "Thumbelina," was nominated for an Academy Award. "On a Slow Boat to China," a leading song hit of 1948, was written and published independently.

Loesser has also enjoyed a highly fruitful career as a composer for the Broadway theatre. Even his first musical comedy, *Where's Charley?,* which opened on October 11, 1948, was a smash box office success. This George Abbott musical comedy adaptation of Brandon Thomas' farce *Charley's Aunt* starred

Ray Bolger as Charley. Its two hit songs were "Once in Love with Amy" and "My Darling, My Darling."

Loesser's next Broadway play proved to be a major triumph of our musical theatre, one of the best musical comedies ever produced. This was *Guys and Dolls*, which opened in New York on November 24, 1950, to run for twelve hundred performances. Damon Runyon's characters and stories gave Jo Swerling and Abe Burrows the material for a brisk, hard-boiled, and racy play filled with Broadway eccentrics and tinhorn gamblers. Michael Kidd's memorable ballet episodes were in character (including a fast-moving opening scene of life and personalities on Broadway, and a dice game in the depths of a sewer). And Loesser's score was a veritable cornucopia of brilliant lyrics and remarkably varied melodies: love songs—"I'll Know," "I've Never Been in Love Before," and "If I Were a Bell"; and humorous ditties —"A Bushel and a Peck," the "Fugue for Tin Horns" (a three-part canon in which horse players are trying to pick the winners for the day), "Adelaide's Lament" about her psychosomatic cold, and "Take Back Your Mink." For the motion picture adaptation produced by Goldwyn and starring Marlon Brando and Frank Sinatra, Loesser wrote a new hit ballad, "A Woman in Love."

With *The Most Happy Fella*, produced on May 3, 1956, Loesser extended his creative horizon by writing the text, as well as music and lyrics, for an adaptation of Sidney Howard's Pulitzer Prize play, *They Knew What They Wanted*. The music was conceived on a more ambitious scale than anything Loesser had attempted up to this time, and embraced thirty numbers: arias, recitatives, duets, canons, choral pieces, folk hymns, parodies, and instrumental interludes. "Stand-in' on the Corner," "Happy to Make Your Acquaintance," and "Big D" were of the Hit Parade variety. Others were more subtle in penetrating into the personality of the characters who sang them, or in projecting a mood. The best of these were the vocal quartet "How Beautiful the Days," "My Heart Is So Full of You," and the waltz "Young People." *The Most Happy Fella* was voted by the Drama Critics Circle as the best musical of the year, and on April 21, 1960, it opened at the Coliseum Theatre in London

where it ran most of the year. Other companies presented this musical in Sweden and Australia.

Greenwillow, which had only a brief New York run in 1960, was described in the program as "a comedy drama." The book, by Lesser Samuels and Frank Loesser, was based on B. J. Chute's novel of the same name. To the critic of *Variety*, *Greenwillow* had "a Dickensian, old-English flavor . . . [with] the quality of Pickwick and the suggestion of Dingley Dell to carry on the quaint Christmasy tone." "Summertime Love" and "Faraway Boy" were two outstanding features in this score.

Loesser regained his winning stride on Broadway in the fall of 1961 with *How to Succeed in Business Without Really Trying*, adapted from Shepherd Mead's book by Abe Burrows, Jack Weinstock, and Willie Gilbert. Rudy Vallee and Robert Morse were starred in this highly acclaimed musical which, as *Show* reported, "marks composer Frank Loesser's return to the sassy big-city arena he captured so well in *Guys and Dolls*."

ABOUT:

American Magazine, February 1946; Life, December 1952; New York Times Magazine, May 20, 1956; Notes, March 1950; Theatre Arts, May 1956.

Frederick Loewe 1904-

FREDERICK ("FRITZ") Loewe was born in Vienna, Austria, on June 10, 1904. His father was a famous Viennese operetta tenor who had created the role of Prince Danilo in Lehár's *The Merry Widow*. Frederick began to study piano when he was five and at thirteen became the youngest pianist ever to appear as soloist with the Berlin Symphony. Composition also began early. He wrote his first popular song when he was a child; during his early boyhood he completed several musical numbers that were used in his father's act in a variety theatre; and when he was thirteen, his song "Katrina" sold over a million copies of sheet music in Europe.

Despite his activity and interest in popular music, Loewe received comprehensive training as a serious musician. He studied piano with Ferruccio Busoni and Eugène d'Albert and composition with Nikolaus Reznicek. In 1923 he received the Hollaender medal for piano.

He came to the United States in 1924 to further his career as a piano virtuoso. Unable to get a hearing from managers, he decided to give up serious music. For a while he supported himself by playing piano in a Greenwich Village night club and working as a bus boy in a cafeteria. Then, for several years, he led a nomadic existence, wandering across the United States, taking on any job that came along. He prospected for gold; he punched cattle in Montana; he was a riding instructor at a resort in New Hampshire; he delivered mail by horseback; he engaged in professional boxing bouts in the bantamweight class in a Brooklyn athletic club (winning eight of the nine fights in which he took part). He also played piano on cruise ships and in beer halls in the Yorkville section of New York.

In the early 1930's he started to write popular songs. In 1934 "Love Tiptoed Through My Heart" was used in *Petticoat Fever,* a nonmusical Broadway play starring Dennis King. A year later, Loewe formed a partnership with Earle Crooker, a radio and Hollywood script writer, with whom he wrote the song "A Waltz Was Born in Vienna," introduced by Gomez and Winona in *The Illustrators Show.* Loewe and Crooker then wrote the score for *Salute to Spring,* a musical comedy produced in St. Louis in the summer of 1937. Dwight Deere Wiman, who happened to see the show, was so impressed by the songs that he offered a contract to Loewe and Crooker to write the complete score for a Broadway operetta, *Great Lady.* The operetta opened on December 1, 1938, but ran for only twenty performances.

A change of fortune for Loewe came about as a result of a meeting with Alan Jay Lerner at the Lambs Club in New York. Lerner was a Harvard graduate who had written sketches and lyrics for two Hasty Pudding shows. After college, Lerner had worked for radio, creating over five hundred scripts in two years. But his ambition was to write texts and lyrics for the Broadway theatre. His meeting with Loewe brought him a composer with similar dreams of Broadway. They decided to work together.

Loewe proposed that Lerner revise some of the lyrics of *Salute to Spring* for a possible Detroit production. Renamed *Life of the Party,* the show opened on Broadway in October 1942, with Dorothy Stone in the star-

FREDERICK LOEWE

ring role. Then Lerner and Loewe went to work on another Broadway show. *What's Up?* (1943), for which Lerner wrote text as well as lyrics, starred Jimmy Savo as an East Indian potentate. It stayed on the boards for only eight weeks.

The Day Before Spring (1945) was their first modest success, though much more so with the critics than with the public. This was a fantasy with interesting psychological overtones. Loewe's musical style, previously continental, began to assume an American identity for the first time. The best numbers were "You Haven't Changed at All," the title number, and "I Love You This Morning."

Brigadoon, which had its New York première on March 13, 1947, was Lerner and Loewe's first box office triumph, with a run of 581 performances. *Brigadoon* was also a fantasy, the title referring to an enchanted Scottish village that once in a century comes to life for a single day. The plot concerned two Americans' discovery of this town during its one-day existence and their part in its eerie, storybook life. Lerner's lyrics and dialogue maintained a fine balance between reality and fantasy, sentiment and whimsy. Loewe's music maintained the sensitive moods of the play. "Almost Like Being in Love" became a hit song in 1947. "The Heather on the Hill" and "Come to Me, Bend to Me" were delightfully touched with piquant Scottish flavors.

Brigadoon was the first musical to win the Drama Critics Award as the best play of the year. Its four-year run in London was one of the longest ever enjoyed by any musical in England. When *Brigadoon* was successfully revived in New York in 1957, Richard Watts, Jr., said of Loewe's music: "I had forgotten . . . what a delightful score Frederick Loewe composed for this Alan Jay Lerner fantasy. . . . It came to me as almost a revelation . . . that *Brigadoon* was filled with enchanting melodies."

The next Broadway production of Lerner and Loewe was *Paint Your Wagon* (1951), a far better musical than its comparatively modest run of 289 performances might suggest. Set in northern California during the Gold Rush, *Paint Your Wagon* gave a fascinating picture of the development of a mining camp into a boom town and its disintegration into a ghost town. The play, conceived by Lerner as "a musical that would embrace all the robustness and vitality and cockeyed courage that is so much a part of our American heritage," had an inviting folk flavor, which was further enhanced by the picturesque folk choreography of Agnes De Mille. Loewe's score included such delightful songs as "All for Him," "Wand'rin' Star," "I Talk to the Trees" and "Another Autumn."

With the epoch-making *My Fair Lady*, Lerner and Loewe took a place beside Rodgers and Hammerstein as a words-and-music partnership. *My Fair Lady*, a musical adaptation of Bernard Shaw's *Pygmalion*, appeared in New York on March 15, 1956, and received the unanimous vote of the critics as one of the best musical productions seen on Broadway in many years. "This is a legendary evening," reported William Hawkins. Brooks Atkinson said: "It gets close to the genius of creation." To the penetrating social viewpoint of the Shaw play, to its mocking appraisal of class distinctions in England, and to the satirical Shavian commentary, Lerner added winning sentiment and heart-warming romantic ardor. The result was an evening that carried a radiance and glow across the footlights into the hearts of the audience. Beyond Lerner's artistry in making the adaptation, and his consummate skill and invention in writing dialogue and lyrics, the play profited from unforgettable performances by Rex Harrison and Julie Andrews, highly imagina-

tive direction by Moss Hart, the striking choreography of Hanya Holm, and the tasteful sets and costumes of Oliver Smith and Cecil Beaton respectively. Loewe's music was a strong suit, beautifully attuned to the spirit of a play set in England in 1912. The overtones of that era were caught in pieces like the "Ascot Gavotte" and the "Embassy Waltz." Two other Loewe songs became immediate hits, "I Could Have Danced All Night" and "On the Street Where You Live," both in a romantic style, as was also "I've Grown Accustomed to Her Face." The best comedy numbers included the cockney songs, "With a Little Bit of Luck," and "Get Me to the Church on Time," and two patter songs, "Why Can't the English?" and "A Hymn to Him."

My Fair Lady made stage history with a bigger five-year gross at the box office than any previous Broadway play; a run surpassing the record previously held by *Oklahoma!;* and an extraordinary number of touring companies in all parts of the world, including the Soviet Union, where the audience and critics hailed the première in Moscow on April 18, 1960. The long-playing record made by the original cast sold more than two million discs—only one of many different recordings in every possible style and arrangement. *My Fair Lady* captured one third of the Antoinette Perry Awards, a record previously held only by *South Pacific* and *Damn Yankees.*

In 1957 Lerner and Loewe completed an all-important assignment for Hollywood, the adaptation of Colette's *Gigi* into a screen musical. In story, feeling, and treatment, *Gigi* proved to be another *My Fair Lady*, and like the stage musical which it emulated it went on to make history. It received nine Academy Awards (the first time a single motion picture received that many), including that for the best picture of the year, and one to Lerner and Loewe for the title song. Other memorable songs included "Thank Heaven for Little Girls," "The Night They Invented Champagne," "I'm Glad I'm Not Young Any More," and "I Remember It Well."

When *Camelot*—the Lerner and Loewe successor to *My Fair Lady*—opened on Broadway on December 4, 1960, it arrived with the largest advance sale in stage history, about three million dollars. It aroused great expectations, which were not completely fulfilled. *Camelot,* adapted from *The Once and Future King,* a novel by T. H. White, was a musical stage setting of the legend of King Arthur and the Knights of the Round Table. The show was sumptuously mounted; it boasted outstanding performances by Julie Andrews as Guinevere, Richard Burton as King Arthur, and Robert Goulet as Lancelot; it had several delightful musical numbers, including the title song, "What Do Simple Folks Do?," "If Ever I Would Leave You," and "How to Handle a Woman"; and it profited from some stunning choreography by Hanya Holm. But the critical consensus was that this was no *My Fair Lady* by any stretch of the imagination. "Graceful and sumptuous though it is," said Howard Taubman in the New York *Times,* "*Camelot* leans dangerously in the direction of old-hat operetta. It has intervals of enchantment . . . but it cannot be denied that they [Lerner and Loewe] badly miss their late collaborator—Bernard Shaw." "There is a curious air of heaviness hanging over it," remarked Richard Watts, Jr., "and it has an unfortunate way of getting lost from time to time between its fantasy, its satirical humor, and its romantic wistfulness." "To tell the truth," said Robert Coleman bluntly, "*Camelot* is an expensive disappointment."

Arthur Freed, the Hollywood producer of *Gigi,* once disclosed to Ira Gershwin how Lerner and Loewe operated as collaborators. Writes Ira Gershwin: "Fritz waits until Alan comes up with a title that both agree is an inevitable or feasible one. Then Fritz musicalizes the title (sometimes in a variety of ways); and when both are agreed that the tune suits the mood and background, Alan then fills in the lyric. But nothing is gospel. Alteration in lyric or music line may later occur. And sometimes a song that has been sweated over for weeks suddenly sounds impossible and is thrown out. But when the score is finally completed and 'that's it!,' Fritz insists that it be done exactly as conceived. He is adamant about every phase of it. There can be no change in tempo, inflection, or orchestration; and no matter who the star or conductor, what the audience hears musically is scrupulously Fritz's intent."

Partly because his collaboration with Lerner on *Camelot* had not progressed harmoniously, and partly because he had suffered a serious heart attack, Frederick Loewe announced in 1961 that he would take an indefinite leave of absence as Lerner's partner. Soon after that, Lerner and Richard Rodgers revealed that they had set up a working arrangement for a new musical production for 1962 or 1963.

ABOUT:
Green, Stanley. The World of Musical Comedy.
Business Week, July 28, 1956; New York Times Magazine, March 15, 1959.

Gustav Luders *1865-1913*

GUSTAV LUDERS was born in Bremen, Germany, on December 13, 1865. He received his musical education in Europe, and came to the United States in 1888 to settle in Milwaukee. For several years he conducted popular orchestras in restaurants, theatres, and beer gardens. Attracting the interest of Charles K. Harris, he was induced by the composer of "After the Ball" to pursue a career in music publishing in Chicago. Luders found employment in the local Witmark office as an arranger; one of his highly successful arrangements was of Barney Fagan's ragtime melody, "My Gal's a High Born Lady" (1896). Luders also directed theatre orchestras in Chicago, and began to write songs which Isidore Witmark described as "tuneful, bright, and gay."

In 1899, Luders' first operetta, *Little Robinson Crusoe,* starring Eddie Foy, was produced. Henry W. Savage now became interested in Luders and commissioned him to write a score for *The Burgomaster,* an operetta produced in Chicago with Raymond Hitchcock. It was here that Luders' first successful song, "The Tale of the Kangaroo," was heard. It was here too that Luders made a working arrangement with Frank Pixley, editor of the Chicago *Times-Herald,* by which Pixley wrote texts and lyrics to Luders' music. *King Dodo* (1902) had a bright score that included the song "The Tale of the Bumble Bee," a ballad, "Diana," and a march, "The Lad Who Leads."

Luders achieved his greatest success with *The Prince of Pilsen.* This play, which opened on Broadway on March 17, 1903, was one of the most successful operettas of the New York stage in the early 1900's. Besides its long initial New York run, it enjoyed a

From AFTER THE BALL, copyright
renewed 1953 by James J. Geller; by
permission of the copyright owner

GUSTAV LUDERS

five-season tour of the country, and three
additional returns to Broadway. Pixley's
book, set on the French Riviera, involves mistaken identity; a Cincinnati brewer is mistaken for a prince—a state of affairs all too
willingly accepted by the prince, who is eager
to travel incognito. Luders' rich score included two outstanding songs: "The Tale of
the Sea Shell" and "The Message of the
Violet," as well as a stirring choral number,
"The Heidelberg Stein Song."

Luders continued to work with Pixley
on many operettas. The most successful were
Woodland (1904), a fantasy in which all
characters were birds, and for which they
wrote the tuneful "The Tale of the Violet";
The Grand Mogul (1907); *Marcelle* (1908),
which featured "The Message of the Red,
Red Rose"; and *The Gipsy* (1912).

During this period Luders also wrote
music to texts and lyrics by George Ade. The
most important of these productions were
The Sho Gun (1904) and *The Fair Co-Ed*
(1909). The former, set in Ka Choo, an
imaginary island between Japan and Korea,
satirized American big business and high-
pressure methods. Its principal songs were
"I'll Live for You," "Flutter Little Bird,"
and "I Am Yours Truly." *The Fair Co-Ed*
had a college town setting, and two of its

most charming songs were "Here in the Starlight" and "I'll Dream of That Sweet Co-Ed."

In 1913 Luders wrote his thirteenth operetta, *Somewhere Else.* It was so severely
criticized by the press that it closed after
the eighth performance. Luders, having suffered a long and serious illness just before
writing *Somewhere Else,* died of a heart attack late in January 1913, the day after this
show closed.

ABOUT:
Ewen, David. Complete Book of the American Musical Theater.

Jimmy McHugh 1895-

JIMMY McHUGH was born in Boston,
Massachusetts, on July 10, 1895. Both
his parents were musical; his mother, an excellent pianist, gave him his first music lessons. He studied at St. John's Preparatory
School and Staley College in Boston. After
helping out in his father's plumbing establishment, Jimmy found an opening at the
Boston Opera House as an office boy. There
he frequently delighted opera stars and conductors with his improvisations on famous
opera arias.

McHugh went to work for the Boston
branch of the Irving Berlin Publishing Company as a pianist and part-time song plugger
in local theatres and five-and-ten-cent stores.
In 1921 he went to New York and joined
the Mills Publishing Company. It was here
that he wrote and published his first song,
"Emaline." For nine years after that, he
wrote songs for the Cotton Club, the Harlem
night club, where he is reputed to have introduced and helped to popularize Duke
Ellington and his orchestra. The shows
that he wrote and produced at the Cotton Club
contained several song hits, "When My Sugar
Walks Down the Street" (lyrics by Irving
Mills and Gene Austin) and "I Can't Believe
That You're in Love with Me" (lyrics by
Clarence Gaskill). The latter was used as
the main theme in the motion picture *The
Caine Mutiny* about thirty years later.

In 1927 McHugh met Dorothy Fields, a
member of the celebrated theatrical family
headed by Lew Fields, half of the comedy
team of Weber and Fields. Dorothy's brother Herbert was a writer of musical comedy
texts, and for many years he collaborated with

Rodgers and Hart. Joseph, another brother, distinguished himself as a playwright and as librettist for musical comedies by Sigmund Romberg and Rodgers and Hammerstein. When he met Dorothy Fields, she was a school teacher, but her ambition was to write songs lyrics. McHugh, recognizing her talent, introduced her work at the Cotton Club in 1927. It proved a happy arrangement. In 1928, the team of McHugh and Fields wrote the songs for the Negro revue *Blackbirds of 1928*. This show, which starred Bill Robinson and Adelaide Hall, was a tremendous success; it ran on Broadway for three years, and sent three companies on tour. Several songs from this revue became formidable hits, notably "I Can't Give You Anything but Love, Baby," "Digga Digga Doo," and "I Must Have That Man."

In 1928 Jimmy McHugh and Dorothy Fields also wrote the songs for another Broadway musical, *Hello Daddy*, produced by and starring Lew Fields. In 1930 McHugh and Fields contributed "On the Sunny Side of the Street" and "Exactly Like You" for Gertrude Lawrence and Harry Richman in the *International Revue*, and "Blue Again" to the *Vanderbilt Revue*.

In 1930 he left New York temporarily for Hollywood, where he became one of the most prolific and successful creators of songs for the screen. His first Hollywood assignment was *Love in the Rough*, for which he and Dorothy Fields wrote "Go Home and Tell Your Mother" for Robert Montgomery. The McHugh-Fields team continued to write for about twelve motion pictures, also contributing occasional songs to night club productions and to the Broadway stage. Their greatest hits included: "Cuban Love Song" (title song of the film starring Lawrence Tibbett); "Singing the Blues" and "It's the Darndest Thing" (*Singing the Blues*); the ever popular "Don't Blame Me" for the Broadway show *Clowns in Clover;* "Lost in a Fog" and "Thank You for a Lovely Evening," written for the Palais Royale revue; "I'm in the Mood for Love" and "I Feel a Song Comin' On" from the film *Every Night at Eight;* and "Hooray for Love" and "You're an Angel" from *Hooray for Love*. In 1937 McHugh and Fields wrote and appeared in the first stage show produced at the Radio City Music Hall in New York.

JIMMY McHUGH

In 1936 Jimmy McHugh started to write music to Harold Adamson's lyrics. This collaboration began with three songs for the motion picture *Banjo on My Knee*, and continued with a long, rich succession of song hits for the screen: "You're a Sweetheart" for the film of the same name; "I Hit a New High" for the Lily Pons film *Hitting a New High;* "This Is a Lovely Way to Spend an Evening" and "I Couldn't Sleep a Wink Last Night" for the Frank Sinatra film *Higher and Higher;* "Don't Believe Everything You Dream" for *Around the World;* "Where Are You?" for *Top of the Town;* "Picture You Without Me" for the Shirley Temple film *Dimples;* "I Wish We Didn't Have to Say Goodnight" and "I'm in the Middle of Nowhere" for *Something for the Boys;* "Here Comes Heaven Again" and "Dig You Later" for Perry Como's first motion picture, *Doll Face;* "I Walked In with My Eyes Wide Open" for *Nob Hill;* "Life Can Be Beautiful" for *Smash-up;* "My How the Time Goes By" for the Eddie Cantor picture *If You Knew Susie;* and "It's a Most Unusual Day" for Jane Powell in *A Date with Judy*. For four years Jimmy McHugh also wrote many songs for Deanna Durbin's motion pictures.

In 1943 McHugh wrote two outstanding World War II songs, "Comin' In on a Wing and a Prayer" and "Say a Prayer for the Boys Over There," the latter featured in the Deanna Durbin picture *Hers to Hold.* These two songs, with McHugh's active promotion of war bond sales, brought him the Presidential Citation from President Truman in 1947.

Though McHugh proved most productive with Harold Adamson, he did write several outstanding screen songs with other lyricists. With Ted Koehler he composed "I'm Shooting High" and "Lovely Lady" for *King of Burlesque;* and with Frank Loesser he wrote "Let's Get Lost" for *Happy Go Lucky* starring Mary Martin.

McHugh returned to Broadway with *Streets of Paris* (1939), with Al Dubin as his lyricist. It was here that Carmen Miranda introduced another of McHugh's all-time favorites, "South American Way," now a rumba classic. In 1940, again with Dubin, he provided the songs for the musical comedy *Keep Off the Grass.* In 1948, with Harold Adamson, he provided an excellent score for the outstanding musical comedy success *As the Girls Go,* a Mike Todd production. Its principal numbers were "I Got Lucky in the Rain," "Nobody's Heart but Mine," and "You Say the Nicest Things, Baby."

In 1951 McHugh was one of several Hollywood personalities chosen to do a command performance for Queen Elizabeth of England (mother of Elizabeth II). After the show the Queen said to McHugh: "Mr. McHugh, you seem to have written all of my favorite songs; and not only that, but I sing them also."

In the years that followed, McHugh organized an act made up of four beautiful and gifted young singers, which for several years toured the country appearing in night clubs and on television shows. McHugh has also made numerous personal appearances on major television productions featuring his principal song hits. In 1952 he was the subject of a "This Is Your Life" telecast.

In the summer of 1959 McHugh's thirty-fifth anniversary as a composer was celebrated with a concert in the Hollywood Bowl. "Covering a time span from the twenties to the present," said the Los Angeles *Times,* "McHugh's songs have the kind of durability whereby they sound as good as ever today."

Towards the end of 1959 Jimmy McHugh formed his own publishing house, the Jimmy McHugh Publishing Company. Outside of music, he has been active as president of the Beverly Hills Chamber of Commerce and as the founder of the Jimmy McHugh Polio Foundation, now called the Jimmy McHugh Charities.

Since the mid-1950's, Jimmy McHugh has contributed songs to the following successful motion pictures: *The Helen Morgan Story* (1957), *Home Before Dark* (1958), and *Let No Man Write My Epitaph* (1960).

Hugh Martin 1914-

HUGH MARTIN was born in Birmingham, Alabama, on August 11, 1914. He attended the local public schools and Phillips High School, and spent two years at Birmingham-Southern College. When he was five he started to take piano lessons with Edna Gussen at the Birmingham Conservatory. Later he studied piano with Dorsey Whittington.

Though trained as a classical musician, Hugh Martin was inspired by George Gershwin's music to enter the field of popular music. In 1937 he appeared as a singer in the Broadway musical *Hooray for What.* Soon afterwards he put his knowledge of jazz harmony into practice by preparing arrangements for his own vocal quartet, called "The Martins," which included Ralph Blane. This quartet was featured on Fred Allen's radio program and in 1939 in the Irving Berlin musical *Louisiana Purchase.* Martin also functioned as vocal director and arranger for this and other plays, including the Rodgers and Hart musical *The Boys from Syracuse;* Cole Porter's *Du Barry Was a Lady;* Vernon Duke's *Cabin in the Sky; High Button Shoes; Gentlemen Prefer Blondes;* and *Top Banana.*

In 1941 Hugh Martin and Ralph Blane were commissioned to write the complete score for *Best Foot Forward* by Richard Rodgers, an unlisted producer of the play. *Best Foot Forward,* produced by George Abbott, opened on Broadway on October 1, 1941. It starred Nancy Walker in a youthful frolic set in the school town of Winsocki, near Philadelphia. For it Martin and Blane wrote their first important songs, including "Buckle Down, Winsocki" (an outstanding song hit of 1941), "Ev'ry Time," "Wish I May," and "What Do You Think I Am?" In 1942 Martin and Blane were engaged by MGM to go to Hollywood. They wrote the

HUGH MARTIN

songs for the successful *Meet Me in St. Louis,* starring Judy Garland. Its leading musical numbers were "The Trolley Song," "The Boy Next Door," and "Have Yourself a Merry Little Christmas." (In 1960, a stage adaptation of *Meet Me in St. Louis* toured the summer circuit.) Martin and Blane also wrote "Love," which Lena Horne introduced in *Ziegfeld Follies,* and "Pass That Peace Pipe" (*Good News*).

During World War II Martin served with the American armed forces in the European theatre of operation. After his discharge in 1946, he wrote the music and lyrics for another Broadway musical starring Nancy Walker, *Look Ma, I'm Dancin'* (1948). Its score included "Gotta Dance," "I'm Tired of Texas," "Tiny Room," and "I'm the First Girl in the Second Row." In 1951 he wrote the score (lyrics and music) for a musical comedy adaptation of Ferenc Molnar's *The Good Fairy,* entitled *Make a Wish.* "When Does This Feeling Go Away?," "Suits Me Fine," "Who Gives a Sou?" and "The Tour Must Go On" were some of its features.

Hugh Martin has also written scores for several musicals produced in London. The most important of these was *Love from Judy* (1952) in which Jeannie Carson had her first starring role.

In 1950 Martin wrote the music for a motion picture short about Grandma Moses,

from which Alec Wilder prepared an orchestral suite, *The New England Suite.* In 1954 he was vocal director and arranger for the motion picture *A Star Is Born.* Martin has also written the music, or served as vocal director and arranger, for several major television programs. Among these were the Hallmark Hall of Fame program *Hans Brinker or the Silver Skates,* for which he wrote lyrics and music; the series "Washington Square," starring Ray Bolger; and the Patrice Munsel show. In addition, Martin has distinguished himself as a vocal coach for several leading Hollywood stars including Judy Garland, Lena Horne, Nanette Fabray, Rosalind Russell, and Ray Bolger.

Bob Merrill *1921-*

BOB MERRILL was born in Atlantic City, New Jersey, on May 17, 1921. He was raised in Philadelphia, where he attended grade school. As a high school student he often traveled around the country supporting himself by picking up jobs as he went along. He loaded boats and picked crops; he was an usher in movie houses; he did some performances in night clubs. In 1939 he attended the Bucks County Playhouse where he studied acting with Richard Bennett.

From 1940 to 1942 he was in uniform, for a time in the Cavalry, then in Special Services where he wrote and produced radio shows for the armed forces. Immediately after his separation from the service, he hitchhiked to California where he found a job as supervisor of writers at NBC. From 1943 to 1948 he was dialogue director at Columbia Pictures, where he also played some minor roles in several productions. From 1948 to 1949 he was casting director for CBS-TV.

He had been writing popular songs for several years before he scored his first hit, in 1950, with "If I Knew You Were Comin' I'd've Baked a Cake." He wrote the song with Al Hoffman and Clem Watts; Eileen Barton's recording of it sold over a million discs and helped to make it one of the year's outstanding successes. That year Merrill also wrote "Candy and Cake," for which (as for all his later songs) he wrote his own lyrics. In 1951 "Truly, Truly Fair" and "Sparrow in the Tree Top" followed. Subsequent hit

BOB MERRILL

songs included "Doggie in the Window," "Mambo Italiano," and "Honeycomb"; the last sold over a million discs in Jimmie Rodgers' recording. Merrill had no fewer than eighteen songs in the top ten of the Hit Parade between 1950 and 1954.

From 1951 to 1956 Merrill was the television production consultant for Liggett and Myers. In 1956 he signed the first four-way contract ever given by MGM—as producer, composer, writer, and publisher. His initial Hollywood assignment was to prepare a score for a film musical based on Eugene O'Neill's Pulitzer Prize drama *Anna Christie*. The film never materialized, but the idea of making a musical out of *Anna Christie* was born. In George Abbott's skillful stage adaptation, and with music and lyrics by Merrill, the *Anna Christie* musical, called *New Girl in Town*, opened on Broadway on May 14, 1957, starring Gwen Verdon as Anna and featuring Thelma Ritter. Merrill's score included an outstanding ballad, "Sunshine Girl," and other fine numbers—"Look at 'Er," "It's Good to Be Alive," and "Did You Close Your Eyes?"

When Merrill wrote his next score for Broadway it was once more for a musical comedy adaptation of an O'Neill play—the nostalgic American comedy *Ah, Wilderness*. Renamed *Take Me Along*, and starring Jackie Gleason, it opened on Broadway on

October 22, 1959, and was described by Richard Watts, Jr., as "bright, warm-hearted, likable, and filled with talented people." Merrill's best songs were "Promise Me a Rose," "We're Home," and "I Get Embarrassed."

With *Carnival*, which appeared on April 13, 1961, Bob Merrill achieved his greatest Broadway success up to that time. This was a musical-comedy adaptation of the charming motion picture *Lili*, and it starred Anna Maria Alberghetti. *"Carnival,"* reported Richard Watts, Jr., "captures the quality of magic. . . . Its charm, warmth and humor, abetted by a fresh and beautiful production, a delightful cast, a bright and attractive score by Bob Merrill, zestful dances, a colorful background and a pleasant romantic story make it a wonderfully winning and thoroughly enchanting entertainment." Frank Aston summed up: *"Carnival* gets my vote as the best musical of the season." As if in confirmation, the Drama Critics Circle selected it as such. A poll by the first-string New York drama critics picked out Merrill's score as the cream of the theatrical crop. Within that score were found such appealing items as "Love Makes the World Go Round," "A Very Nice Young Man," "Always, Always You," and "Mira."

ABOUT:
Green, Stanley. The World of Musical Comedy.

Theodore Metz *1848-1936*

THEODORE A. METZ was born in Hanover, Germany, on March 14, 1848. He began to take violin lessons at the age of five. He subsequently attended the Hanover Conservatory and completed violin study with Joseph Joachim. After coming to the United States, he settled temporarily in Brooklyn, New York, earning his living as a druggist's assistant while devoting his evenings to musical activities. After moving to Indianapolis, he worked as an instructor in swimming and gymnastics. During this period he took lessons in orchestration from a local conductor, in whose orchestra he soon became concertmaster.

In 1868 Metz went to Chicago, where he labored by day as a builder's assistant, and at night filled engagements as a violinist. He soon started to conduct various bands and orchestras, and at these performances became one of the first to offer ragtime versions of semiclassics. In time he became principal conductor of the minstrel company headed by McIntyre and Heath. It was in this post that, in 1886, he came to write the song by which his name survives, "A Hot Time in the Old Town Tonight" (lyrics by Joe Hayden).

Metz has provided the story of how this song came to be written. During one of the tours of the McIntyre and Heath company, it arrived at a station named Old Town, Louisiana. From his railroad car window, Metz happened to notice a group of young children starting a fire near the tracks. "There'll be a hot time in the Old Town tonight," remarked a minstrel near him. Metz wrote down that sentence on a scrap of paper, intending to use it as the title for some march music. He wrote his march the very next day, and it was soon used in the street parade of the McIntyre and Heath minstrels. It achieved considerable popularity as an instrumental number before lyrics were added to it by Joe Hayden, a singer in the McIntyre and Heath company. In this new version it became a favorite as the opening chorus of minstrel shows everywhere, and in 1896 it was finally published. During the Spanish-American War it was the song most popular with Theodore Roosevelt's Rough Riders; for this reason, the song is most often associated with that war.

Though "A Hot Time in the Old Town Tonight" is Metz's best-known song, he wrote many others during his long and active career, usually to his own lyrics. The most important are "Mother's Dear Old Face," "When the Roses Are in Bloom," "A Warm Baby" (an early example of a ragtime song), "Another Baby," "Never Do Nothin' for Nobody," "Merry Minstrels," "Once Again," "Diana Waltz," "Olympic March," and "One Sweet Smile." He also wrote one operetta, *Poketa*, on an Indian subject, with a libretto by Monroe H. Rosenfeld.

In the 1890's Metz entered the music publishing business in Stamford, Connecticut, later moving these publishing activities to New York City. After World War I, he lived in retirement in New York. When he was eighty-seven he received a stirring ovation at Madison Square Garden, the or-

THEODORE METZ

chestra striking up the strains of "A Hot Time in the Old Town Tonight," in his honor. He died soon after that in New York City, on January 12, 1936.

ABOUT:
Musical America, January 25, 1936; Musical Courier, January 18, 1936.

George W. Meyer 1884-1959

GEORGE W. MEYER was born in Boston, Massachusetts, on January 1, 1884. He taught himself piano while attending public school. His formal education ended when he graduated from Roxbury High School. He worked for several years as an electrician, and then in the accounting department of a Boston store. After moving to New York he was employed by several department stores before he found a position as a song plugger in Tin Pan Alley.

His first published song, "Lonesome," was written in 1909 in collaboration with Kerry Mills and to lyrics by Edgar Leslie; it sold almost a million copies of sheet music. A success of such magnitude with his maiden effort convinced him that songwriting was his forte. He gave up song plugging and devoted himself entirely to composition. Over a period of several years he produced a great many songs. The best of these were "You Taught Me How to Love You, Now Teach

ASCAP

GEORGE W. MEYER

Me to Forget" (lyrics by Jack Drislane and Alfred Bryan); "I'm Awfully Glad I Met You" (lyrics by Drislane); "Somebody Else, It's Always Somebody Else" (lyrics by Drislane); "There's a Dixie Girl Who's Longing for a Yankee Doodle Boy" (lyrics by Robert F. Roden); "That Was Before I Met You" (lyrics by Bryan); "A Ring on the Finger Is Worth Two on the Phone" (lyrics by Jack Mahoney); "Honey-Love" (lyrics by Drislane); "A Girlie Was Made to Love" (lyrics by Joe Goodwin); "Bring Back My Golden Dreams" (lyrics by Bryan); "That Mellow Melody" (lyrics by Sam M. Lewis); and "Dear Old Rose" (lyrics by Drislane).

Despite his prolific output it was not until 1914 that Meyer once again achieved a success of major proportions. It came with "When You're a Long, Long Way from Home" (lyrics by Lewis). This was followed in 1915 by "There's a Little Lane Without a Turning" and "My Mother's Rosary," both to Lewis' lyrics; and in 1916, by "Where Did Robinson Crusoe Go with Friday on Saturday Night?" (lyrics by Lewis and Joe Young), introduced with outstanding success by Al Jolson in his Winter Garden extravaganza, Robinson Crusoe, Jr.

The greatest success of Meyer's career came in 1917 with "For Me and My Gal" (lyrics by Leslie and E. Ray Goetz). It sold over three million copies of sheet music,

and was sung by most of the leading entertainers of the day, including Al Jolson, Belle Baker, Sophie Tucker, Eddie Cantor, and George Jessel. In 1942 "For Me and My Gal" was successfully revived by Judy Garland in a screen musical of the same name.

Among Meyer's most important songs after 1917 were "Everything Is Peaches Down in Georgia," which he wrote in collaboration with Milton Ager to Grant Clarke's lyrics; "Bring Back My Daddy to Me" (lyrics by William Tracey and Howard Johnson); "If He Can Fight Like He Can Love" (lyrics by Clarke and Howard E. Rogers); "In the Land of Beginning Again" (lyrics by Clarke), revived in 1946 by Bing Crosby in the film The Bells of St. Mary's; "Now I Lay Me Down to Sleep" (lyrics by Sidney Mitchell), long used by Bert and Betty Wheeler in their vaudeville act; "Tuck Me to Sleep in My Old 'Tucky Home" (lyrics by Lewis and Young), which sold several million copies of sheet music and a million records; "Brown Eyes, Why Are You Blue?" (lyrics by Bryan); "Sittin' in a Corner" (lyrics by Gus Kahn); "Happy Go Lucky Lane" (lyrics by Lewis and Young); "If I Only Had a Match" (lyrics by Arthur Johnston and Lee Morris), successfully recorded by Al Jolson; and "The Story of Annie Laurie" (lyrics by Young and Peter Wendling).

Meyer also wrote the scores for several Broadway musicals, but none were successful. With the advent of talking pictures he contributed songs to several screen productions, including "If I Can't Have You" (lyrics by Bryan) for Footlights and Fools, "My Song of the Nile" (lyrics by Bryan) for Drag, and "Maybe It's Love" (lyrics by Mitchell) for The Girl from Woolworth's.

From 1939 to 1951 George W. Meyer was a director and secretary of ASCAP. He died as a result of a fire in his hotel room in New York City on August 28, 1959, apparently having fallen asleep while smoking.

Joseph Meyer 1894-

JOSEPH MEYER was born on March 12, 1894, in Modesto, California, where his parents had immigrated from Alsace-Lorraine. In Modesto Joseph attended public school, but at thirteen he left school temporarily to study violin for a year in Paris. After returning to the United States in 1908, he resumed his formal schooling. Upon graduating from high school he followed a mercantile career for a while, but finally abandoned it to study harmony and counterpoint and play violin in a café orchestra in San Francisco. During World War I he served in the United States Army. After the war he was associated with a wholesale dry goods business. But music remained his main interest. After a year in business in San Francisco, he went to New York to pursue an active career in music. His first song, published in 1922, was "My Honey's Lovin' Arms," with lyrics by Herman Ruby. Success was not slow to follow. "California, Here I Come" (lyrics by Buddy De Sylva), was interpolated by Al Jolson into his Winter Garden extravaganza *Bombo* in 1922, and became one of his outstanding hits.

In 1925 Meyer wrote "Clap Hands, Here Comes Charley" (lyrics by Billy Rose and Ballard MacDonald) and "If You Knew Susie" (lyrics by Buddy De Sylva). The latter was intended for Jolson, but after he introduced it without success, Eddie Cantor took it over and made it one of his specialties. (In 1948 the title of the song was used as the name of a screen musical starring Eddie Cantor.) Subsequent hit songs by Meyer included: "A Cup of Coffee, a Sandwich, and You" (lyrics by Rose and Al Dubin), featured on Broadway in *Charlot's Revue of 1925;* "Isn't It Heavenly?" (lyrics by E. Y. Harburg) ; "Falling in Love with You" (lyrics by Benny Davis); "I Wish I Were Twins" (lyrics by Eddie De Lange and Frank Loesser) ; and "Meadows of Heaven" (lyrics by Joseph McCarthy, Jr.).

In 1925 Meyer wrote the complete score for *Big Boy* starring Al Jolson, and in 1929 for *Lady Fingers.* His songs were also interpolated into several other productions. "Crazy Rhythm" (lyrics by Irving Caesar), composed in collaboration with Roger Wolfe Kahn, became a hit number in *Here's Howe* (1928). In 1934 a few of Meyer's songs were presented in the Ziegfeld *Follies.* He wrote special material for Fanny Brice in collaboration with Billy Rose. Several songs were also heard in motion pictures between 1930 and 1935, including *Remote Control, George White's Scandals of 1935,* and

JOSEPH MEYER

Possessed. The best of these numbers were "It's an Old Southern Custom" (lyrics by Jack Yellen) and "According to the Moonlight" (lyrics by Jack Yellen and Herb Magidson) from *George White's Scandals of 1935* and "How Long Will It Last?" (lyrics by Max Leif) from *Possessed.*

Kerry Mills *1869-1948*

FREDERICK ALLEN MILLS, better known as Kerry Mills, was born in Philadelphia, Pennsylvania, on February 1, 1869. From his sixth year on he studied violin with private teachers. In 1892 he became head of the violin department of the University of Michigan School of Music. A year later he opened his own violin studio in Ann Arbor, Michigan, and began to give concerts.

In 1893 he wrote a two-step march in ragtime, *Rastus on Parade,* with which the cakewalk is believed to have first become popular in commercial music. After moving to New York in 1895 and organizing the publishing firm of F. A. Mills, he published this piece, following it with *Happy Days in Dixie* (a minor success in 1896) and *Georgia Camp Meeting* (a major one in 1897). These numbers, particularly *Georgia Camp Meeting,* were influential in popularizing the use of syncopation in Tin Pan Alley. Still another of his highly popular ragtime piano tunes was

Whistling Rufus in 1899, to which W. Murdock Lind later provided lyrics. In an entirely different style were "Let Bygones Be Bygones" (lyrics by Charles Shackford) in 1897, and "Meet Me in St. Louis," a nostalgic waltz written in 1904 for the St. Louis Exposition, of which it became the theme music. "Meet Me in St. Louis" was successfully revived in 1944 for the motion picture of the same name starring Judy Garland. In 1904 Mills also wrote the hit song "When the Bees Are in the Hive" (lyrics by Alfred J. Bryan), and in 1907 came "Take Me Around Again" (lyrics by Ed Rose) and "Red Wing" (lyrics by Thurland Chattaway). The following year he published "Any Old Port in a Storm" (lyrics by Arthur J. Lamb) and "The Longest Way 'Round Is the Sweetest Way Home" (lyrics by Ren Shields).

After World War I Mills devoted himself primarily to his publishing business. He died in Hawthorne, California, on December 5, 1948.

Jimmy Monaco *1885-1945*

JAMES V. MONACO was born in Genoa, Italy, on January 13, 1885. He studied piano by himself. His family came to the United States in 1891 and settled in Chicago. James earned his living playing ragtime music at the Savoy and other Chicago night clubs. In 1910 he went to New York where he performed piano rags at the Bohemia Café on West 29th Street and in several Coney Island saloons. One year after his arrival, "Oh, You Circus Day," his first published song, appeared (lyrics by M. Lessing); it was introduced by Florence Moore and Billy Montgomery in the Broadway musical *Hanky-Panky.* In 1912 he wrote two substantial song hits which established his reputation in Tin Pan Alley. One was "Row, Row, Row" (lyrics by William Jerome), which Lillian Lorraine first made famous in the Ziegfeld *Follies* of 1912; the other, "You Made Me Love You" (lyrics by Joseph McCarthy), a song that twenty-five years later helped to make a star of Judy Garland in the motion picture *Broadway Melody of 1937.*

Monaco's most popular songs in Tin Pan Alley after that included the following: "If We Can't Be the Same Old Sweethearts" (lyrics by McCarthy); "What Do You Want to Make Those Eyes at Me For?" (lyrics by Howard Johnson and McCarthy); "Dirty Hands, Dirty Face" (lyrics by Edgar Leslie and Grant Clarke), an Al Jolson specialty which he featured again in his epoch-making movie *The Jazz Singer;* "Crazy People" (lyrics by Leslie); "You're Gonna Lose Your Gal" (lyrics by Joe Young); "Six Lessons from Madame La Zonga" (lyrics by Charles Newman); "More Now than Ever" (lyrics by Ted Koehler); and "Crying for Joy" (lyrics by Billy Rose).

In 1927 Monaco contributed several songs to the revue *Harry Delmar's Revels,* in which Bert Lahr made his Broadway stage debut. After 1930 Monaco was active in Hollywood where he wrote songs for about fifteen screen musicals. Between 1937 and 1940 his songs, written to Johnny Burke's lyrics, were performed in six screen musicals starring Bing Crosby. The best of these were "My Heart Is Taking Lessons" and "On the Sentimental Side" (*Doctor Rhythm*); "I've Got a Pocketful of Dreams" (*Sing, You Sinners*); "An Apple for the Teacher" (*The Star Maker*); and "Only Forever" (*Rhythm on the River*). For several other successful motion pictures, Monaco wrote music to lyrics by Mack Gordon. Among these songs were "I'm Making Believe" (*Sweet and Low Down*), and "I Can't Begin to Tell You" (*The Dolly Sisters*).

Jimmy Monaco died of a heart attack in Beverly Hills, California, on December 17, 1945.

Theodore F. Morse *1873-1924*

THEODORE F. MORSE was born in Washington, D.C., in 1873. As a boy he studied both violin and piano. When he was fourteen he ran away from the Maryland Military Academy, which he was then attending, to New York. His first job there was as a clerk in a music shop on 125th Street, exchanging his services for room and board. A year later he found a salaried position with the New York branch of Oliver Ditson. While employed there as a salesman, he also played the violin with a trio that performed at weddings and other social events, and devoted his free time to writing instrumental compositions.

In 1897 he formed his own publishing firm in Tin Pan Alley, the Morse Music Company, and immediately placed it on a solid footing by issuing a hit song of the Spanish-American War, "Goodbye, Dolly Gray," written by Will Cobb and Paul Barnes. He sold the firm in 1900, and soon afterwards entered the employ of Howley, Haviland and Dresser. In 1902 he wrote the song "In the Moonlight," which Christie MacDonald featured that year in *The Toreador.* A year later he achieved his first successes as a composer with "Dear Old Girl" (lyrics by Richard Henry Buck) and "Hurray for Baffin's Bay" (lyrics by Vincent Bryan). The latter was introduced by Montgomery and Stone in the Broadway extravaganza *The Wizard of Oz.*

In 1904 Morse became a full partner of the newly formed publishing firm of F. B. Haviland. He also became its principal composer. During the next few years he wrote for his new firm a succession of hits to lyrics by Edward Madden: "Blue Bell," "I've Got a Feelin' for You," "A Little Boy Called Taps," "Nan! Nan! Nan!" "Please Come and Play in My Yard," "Daddy's Little Girl," "Two Little Baby Shoes," "The Leader of the German Band," "Two Blue Eyes," "She Waits by the Deep Blue Sea," and "Starlight."

During this period he worked with other lyricists as well. With Richard H. Buck he wrote "Where the Southern Roses Grow," and with William Cahill, "One Called Mother and the Other Home Sweet Home." With Jack Drislane as his lyricist he was particularly prolific, producing within the span of several years "Arrah Wanna," "The Good Old U.S.A.," "Keep a Little Corner in Your Heart," "Longing for You," "Keep on the Sunny Side," "Nobody's Girl," and "It's Great to be a Soldier."

Still another lyricist with whom he worked was Theodora Terris, his wife. Although the most successful songs for which she created lyrics were written by other composers (with Julian Robeldo she wrote "Three O'Clock in the Morning" and with Ernest Lecuona, "Siboney"), this collaboration is of interest as the first husband-and-wife songwriting team in Tin Pan Alley.

In 1907 and 1908 Morse's best songs were again written to Madden's lyrics; they included "I'd Rather Be a Lobster Than a Wise Guy," "When You Wore a Pinafore," "The Lanky Yankee Boys in Blue," "I've Taken Quite a Fancy to You," "Down in Jungle Town," and "Consolation." Among his later songs were "M-o-t-h-e-r" (lyrics by Howard Johnson) and "We'll Knock the Heligo-Into Heligo-Out of Heligoland" (lyrics by John O'Brien).

Morse also wrote several ragtime tunes to his own lyrics; the best were "Another Rag" (1911) and "When Uncle Joe Plays a Rag on His Old Banjo" (1912).

Paradoxically enough, of his vast song output, what has survived to the present time is not one of his original numbers but an adaptation. In 1917 he borrowed the melody of the "Pirates' Chorus" from *The Pirates of Penzance* by Gilbert and Sullivan for lyrics by his wife (who here utilized the pen name of D. A. Esrom); the result was the still popular ditty "Hail, Hail, the Gang's All Here."

Morse wrote the score for a single Broadway musical production, *Playing the Ponies* (1908), which starred the comedy team of Gus Yorke and Nick Adams.

Theodore F. Morse died in New York City on May 25, 1924.

Lewis F. Muir

BIOGRAPHICAL data on Lewis F. Muir are meager. The date and place of his birth are unknown, as are those of his death. We do know that in 1904 he began his career as a popular musician by playing ragtime in the honky-tonks of St. Louis during the Exposition. Like Irving Berlin after him, he was able to play piano in only one key, but apparently his playing had considerable impact, for he was a favorite with his clientele. After moving to New York, his first hit song was published in 1910, "Play That Barber Shop Chord." Ballard MacDonald wrote the original lyric, but for some unexplained reason William Tracey was called in to revise it, and when the song was issued MacDonald's name was omitted from the printed sheet music. Bert Williams introduced the song in the Ziegfeld *Follies* of 1910 and made it an instantaneous success. So popular did the song become that before long Ballard MacDonald went to the law courts to bring suit against the publishers for having omitted his name from the published music; he was awarded damages of $37,500.

In 1911 Muir created an outstanding ragtime tune in "When Ragtime Rosie Ragged the Rosary" (lyrics by Edgar Leslie). L. Wolfe Gilbert, a lyricist, wrote a scathing review of the song in the New York *Clipper*. Yet, despite his apparently low opinion of both the song and the composer, Gilbert asked Muir to write the music for one of his lyrics which had been inspired by a scene at a levee in Baton Rouge, Louisiana: a group of Negroes unloading freight from a Mississippi River boat, the Robert E. Lee. Muir wrote his music to Gilbert's lyrics in 1912, creating one of the enduring classics of ragtime, "Waiting for the Robert E. Lee." Curiously, when the publisher F. A. Mills first heard Gilbert sing it he turned it down. But when Gilbert returned to the Mills office to pick up some music he had forgotten, the publisher asked him to play it again, and this time he bought it. The song was a sensation. Outstanding stars like Al Jolson, Ruth Roye, and Belle Baker, among many others, sang it on the stage throughout the country.

In 1912 Muir also wrote, with Gilbert, two other fine ragtime tunes: "Here Comes My Daddy Now" and "Mississippi River Steamboat"; and, to lyrics by Maurice Abrahams, "Ragtime Cowboy Joe" and "Hitchy-Koo." Muir was now often found at the offices of his publisher, delighting visitors with his ragtime performances; one of his admirers during this period was the young Irving Berlin. (Muir, like Berlin, had a special mechanism on his piano enabling him to play any composition in the one key of his preference.) L. Wolfe Gilbert recalls: " 'Waiting for the Robert E. Lee' was written in two keys: the verse in C and the chorus in F. If Muir played for you, when you got to the end of the verse, you would have to hold the note until Muir moved the handle under the piano and the entire keyboard moved to the key of F. Then you sang the chorus."

It is generally acknowledged that the ragtime songs of Muir were a powerful influence in creating a vogue for this type of music in England. Albert Decourville, an English pro-

ducer, heard L. Wolfe Gilbert and a vocal group sing Muir's songs in a Coney Island night club called the College Inn. Decourville invited the group to make appearances in London where they were billed as "The Ragtime Octet." Later on, Muir was also invited to London to perform his ragtime music, and he enjoyed an immensely successful engagement at the Oxford Theatre. During his stay in England, Muir completed a score for a London revue, which he wrote in collaboration with Ruggiero Leoncavallo, the composer of the opera *Pagliacci*.

Among Muir's other successful songs were "Mammy Jinny's Jubilee" and "If I Had a Pal," both to Gilbert's lyrics, and "Hicky Koi" to lyrics by Stanley Murphy.

ABOUT:
Gilbert, L. Wolfe. Without Rhyme or Reason.

Alfred Newman *1901-*

ALFRED NEWMAN, one of the most prolific and successful composers for motion pictures, was born in New Haven, Connecticut, on March 17, 1901. He was the oldest of ten children. His mother, recognizing that he was musical, had him start piano lessons when he was five. After an additional period of study with Edward A. Parsons, Newman gave a concert in New Haven to finance his advanced education. Newman continued his studies in New York with Sigismond Stojowski at the Von Ende School of Music; in 1914 he received a silver medal, and a year later a gold medal, for piano playing. He supplemented piano study with lessons in harmony, counterpoint, and composition with Rubin Goldmark and George Wedge. At a later date he studied composition with Arnold Schoenberg for three years.

Newman began supporting himself in his thirteenth year, when he appeared for twelve weeks as piano soloist at the Strand Theatre in New York, performing portions of famous concertos and other concert numbers. After that he worked for a while at Reisenweber's Restaurant. Grace La Rue heard him there and engaged him as her accompanist for a tour of the Keith vaudeville circuit. When Grace La Rue was starred on Broadway in *Hitchy-Koo* of 1916, she arranged for Newman to play the piano in the pit orchestra.

The conductor, William Daly, gave Newman instruction in conducting and persuaded him to consider a career as music director of Broadway productions.

Newman was the conductor for several unsuccessful shows. Then, on George Gershwin's recommendation, he became music director of the George White *Scandals* of 1920 and 1921. He later conducted several successful Broadway musicals, including *Big Boy* starring Al Jolson, Kern's *Criss Cross*, and Gershwin's *Funny Face*.

In 1930 Irving Berlin asked him to assume the musical direction of a motion picture, *Reaching for the Moon*, for which Berlin had written the title song. Newman went out to Hollywood on a three-month contract but decided to remain. When he completed his assignment on *Reaching for the Moon*, he was employed by Samuel Goldwyn as music director of *Whoopee*, starring Eddie Cantor, and then was commissioned to write the background music for *Street Scene*. While working for Goldwyn, Newman also adapted and conducted Charlie Chaplin's music for *City Lights* and *Modern Times*.

After working for several years on the Goldwyn lot, Newman was offered a contract in 1939 to serve as general music director at Twentieth Century-Fox. He held this post twenty-one years. Earlier, in 1935, he had written and recorded the fanfare trademark for Twentieth Century (later Twentieth Century-Fox)—a theme which has been used since that time.

Newman has conducted and/or composed the music for almost two hundred and fifty motion pictures, a record without equal among Hollywood composers. Some of the films for which he served as music director, adapter, and composer of incidental music were Cole Porter's *Born to Dance*; Irving Berlin's *Alexander's Ragtime Band, Call Me Madam*, and *There's No Business Like Show Business*; Kern's *Centennial Summer*; and Rodgers and Hammerstein's *Carousel, The King and I, South Pacific, Flower Drum Song*, and *State Fair*. Newman received Academy Awards for *Alexander's Ragtime Band, Tin Pan Alley, Mother Wore Tights, With a Song in My Heart, Call Me Madam*, and *The King and I*.

Newman also received Academy Awards for his background music for *The Song of*

ALFRED NEWMAN

Bernadette and *Love Is a Many-Splendored Thing*. Other distinguished motion pictures with Newman's dramatic background music were *Wuthering Heights, How Green Was My Valley, The Robe*, and *The Diary of Anne Frank*, the last of which received an Academy Award nomination in 1959 for Newman's scoring.

Alfred Newman has also been highly successful as a composer of popular songs. The first came in the 1920's while he was still working as a Broadway conductor: "Concentrate" and "Voodoo Man," both to lyrics by Otto Harbach. The following are some of his best songs introduced in motion pictures: "The Moon of Manakoora" (lyrics by Frank Loesser) in *The Hurricane*; "Your Kiss" (lyrics by Loesser) and "Someday You'll Find Your Bluebird" (lyrics by Mack Gordon) in *The Bluebird*; "Blue Tahitian Moon" (lyrics by Gordon) in *The Black Swan*; "Through a Long and Sleepless Night" (lyrics by Gordon) in *Come to the Stable*; "Castle in the Sand" (lyrics by Ralph Blane) in *Half Angel*; "Song from Désirée" (lyrics by Ken Darby) in *Désirée*; "The Girl Next Door" (lyrics by Sammy Cahn) in *The Seven Year Itch*, starring Marilyn Monroe; the title song (lyrics by Paul Francis Webster) in *Anastasia*, starring Ingrid Bergman and Yul Brynner; the title song and "Lonely Lover" (lyrics by Cahn) in *The Best of Everything* (the former nominated for an Academy Award in 1959); the title song for *The Pleasure of His Company* (lyrics by Sammy Cahn).

Besides songs, Alfred Newman has contributed successful instrumental numbers for various pictures: *Street Scene* for the film of the same name; *Cathy* for *Wuthering Heights; How Green Was My Valley* for the film of the same name; *The Vision* for *The Song of Bernadette; Pinky* and *The President's Lady* for those films; *Conquest*, a march for *The Captain from Castile;* and *The Diary* and *Love Music* for *The Diary of Anne Frank.*

ABOUT:
Overture, January 1953.

Chauncey Olcott *1858-1932*

CHANCELLOR JOHN OLCOTT, better known as Chauncey Olcott, achieved fame as a singer of Irish ballads in American musicals. But he was also both a lyricist and a composer of popular songs. He was born in Buffalo, New York, on July 21, 1858, and was educated in the city public schools and with the Christian Brothers. His first public appearance was as a singer of ballads at the Academy of Music in Buffalo. In the 1880's he appeared as a blackface minstrel with the Thatcher, Primrose and West

CHAUNCEY OLCOTT

troupe. In 1888 he sang in a vocal quartet featured in Denman Thompson's original production of *The Old Homestead,* and soon thereafter he assumed the leading role in Edward Solomon's *Pepita,* produced by the Lillian Russell Opera Company in Union Square, New York. He went to London in 1890 to study voice and while there made several appearances in light opera. Upon returning to the United States he succeeded the recently deceased actor-singer William J. Scanlan as an Irish singer in musical plays put on by Augustus Pitou to his own librettos. For many of these plays, Olcott wrote the musical score, among them *Minstrel of Clare* (1896), *Sweet Inniscarra* (1897), *A Romance of Athlone* (1899), *Garrett O'Magh* (1901), and *Old Limerick Town* (1902).

Olcott's most famous song was "My Wild Irish Rose," written to his own lyrics, which was heard in *A Romance of Athlone.* Other successful songs included "Olcott's Home Song" from the *Minstrel of Clare;* "Kate O'Donahue," "Old-Fashioned Mother," and the title song from *Sweet Inniscarra;* "Olcott's Lullaby" from *A Romance of Athlone;* and "Voice of the Violet" from *Old Limerick Town.*

Among the later operettas for which Olcott wrote songs were *Edmund Burke* (1905), from which came "Your Heart Alone Must Tell"; *Eileen Asthore* (1906); *O'Neill of Derry* (1907), its principal song being "Every Star Falls in Love with Its Mate"; *Barry of Ballymore* (1911); *Isle o' Dreams* (1912); *Shameen Dhu* (1913); and *Terence* (1914).

Chauncey Olcott was associated for many years and in several different capacities with Ernest R. Ball, the ballad composer. Some of Ball's best-loved songs were introduced by Olcott. In addition, Olcott collaborated with Ball in writing the music for "Mother Machree," which was first heard in *Barry of Ballymore,* starring Olcott, and "I Love the Name of Mary." To Ball's music, Olcott, in collaboration with George Graff, Jr., wrote the lyrics for "When Irish Eyes Are Smiling."

Several more songs by Olcott deserve mention: "In the Sunshine of Your Love," "Goodbye My Emerald Isle," "Day Dreams," "Wearers of the Green," "Laugh with a Tear in It," "Last Love Song," and "Tic-Tac-

Toe." Indicative of his immense popularity as a singer-composer-lyricist was the line in Jean Schwartz's popular song "Bedelia" alluding to Olcott as the object of admiration of all women: "I'll be your Chauncey Olcott."

Olcott suffered a physical collapse while appearing in *The Rivals* in Ann Arbor in 1925. He never recovered his health and was forced to go into retirement. He lived in a chateau in Monte Carlo, where he adopted and helped raise a prodigy pianist. He died in Monte Carlo on March 18, 1932.

Olcott's screen biography, *My Wild Irish Rose*, with Dennis Morgan playing Olcott, was released in 1947.

ABOUT:
Spaeth, Sigmund. A History of Popular Music in America; Witmark, Isidore. From Ragtime to Swingtime.

ASCAP
COLE PORTER

Cole Porter 1893-

COLE ALBERT PORTER was born in Peru, Indiana, on June 9, 1893. The Porters were wealthy, the family fortune having been amassed by Cole's grandfather through speculation in coal and timber. Cole's father was the manager of a seven-hundred-acre fruit farm in Peru and helped to operate his own father's vast holdings.

Cole was directed to music by his mother at an early age. When he was six he took his first lessons on the violin; at eight he began to study piano as well. At the age of ten he wrote the words and music of an operetta, and the following year one of his instrumental compositions, *The Bobolink Waltz*, was published in Chicago.

Porter's grandfather insisted that he be trained for the law. After graduating from the Worcester Academy in Massachusetts, Porter matriculated at Yale in 1909. While pursuing his academic studies he engaged in many musical activities. He sang in, and afterwards conducted, the college glee club, helped to write and produce college shows, and composed two football songs that have retained their popularity, the Yale "Bulldog" song and "Bingo Eli Yale." (Another song, "Bridget," his first to be published, was issued by Remick in 1910.) He was voted by his class "the most entertaining man."

In 1913 he graduated from college and entered Harvard Law School. The Dean of

the Law School, Ezra Ripley Thayer, urged him to give up law for music. As a student in the School of Music, Porter collaborated with Lawrason Riggs on a musical comedy in the style of Gilbert and Sullivan. It was called *America First* and was described on the program as "a patriotic comic opera." It was produced on Broadway in 1916 with Clifton Webb in the leading role, proved a dismal failure, and closed after two weeks.

There followed for Porter a period of travel and adventure during which he joined the Foreign Legion. He carried along a small portable piano, strapped to his back, on which he would accompany himself as he entertained his companions with sprightly songs of his own invention.

When America entered the First World War, Porter was transferred to France and attended the French Officers Training School at Fontainebleau. He was later assigned to teach French gunnery to American soldiers. While stationed at Fontainebleau, he lived in a beautifully furnished apartment in Paris which became a meeting place for the social élite of the French capital. Here he met Linda Lee Thomas, the divorced wife of an American publisher, whom he married when the war ended.

Soon after the war, on board a steamship on a visit to the United States, Porter met

Raymond Hitchcock. Hitchcock at the time produced and starred in an annual series of Broadway revues called *Hitchy-Koo.* While en route, Porter impressed Hitchcock with some of his recent songs and was commissioned to write the music for the next edition of *Hitchy-Koo.* Porter contributed about twelve songs for the *Hitchy-Koo* of 1919; they included "An Old-Fashioned Garden" and "When I Had a Uniform On." (Joe Cook made his New York stage debut in the latter.) Porter always wrote the lyrics as well as the music of his songs.

Porter now established a permanent home on the Rue Monsieur in Paris where he held sumptuous parties regularly. For one of these affairs, Porter engaged the Monte Carlo Ballet to entertain his guests. Sometimes the setting of the festivities was Venice, where the Porters rented the Rezzonico Palace, the place of Robert Browning's death. Sometimes the parties were held on the Riviera. The most honored members of the social and theatrical world were guests —the Princess de Polignac, Noël Coward, the Prince of Wales, Elsa Maxwell, Cecil Beaton. Days and nights were lively with elaborate costume balls, treasure hunts, and similar diversions.

Not the least of the attractions at these gay soirées were the sophisticated and often naughty songs Porter wrote and sang. "You are much too good," Elsa Maxwell once told him. "Your standards are too high. But one day you will haul the public up to your own level and then the world will be yours."

Despite the demands that these social activities placed upon him, Porter continued to write songs and to study music with Vincent d'Indy at the Schola Cantorum in Paris. In 1924 he reentered the Broadway theatre with five songs that were performed in the *Greenwich Village Follies;* none of these attracted interest. But in 1928 he contributed five songs to *Paris,* a sophisticated musical comedy starring Irene Bordoni, and made his first strong impression. Among the hits that made the show a box office success was "Let's Do It," whose lyrics and music captured the sophisticated, cultured, provocative style that would identify him. Even greater recognition heralded Porter in 1929 with *Fifty Million Frenchmen;* its best songs were "You Do Something to Me" and "Find Me a

Primitive Man." ("Let's Do It" and "You Do Something to Me" were revived in 1960 in the motion picture *Can-Can.*) Two subsequent song classics—"What Is This Thing Called Love?" from *Wake Up and Dream* in 1929 and "Love for Sale" from *The New Yorkers* in 1930—established Porter's identity as a lyricist and composer.

Porter maintained an imperial position in the Broadway theatre as lyricist-composer during the next two decades. In the 1930's he wrote the songs for such outstanding musicals as *The Gay Divorce* (1932), *Anything Goes* (1934), *Leave It to Me* (1938), and *Du Barry Was a Lady* (1939).

The Gay Divorce, which opened on November 29, 1932, starred Fred Astaire and Luella Gear and introduced one of Porter's most memorable ballads, "Night and Day." (This title was changed to *The Gay Divorcee* when the musical was adapted for motion pictures.) *Anything Goes* (November 21, 1934) cast Victor Moore as Public Enemy No. 13 disguised as a clergyman, William Gaxton as a dapper playboy, and Ethel Merman as an evangelist turned night club entertainer. Ethel Merman sang "I Get a Kick Out of You," and "Blow, Gabriel, Blow," and presented, with Gaxton, one of Porter's sprightliest patter songs, "You're the Top." *Leave It to Me* (November 9, 1938) was a satire on the Soviet Union, with Victor Moore in the role of a homesick American ambassador. A new star emerged in this production, Mary Martin; her rise to fame was made with one of Porter's most provocative songs, "My Heart Belongs to Daddy." In *Du Barry Was a Lady* (December 6, 1939) Bert Lahr appeared as Louis XV madly pursuing Mme. du Barry, enacted by Ethel Merman. Here Porter's principal numbers were "Do I Love You?," "Katie Went to Haiti," and "Friendship."

During the 1930's several other Broadway stage productions featured Porter's music. Some of these may have been box office failures, but they have been remembered as the showcases for Porter songs—for example, "Begin the Beguine" in *Jubilee* (1935), and "It's De-Lovely" in *Red, Hot and Blue* (1936). "Begin the Beguine" passed unnoticed when it was introduced in *Jubilee* and for a long time was completely forgotten. Then, in the 1940's, it was revived on records in lush orchestrations—the most successful was Artie Shaw's—and it caught on permanently.

On October 30, 1940, Porter was represented on Broadway with still another major box office success in *Panama Hattie*, in which Ethel Merman starred. The impact of World War II on the American way of life was reflected in Porter's next two musicals: *Let's Face It* (October 29, 1941), in which Danny Kaye had his first Broadway starring role, and *Something for the Boys* (January 7, 1943) with Ethel Merman. *Mexican Hayride* (January 28, 1944) was, on the other hand, an escape from war's grim realities. The setting was exotic Mexico, and the heroine was, of all things, a bullfighter. The three best songs from these Broadway productions were "Let's Be Buddies" from *Panama Hattie*, "Everything I Love" from *Let's Face It*, and "I Love You" from *Mexican Hayride*. But the greatest triumph achieved by any Cole Porter song during this period came from Hollywood. It was the cowboy ditty, "Don't Fence Me In," originally written and discarded in 1934, and revived in 1944 by Roy Rogers for the motion picture *Hollywood Canteen*. "Don't Fence Me In" sold several million records and copies of sheet music and for many weeks held first place on the Hit Parade.

Porter's most successful and brilliant musical comedy was *Kiss Me Kate*, which started a Broadway run of over one thousand performances on December 30, 1948. The story, by Bella and Samuel Spewack, involves a contemporary theatrical troupe that is to perform Shakespeare's *The Taming of the Shrew*. The personal lives of the stars are complicated, since they are divorced and have had other amatory involvements; but they are still very much in love with each other. Within the performance of the Shakespeare comedy they manage first to vent their anger against each other and then to achieve a new understanding and reconciliation.

Porter's remarkable score ranged from satire and burlesque to the sentimental and sensuous with startling virtuosity. The main love songs were "So in Love" and "Were Thine That Special Face"; a lighter, merrier spirit was caught in "Wunderbar," "Brush Up Your Shakespeare," "I Hate Men" and "Where Is the Life That Late I Led." Some

of these melodies were admirably adapted by Robert Russell Bennett into a symphonic synthesis.

After its long run on Broadway *Kiss Me Kate* enjoyed a highly successful national tour and then was made into a motion picture. It was also acclaimed in Europe. At the Volksoper in Vienna it proved to be the greatest hit in the more than fifty-year history of that theatre; in Poland, where it was the first American musical ever given, it played two hundred times to sold-out houses.

Porter's subsequent Broadway musicals were *Can-Can* (1953) and *Silk Stockings* (1955). The former, set in the Bohemian Paris of 1893, was highlighted by songs with a distinctly Parisian air, such as "I Love Paris," "C'est Magnifique," and "Allez-vous En." *Silk Stockings* was a musical comedy adaptation of a famous motion picture satire on the Soviet Union, *Ninotchka*, which had starred Greta Garbo. Here the most important songs were "Paris Loves Lovers" and "All of You."

Porter has also written a great number of songs for motion pictures. The most important are "I've Got You Under My Skin" for *Born to Dance;* "In the Still of the Night" *(Rosalie);* "You'd Be So Nice to Come Home To" *(Something to Shout About);* and "True Love" *(High Society)*. The last was introduced by Bing Crosby and Grace Kelly. In 1946 Porter's screen biography, entitled *Night and Day*, was released. It starred Cary Grant as the composer and presented a cavalcade of fourteen of Porter's most famous songs of stage and screen.

Most of Porter's best writing took place under conditions of intense suffering. As far back as 1937, while riding horseback on Long Island, he had suffered a serious accident in which his legs were crushed and his nerve tissues seriously damaged. Over a period of many years he underwent more than thirty operations in an effort to save his legs. For more than two years he had to be hospitalized, and for five years he was confined to a wheelchair. Finally, in 1958, his right leg was amputated.

On May 15, 1960, the Metropolitan Opera House in New York presented a magnificent "salute to Cole Porter," sponsored by ASCAP, in which several of America's foremost songwriters and some of Broadway's most luminous stars participated. Cole Porter, confined to his apartment in the Waldorf Towers after the amputation of his leg, could not attend. On June 9, 1960, Yale University conferred an honorary degree on Porter. The occasion shattered tradition since the degree was bestowed at a private ceremony in his own apartment.

ABOUT:
Lounsberry, Fred, editor. 103 Lyrics by Cole Porter.

New Yorker, January 29, 1949; Newsweek, May 18, 1953; New York Times Magazine, February 20, 1955; Theatre Arts, July 1955.

André Previn *1929-*

ANDRÉ PREVIN was born in Berlin, Germany, on April 6, 1929. As a child in Germany he was a student at the Berlin Conservatory for two years. He came to the United States in 1938 (he was naturalized in 1943) and while attending elementary school and high school in Los Angeles studied composition first with Joseph Achron and then with Mario Castelnuovo-Tedesco. Previn was still in high school when the MGM studios engaged him to arrange the score for *Holiday in Mexico,* a screen musical starring José Iturbi, At nineteen he was offered a contract as a composer-conductor for MGM, a post he held until 1960. During his stay at MGM he also performed various assignments

ANDRÉ PREVIN

while on loan to other studios. Since 1960 he has been a free-lance composer.

Previn has been one of Hollywood's most prominent and gifted composers. He has written the background music for more than thirty motion pictures, including *Bad Day at Black Rock, Invitation to the Dance, Designing Woman, House of Numbers, Who Was That Lady?, The Subterraneans, Elmer Gantry,* and *The Four Horsemen of the Apocalypse.* He has been music director for many outstanding screen musicals. The best were *Three Little Words* (the screen biography of the songwriting team of Ruby and Kalmar); Cole Porter's *Kiss Me Kate* and *Silk Stockings; Kismet;* Lerner and Loewe's *Gigi;* the elaborate Samuel Goldwyn production of Gershwin's opera *Porgy and Bess;* Styne's *Bells Are Ringing,* with Judy Holliday; and the screen adaptation of *Irma la Douce.* He was twice honored with Academy Awards for scoring: for *Gigi* and (with Ken Darby) for *Porgy and Bess.* In addition he received the Screen Composers Association Award for *Invitation to the Dance,* and the Berlin Film Festival Award for *Bad Day at Black Rock.*

Previn has written the complete scores for two important screen musicals: *It's Always Fair Weather,* for which Betty Comden and Adolph Green wrote the lyrics; and *Pepe* (lyrics by Previn's wife, Dory Langdon). From *It's Always Fair Weather* have come "Time for Parting," "Thanks a Lot but No Thanks," "I Like Myself," and "Music Is Better than Words." The main songs from *Pepe* are "The Far-Away Part of Town" (nominated for an Academy Award in 1961), "That's How It Went All Right," and "The Rumble."

Other significant songs by Previn include the following: "Why Are We Afraid?" (lyrics by Langdon) from *The Subterraneans;* the title song from *Designing Woman* (lyrics by Jack Brooks); "Lost in a Summer Night" (lyrics by Milton Raskin) from *Hot Summer Night;* "Your Smile" (lyrics by Langdon) from *Who Was That Lady?;* and the title song from *Tall Story* (lyrics by Langdon). With his wife as lyricist, Previn has written some notable songs which were not intended for the screen but which were recorded by Judy Garland, Eileen Farrell, and Doris Day, among others. These include: "Yes," "Control Yourself," "River Shallow," "Mine for the Moment," and "Like Love." Previn has recorded for Columbia Records some of his best instrumental numbers, among which are *Touch of Elegance, Lost Letter, When Will I Hear From You?* and *Where I Wonder.* Previn was the music director of the Academy Award festivities in Hollywood in 1960 and 1961.

Previn has been active as pianist in both concert and jazz performances. He has been a soloist with most of the major American orchestras and has made numerous television appearances. He became interested in jazz after hearing performances by Art Tatum and made his first jazz records in 1945. He has since made a number of appearances and has performed on records with Shelly Manne (drums), and Red Mitchell (bass). "His jazz manner," said *Time,* "is all his own: a fanciful, highly individualistic style, characterized by kaleidoscopic rhythmic shifts, triple-hammered treble runs and a discreetly swinging left hand punctuated by sudden stops and breaks." On six different occasions Previn has been recipient of *Downbeat* Awards for his jazz performances.

Previn has also been active as a conductor and as a lecturer and teacher at the University of California in Los Angeles. As a composer of concert music he has produced two symphonies, a string quartet, a cello sonata, a flute quintet, and numerous compositions for piano solo.

ABOUT:
Time, April 20, 1959.

Ralph Rainger *1901-1942*

R ALPH RAINGER was born on New York City's East Side on October 7, 1901. He began to take piano lessons early; when he was thirteen he started to study theory and composition from texts. While attending high school in Newark, New Jersey, he helped support himself by playing the piano for school dances. A scholarship brought him to the Institute of Musical Art in New York. After he had attended that school for about a year, his father insisted he give up all thoughts of becoming a professional musician. He entered law school, earned a degree, and then worked as a clerk in a New

York law firm for twenty-five dollars a week. But law bored him. For a while he found escape from routine by playing the piano at night with a dance orchestra. Finally, in 1926, he gave up law for good. His first permanent job in music was as rehearsal pianist, then as pianist in the pit orchestra, for the Broadway musical *Queen High.* After that show closed, he was hired as accompanist for the touring vaudeville act of Clifton Webb and Mary Hay.

In 1929 Webb was engaged as one of the stars of a new, intimate, and sophisticated Broadway revue called the *Little Show.* Webb found Rainger a job as pianist in the pit orchestra. During rehearsals, it was found that a number was needed for Webb. Rainger wrote it for him—"Moanin' Low" (lyrics by Howard Dietz)—and it became one of the smash song hits of the show. This was Rainger's first song in a Broadway musical, his first published song, and his first hit. A year later he had a second hit, though of lesser proportions, in "I'll Take an Option on You" (lyrics by Leo Robin), featured in the Broadway revue *Tattle Tales.*

Between 1930 and 1942 Ralph Rainger was a staff composer for Paramount Pictures. To Leo Robin's lyrics he produced songs for almost fifty motion pictures, the most successful of these being the following: "Love in Bloom" for *She Loves Me Not,* which starred Bing Crosby (the song subsequently became Jack Benny's theme music on radio and television) ; "June in January," for another Bing Crosby musical, *Here Is My Heart;* and "Thanks for the Memory," Bob Hope's radio and television theme music, which Hope himself introduced in *The Big Broadcast of 1938* and which received an Academy Award.

Among other songs written by Rainger for the screen are "Do I Love You?" from *Shoot the Works;* "I'm Talking Through My Heart" and "La Bomba" from *The Big Broadcast of 1937;* "Blue Hawaii" and "Sweet Is the Word for You," the latter to Harry Owens' lyrics, from *Waikiki Wedding,* starring Bing Crosby; "What Goes On Here in My Heart?" from *Give Me a Sailor,* with Bob Hope; and "You're a Sweet Little Headache" from the Bing Crosby picture *Paris Honeymoon.*

Ralph Rainger died in an airplane crash on October 23, 1942.

Harry Revel *1905-1958*

HARRY REVEL was born in London on December 21, 1905. He began to study the piano when he was nine and continued his musical education during his boyhood in Germany and Austria. When he was fifteen he became a member of a Hawaiian group in Paris, a group with which he remained for two years. While working with this ensemble he wrote "Oriental Eyes," a song published in Italy. He then joined the New York Jazz Band, a European group which toured the leading capitals of the Continent. During a stay in Berlin, Revel wrote the music for a German operetta, *Was Frauen Traumen.* (This was his first association with the stage.) In 1925 he gave a command performance as pianist for the royal family of Italy, and in 1928 he contributed several songs to *Charlot's Revue* in London. An admirer of American popular music—and particularly of the music of Gershwin, Kern, and Berlin—he wrote several songs in which both the melodies and the lyrics had a pronounced American flavor even though he had never visited the United States. The most successful was "I'm Going Back Again to Old Nebraska," which was published in London and sold over a million copies.

In 1929 Revel finally arrived in the United States, where he established permanent residence and became a citizen. A meeting with Mack Gordon, a vaudevillian and part-time lyricist, was decisive for him. For a while, Revel toured the vaudeville circuit as Gordon's accompanist. Then they started writing songs —Revel the music and Gordon the lyrics. This collaboration flourished for many years and brought Revel his greatest successes.

In 1931 Gordon and Revel were engaged by Florenz Ziegfeld to write several songs for the last edition of the *Follies* produced by Ziegfeld himself; two of their more interesting numbers from this production were "Help Yourself to Happiness" and "Sunny Southern Belle." In the same year (1931) they also wrote music for a Negro revue, *Fast and Furious.* In 1932 their songs were heard in *Smiling Faces,* in which Fred and Dorothy Stone were starred, and *Marching By.*

During 1932 they also wrote their first successful independent songs: "Underneath the Harlem Moon," "Listen to the German

Band," "A Boy and a Girl Were Dancing," and "It's Within Your Power." In 1933 they wrote "An Orchid to You," dedicated to Walter Winchell in gratitude for the frequent mentions of their songs made by Winchell in his newspaper column.

Their most formidable song hits were written in Hollywood, where they arrived in 1933 to write music for *Sitting Pretty;* in this screen musical can be found their first resounding Hollywood success, "Did You Ever See a Dream Walking?" After that they wrote songs for all of Shirley Temple's motion pictures in the 1930's, as well as for many other important films. Among their leading motion picture songs were "You're My Past, Present and Future" and "Doin' the Uptown Lowdown" for *Broadway Through a Keyhole;* "With My Eyes Wide Open I'm Dreaming" for *Shoot the Works;* "Stay As Sweet As You Are" for *College Rhythm;* "Love Thy Neighbor," "May I?" and "Good Night, My Love" for *We're Not Dressing,* starring Bing Crosby; "Don't Let It Bother You" for *The Gay Divorcee;* "The Words Are in My Heart" and "From the Top of Your Head to the Tip of Your Toes" for *Two for Tonight;* "The Loveliness of You" for *Love in Bloom;* and the title song for *Paris in the Spring.* The last four songs were released in 1935, a year in which Gordon and Revel received nine awards from ASCAP for as many songs.

Other distinguished songs written for later motion pictures by Gordon and Revel included "When I'm with You" and "A Star Fell Out of Heaven" for the Shirley Temple picture *The Poor Little Rich Girl;* "May I Have the Next Romance with You?" for *Head Over Heels in Love;* "I Feel Like a Feather in the Breeze" for *Collegiate;* "There's a Lull in My Life," "Never in a Million Years," and the title song for *Wake Up and Live.*

The partnership of Gordon and Revel was dissolved during the early part of World War II. Revel devoted himself to war work, supervising the USO unit in Hollywood, organizing stage shows touring hospitals and military bases, and editing a magazine for hospitalized veterans.

In 1945 Revel returned to the Broadway stage to write the music, to Arnold B. Horwitt's lyrics, for the musical comedy *Are*

You With It? He also continued producing songs for the screen, principally to lyrics by Paul Francis Webster. But he did not confine his activity exclusively to stage and screen. He created therapeutic music recorded by Capitol Records—albums like *Music Out of the Moon* and *Music for Peace of Mind;* and he wrote, on a commission from Corday Parfums, an orchestral suite entitled *Perfume Set to Music,* which was introduced at Carnegie Hall, New York, in the spring of 1954. He was also director of his own music publishing firm in New York.

Revel was fatally stricken with a cerebral hemorrhage in New York City on November 3, 1958.

Richard Rodgers *1902-*

R ICHARD CHARLES RODGERS was born in Hammels Station, near Arverne, Long Island, on June 28, 1902. He was the younger son of Dr. William Rodgers, a successful general practitioner, and Mamie Rodgers, an excellent amateur pianist. Dick gravitated to music naturally and inevitably. He started to piece out little melodies on the piano when he was four, and at six began to take formal piano lessons with his aunt. He was continually at the piano, improvising, creating little tunes of his own, trying to reproduce the Broadway songs his father sang repeatedly. His passion for music was equaled only by his enthusiasm for the musical theatre, which he began to attend when he was six. His interest, initially aroused by the operettas of Victor Herbert, was further stimulated by Jerome Kern's musical comedies.

Richard attended elementary school in New York City, and he sometimes played the piano at assemblies. At his graduation exercises at P.S. 166 in 1916, he performed a potpourri of opera melodies which he had adapted himself. In summer he went to a boys' camp in Maine; it was there that in 1916 he wrote his first songs, "Campfire Days" and "The Auto Show Girl." While at De Witt Clinton High School he not only continued to write songs but also started to attend symphony concerts and operas.

In 1917 a club to which his brother belonged planned an amateur musical production at the Hotel Plaza. Dick was recruited to

RICHARD RODGERS

write the music. Thus Rodgers' bow as a composer for the stage took place with his seven songs for *One Minute Please,* which was performed on December 29, 1917.

He wrote songs for two other amateur productions. One took place at the Waldorf-Astoria Hotel in 1919, on which occasion Rodgers also made his first attempt at conducting. The other was given at the 44th Street Theatre in New York for the benefit of the Soldiers and Sailors Welfare Fund.

Up to this point Rodgers had written his music to the lyrics of several individuals, including his brother, or friends of the family. In 1918 he was introduced to Lorenz Hart, a creative young man who had attended Columbia College and had translated German operetta librettos into English. Hart's ambition was to be a lyricist; and he had definite and unique ideas on how an intelligent and sophisticated song lyric should be written. Young Rodgers and Hart hit it off well from the very first meeting, "It was a case of love at first sight," Rodgers later recalled. "In one afternoon I acquired a career, a partner, a best friend—and a source of permanent irritation."

In a few weeks they wrote about fifteen songs. One was "Any Old Place with You," which was interpolated into a Broadway musical comedy, *A Lonely Romeo* (August 26, 1919). That fall Rodgers entered Columbia

College. In Rodgers' first year he and Hart (who had left Columbia) wrote the college Varsity show, *Fly with Me* (produced at the Hotel Astor on March 24, 1920); it was the first time that the work of a freshman had been accepted for these productions. "We had not heard of Richard Rodgers before," reported S. Jay Kaufman in the New York *Globe*. Then he added prophetically: "We have a suspicion we shall hear of him again."

Rodgers' music for this Varsity show made such a deep impression on the noted Broadway actor and producer Lew Fields (one-time partner in the comedy team of Weber and Fields) that he invited Rodgers and Hart to contribute some songs to one of his Broadway musicals. Rodgers and Hart wrote seven songs for *The Poor Little Ritz Girl*, which opened on Broadway on July 28, 1920. (The remaining eight songs were by a veteran Broadway composer, Sigmund Romberg.) Rodgers' songs elicited the following comment from H. T. Parker, the noted Boston music and drama critic: "He writes uniformly with a light hand; now and then with neat modulations or pretty voices; and once again with a hint of grace and fancy."

It was several years before Rodgers and Hart appeared again in the Broadway theatre. Meanwhile they accepted any assignment that came along, usually from amateur groups. But the Broadway producers and the publishers in Tin Pan Alley remained aloof. Impelled partly by discouragement, partly by a need for more training, Rodgers entered the Institute of Musical Art in New York in 1922. He remained for two years, studying harmony, counterpoint, theory, and music appreciation; on three occasions he helped to prepare the school's annual musical productions.

After this period of study, Rodgers resumed his songwriting with Hart, mainly for shows put on by a private school for girls in New York. In 1924 they also were able to find a producer for *The Melody Man*, a play which they had written in collaboration with Herbert Fields. It ran for fifty-six performances.

Rodgers was about to give up songwriting and the theatre to work as a salesman for a children's underwear firm when he and Hart were asked to take part in the presentation of an intimate and sophisticated revue planned by some of the younger members of the Theatre Guild. The immediate aim of this revue was to raise the money for two tapestries to be hung in the Guild's new 52nd Street theatre, which was under construction. *The Garrick Gaieties*, as this revue was called, was originally intended for two performances on May 17 and 18, 1925. But the critics' accolades and the audience's enthusiasm were so strong that the show was scheduled for a regular run. Seven songs by Rodgers and Hart were featured in it. One was the still popular "Manhattan"; another was "Sentimental Me." "They clicked," reported *Variety*, "like a colonel's heels at attention."

The Garrick Gaieties marked the beginning of Rodgers' success on Broadway. From then on his fame and success would reach higher peaks. With Herbert Fields as librettist and Lorenz Hart as lyricist, Richard Rodgers helped to bring to the Broadway stage some of the freshest, most imaginative, and most exciting musical productions of the 1920's. *Dearest Enemy* (September 18, 1925) was based on an episode from the Revolutionary War: Mrs. Robert Murray detains British officers at her home on Murray Hill long enough to allow the Continental Army to make a strategic and safe withdrawal. For this play Rodgers and Hart wrote the remarkable ballad "Here in My Arms." *The Girl Friend* (March 17, 1926) was a more intimate musical whose vivacious score included the lively title song, and "Blue Room." Both were among the leading song hits of that year. *Peggy-Ann* (December 27, 1926) was a brilliant and daring experiment in dream fantasies, carried out not only in the text but also in the choreography and in much of the mood music for several dream sequences. For *A Connecticut Yankee* (November 3, 1927) the authors went to Mark Twain, bringing to this famous story some of the wittiest lines, breeziest lyrics, most infectious melodies the musical stage of the 1920's could boast. One of these Rodgers and Hart songs which became a formidable hit, "My Heart Stood Still," was not written directly for this production but was taken over from a London revue produced by Charles Cochran for which Rodgers and Hart had written the score. *Present Arms* (April 26, 1928) was most notable for its songs—"the most beautiful element in the production," according to Brooks Atkinson; and the best of these was "You Took Advantage of Me." *Chee-Chee* (September 25, 1928) may have been a box office disaster, but it was nonetheless a significant experiment in the musical play as opposed to musical comedy—in integrating book and music into a single artistic effort. So basic were the songs and instrumental episodes to the action that no attempt was made to list the separate numbers in the program. The main importance of *Spring Is Here* (March 11, 1929) is that it became the frame for one of Rodgers and Hart's song classics, "With a Song in My Heart." *Simple Simon* (February 18, 1930), in which Ed Wynn starred, introduced still another of their musical gems, "Ten Cents a Dance." And *America's Sweetheart* (February 10, 1931), a satire on Hollywood, had still another musical delight in "I've Got Five Dollars."

Rodgers and Hart left the Broadway scene for about five years after *America's Sweetheart*. During this period they worked in Hollywood, writing for several delightful motion pictures. The most important of these films was *Love Me Tonight*, in which Maurice Chevalier starred; its best songs included "Mimi," "Isn't It Romantic?" and "Lover." They also wrote songs for pictures starring Bing Crosby, George M. Cohan, and Al Jolson. But what was perhaps their best song during this Hollywood period never reached the screen. "Blue Moon," which had been written to two different sets of lyrics and with different titles for two motion pictures only to be discarded, was finally published as an independent number. The sheet music sale of this song was greater than any thus far achieved by Rodgers and Hart—over a million copies.

In 1936 Rodgers and Hart returned to Broadway with *Jumbo*, an elaborate circus spectacle produced at the Hippodrome by Billy Rose. For this mammoth production Rodgers created one of his best scores, which included the intoxicating waltzes "The Most Beautiful Girl in the World" and "Little Girl Blue," and the unforgettable ballad "My Romance."

From this time on, Rodgers and Hart grew increasingly venturesome in their choice of texts and materials for musical comedy;

in so doing they helped to create a rich new epoch for the American musical theatre. As Hart told an interviewer at that time, both he and Rodgers envisioned "a new form of musical show. It will not be musical comedy and it will not be operetta. The songs are going to be part of the progress of the piece, not extraneous interludes without rhyme or reason." During this period Rodgers said: "I should like to free myself for broader motifs, more extended designs—but within the framework of the theatre."

On Your Toes (April 11, 1936)—with book by Rodgers and Hart in collaboration with George Abbott—explored the world of ballet. Since the plot involved dancers as principal characters and the terpsichorean world as a background, ballet was made basic to the story. One such sequence brought the play to a dramatic climax. Called "Slaughter on Tenth Avenue," it was a satire on gangsters expressed in modern American dance terms. For this episode Rodgers wrote an ambitious jazz score, one of his finest achievements in a symphonic medium. In a more traditional song form, Rodgers composed the charming "There's a Small Hotel," and an effective ballad, "Quiet Night." Hart's increasing virtuosity in writing sophisticated lyrics was demonstrated in "Too Good for the Average Man" and "The Three B's."

Babes in Arms (April 14, 1937)—with book by Rodgers and Hart—was a play within a play. In it the children of traveling vaudevillians put on their own show at their home on Long Island in order to keep out of work camp while their parents are away. This musical was a "zestful, tuneful and brilliantly danced affair," as John Mason Brown reported, "filled with talented striplings and bubbling over with the freshness and energy of youth." The production also overflowed with wonderful songs: "Where or When?" "My Funny Valentine," "The Lady Is a Tramp," "I Wish I Were in Love Again," "Johnny One Note," and "All at Once."

In *I'd Rather Be Right* (November 2, 1937), for which George S. Kaufman and Moss Hart contributed the book, Rodgers and Hart ventured for the first time into the realm of politics. George M. Cohan played the part of a President of the United States who bears a striking resemblance to Franklin D. Roosevelt. He appears in the hero's dream to solve the young man's personal problem: the hero wants to get married but he can't afford to do so without a raise, and a raise will not be forthcoming unless the national budget is balanced. Within the dream, the President promises to do all he can to balance the budget but encounters all kinds of political and social problems in the attempt. At the end, the President advises the hero to get married without his raise, advice the hero follows eagerly when he awakens the following morning. Within this framework the authors found ample opportunity to mock the New Deal, federal subsidized theatre, taxes, laws, labor, the "brain trust," and other political and social problems of the 1930's. The songs also had a pronounced political slant, and were so inextricably wedded to the action of the play that they had little interest apart from the text. The single exception was "Have You Met Miss Jones?"

I Married an Angel (May 11, 1938) was a delightful fantasy adapted by Rodgers and Hart from a play by John Vaszary. A man disillusioned with women marries an angel who comes flying through the window; but he soon discovers that being married to an angel has its shortcomings. With Vera Zorina, a famous ballerina, as the star, the production placed a strong accent on ballet. The choreography was created by Georges Balanchine. The ballet music and two extended musical episodes revealed greater spaciousness in Rodgers' musical thinking. The main songs were the title number and "Spring Is Here."

The Boys from Syracuse (November 23, 1938) was the first attempt in the popular American musical theatre to adapt Shakespeare. This broad travesty filled with bawdy episodes was a George Abbott adaptation of Shakespeare's *A Comedy of Errors*. The waltz "Falling in Love with Love" was its most important song.

The most unconventional of all the Rodgers and Hart musicals was *Pal Joey*, based on John O'Hara's sketches, which opened on Broadway on December 25, 1940. Never before had American musical comedy attempted to depict such disreputable characters or questionable activities. This was realistic musical theatre on an adult level, and the same bold approach was found in its principal song, "Bewitched, Bothered and Bewildered." Another song hit was the ballad "I Could Write a Book." When *Pal Joey* was revived on Broadway in 1952, it had the longest run of any New York stage revival.

The last of the Rodgers and Hart musicals was *By Jupiter* (June 2, 1942), based on J. F. Thompson's *The Warrior's Husband*. A substantial box office success, this musical marked the end of the Rodgers and Hart collaboration. (They were involved in one more effort after that, a 1943 revival of *A Connecticut Yankee*, for which they wrote several new numbers, including "To Keep My Love Alive.")

Lorenz Hart had never been easy to work with. Erratic, unreliable, undisciplined, he preferred to do tomorrow what should be done today. To keep him at any given task at a given time was a task to try the patience of a saint. In the last years of his collaboration with Rodgers, Hart's lackadaisical ways and irresponsibility grew into a general disintegration of health and spirit. He started to drink and to lose all interest in his work and career. By 1943 it became apparent to Rodgers he would have to seek a new lyricist if he wished to continue functioning as a composer for the stage. (Hart died on November 22, 1943. His fabulous songwriting career with Rodgers was dramatized posthumously in the motion picture *Words and Music*, released in 1948, with Tom Drake portraying Rodgers and Mickey Rooney as Hart.)

Rich as had been the achievement of Rodgers with Hart, an even more eventful epoch was to unfold for him after 1943 with a new collaborator, Oscar Hammerstein II. Indeed, their very first stage effort became a red-letter day for the American theatre: *Oklahoma!*, a folk play with music, adapted from a Theatre Guild play by Lynn Riggs, *Green Grow the Lilacs*. Here was the goal toward which Rodgers and Hart had been reaching for so many years: a musical play in which every element was basic to the artistic whole, in which the clichés, formulas, and the long-established rituals of musical comedy were abandoned for fresh, new, imaginative procedures. In place of a hackneyed love situation set against a stilted background, *Oklahoma!* provided a story rich in dramatic interest and vibrant in characterization. Formal dance and chorus girl routines were replaced by Western folk ballets conceived by Agnes De Mille; comedy was used only when it evolved naturally from the characters or action; tragedy and even murder were not avoided, since they were essential to the plot. And every bit of music—songs, dances, instrumental interludes—was intrinsic in the texture of the play and contributed to the dramatic action.

Oklahoma! opened at the St. James Theatre on March 31, 1943. Almost everyone connected with the production had prophesied it would be a box office fiasco—too highbrow and off-beat for public consumption, too artistic to provide entertainment for tired business men. But the critics were enchanted. Lewis Nichols described it as a "folk opera," and John Anderson said of it that it was "beautiful . . . delightful . . . fresh . . . imaginative." The next morning queues formed outside the theatre; and crowds continued to come until *Oklahoma!* achieved the longest run of any musical in Broadway history up to that time—2,248 performances over a five-year period, with a gross profit of seven million dollars. A national company was on tour for ten years, and the original New York company also toured seventy cities in fifty-one weeks. In ten years, almost thirteen million Americans had paid more than forty million dollars to see this play. It was also presented with sensational results in the capitals of Europe, the Union of South Africa, and Australia; in London it had the longest run in the three-hundred-year history of the Drury Lane Theatre. *Oklahoma!* was given a special award by the Pulitzer Prize Committee; the original-cast recording, the first recording ever made of the complete score of a musical, sold over a million albums; and in 1955 a motion picture version in the new Todd-AO process was released. Each investor of fifteen hundred dollars in the original production earned over fifty thousand dollars; the Theatre Guild earned over four million dollars in profit; and Rodgers and Hammerstein earned over a million dollars each.

Stimulated by the poetry and humanity of Oscar Hammerstein's dialogue and lyrics, Richard Rodgers revealed new depth and warmth in his writing. With a simple, economical approach, Rodgers produced songs with the flavor of American folk music: "Oh, What a Beautiful Mornin' " and "The Surrey with the Fringe on Top." To other songs he brought a lyrical glow and a sensitive emotion rarely encountered before in his music, as in "Many a New Day," "Out of My Dreams" and "People Will Say We're in Love," the last a hit song in 1944. And in numerous orchestral episodes and interludes, and in the ballet sequences, his writing revealed a new symphonic dimension.

On the strength of their success with *Oklahoma!* Rodgers and Hammerstein formed their own music publishing firm (named Williamson Music, Inc., because the fathers of both Rodgers and Hammerstein had been called William), and their own producing organization. In 1944 they also accepted a contract from Hollywood to write songs for *State Fair*, one of which—"It Might as Well Be Spring"—received the Academy Award in 1946. Another substantial hit from this picture was "It's a Grand Night for Singing."

Oklahoma! was succeeded on April 19, 1945, by *Carousel*. "This is the most glorious of the Rodgers and Hammerstein works," Brooks Atkinson has written. "*Carousel* is a masterpiece that grows in stature through the years." This musical was an adaptation of Ferenc Molnar's Theatre Guild play *Liliom*, with its setting transferred from Budapest to the New England of 1873, and some basic changes in plot structure. The opulent Rodgers score included the extended narrative "Soliloquy"; the love duet "If I Loved You"; a spiritual ballad, "You'll Never Walk Alone"; and the idyll "June Is Bustin' Out All Over." A waltz prelude of symphonic proportions, played under the opening scene, further demonstrated the composer's growing breadth of style; and the song "What's the Use of Wond'rin'?" reflected a heightened lyrical expressiveness. *Carousel* has often been revived, and in 1958 it was chosen to represent the American theatre at the World's Fair in Brussels.

Allegro, which opened on October 10, 1947, was more interesting as an experiment than as a musical play. The text, by Oscar Hammerstein II, traced the biography of a physician through various stages in his successful career to his final renunciation of materialism and empty living. Many of the biographical episodes were told by means of ballets or extended vocal and choral sections. Lights and colors were used to point up moods and emotions, while much of the action took place on an empty stage. A kind of Greek chorus was employed to comment on what was happening—sometimes in song, sometimes in speech. Although Robert Coleman described *Allegro* as a "stunning blending of beauty, integrity, imagination, taste and skill," *Allegro* did not succeed at the box office, and it has never been revived. Two of Rodgers' songs have survived: "A Fellow Needs a Girl" and "The Gentleman Is a Dope."

South Pacific, which followed on April 7, 1949, is undoubtedly one of the glories of our musical theatre, a critical and box office success of the first magnitude. It was based on James A. Michener's Pulitzer Prize-winning book of World War II stories, *Tales of the South Pacific;* the adaptation was made by Oscar Hammerstein II in collaboration with Joshua Logan, and it opened with Ezio Pinza and Mary Martin in the starring roles. *South Pacific* was hailed by the critics; Howard Barnes described it as a "show of rare enchantment, novel in texture, rich in dramatic substance, and eloquent in song." It won its audiences just as decisively. Its run of 1,925 performances on Broadway and its gross profit of nine million dollars made stage history. The national company toured for several years; the sheet music sold several million copies; the original-cast long-playing recording of the entire score sold more than a million copies. In addition, *South Pacific* received the Pulitzer Prize for drama in 1950, the Drama Critics Award, seven Toni Awards, and nine Donaldson Awards. Some of the songs that made *South Pacific* a delight were "Some Enchanted Evening," "I'm Gonna Wash That Man Right Outa My Hair," "This Nearly Was Mine," "I'm in Love with a Wonderful Guy," "Bali Ha'i," "Younger than Springtime" and "There Is Nothing Like a Dame."

Never the ones to follow a set pattern, Rodgers and Hammerstein created a completely different kind of musical play after *South Pacific.* Named *The King and I,* this musical was based on Margaret Landon's book *Anna and the King of Siam.* The setting was exotic Siam, the characters Oriental except for the heroine. A climactic point in the story was reached with a ballet conceived by Jerome Robbins; in it the story of *Uncle Tom's Cabin* was retold in terms of the Siamese dance against a rhythmic background produced by wood block and ancient cymbals and the spoken commentary of a chorus.

The King and I opened on Broadway on March 29, 1951, with Yul Brynner as the king and Gertrude Lawrence as the Welsh schoolmistress. It was an unqualified triumph, a "flowering of all the arts of the theatre with moments . . . that are pure genius," as Danton Walker wrote. Rodgers' music, occasionally tinted with Oriental hues, was beautifully in spirit with the entire production; yet it never lost the popular touch. One of the best numbers was the king's narrative "A Puzzlement," and one of the most eloquent songs was Anna's ballad "Hello, Young Lovers." Other appealing musical moments included the orchestral march of the royal Siamese children, "I Whistle a Happy Tune," "Getting to Know You," "We Kiss in the Shadow," "Shall We Dance?" and "I Have Dreamed."

Two lesser Rodgers and Hammerstein productions followed, neither one a success. *Me and Juliet* (1953) was concerned with the backstage life of a company producing a musical comedy. *Pipe Dream* (1955), based on a novel by John Steinbeck, was set in Cannery Row in California and involved a strange assortment of characters including the proprietress of a brothel, an indigent scientist, a girl vagrant, and a group of misfits who inhabit a flophouse. A few musical episodes from each of these plays are worth mentioning: "No Other Love," and an eloquent narrative about theatre audiences entitled "The Big, Black Giant," from *Me and Juliet;* and "Everybody's Got a Home but Me" and "All at Once You Love Her" from *Pipe Dream.*

Rodgers and Hammerstein recovered their stride with *Flower-Drum Song* in 1958 and *The Sound of Music* in 1959, both outstanding box office attractions, although critical opinion was divided about their artistic merit. *Flower-Drum Song,* based on a novel by C. Y. Lee, was more of a musical comedy than a musical play. Set in San Francisco's Chinatown, and devoted to the conflict of interests and viewpoints between East and West, between the older and younger generations of Chinese immigrants, *Flower-Drum Song* was great entertainment. It featured a buck-and-wing dance, a strip tease, and pert Pat Suzuki singing "I Enjoy Being a Girl."

The Sound of Music—the story of the Trapp Family Singers and specifically of Baroness von Trapp—was criticized by some as leaning too heavily upon operetta traditions. With Mary Martin as its heroine, it flooded the theatre with gladness, warmth, gaiety, and charm. Rodgers' writing displayed remarkable resiliency, ranging from the polyphonic style demanded by the church scenes to the peasant style of Austrian folk music. "Do, Re, Mi," the title song, "My Favorite Things" provided a contrast of grace, charm, and sweetness to other more emotionally compelling and dramatic musical sequences, as, for example, "Climb Every Mountain."

Most of the Rodgers and Hammerstein musical plays have been made into highly successful motion pictures. *Oklahoma!* was the first film to be made in the Todd-AO process. *South Pacific,* according to a tabulation in *Variety* in 1961, accumulated the sixth highest gross in the United States and Canada in the history of motion pictures, over sixteen million dollars.

With *The Sound of Music,* the historic partnership of Rodgers and Hammerstein came to an end: Oscar Hammerstein II died of cancer at his home in Doylestown, Pennsylvania, on August 23, 1960. In 1961 Rodgers became his own lyricist in several new songs for a screen remake of the old Rodgers and Hammerstein motion picture musical *State Fair.*

In the spring of 1961 Richard Rodgers and Alan Jay Lerner announced that they would collaborate on a new musical play scheduled for production some time in 1962 or 1963. Meanwhile, Richard Rodgers completed both the music and the lyrics for still another musical, *No Strings,* with a text by Samuel Taylor based on an idea suggested by Rodgers. Set in Paris, it centers on the romance of a Negro model and a white author.

In addition to their stage productions and their one Hollywood assignment, Rodgers and Hammerstein wrote a musical play for television: *Cinderella,* which starred Julie Andrews over the CBS-TV network on March 31, 1957.

Rodgers' output also includes a number of other works. He composed the music for a ballet, *Ghost Town,* introduced by the Ballet Russe de Monte Carlo in New York on November 12, 1939. In 1952 he wrote the background music for a series of documentary films on World War II naval operations, collectively entitled *Victory at Sea.* For these twenty-six half-hour installments Rodgers' score was thirteen hours long. The television series was first presented over NBC in 1952 and received the George Foster Peabody Citation and the Sylvania Award. "Hardly enough can be said for the score of Mr. Rodgers," reported Jack Gould in the New York *Times.* "His work has a compelling beauty and vigor that adds incalculably to the emotional intensity of the series." Robert Russell Bennett adapted the best pages of this score into a nine-movement orchestral suite that has been recorded and performed by many important American symphony orchestras. Two of the most popular excerpts from this suite are the stirring "Guadalcanal March" and a seductive tango melody which Rodgers borrowed for his song "No Other Love" in *Me and Juliet.*

In 1960 Rodgers wrote the background music for still another monumental television series, produced in 1960-1961—a documentary based on the career of Sir Winston Churchill, *Winston Churchill: The Valiant Years.*

Rodgers has been the recipient of numerous honors, as befits a composer who has dominated the American popular musical theatre and popular music world for more than forty years. He received the Medal of Excellence from Columbia University in 1949, the Award of the Hundred Year Association in 1950, the Distinguished Public Service Award from the United States Navy in 1953, and the Alexander Hamilton Award of Columbia College in 1956. In 1955 the Library of Congress presented in Washington, D.C., an exhibit of his manuscripts together with other documents and photographs relating to his career and achievements; only once before—with a Stephen Foster exhibit —had the Library of Congress paid this homage to a popular composer.

Rodgers' daughter, Mary, is also a composer of popular music. Her musical comedy *Once upon a Mattress* received a highly successful off-Broadway production in 1959; it was moved to Broadway for an extended run, after which it went on the road.

ABOUT:
Ewen, David. *Richard Rodgers*; Rodgers, Richard, editor. *The Rodgers and Hammerstein Song Book*; Rodgers, Richard, editor. *The Rodgers and Hart Song Book*; Taylor, Deems. *Some Enchanted Evenings.*
Harper's Magazine, August 1953; Ladies' Home Journal, November 1950; New York Times Magazine, March 18, 1951; New Yorker, May 28, June 4, 1938; November 18, 1961.

Sigmund Romberg *1887-1951*

SIGMUND ROMBERG, last in the royal line of American operetta composers that began with De Koven and Victor Herbert, was born in the Hungarian town of Szeged on July 29, 1887. His father was a gifted amateur in music and a bon vivant, his mother a poet and short-story writer. Soon after Sigmund was born, his family moved to the town of Belisce where his father became the director of a factory. It was there that the boy's musical training was begun: the violin when he was six, and the piano two years after that. The child's absorption with music gave his parents considerable concern since they did not want him to divert his energies and interests from the preparation for some practical profession. The one they finally selected for him was engineering. For his preliminary education, Sigmund was enrolled in the Osiek Realschule, where his interest in music was kept alive by one of the professors who directed the school orchestra. When this professor heard Romberg play the violin he waived an existing rule forbidding students to join the orchestra before their fifth school year.

After five years at the Realschule, Romberg was transferred in quick succession to two other preparatory schools. At the first he became a member of the orchestra and played the organ at church services; at the second, he wrote his first piece of music to be performed, a march dedicated to the Grand Duchess, patroness of a local Red Cross drive, who used her influence to have Romberg conduct it with an orchestra formed especially for the town's Red Cross celebration.

Romberg completed his engineering studies at the Politechnische Hochschule in Vienna. The excitement and adventure of Vienna's musical life infected Romberg. He began to study composition and harmony with Victor Heuberger; was a frequent visitor to the salon of Albert Gruenfeld, an eminent Viennese musician; attended every opera, concert, or operetta he could afford. A friend enabled him to gain admission backstage at the Theater-an-der-Wien where he could watch for hours rehearsals of operettas. For a brief period he even found employment in that theatre as assistant stage manager.

After receiving his degree in engineering, Romberg was compelled to enter military service. He joined the 19th Hungarian Infantry Regiment stationed in Vienna and served for a year and a half. By the time he had completed his military commitments, he had become convinced that he wanted to be a musician. He also became convinced that if he were to make his way in music it would have to be in a center of music-making with far less competition from brilliant musicians than Vienna. He was thinking specifically of New York.

In his twenty-second year he arrived in the United States. His entire financial resources consisted of $300. His first job in New York was in a pencil factory at a wage of seven dollars a week. While wandering the streets of New York in search of some musical job, he found a café on Second Avenue in need of a house pianist. He was hired for fifteen dollars a week. From there he went on to the Pabst-Harlem Restaurant where, within a short period of time, he was earning forty-five dollars a week. By 1912 he was hired by Bustanoby's, one of New York's finest restaurants. His job was to conduct an orchestra in salon and light music. One day he decided upon an innovation: the inclusion, in his nightly program, of popular American music meant for social dancing. Despite the fact that during that period dancing was virtually unknown in restaurants, this innovation caught on and made Bustanoby's a favored rendezvous. Business thrived; Romberg's weekly salary leaped to one hundred fifty dollars a week. He supplemented his conducting duties with the writing of his own American dance music. Three of these compositions were published in Tin Pan Alley: "Leg of Mutton" and "Some Smoke," both of these one-steps, and a waltz entitled "Le Poème."

When Louis Hirsch resigned as staff composer for the Shuberts, J. J. Shubert hired Romberg as a replacement. The first Broadway musical for which Romberg supplied the music was *The Whirl of the World,* a Winter Garden extravaganza in 1914 starring the Dolly Sisters and Eugene and Willie Howard. From then on, Romberg was kept busy writing music for many Shubert productions. By 1917 he had written 275 numbers for 17 musicals, including several editions of *The Passing Show,* several extravaganzas starring Al Jolson at the Winter Garden, and an operetta in a Continental style, *The Blue Paradise* (1915), for which he wrote his first famous song, "Auf Wiedersehen" (lyrics by Herbert Reynolds).

Though Romberg continued writing music for the Shuberts—revues, musical comedies, extravaganzas—it was with operettas in the European tradition that he soon achieved his identity as a composer and his first major successes. *Maytime,* produced on August 16, 1917, had for its setting eighteenth century New York; nevertheless, it was thoroughly European in style and approach. It was such an outstanding box office success that within a year of its Broadway opening a second company was formed to present it in a nearby theatre, the first such occurrence on Broadway. Its principal song was the lilting waltz "Will You Remember?" (lyrics by Rida Johnson Young), now a Romberg standard.

After *Maytime,* Romberg contributed several scores for traditional Broadway musical comedies and revues, including several starring Al Jolson and Fred and Adele Astaire, among others. During World War I, Romberg served in the United States Army; his assignment was to write music for army shows and to travel from one camp to another entertaining the troops. After the war, Romberg briefly tried his hand at producing Broadway musicals but, after two dismal failures, decided to concentrate on composition.

His next Broadway triumph arrived on September 29, 1921—*Blossom Time,* adapted

SIGMUND ROMBERG   ASCAP

from a German operetta and freely based on the life and music of Franz Schubert. With Schubert's beloved melodies as his point of departure, Romberg created an outstanding score, to lyrics by Dorothy Donnelly. Its greatest hit was "Song of Love," the principal melody derived from the *Unfinished Symphony.* Other delightful Romberg songs derived from Schubert's melodies included "Three Little Maids," "Tell Me Daisy," "Lonely Heart," and "My Springtime Thou Art." So successful was *Blossom Time* that besides a Broadway run of almost six hundred performances it boasted no fewer than four road companies traveling simultaneously.

After that, Romberg's most famous operettas were *The Student Prince* (which opened December 2, 1924), *The Desert Song* (November 30, 1926), and *The New Moon* (September 19, 1928).

The Student Prince (like *Blossom Time*) came from a successful German operetta, rewritten for American consumption. The setting is Heidelberg, Germany, in 1860. The principal characters are a German prince and a Heidelberg waitress with whom he falls in love but whom he must finally desert for reasons of state. The score was one of the best of Romberg's career, featuring "Deep in My Heart," "Serenade," "Golden Days," and the vigorous male chorus, "Drinking Song." All the lyrics were by Dorothy Donnelly, who was also responsible for the American text.

The Desert Song was a homegrown product, with book and lyrics by Otto Harbach, Oscar Hammerstein II, and Frank Mandel. But it was still an operetta, with an exotic setting (French Morocco) and colorful storybook characters (a bandit chief, the Caid of the Riff tribe, the governor of a French Moroccan province, and so forth). "Pageantry, romance, ringing music, vitality and humor," as one critic reported, were the strong points of this play. The "ringing music" could be found in two stirring choruses, "Sabre Song" and "French Marching Song." In a more romantic vein were two beautiful love songs, "One Alone" and the title number.

The New Moon, the last of the great Romberg operettas, was based on the historical character of Robert Mission, a French aristocrat of the eighteenth century living in New Orleans. There were three outstanding sentimental numbers in the Romberg score, written to lyrics by Oscar Hammerstein II: "Lover Come Back to Me" (its main melody taken by Romberg from a piano piece by Tchaikowsky), "One Kiss," and "Softly as in a Morning Sunrise." The score also boasted a rousing, virile number in "Stout-Hearted Men."

Romberg went to Hollywood in 1929 on his first screen assignment, *Viennese Nights.* He continued to write songs for the screen for the next few years, but only one matched the success and the durability of his best numbers for Broadway: "When I Grow Too Old to Dream" in *The Night Is Young.*

Soon after Pearl Harbor, the William Morris Agency prevailed on Romberg to form an orchestra and tour the country in performances of semiclassical music. The first tour began in Baltimore on October 20, 1942. This tour and the two that followed resulted in deficits. But a fourth tour, which began with a Carnegie Hall concert on September 10, 1943, broke attendance records in several cities. Henceforth these concerts, billed as "An Evening with Sigmund Romberg," were an assured success wherever given.

In the last years of his life Romberg enjoyed one more major success on the Broadway stage—but this time with an American musical comedy rather than a European operetta. *Up in Central Park,* which opened on January 27, 1945, had a fourteen-month run on Broadway before embarking on an extended nation-wide tour and being adapted for motion pictures. With the background of New York in the 1870's, during the rule of the infamous Tweed Ring, this musical proved to be a tender and nostalgic recollection of a bygone era. Romberg's songs (lyrics by Dorothy Fields) were the strong suit of this winning production. The most successful were "Carousel in the Park" and "Close as Pages in a Book." Another powerful asset to the production was an ice-skating ballet against a Currier and Ives background, with choreography by Helen Tamiris.

Sigmund Romberg died in New York City on November 9, 1951. Just before his death he had completed the score for his last musical comedy, *The Girl in Pink Tights,* produced posthumously on March 5, 1954. With a plot based upon the production of *The Black Crook* in New York in 1866, *The Girl in Pink Tights* missed fire completely. "A curious air of heaviness hung over the proceedings," remarked Richard Watts, Jr., sadly. Nevertheless a few ingratiating moments could be found in two Romberg songs (lyrics by Leo Robin): "Up in the Elevated Railway" and "Lost in Loveliness."

After Romberg's death, his screen biography was produced by MGM and released in 1954. It was called *Deep in My Heart* and starred José Ferrer as the composer.

ABOUT:
Arnold, Elliott. Deep in My Heart.
International Musician, November 1950; Music Journal, September 1954; Opera and Concert, April 1947.

Harold Rome 1908-

HAROLD ROME was born in Hartford, Connecticut, on May 27, 1908. He attended public schools and Trinity College in his native city and received his bachelor of arts degree from Yale in 1929. For two years he attended Yale Law School, but in 1930 decided upon architecture as a career and completed his training at the Yale School of Architecture in 1934. At school he helped support himself by playing the piano in dance bands and for dancing classes. He also wrote some music for several organizations and was a member of the Yale Band, with which he toured Europe. Though music was a major interest and though he had taken courses in it while in college, it did not occur to Rome at that time to enter the field professionally.

Equipped with a B.F.A. degree, Rome went to New York in 1934 to seek a job as an architect. The Depression was then at its lowest point and such jobs were few and far between. He compromised by accepting a post with a WPA Project for $23.80 a week. After that he worked for a well-known New York architect who promised him valuable experience but no salary. Rome now had to find some way of earning a living until architecture paid. Since music was the only field outside architecture for which he had some aptitude, he turned to it for an income. He began to write songs, sometimes the melody, sometimes the lyrics, sometimes both. Gypsy Rose Lee commissioned a song from him. Another of his numbers was used by the Ritz Brothers in one of their motion pictures. When he discovered that writing songs was more profitable than architecture, he decided to concentrate on music exclusively. While waiting for success, he worked for several summers at Green Mansions, an adult camp in the Adirondacks, for whose weekly stage productions he wrote songs, sketches, and other material, besides playing the piano at times in the pit orchestra. Meanwhile he had continued to study music in New York with various private teachers—piano with Arthur Lloyd and Loma Roberts, and composition with Joseph Schillinger, Lehman Engel, and Meyer Kupferman.

His songs attracted the interest of Louis Schaeffer, of the International Ladies' Garment Workers' Union. That union was in the process of producing a musical revue with a cast composed entirely of union members and material slanted politically and socially. Schaeffer asked Rome to write the songs and to assist in the over-all production. Named *Pins and Needles,* the revue opened in New York on November 27, 1937, for what had been planned as a limited run. It stayed on in New York for 1,108 performances—the longest run of any revue in

HAROLD ROME

Broadway history. With its trenchant and satirical commentary on the political and social problems of the day, *Pins and Needles* was an exciting experience in musical theatre, a "Puckish proletarian romp" as the New York *Post* described it. Fascism and Big Business were attacked with laughter and ridicule; unionism was glorified; the working man's pleasures were sentimentalized. Rome's songs (for which he wrote lyrics as well as music) included "Sunday in the Park," which won an ASCAP award in 1937. Another of his songs set the tone for the entire production: "Sing Me a Song of Social Significance."

Pins and Needles established Rome's reputation as a composer-lyricist. In 1938 Max Gordon offered him a contract to write the songs for another politically conscious revue, *Sing Out the News.* One of Rome's best political numbers was featured in this production, "Franklin D. Roosevelt Jones," for which he again won an ASCAP award. In 1940 Rome contributed songs to the revue *Streets of Paris* and the entire score for *The Little Dog Laughed.* In 1942 he contributed to still another revue with a social theme, *Let Freedom Ring.*

When World War II broke out, Rome created material for a series of revues collectively entitled *Lunchtime Follies* which were given in defense plants. He also had some of his songs and special material interpolated into *Star and Garter* (1942) and the Ziegfeld *Follies* of 1943.

In 1943 Rome entered the army and for a time was stationed at the New York Port of Embarkation in the office of Special Services. His assignment was to write material for army shows as well as orientation songs. One of his productions, *Stars and Gripes*, toured army camps in the United States and combat areas in the Pacific. Another, *Skirts*, was produced in England.

After his discharge from the armed forces in 1945, Rome wrote the music and lyrics for one of the most successful revues produced on Broadway in the postwar era: *Call Me Mister*, which began a run of 734 performances on April 18, 1946. The hit song was "South America, Take It Away," with which Betty Garrett became a star. Another successful number, but in a more sentimental vein, was "The Face on the Dime," a moving tribute to President Roosevelt.

In 1950 Rome wrote songs for two more revues, Mike Todd's *Peep Show* and *Bless You All*. His first significant attempt to write music and lyrics for a musical comedy was *Wish You Were Here*, a major success which opened on June 25, 1952. This was a musical comedy adaptation of Arthur Kober's stage comedy *Having Wonderful Time*. The title song of *Wish You Were Here* was one of the outstanding hit songs of the year. (Rome had previously written the scores for several musical comedies that expired before reaching New York. Out of one of these, however, came a highly successful song, "Money, Money, Money.")

Rome's next two Broadway musical comedies were also substantial successes: *Fanny* (November 4, 1954) and *Destry Rides Again* (April 23, 1959). *Fanny*, starring Ezio Pinza, was a tender and sensitive musical comedy adaptation of Marcel Pagnol's trilogy of plays: *Marius, Fanny*, and *César*. Rome's score was the most ambitious he had yet written. It included the poignant idylls "Fanny" and "Love Is a Very Light Thing"; several numbers that provided a penetrating insight into the characters who sang them; and music of symphonic stature for the ballet episodes. *Fanny* was successfully produced in Munich, Germany, in 1955. When *Fanny* was made into a motion picture, none of

Rome's songs was retained with the exception of the title number, used as background music.

Destry Rides Again, with Andy Griffith, was a "Western musical" based on a story of Max Brand which had previously been used for a motion picture starring James Stewart and Marlene Dietrich. "Beginning with a razzle-dazzle overture," reported Brooks Atkinson, "Mr. Rome has written an entertaining score in the traditional mood of cowboy music with some ragtime flourishes for the saloon festivities." Its most notable musical numbers were "Anyone Would Love You," "Ballad of the Gun," and "I Know Your Kind."

In 1961 Rome completed the score for a new musical comedy, *I Can Get It For You Wholesale*, adapted from Jerome Weidman's best-selling novel.

Rome wrote an album for children, "Sing Song Man," recorded for Decca by Frank Luther. He also made several albums in which he sang his own songs to his own accompaniment; one of these, "Harold Rome Sings *Fanny*," on the Heritage label, won the music critics' award as one of the ten best "pop" albums of the year.

ABOUT:

Ewen, David. Complete Book of the American Musical Theater; Green, Stanley. The World of Musical Comedy.

George Frederick Root *1820-1895*

GEORGE FREDERICK ROOT was born in Sheffield, Massachusetts, on August 30, 1820. After receiving some musical training from George J. Webb in Boston, he went to New York in 1845 and there taught music at the Abbott Institute for Young Ladies and played the organ at the Church of the Strangers. In 1850 he spent a year traveling and studying music in Europe. Upon returning to the United States he devoted himself to music education, assisting Lowell Mason at the Academy of Music in Boston and later helping to found the New York Normal Institute, which trained music teachers.

He started to write popular songs (lyrics as well as music) in 1851, publishing them under the pen-name of "Wurzel" (the German word *Wurzel* being a translation of *root*). His first success was "The Hazel Dell," published in 1853. Two years later he had an even more substantial success in the sentimental ballad "Rosalie, the Prairie Flower." Root offered to sell "Rosalie" outright to his publishers for one hundred dollars, but they felt that the sale of the sheet music would be limited and preferred to offer royalty payments—an arrangement which eventually brought the composer several thousand dollars. Other songs written by Root during this period included "Flee as a Bird" (lyrics by Mary S. B. Dana) and "There's Music in the Air" (lyrics by Frances Jane Crosby). The latter became popular as a college song many years later. Root's highly successful evangelical hymn "The Shining Shore" was written to verses by the Reverend David Nelson.

Root went to Chicago in 1859 and worked at the music publishing house of Root and Cady, which his older brother had founded a year earlier. When the Civil War broke out, Root directed his songwriting activity into martial channels, creating both the lyrics and the music. His first war song, "The First Gun Is Fired" was a failure. But with his second war song, in 1863, he achieved immortality; the song was "The Battle Cry of Freedom."

"The Battle Cry of Freedom" was inspired by President Lincoln's second call for volunteers. One day, a singing duo, Frank and Jules Lombard, came into the shop of Root and Cady to choose some war song for presentation that evening at a rally in the Chicago Court House Square. Root showed them the manuscript of his newly completed song and the Lombards accepted it immediately. They scored such a success with it that evening that, at one point, the audience joined spontaneously in singing a repetition of the refrain. "The Battle Cry of Freedom" then entered into the permanent repertory of the Hutchinsons, a famous singing troupe that helped to popularize the song throughout the North. The song also became a strong favorite with soldiers everywhere, putting "as much spirit and cheer into the army" (as one enthusiastic Union soldier maintained) "as did a splendid victory; day and night you could hear it by every campfire and in every tent."

Root wrote several more Civil War songs that have survived to the present time. These include three highly effective sentimental bal-

GEORGE FREDERICK ROOT

lads: "Just Before the Battle, Mother" (which, during the war, was almost as popular in the South as it was in the North), "Tramp, Tramp, Tramp," and "The Vacant Chair." "Just After the Battle" was a sequel to "Just Before the Battle" and "On, On, On the Boys Came Marching" a sequel to "Tramp, Tramp, Tramp."

After the Civil War, Root continued to work for Root and Cady. In 1872 the degree of doctor of music was conferred on him by the University of Chicago. He died on Bailey Island, Maine, on August 6, 1895.

ABOUT:

Root, George Frederick. Story of a Musical Life; Thompson, David. Songs That My Mother Used to Sing.

Notes, June 1944-1946.

David Rose 1910-

DAVID ROSE was born in London on June 15, 1910. He was only four when his family came to the United States and settled in Chicago. There he attended public elementary school and high school and received his musical training at the Chicago Musical College. After that he became arranger and pianist for the local radio outlet of NBC and pianist for the Ted Fiorito orchestra.

In 1938 he went to Hollywood, where he became affiliated with the Mutual network as

DAVID ROSE

music director. During World War II he served for four years with the Air Force. In 1943 he was music director of, and composer of the music for, Moss Hart's Air Force production, *Winged Victory*. In the same year he wrote and published an outstandingly successful instrumental composition which is still his most famous single work —*Holiday for Strings*. It caught on immediately, was heard extensively over the radio, was recorded by a dozen different companies, and in time sold several million records.

After the war, Rose returned to Hollywood to resume his professional career as a conductor of radio orchestras. He became the first to employ the echo chamber not only on radio but also in recordings. Since then, he has been uniquely active and prominent as a music director on radio, television, and records and as a composer of background music for motion pictures. Among the many important television programs on which he has served as music director are the Red Skelton show, the Fred Astaire shows (for the first Rose received an "Emmy" award), the Bob Hope show, the Dean Martin show. Among the many motion pictures for which he has contributed either the scoring or the background music are *Everything I Have Is Yours, Young Man in a Hurry, Young and Pretty, Jupiter's Darling, Operation Petticoat*, and *Please Don't Eat the Daisies*.

Among Rose's most popular instrumental compositions in a popular style, besides *Holiday for Strings,* are *Our Waltz, Dance of the Spanish Onion, Nostalgia,* and *Holiday for Trombones.* Most of these are now considered "standards." A national survey in 1959 revealed that David Rose's instrumental music was being used as theme songs for twenty-two different television programs including "Highway Patrol," "Sea Hunt," and "Bonanza." He has been honored by the BBC in London with a special David Rose Tribute Show featuring these compositions. He has also written many popular piano pieces.

Rose is the composer of such successful popular songs as "One Love," "Once Upon a Lullaby," and "Just in Love." The last (lyrics by Leo Robin) was heard in the film *Wonder Man,* starring Danny Kaye, and was nominated for an Academy Award.

Rose has appeared extensively as a guest conductor of major orchestras in the United States, Paris, Berlin, Copenhagen, and Rome. In May 1960 he undertook a six-week tour of Japan as a conductor.

Harry Ruby 1895-

HARRY RUBY was born Harry Rubinstein on the lower East Side of New York City on January 27, 1895. He was the fourth of six children. As a boy his main interest was baseball, a passion that has remained with him to the present time. "I went to bat against the great Walter Johnson in 1931 in an exhibition game between the Washington Senators and the Baltimore Orioles," he writes. "I also played in a few major league exhibition games, and in four official games in the Coast League with the Hollywood Stars and Los Angeles Angels. All this, you will admit, is more than Mozart, Berlin, Gershwin, and Chopin can say."

In his boyhood his days were spent in the city streets and on sand lots playing ball, much to the detriment of his school studies, which he detested. He continually played hooky and was continually brought to task by his teachers for failing to show interest in his work. Nevertheless, he managed to complete elementary school and attended high school for a short time. He also managed to teach himself to play the piano. When he was sixteen he was earning five dollars a week and board by playing the piano in a trio performing at a resort in Long Branch, New Jersey.

His father wanted him to study medicine, but Ruby knew he was no scholar. In fact he was politely "invited" to leave the High School of Commerce after thirty days, and Mount Morris High School after only two, because of his complete apathy to the activities of the classroom. When he refused to consider medicine as a career, a compromise was reached by having him study commercial subjects in a business school. After four months in two different business schools, Ruby abandoned his education for good. (Much later in life, Ruby became an avid bibliophile and a passionate reader of literature and books on science.)

He soon found a job as staff pianist and song plugger in the publishing house of Gus Edwards in Tin Pan Alley. Sometimes assisted by young Walter Winchell (then also a song plugger) he would visit the Woolworth stores in the city to demonstrate the songs of his firm. After that, Ruby worked as a song plugger for Harry Von Tilzer in restaurants and rathskellers; played the piano for illustrated song slides then being featured in motion picture houses; appeared in vaudeville with the Messenger Boys Trio; performed in nickelodeons in an act called Edwards and Ruby (the "Edwards" in this act later became the powerful Hollywood executive Harry Cohn).

While working as a song plugger for the firm of Kalmar and Puck, Ruby met and became a friend of one of the two partners, Bert Kalmar. Kalmar was a successful vaudevillian who spent some of his free time writing song lyrics. When a knee injury compelled Kalmar to retire from the stage, he decided to devote himself seriously to lyrics and induced Ruby to write the music for them. One of their first efforts was "He Sits Around," performed in vaudeville by Belle Baker.

Between 1917 and 1920 Ruby wrote several important songs with other lyricists: "When Those Sweet Hawaiian Babies Roll Their Eyes" and "Come on Papa" (lyrics by Edgar Leslie); "What'll We Do Saturday Night When the Town Goes Dry?" (his own lyrics); "Daddy Long Legs" (lyrics by Sam

HARRY RUBY

Lewis and Joe Young); "And He'd Say 'Oo-La-La Wee-Wee'" (lyrics by George Jessel). But in 1920 he resumed working with Kalmar, with whom, during the next few years, he wrote many outstanding hits: "So Long Oo Long," "Timbuctoo," "She's Mine, All Mine," "Where Do They Go When They Row, Row, Row?," "The Vamp from East Broadway" (written in collaboration with Irving Berlin and introduced by Fanny Brice in the Ziegfeld *Follies* of 1920), "My Sunny Tennessee" (which sold a million and a half records and a million copies of sheet music), and "I Gave You Up Just Before You Threw Me Down" (lyrics by Ruby and Kalmar to Fred Ahlert's music). For "Who's Sorry Now?," a leading song hit of 1923, Ruby and Kalmar wrote the lyrics to Ted Snyder's music.

Now leading figures in Tin Pan Alley, Ruby and Kalmar were offered contracts to write songs for the Broadway theatre. Their first musical comedy was *Helen of Troy, New York,* a satire on advertising and the business world with book by George S. Kaufman and Marc Connelly. Ruby's best songs here were in a comic vein: "I Like a Big Town" and "What Makes a Business Man Tired"; in a sentimental style the principal number was "It Was Meant to Be."

Ruby and Kalmar continued to write songs for the stage for the next five years. *The Ramblers* (1926) starred Clark and McCullough; it had an outstanding song in "All Alone Monday." The score of *Five O'Clock Girl* (1927) included "Thinking of You," "Up in the Clouds," and "Happy Go Lucky." *Good Boy* (1928) starred Helen Kane, the "boop-boop-a-doop girl" who stopped the show nightly with "I Wanna Be Loved By You." *Animal Crackers* (1928) starred the four Marx Brothers; its best songs were two in a romantic vein, "Watching the Clouds Roll By" and "Who's Been Listening to My Heart?" A third song, "Hooray for Captain Spaulding" was used by Groucho Marx as his TV theme music for over a decade.

Ruby went to Hollywood in 1930 and from that time his best songs were written for the screen. His very first effort for motion pictures proved a major hit—"Three Little Words," for the Amos 'n' Andy picture, *Check and Double Check*. Later screen musicals brought "I Love You So Much" for *The Cuckoos*, "Everyone Says I Love You" for *Horsefeathers*, starring the Marx Brothers, and "A Kiss to Build a Dream On" for *The Strip* (the last of these with lyrics by Kalmar in collaboration with Oscar Hammerstein II). "Nevertheless," which Ruby and Kalmar wrote as an independent number in 1931, became one of their biggest successes. In Hollywood Ruby also distinguished himself as a lyricist. To Ruby Bloom's music he wrote "Give Me the Simple Life," and "I Wish I Could Tell You" for *Wake Up and Dream* and the title song for *Do You Love Me?* To Ernesto Lecuona's music he wrote "Another Night Like This" for *Carnival in Costa Rica*. "Maybe It's Because," an independent number for which Ruby provided the lyrics to Johnny Scott's music, was heard for ten weeks on the "Hit Parade."

In 1941 Ruby and Kalmar wrote the songs for the Broadway musical *High Kickers,* starring George Jessel and Sophie Tucker. A few years later they wrote the original story for the Warner Brothers screen biography of Marilyn Miller, *Look for the Silver Lining*, which received the Box Office Blue Ribbon Award. They also wrote several other screen plays (some of them nonmusicals), including those for *The Kid from Spain* starring Eddie Cantor (for which they also wrote the score), *Bright Lights* with Joe E. Brown, and *Duck Soup* with the Marx Brothers.

Since Bert Kalmar's death in 1947, Ruby has for the most part been writing his own lyrics. A screen musical based on the career of Ruby and Kalmar, *Three Little Words,* was released in 1950. The picture was a box office triumph, but for Ruby it also had elements of sadness. "Kalmar signed the contract for the movie just two days before he passed away," he reveals. "My father, who waited for the movie of his son, counted the days and minutes for its release. He died the morning the picture opened in New York."

Since 1950 Ruby has made numerous appearances on major television programs, and in 1961 was a subject of "This Is Your Life."

Henry Russell *1812-1900*

HENRY RUSSELL was America's first important composer of sentimental ballads. He was born in Sheerness, England, on December 24, 1812, and began his career in music as a boy singer. In his youth he went to Bologna and Milan for music study that included lessons in composition and orchestration with the celebrated opera composer Vincenzo Bellini. He also became acquainted with Rossini and Donizetti. After a brief stay in Paris, where he befriended Meyerbeer, he returned to England. Unable to earn his living there through music, he decided to seek a career in other parts of the world. His destination was Canada, which proved disappointing to him since he found that country to be uninterested in culture. A friend then persuaded him to come to the United States. In 1833 he arrived in Rochester, New York, where he remained for eight years, serving most of that time as organist of the First Presbyterian Church.

It was in the United States that Russell began to write sentimental ballads. He explained that his immediate stimulus was Henry Clay's speeches. "Why," he asked himself, "should it not be possible for me to make music the vehicle of grand thoughts and noble sentiments, to speak to the world through the power of poetry and song?" He answered this question by writing his first ballad: a musical setting of Charles Mackay's "Wind of the Winter Night."

In 1837 he wrote one of his most famous ballads, "Woodman, Spare That Tree," to words by George P. Morris, a New York newspaperman. John Hill Hewitt, in his book *Shadows on the Wall,* tells of the profound impact this ballad made on audiences when Russell sang it publicly: "He had finished the last verse. . . . The audience was spellbound for a moment, and then poured out a volume of applause that shook the building to its foundation. In the midst of this tremendous evidence of their boundless gratification, a snowy-headed gentleman with great anxiety depicted in his venerable features, arose and demanded silence. He asked with tremulous voice: 'Mr. Russell, in the name of Heaven, tell me, was the tree spared?' 'It was, sir,' replied the vocalist. 'Thank God! Thank God! I breathe again!' and he sat down perfectly overcome by emotion."

In 1837 Russell also wrote one of America's first popular songs about the Indian, "The Indian Hunter." A year after that came an early example of American popular music about the sea, "A Life on the Ocean Wave," which in 1899 was made the official song of the British Royal Marines. In 1840 Russell wrote what is undoubtedly one of the first "mammy" songs, "The Old Arm Chair." He continued to write sentimental ballads on every conceivable subject after that. The most famous are "The Old Family Clock," "The Old Spinning Wheel," "The Old Bell," "The Old Sexton," and "That Old Gang of Mine." Other ballads had a highly dramatic character with a kind of gruesome realism in the words: "The Gambler's Wife," "The Ship on Fire," "The Dream of the Reveller," and "The Maniac." In all, Russell wrote about eight hundred songs, most of them to his own lyrics.

After settling in New York, Russell joined several of his London friends in a vocal group that performed successfully throughout the East. This venture encouraged him to set out on his own in solo concerts, his *tour de force* being the performance of his own ballads to his piano accompaniments. Despite the immense popularity of his songs throughout the United States, Russell's livelihood came not from the sale of sheet music but from the fees he earned from his concerts. As he himself explained in his autobiography, *Cheer, Boys, Cheer* (named after one of his highly successful songs, published

Courtesy of The New York Public Library, Music Division

HENRY RUSSELL

in 1850): "There was no such thing as royalty in those days and when a song was sold it was sold outright. My songs brought me an average of ten shillings each . . . though they made the fortune of several publishers. Had it not been that I sang the songs myself . . . the payment for their composition would have meant simple starvation."

"In person," wrote John Hill Hewitt, "he was rather stout but not tall. His face was prepossessing . . . dark and heavy whiskers and curly hair. He was an expert at wheedling applause out of audiences and adding to the effect of his songs by a brilliant pianoforte accompaniment. With such self-laudation he used often to describe the wonderful influence of his descriptive songs over audiences."

During the last few years of his stay in the United States, Russell wrote many songs propagandizing social causes: abolition of slavery, reforms in lunatic asylums, and temperance. He left the United States in 1841 and returned to London, where he went into retirement in 1865 and where he died on December 8, 1900.

Henry Russell was the father of two sons who achieved outstanding recognition in English music. One was Henry Russell, a distinguished impresario, who managed the opera company at Covent Garden, the Henry Russell Opera Company, and the Boston

Opera Company. Another son was Sir Landon Ronald, one of England's most eminent conductors.

ABOUT:
Hewitt, John Hill. Shadows on the Wall; Russell, Henry. Cheer, Boys, Cheer.

William J. Scanlan *1856-1898*

WILLIAM J. SCANLAN—who distinguished himself both as a songwriter and as a singing star of musical productions —was born in Springfield, Massachusetts, on February 14, 1856. At the age of thirteen he became known throughout New England as a boy temperance singer. For about seven years he traveled with various temperance lecturers providing entertainment at their meetings by singing ballads. After that he formed a vaudeville act with the Irish comedian William Cronin and toured the circuit for many years.

It was during this period of his life that Scanlan is believed to have written the famous ballad "Jim Fisk." Fisk was a corrupt New York politician who became involved in disreputable deals in Wall Street and Tammany Hall. In 1872 he was murdered by Edward Stokes outside the Grand Central Hotel. His career and death were immortalized in "Jim Fisk," in which he was elevated to heroic stature as a kind of Robin Hood with heart of gold who stole from the rich to give to the poor. Sigmund Spaeth points out that when this ballad was first published, the sheet music identified the composer-lyricist merely with the initials "J.S." though later editions used Scanlan's full name. However, Spaeth notes, since that time serious doubts have arisen as to whether Scanlan was really the author of the ballad; it is the practice today to place it among American folk songs of undetermined origin.

After appearing for two years in musical productions with Minnie Palmer, Scanlan began to produce musicals and to star in them. One of these was Bartley Campbell's *Friend and Foe* (1881), in which Scanlan introduced one of his most successful songs, "Peek-a-Boo"; other musical highlights of this play were the ballad "Moonlight at Killarney," the waltz "Over the Mountain," and "There's Always a Seat in the Parlor for You." In or about 1883 he began to star as a singer-actor and to write songs (lyrics as well as music) for productions put on by Augustus Pitou. For *The Irish Minstrel* (1883) he wrote another of his outstanding song hits, "My Nellie's Blue Eyes," as well as "Scanlan's Rose Song," "I Love Music," "Bye, Bye, Baby" and "What's in a Kiss?" For *Shane-na-lawn* (1885) he wrote "Peggy O'Moore," "You and I, Love," "Gathering the Myrtle with Mary," "Remember Boy, You're Irish," and "Why Paddy's Always Poor." In *Myles Arroon* (1888) "Swing Song," "My Maggie" and "Live, My Love, O Live" were introduced and in *Mavourneen* (1891) the title number and "Molly O!"

On September 28, 1891, Scanlan opened at the Fourteenth Street Theatre in New York in *Mavourneen*. During the run of the show he began to show unmistakable signs of mental disturbance. He continued to perform, however, until December 25, by which time he was completely insane. On January 7, 1892, he was committed to the Bloomingdale Asylum in White Plains, New York, where he was confined until his death on February 19, 1898.

ABOUT:
Spaeth, Sigmund. A History of Popular Music in America.

Victor Schertzinger *1890-1941*

VICTOR SCHERTZINGER, a successful composer for the screen in the early days of talking pictures, was born to musical parents in Mahanoy City, Pennsylvania, on April 8, 1890. While attending the Brown Preparatory School in Pennsylvania he received private violin instruction. As a boy of eight he appeared as violinist with the Victor Herbert Orchestra in Washington Park, Pennsylvania. Afterwards he gave several other successful performances as a prodigy violinist with musical organizations led by John Philip Sousa, Victor Herbert, and others. In his early teens he toured both Europe and America in violin recitals.

Schertzinger abandoned the violin for the baton when he became a conductor of several theatre orchestras in Los Angeles. He later transferred his conducting activities to the Broadway musical comedy stage, but then returned to Los Angeles. Meanwhile, in 1913, he had published two highly successful songs.

One was "Marcheta," to his own lyrics; the other was "My Wonderful Dream Girl" (lyrics by Oliver Morosco).

Schertzinger was conducting a theatre orchestra in Los Angeles when he first became associated with motion pictures as a composer of background music. One of these productions was *Civilization*, perhaps the earliest full-length silent motion picture to have an original score as background music. With the coming of sound, Schertzinger became one of Hollywood's most active composers. The first talking pictures to feature his songs were *The Laughing Lady* and *Manhattan Cocktail*, in 1927 and 1928 respectively, for which he wrote "Another Kiss" and "Gotta Be Good." In 1929 he wrote the songs for *The Love Parade*, in which Maurice Chevalier was starred; its principal numbers (lyrics by Clifford Grey) were the title song, "Dream Lover," and "Paris Stay the Same." His best songs for the screen after that included the following: the title numbers (written to lyrics by Gus Kahn) for *Love Me Forever* and *One Night of Love* (the latter was the film in which Grace Moore scored her first success on the screen); "I Don't Cry Any More" (lyrics by Johnny Burke) for a Bing Crosby musical, *Rhythm on the River;* "Willow Tree" (lyrics by Burke) for the Bing Crosby-Bob Hope musical *Road to Singapore;* the title number and "I'll Never Let a Day Pass By" (lyrics by Frank Loesser) for *Kiss the Boys Goodbye;* and "I Remember You" (lyrics by Johnny Mercer) for *The Fleet's In.*

Victor Schertzinger died in Hollywood on October 26, 1941.

ABOUT:
Metronome, December 1941.

Arthur Schwartz 1900-

ARTHUR SCHWARTZ was born in Brooklyn, New York, on November 25, 1900. He showed unusual interest in music during his boyhood by playing the harmonica, inventing little songs, and learning by himself to play the piano. By the time he was fourteen he was sufficiently adept as a pianist to get a job accompanying silent films at the Cortelyou Theatre in Brooklyn. But his father, a lawyer, insisted that Arthur follow

ARTHUR SCHWARTZ   ASCAP

in his footsteps. He attended elementary schools and Boys' High School in Brooklyn and received a bachelor of arts degree from New York University in 1920 and a master's degree from Columbia University in 1921. He then attended Columbia Law School and was admitted to the bar in 1924.

During this period music was not neglected. For several years he helped write and produce shows at Brant Lake Camp, a boys' summer camp where, for one season, he was assisted by Lorenz Hart, later the lyricist of Richard Rodgers. At New York University, Schwartz wrote marches and college songs; he also took a course in harmony, his first and only application to formal music study. While attending law school (and supporting himself by teaching English in a New York high school) he wrote popular songs. His first published song, "Baltimore, Md., You're the Only Doctor for Me," came out in 1923 and brought him eight dollars in royalties.

His extracurricular activity of songwriting continued without interruption while he practiced law. Two of his songs were heard in the *Garrick Gaieties of 1926*: "A Little Igloo for Two" and "Polar Bear Strut." He also wrote special material for vaudeville acts and some songs under a pen name for a show that expired out of town.

In 1925 he played some of his songs for George Gershwin, and began one that paid sentimental tribute to Gershwin's genius and quoted the *Rhapsody in Blue.* "I sat down nervously at the piano," recalls Schwartz. "As he stood behind me patiently, I played a long, aimless introduction and cleared my throat much more than was necessary. Suddenly I wished I had never asked for this preposterous audition, for I began to realize the full extent of my audacity in writing this lily-gilding song. . . . How *dared* I? I could go no further, in spite of George's friendly insistence. When I told him I was withdrawing my composition right then and there, he didn't quarrel with my decision. Mercifully changing the subject he asked me to play some of my other tunes. I found his reactions the warmest, most encouraging I had yet received."

Lorenz Hart encouraged him to give up his law practice in 1928 and to concentrate on songwriting. That year Schwartz attended a performance of an intimate Broadway revue, *Merry-Go-Round,* for which a young man by the name of Howard Dietz had written some of the lyrics. Dietz, who was publicity director for MGM—it was he who conceived the trademark of a roaring lion for the company as well as its slogan *"Ars Gratia Artis"*—spent his free hours writing song lyrics; some of these had been heard in the Broadway musical *Poppy* (starring W. C. Fields) and *Dear Sir* (for which Jerome Kern had written the score). Coming into contact with Dietz's brilliant versification and wit, Schwartz knew that he had found the man with whom he wanted to work on a permanent basis. He badgered Dietz until the latter finally agreed to write lyrics to his music. Their first collaboration proved the wisdom of that decision: the score for the *Little Show* (1929), one of the most outstanding sophisticated intimate revues of that period, in which Fred Allen, Libby Holman, and Clifton Webb were starred. Three of the Schwartz-Dietz songs were memorable: "I Guess I'll Have to Change My Plan," "I've Made a Habit of You," and "Little Old New York." Since the first was particularly successful in Clifton Webb's suave delivery, it is interesting to note that Schwartz had written this melody several years earlier (to other lyrics, by Hart) for one of his productions at Brant Lake Camp.

The *Second Little Show* (1930), for which Schwartz and Dietz wrote most of the songs, was a failure; one of its songs, however, "Lucky Seven," deserves to be remembered. But in the same year of 1930 they achieved a second triumph in *Three's a Crowd,* a sophisticated revue in the style and manner of the first *Little Show,* and with the same stars. "Something to Remember You By," introduced by Libby Holman, was one of the musical highlights.

The *Bandwagon* (1931), for which George S. Kaufman and Dietz wrote the book, was also a resounding box office success; it included one of Schwartz's best songs, "Dancing in the Dark." (*The Bandwagon* was twice adapted for the screen, and on the first occasion the picture was named after this hit song.) "I Love Louisa" and "New Sun in the Sky" were two other important songs from this revue.

Succeeding revues for which Schwartz and Dietz wrote songs included *Flying Colors* in 1932 ("Alone Together," "Louisiana Hayride," and "A Shine on Your Shoes"); *At Home Abroad* in 1935 ("Love Is a Dancing Thing"); and *Inside U.S.A.* in 1948 ("Haunted Heart" and "Rhode Island Is Famous for You").

Schwartz's songs were also being heard in motion pictures. "After All You're All I'm After" (lyrics by Edward Heyman) was featured in *She Loves Me Not,* starring Bing Crosby, in 1934. In 1936 five of Schwartz's songs, again to Heyman's lyrics, were presented in *That Girl from Paris,* starring Lily Pons, the best being "Seal It with a Kiss."

Schwartz had also been engaged in writing scores for Broadway musical comedies, but with less happy results. As a matter of fact, in the field of musical comedy he suffered six successive failures before finally hitting a winning stride. One of these failures, *Between the Devil* (1937), had an excellent song, "I See Your Face" (lyrics by Dietz). And another, *Revenge with Music* (1934) deserves special attention as an ambitious popular treatment of a plot previously used in a ballet (Manuel de Falla's *The Three-Cornered Hat*) and an opera (Hugo Wolf's *Der Corregidor*). Though Schwartz's plot, setting, and characters were fresh, *Revenge with Music* made little impression upon audiences and critics (nor did it stir additional excitement when it was revived on television on October 21, 1954). But two of the songs from Schwartz's score must be numbered with his greatest: "You and the Night and the Music" and "If There Is Someone Lovelier than You" (lyrics by Dietz).

In 1936 Schwartz wrote the music for a thirty-four-week radio serial, "The Gibson Family." In 1941 he returned to Hollywood where he concentrated his principal activity for the next few years. Among the screen productions in which his songs were heard were *Cairo* with Jeanette MacDonald, and *Thank Your Lucky Stars,* a revue in which Bette Davis sang a World War II lament, "They're Either Too Young or Too Old" (lyrics by Frank Loesser). Schwartz subsequently became the producer of several major film musicals, including Jerome Kern's *Cover Girl* and the Cole Porter screen biography, *Night and Day.*

Schwartz's return to Broadway took place in 1951 with his first musical comedy success, *A Tree Grows in Brooklyn.* This was a nostalgic adaptation, starring Shirley Booth, of Betty Smith's best-selling novel. Schwartz created several memorable songs (to lyrics by Dorothy Fields), among them "Love Is the Reason" and "I'll Buy You a Star." Shirley Booth was also the star of Schwartz's next Broadway musical comedy, *By the Beautiful Sea* (1954); this play (with text by Herbert and Dorothy Fields), was set in Coney Island at the turn of the century. "Alone Too Long" and "More Love than Your Love" (lyrics by Dorothy Fields) were the two best numbers.

Arthur Schwartz and Howard Dietz worked together again in 1961, writing the songs for the Broadway musical *The Gay Life,* which opened late in the fall of that year. *The Gay Life* was a musical-comedy adaptation by Michael and Fay Kanin of Arthur Schnitzler's 1911 play, *Anatol.*

ABOUT:
Ewen, David. Complete Book of the American Musical Theater; Green, Stanley. The World of Musical Comedy.
Collier's, October 14, 1944.

Jean Schwartz *1878-1956*

JEAN SCHWARTZ was born in Budapest, Hungary, on November 4, 1878. A musical child, he received piano instruction from his sister, a pupil of Liszt. He was about thirteen when his family came to the United States and settled on New York's Lower East Side. There for several years they knew the most abject poverty. They could not find, let alone own, a piano on which to practice. To help support his family, Jean held various jobs: he was a night cashier at a Turkish bath; he played the piano with an ensemble in Coney Island; he demonstrated popular songs in the first sheet music department ever opened in a New York department store (Siegel-Cooper); and finally he became staff pianist and song plugger at Shapiro-Bernstein in Tin Pan Alley. Schwartz's first publication, a piano cakewalk entitled *Dusky Dudes,* was issued in 1899.

In 1901 Schwartz met and became a friend of William Jerome, already an established lyricist in Tin Pan Alley. Schwartz initiated a songwriting partnership that continued successfully for many years. One of their earliest efforts was "When Mr. Shakespeare Comes to Town," interpolated into the Weber and Fields' 1901 burlesque *Hoity-Toity,* a production in which Schwartz was serving as an onstage pianist. In 1901 Schwartz and Jerome also wrote "Rip Van Winkle Was a Lucky Man" and "Don't Put Me Off at Buffalo Any More." One year later their leading songs included "Hamlet Was a Melancholy Dane," which was successfully introduced at the Iroquois Theatre in Chicago by Eddie Foy; "Since Sister Nell Heard Paderewski Play" and "I'm Unlucky," both interpolated into the Broadway musical *The Wild Rose;* and "Mister Dooley," heard in *The Chinese Honeymoon.* Their smash hit song, "Bedelia," was introduced in 1903; almost three million copies of sheet music were sold after the song was popularized by Blanche Ring in *The Jersey Lily.*

Success as songwriters brought Schwartz and Jerome an engagement on the vaudeville circuit. They remained headliners for many years. Schwartz was also the piano accompanist for the Dolly Sisters when they played in vaudeville, and one of them (Rozika) became his wife.

Schwartz and Jerome wrote their first complete Broadway musical comedy score in 1904: *Piff, Paff, Pouf* starring Eddie Foy and Alice Fisher. "Good Night, My Own True Love," "Love, Love, Love," and "The

JEAN SCHWARTZ

ASCAP

Three striking successes which Schwartz wrote to lyrics by Sam M. Lewis and Joe Young were first made famous by Al Jolson at the Winter Garden in *Sinbad* (1917): "Hello, Central, Give Me No Man's Land"; "Why Do They All Take the Night Boat to Albany?"; and "Rock-a-bye Your Baby with a Dixie Melody," revived more than a quarter of a century later in the motion picture *The Jolson Story*. Ben Bernie's radio signature, "Au Revoir, Pleasant Dreams," was composed by Schwartz to words by Jack Meskill.

Between 1931 and 1937, Schwartz wrote several songs in collaboration with Milton Ager: "Little You Know," "Trouble in Paradise," and one which enjoyed a high position among the hits of 1937, "Trust in Me."

Jean Schwartz died in Los Angeles on November 30, 1956.

Ghost That Never Walked" were three of its principal numbers. For the next few years they continued to write music for various Broadway stage productions, most notably *Lifting the Lid* (1905), *Lola from Berlin* (1907), *In Haiti* (1909), and *Up and Down Broadway* (1910). Apart from their compositions for these plays, they also wrote the following popular songs during this period: "Chinatown, My Chinatown"; "The Hat My Father Wore on St. Patrick's Day"; "My Irish Molly-O," introduced by Blanche Ring in *Sergeant Blue* (1905); and "When the Girl You Love Is Loving," heard in the Ziegfeld *Follies* of 1908.

At the beginning of World War I, Schwartz and Jerome went separate ways. In 1914 Schwartz wrote two successful songs to Grant Clarke's lyrics, "Back to the Carolina You Love" and "I Love the Ladies." With the librettist Harold Atteridge as lyricist, he wrote songs for two editions of *The Passing Show* (1913 and 1921), *Artists and Models of 1923*, *Topics of 1923*, and several musical comedies, including *The Honeymoon Express* (1913), *Make It Snappy* (1922), and *Innocent Eyes* (1924). To lyrics by Anne Caldwell, Schwartz wrote songs for several other musical comedies, notably *When Claudia Smiles* (1914), *Hello Alexander* (1919), *A Night in Spain* (1927), and *Sunny Days* (1928).

Raymond Scott 1909-

RAYMOND SCOTT was born Harry Warnow in Brooklyn, New York, on September 10, 1909. His older brother, Mark Warnow, was a distinguished conductor, for many years music director of the "Hit Parade" program on radio and television. Their father had been a concert violinist in Russia and the owner of a record shop in New York.

Raymond's first interest was science, nurtured at the Brooklyn Technical High School. But music—especially the hot jazz of New Orleans—was also a boyhood passion, and upon graduating from high school he decided to make music his career. For several years he attended the Institute of Musical Art and then for a while was a member of his brother Mark's orchestra.

In 1930 Scott was hired as house pianist for the Columbia Broadcasting System. During the next four years he played the piano over the CBS network, performed with radio orchestras, and wrote music for several programs. One of his earliest compositions, *Christmas Night in Harlem*, was introduced on the radio by Mark Warnow and his orchestra in 1932.

In 1936 Scott left his radio job to become pianist with a small jazz group which appeared on "Saturday Night Swing," the first radio program to feature real jazz. The members of the ensemble included Jerry Colonna (later famous as a radio and television comedian) and Bunny Berigan, the trumpet player. In 1937 Scott organized his own jazz quintet with Johnny Williams, Peter Pumiglio, Dave Harris, Louis Schoobe, and Dave Wade. The group made its first recordings in 1937 and in short order became one of the most successful new jazz combinations, sought after for engagements in theatres throughout the country. Scott's novel arrangements and his skillful improvisations sounded a new note for jazz and aroused the enthusiasm not only of jazz lovers but also of serious musicians (among them Stravinsky and Heifetz). Scott also wrote pieces in a jazz style or popular vein. The most memorable were *Twilight in Turkey* and *In an Eighteenth-Century Drawing Room,* the latter a jazz version of the main theme from the first movement of Mozart's Piano Sonata in C major, K. 545.

Scott's popularity brought him a contract for work in Hollywood and there he wrote music for and appeared in pictures starring Eddie Cantor, Shirley Temple, and others. *Toy Trumpet,* written in 1937 and used in the Shirley Temple film *Rebecca of Sunnybrook Farm,* became an outstanding hit.

He remained in Hollywood for only one year before returning to New York to become music director of the Columbia Broadcasting System. With his famous quintet he made numerous appearances and also undertook nation-wide tours. Later (in 1945) he expanded his ensemble into a dance band.

In 1945 Scott wrote incidental music for a Broadway play, *Beggars Are Coming to Town.* One year later he wrote the score for the musical *Lute Song,* in which Yul Brynner and Mary Martin were starred. This was a modernization by Sidney Howard and Will Irwin of a Chinese classic, *Pi-Pa-Ki.* Though well received by the critics, *Lute Song* proved a box office failure both on Broadway and on tour. One of its best songs was "Mountain High, Valley Low" (lyrics by Bernard Hanighen). When *Lute Song* was revived in New York early in 1959, Brooks Atkinson wrote: "*Lute Song* is a pleasant and often touching legend about human beings caught in the rigid ceremonies of ancient Chinese life. . . . [It] is an enchanting fable . . . with sweet and mournful music . . . and some marvelous ballets."

When Mark Warnow died, in 1949, Raymond Scott became the music director

RAYMOND SCOTT

of the "Hit Parade" program, a post he retained for about a decade. During that period Scott's wife, Dorothy Collins, was one of the vocal stars.

The following are some of Scott's best instrumental jazz compositions (besides those already mentioned): *All Around the Christmas Tree, Powerhouse, War Dance for Wooden Indians, Minuet in Jazz, Huckleberry Duck, Singing Down the Road, In a Magic Garden* and *In a Subway Far from Ireland.*

In other compositions Scott has displayed the kind of whimsy indulged in by the French composer Erik Satie, devising such titles as *The Girl with the Light Blue Hair, Duet for Piano and Pistol, Square Dance for Eight Egyptian Mummies* and *Dinner for a Pack of Hungry Cannibals.* He has also written the score for a ballet, *The Gremlins.*

Despite his predisposition for the bizarre and the whimsical, Raymond Scott has been an inventive force in contemporary popular music. His best pieces are his brilliant projections of an authentic jazz idiom and style, but with the introduction of new sound effects and instrumental sonorities and the exploitation of a vivid melodic and harmonic imagination.

ABOUT:
Ewen, David. Men of Popular Music.
Metronome, May 1957.

A. Baldwin Sloane *1872-1926*

A. BALDWIN SLOANE was born in Baltimore, Maryland, on August 28, 1872. After attending the Baltimore public schools and studying music with private teachers he became affiliated with the Baltimore Paint and Powder Club, for whose operetta productions he wrote several scores. In the early 1890's he went to New York to further his career in music. "While Strolling Through the Forest," published in 1894, was one of his earliest songs; his first hit came in 1888 with "When You Ain't Got No More Money, Well, You Needn't Come 'Round" (lyrics by Clarence S. Brewster), made popular by May Irwin. Other songs by Sloane before 1900 included "Lazy Bill" and "I'm Looking for an Angel."

In 1900 Sloane wrote the scores for three Broadway musical comedies: *Broadway to Tokyo, Aunt Hannah,* and *A Million Dollars.* Heard in the first of these comedies was "Susie, Ma Sue" (lyrics by George V. Hobart), and in the second, "My Tiger Lily" (lyrics by Clay M. Greene). In 1902, to lyrics by Sydney Rosenfeld, Sloane wrote two more successful musical numbers: "There's a Little Street in Heaven Called Broadway" for *The Belle of Broadway,* and "What's the Matter with the Moon Tonight?" for *The Mocking Bird.*

Sloane's greatest Broadway stage success was the extravaganza *The Wizard of Oz,* a sumptuously mounted and lavishly produced fantasy starring Fred Stone and David Montgomery which opened on January 21, 1903. Not the least of its attractions were songs like "Niccolo's Piccolo" and "The Medley of Nations," written to lyrics by L. Frank Baum, the author of the Oz books.

Through the years Sloane's music was heard in many Broadway musical productions. Of these musicals the most important were *Lady Teazle* (1904), an adaptation of Sheridan's comedy *The School for Scandal,* starring Lillian Russell; *The Gingerbread Man* (1905); *Coming Through the Rye* (1906); *The Mimic and the Maid* (1907); and *Tillie's Nightmare* (1909) with Marie Dressler, a production that featured what is perhaps Sloane's greatest song success, a satire on sentimental ballads called "Heaven Will Protect the Working Girl." The score

included a second hit number in "Life Is Only What You Make It After All." For both songs his lyricist was Edgar Smith.

Between 1910 and 1920 Sloane proved even more prolific as a composer for the Broadway stage. In 1910 he wrote the music for *The Summer Widowers* with Lew Fields and Irene Franklin, and *The Prince of Bohemia;* in 1911 for *The Hen Pecks,* starring Lew Fields and Vernon Castle; 1912 for *Hokey-Pokey* (in which Weber and Fields were temporarily reunited after an eight-year separation), *Hanky-Panky, Roly-Poly,* and *The Sun Dodgers;* in 1918 for *Ladies First,* in which Nora Bayes was the star; in 1919 and 1920 for the first two editions of the *Greenwich Village Follies.* His best songs were "On the Boardwalk" and "Those Were the Happy Days" from *The Summer Widowers* and "White Light Alley" and "June" from *The Hen Pecks* (lyrics by Glen MacDonough); and "I Want a Daddy Who Will Rock Me to Sleep" from the *Greenwich Village Follies* of 1919 and "Just Sweet Sixteen" from the *Greenwich Village Follies* of 1920 (lyrics by Arthur Swanstrom).

Sloane's last Broadway musical comedy, *China Rose* (1924), was a box office failure. Sloane died in Red Bank, New Jersey, on February 21, 1926.

Chris Smith *1879-1949*

CHRIS SMITH was born in Charleston, South Carolina, on October 12, 1879. Early in life he taught himself to play the guitar and piano. As a boy he supported himself by working as a baker. But he soon joined Elmer Bowman in stage appearances. "Elmer and I left Charleston with a white man who had a medicine show," he recalled. "We were still in short pants. This man was an old actor that had turned to do doctoring, and he promised to pay us six dollars a week. He used to take axle grease and sell it for a nickel a box to colored people for a rheumatism cure. And if you want to know how many miles it is from Georgetown to Columbia, South Carolina, it's seventy-nine. Elmer and I had to walk it when this old man wouldn't give us our wages. That's the way we started in show business."

Smith's career as a composer of popular songs began in 1900 with "Never Let the Same Bee Sting You Twice" (lyrics by Cecil Mack). For several years he continued to write music to Mack's lyrics, some of them comedy numbers achieving modest recognition. Between 1901 and 1910 their best efforts included the following: "Good Morning, Carrie" (melody written in collaboration with J. Tim Brymm); "He's a Cousin of Mine" (melody in collaboration with Silvio Hein), interpolated into the stage musical *Marrying Mary;* "All In, Down and Out"; "You're in the Right Church but the Wrong Pew"; "Down Among the Sugar Cane" (Avery and Hart); and "If He Comes In, I'm Going Out." Several of these songs became popular in minstrel shows and vaudeville theatres in performances by such stars as Marie Cahill and Stella Mayhew.

In 1911 Smith became interested in ragtime. His first composition in that style was *Monkey Rag,* for piano solo. In 1913 he wrote the greatest song hit of his career, "Ballin' the Jack," a ragtime tune to lyrics by Jim Burris. It has never lost its popularity. In 1942 it was revived in the motion picture *For Me and My Gal,* starring Judy Garland and Gene Kelly, and it achieved a prominent spot on the Hit Parade. It has since been featured by Danny Kaye on records and in public appearances.

Besides the songs already mentioned, Chris Smith also wrote "Jasper Johnson, Shame on You" (lyrics by John Larkins); "Fifteen Cents" (lyrics by the composer); "After All That I've Been to You" (lyrics by Jack Drislane); and "Beans, Beans, Beans" (lyrics by Elmer Bowman).

Smith produced little after World War I. He lived in seclusion and neglect in an apartment on St. Nicholas Avenue in New York City until his death in 1949.

Ted Snyder 1881-

TED SNYDER was born in Freeport, Illinois, on August 15, 1881. After attending public schools in Boscobel, Wisconsin, he earned his living posting bills for a Chicago theatre. Later he played the piano in cafés and worked as staff pianist and song plugger for several music publishing firms in Chicago and New York.

One of his earliest published songs was written in 1907, "There's a Girl in This World for Every Boy" (lyrics by Will D. Cobb). In 1908 he formed his own Tin Pan Alley publishing company; one of its first issues was his own song, "If You Cared for Me" (lyrics by Ed Rose). "Beautiful Rose" (lyrics by George Whiting and Carter De Haven) was interpolated into the musical production *Mr. Hamlet of Broadway* in 1909.

Irving Berlin, who started to work for the Ted Snyder Company as a lyricist in 1909, created words for Ted Snyder's melodies. Between 1909 and 1910 they wrote "Next to Your Mother, Who Do You Love?" "Sweet Italian Love," "Kiss Me, My Honey, Kiss Me," and "That Beautiful Rag"—all published by Snyder's company. The collaborators became one of Tin Pan Alley's chief songwriting teams, and in 1910 the Shuberts engaged them to appear in a revue, *Up and Down Broadway,* singing their own hits. In 1911 Berlin and Snyder wrote "That Mysterious Rag"; in 1912, "Take a Little Tip from Father"; in 1913, "My Wife's Gone to the Country" (Berlin's lyric written in collaboration with George Whiting). After 1913 Berlin (by that time writing his own melodies) became a partner in Ted Snyder's firm, renamed Waterson, Berlin and Snyder.

Snyder continued to write melodies to the words of other lyricists, notably those of Bert Kalmar, with whom he created "In the Land of Harmony" and "The Ghost of the Violin." "Moonlight on the Rhine" (lyrics by Kalmar and Edgar Leslie) was interpolated into the 1914 Broadway stage production *One Girl in a Million.*

After World War I, Snyder's leading song hits were "How'd You Like to Be My Daddy?" (lyrics by Sam M. Lewis and Joe Young), interpolated into the Al Jolson Winter Garden extravaganza *Sinbad;* "The Sheik of Araby" (lyrics by Harry B. Smith and Francis Wheeler), inspired by the Rudolph Valentino silent motion picture of the same name and introduced in the 1921 Broadway revue *Make It Snappy;* "I Wonder If You Still Care for Me" (lyrics by Smith and Wheeler); and, in 1923, "Who's Sorry Now?" (lyrics by Kalmar and Harry Ruby). Other songs written with various lyricists, included "My Guitar," "Piano Man," "I

Want to Be in Dixie," "Dreams, Just
Dreams," "My Dream of the U.S.A.," and
"Under the Moon."

Ted Snyder retired as a songwriter and
song publisher in 1930. He settled in Hollywood, where he subsequently entered the
restaurant business.

John Philip Sousa *1854-1932*

JOHN PHILIP SOUSA, the "march king,"
was born in Washington, D.C., on November 6, 1854, the son of a Portuguese
father and a Bavarian mother. From his
father, a trombonist in the United States Marine Band, the child inherited his love for
music. The martial music of army bands in
the streets of Washington during and immediately following the Civil War had a profound impact upon him. When he was not
yet fourteen, he enlisted in the Marine Corps.
Having begun music study in 1864 (violin
with John Esputa) he succeeded in becoming a member of the Marine Band. Two
years later, as a civilian, he engaged in various musical activities in Washington while
studying harmony with G. F. Benkert. He
became a conductor of a theatre orchestra;
then first violinist at the Ford Opera House;
and after that, for five seasons, the music
director of the Milton Nobles Repertory
Company.

He wrote his first march, *Salutation,*
while he was still with the Marines. Soon
after that he wrote a waltz, *Moonlight on the
Potomac;* a second march, *The Review*; and
a galop, *The Cuckoo.* The last two were published by a Philadelphia firm which paid him
with copies of the sheet music.

In the summer of 1877 Sousa was the
first violinist of an orchestra conducted by
Jacques Offenbach at the Philadelphia Centennial. For these concerts he wrote *The
International Congress,* a potpourri of national anthems beginning with a fugal treatment of "Yankee Doodle." Sousa settled for
a while in Philadelphia and for four years
was the first violinist of the Chestnut Street
Theatre. During this period his compositions
included a humorous march, *The Free Lunch
Cadets,* published in 1877, and his first comic
opera, *The Smugglers* (1879).

Between 1880 and 1892 Sousa was the
music director of the Marine Band, which

performed frequently at the White House and
at official government receptions under five
Presidents. Under his leadership the band
achieved renown for its accomplished performances, often playing Sousa's own compositions at concerts. In 1886 he wrote the
march *The Gladiator* and in 1888 *National
Fencibles* and the first of his better-known
marches, *Semper Fidelis.* In 1889 he wrote
The Crusader, The Thunderer, and *The
Washington Post March. Our Flirtation,
High School Cadets,* and *Liberty Bell* followed. Many of these early marches were
sold by Sousa to publishers for thirty-five
dollars each. "I was more interested in producing music which would appeal to the
public heart than in gaining a fortune for
myself," he explained in his autobiography.

In 1892 Sousa formed his own band with
which he made numerous American and European tours. In time the Sousa Band became one of America's most famous musical
ensembles, often a feature attraction of outstanding national events. The band performed
at the World's Fair in Chicago in 1893, the
Atlanta Cotton States Exposition in 1895, the
Buffalo Pan American Exposition in 1901,
the St. Louis World's Fair in 1904, and the
Panama-Pacific Exposition in San Francisco
in 1915. Between 1900 and 1904 it made
four tours of Europe, and in 1910 it toured
the world. During its long and active history, the band gave over ten thousand concerts.

Sousa continued to write march music for
his concerts and for specific occasions. His
first engagement with the Sousa Band at
Manhattan Beach in New York resulted in
Manhattan Beach March, in 1893. He wrote
The Picador and *The Belle of Chicago,* among
other marches, in 1894. For his engagement
at the Cotton States Exposition in 1895 he
wrote *King Cotton. On Parade* was published
the same year. In 1896 a Sousa favorite
was introduced—*El Capitan,* adapted as a
march from the male chorus in the second act
of his comic opera of the same title. *El
Capitan* was played on board Admiral (then
Commodore) Dewey's flagship, *Olympia,*
when it steamed down Manila Bay for battle;
and when Dewey was honored as a national
hero in New York on September 30, 1900,
Sousa and his band performed the march
again. In 1897 Sousa wrote *The Bride Elect*

(also an adaptation of an excerpt from a comic opera) and what is undoubtedly one of the most famous marches ever written, *The Stars and Stripes Forever.*

The story of the writing of this classic is now well known. Sousa was touring Europe when he received the news of the death of his manager, which impelled him to cut his trip short and return at once to America. While crossing the ocean on the *Teutonic,* he was haunted by a vigorous march tune which gave him no peace. As soon as he returned to New York he put the tune down on paper and used it as the basic melody for *The Stars and Stripes Forever,* which he completed on April 26, 1897. In this march, as Sigmund Spaeth has written, Sousa created "a perfect example of his own favorite form, starting with an arresting introduction, then using a light, skipping rhythm for his first melody, going from that into a broader tune and finally reaching the immortal strain itself. This trio is interrupted by an exciting interlude to return finally in a massive climax, with piccolo variations and other ornaments to give fresh colors to the instrumentation." In 1915 the California Music Teachers Association petitioned Congress to have this march designated as the official national anthem of the United States.

Of the later marches composed by Sousa, the finest included *Hands Across the Sea, Invincible Eagle, Fairest of the Fair, America First* (or *March of the States*), *New York Hippodrome March* (for Sousa's first season of Sunday evening concerts at the Hippodrome Theatre in 1915), *Saber and Spurs* (dedicated to the United States Cavalry) and *Nobles of the Mystic Shrine.*

In addition to his marches, Sousa wrote the scores for many comic operas, beginning with *The Smugglers* (1879) and concluding with *Victory* (1915). The most successful was *El Capitan,* produced in New York on April 20, 1896, starring De Wolf Hopper and Edna Wallace Hopper. Set in sixteenth century Peru, the opera had as its principal character the Viceroy, who, when his regime is threatened, assumes the identity of a bandit, El Capitan, and thereby becomes the head of the conspirators seeking to destroy him. Besides the second-act male chorus which Sousa transformed into the famous march, the engaging score included a beautiful duet,

ASCAP
JOHN PHILIP SOUSA

"Sweetheart, I'm Waiting" and an amusing topical song, "A Typical Tune of Zanzibar."

Sousa was the composer of an oratorio, *Messiah of the Nations* (1914), and of a vocal setting of John MacCrae's famous poem *In Flanders Fields* (1918). In addition, Sousa made many brilliant band arrangements of American anthems and ballads. One of these was "The Caisson Song" of the field artillery, which Sousa performed at the Liberty Loan Drive at the Hippodrome in 1918. (For a while Sousa was believed to have been the composer of this march, but it was finally ascertained that it had been written by Edmund L. Gruber in 1908 and that only the brilliant band transcription was Sousa's.) Sousa was also commissioned by the United States Government to edit *National Patriotic and Typical Airs of All Countries.*

During World War I, Sousa served as a lieutenant commander at the Great Lakes Training Station. In 1918 Sousa and his band were featured in the Hippodrome spectacle *Everything.* After that his appearances with his band became less and less frequent. He died in Reading, Pennsylvania, on March 6, 1932.

Among the many honors conferred on Sousa were the Victoria Cross of Great Britain and the Golden Palms and Rosette of the French Academy. In 1938, when a Sousa memorial was proposed, the New York *Times* published the following editorial statement:

"Sousa's band was something grand, something that dispelled and did not invite a mental fog. It played daylight, smiling music. The world that created it is ended. The confused world wants 'escape music' now. But Sousa was a cheerful fellow in his day."

It is not often recalled that Sousa wrote several novels, one of which *(The Fifth String)* was a best seller.

ABOUT:

Berger, Kenneth W. The March King; Lewiton, Mina. John Philip Sousa: The March King; Lingg, Ann. John Philip Sousa; Sousa, John Philip. Marching Along.

International Musician, August 1953; Music Journal, May 1953; Musical Digest, May 1948.

Oley Speaks *1874-1948*

OLEY SPEAKS, whose art songs are so well loved and so widely circulated that they may be considered part of the stream of American popular music, was born in Canal Winchester, Ohio, on June 28, 1874. Before deciding on music as a career, he worked as a clerk in a railroad office in Columbus. After comprehensive musical training with Karl Dufft, J. Armour Galloway, Emma Thursby, Max Spicker, and W. Macfarlane, he became a baritone soloist at a church in Columbus. In 1898 he settled permanently in New York City; he was baritone soloist for four years at the Church of the Divine Paternity, then

(from 1901 to 1906) at St. Thomas' Church. While holding these positions he appeared throughout the United States in recitals and performances of oratorios.

While pursuing a successful career as a singer, he wrote art songs, though for many years he failed to arouse the interest of publishers. His first published song was "Thou Gazest at the Stars." His greatest successes were his setting of Rudyard Kipling's "On the Road to Mandalay," published in 1907, "Morning" (verses by Frank L. Stanton) in 1910, and "Sylvia" (verses by Clinton Scollard) in 1914; sheet music sales of each of these three songs exceeded a million copies, and all established themselves permanently in the American song repertory. Of Speaks' more than 250 songs, the following are of special interest: "The Bells of Youth," "The Secret," "The Prayer Perfect," "The Message," "Little House of Dreams," "Star Eyes," "Life," "To You," "The Lord Is My Light," "Life's Twilight," "Fuzzy Wuzzy," and "Roses after the Rain." Speaks was also the composer of the popular World War I ballad "When the Boys Come Home," as well as of many part songs and anthems.

A facile composer, Speaks usually wrote his songs quickly, sometimes at a single sitting. He would first memorize the lyric, then sit at the piano and piece together his melody while improvising.

In 1924 Speaks became a director of ASCAP, holding this post until 1943, when ill health compelled him to decline renomination. He died in New York City on August 27, 1948.

ABOUT:
Musical America, September 1948.

Dave Stamper *1883-*

DAVID STAMPER was born in New York City on November 10, 1883. He received his academic education in the city public schools, and his musical training by studying alone at the piano. At the turn of the century he worked as pianist in a Coney Island dance hall. Soon after that he found employment as song plugger and demonstration pianist in Tin Pan Alley, and from 1903 to 1907 he was accompanist for Nora Bayes on the vaudeville circuit.

OLEY SPEAKS   ASCAP

While pursuing his career as a pianist, Stamper was writing popular songs. Early recognition, as well as his greatest successes, came with the Ziegfeld *Follies*. His debut as composer for the *Follies* took place in 1912 with "Daddy Has a Sweetheart and Mother Is Her Name" (lyrics by Gene Buck). For the next two decades, his songs, usually with lyrics by Buck, were represented in many editions of the *Follies*. In 1913 he contributed three songs: "Just You and I and the Moon," "Everybody Sometime Must Love Somebody," and "Without You." In 1914 he shared the writing of the basic score for the *Follies* with Raymond Hubbell, and in 1915 with Louis A. Hirsch. His most important *Follies* songs after 1915 were "Sweet Sixteen" and "Tulip Time" in 1919; "Plymouth Rock," "Raggedy Ann" and "Sally, Won't You Come Back?" in 1921; "My Rambler Rose" and " 'Neath the South Sea Moon," in 1922, both written in collaboration with Hirsch; and "Some Sweet Day" in 1923, again with Hirsch's collaboration. The last *Follies* revue in which Stamper's songs were heard (it was also the last produced by Ziegfeld himself) was the 1931 edition, for which Stamper wrote "Broadway Reverie" and "Bring on the Follies Girl." This was Stamper's last significant association with the Broadway theatre.

Besides his contributions to the *Follies*, Stamper wrote the complete scores for several Broadway musical comedies. The most noteworthy were *Take the Air* and *The Lovely Lady*, both produced in 1927. The first, which starred Will Mahoney, had two fine songs, "We'll Have a New Home in the Morning" and "All I Want Is a Lullaby" (lyrics by Buck); the latter musical included a title song, "Make Believe You're Happy," and "Ain't Love Grand" (lyrics by Cyrus Wood).

Since the early 1930's Stamper has been in retirement.

Max Steiner 1888-

MAXIMILIAN RAOUL STEINER, one of the most distinguished creators of background music for motion pictures, was born in Vienna on May 10, 1888. For many years the Steiner family had been steeped in the traditions of Viennese light music. Steiner's grandfather and father had both been close friends of Johann Strauss, the waltz king, and had been active in the production of operettas; Steiner's grandfather, also named Maximilian, had been head of the Theater-an-der-Wien, the leading theatre for operetta performances in Vienna.

Max Steiner attended the Imperial Academy of Music in Vienna, a pupil of Arnold Rosé, Graedener, and Fuchs among others. He completed the five-year course in a single year and was awarded a gold medal. He was only fourteen when he wrote and conducted an operetta, *Beautiful Greek Girl*, presented at the Orpheum Theater in Vienna, where it enjoyed a run of more than a year. From 1904 to 1911 Steiner resided in London, serving as conductor at various theàtres, including Daly's, the Adelphi, the Hippodrome, and the London Pavilion. In 1911 he went to Paris as conductor for the Alhambra Theatre.

In 1914 Florenz Ziegfeld invited Steiner to come to the United States as a conductor of some of his productions. After his arrival, Steiner decided to remain permanently and became an American citizen in 1920. He was active for many years as a conductor of musicals, both on Broadway and on tour. In addition he worked as chief orchestrator for the publishing house of Harms, in New York, where he was in close professional association with such leading composers as Victor Herbert, George Gershwin, Jerome Kern, and Vincent Youmans.

In the winter of 1929, while serving as conductor of the Broadway musical *Sons o' Guns*, Steiner was engaged by William Le Baron to become musical director of the RKO studios in Hollywood. He remained on the RKO lot for several years, then worked for Selznick-International, and next for Warner Brothers. Over a period of more than thirty years he has written and conducted the music for almost a hundred films. On three occasions he has been the recipient of Academy Awards: in 1935, for *The Informer;* in 1943, for *Now, Voyager*, from whose score came a hit song of that year, "It Can't Be Wrong" (lyrics by Kim Gannon); and in 1945, for *Since You Went Away.*

MAX STEINER

The following are some other motion pictures for which Steiner has written outstanding scores: *Battle Cry, Casablanca, The Charge of the Light Brigade, The Corn Is Green, Four Wives, The Garden of Allah, Gone with the Wind, Ice Palace, Johnny Belinda, Key Largo, The Letter, Life with Father, Marjorie Morningstar, Mildred Pierce, Parrish, Passage to Marseille, Saratoga Trunk, So Big, A Star Is Born, A Stolen Life, A Summer Place, Tomorrow Is Forever,* and *The Treasure of Sierra Madre.*

In recognition of his achievements, foreign governments have honored Steiner on several occasions. Like his grandfather and father before him, he was decorated Officier de l'Académie Française by the French government. In 1936 the Belgian government presented him with the Bronze Medal at the Brussels Cinema Exhibition, and in the same year he was honored with the World Cinema Congress Medal in Venice. In 1948 he received from the Cinema Exhibition in Vienna a statuette for his *Treasure of Sierra Madre* score. In 1947 the Hollywood Foreign Correspondents honored him with the Golden Globe Award for his music in *Life with Father.*

Steiner's theme music for *A Summer Place* became an outstanding song success in 1959, and that for *The Dark at the Top of the Stairs* in 1960.

Joseph W. Stern *1870-1934*

JOSEPH W. STERN was born to a well-to-do family in New York City on January 11, 1870. His father was part owner of a neckware manufacturing plant in New York. Joseph attended the city public schools and afterward earned his living as a traveling salesman for a tie manufacturer. He had no musical training. He played the piano "with one hand while faking with the other" (his own description) when he wrote his first song and started a successful career both as a composer and publisher.

An incident reported in the newspapers was the inspiration for that first song. Stern's friend Edward B. Marks—a traveling salesman for a button factory who liked writing song lyrics—came upon a story describing the plight of a little girl in New York found by a policeman who turns out to be her long-lost father. Marks scribbled the verses for a sentimental ballad inspired by this episode and prevailed upon Stern to write the melody. Since they could not find a publisher for this first effort, which they called "The Little Lost Child," they set up a publishing house of their own, Joseph Stern & Company, on 14th Street, New York City, and issued their song in 1894.

A musical comedy star of that period, Della Fox, became interested in "The Little Lost Child" and introduced it effectively on the stage. Soon afterward a Brooklyn electrician originated slides with which still pictures could be flashed on a motion picture screen. With the help of William Fox, then running a slide exchange on 14th Street, slides were used in a motion picture theatre in Union Square to dramatize "The Little Lost Child" pictorially, the words of the ballad flashed beneath the various pictures. This was the first such presentation of a popular song. "The Little Lost Child" became one of the most successful sentimental ballads of the 1890's, its sheet music sales rising to several million copies. Thus the firm of Joseph Stern & Company, and the songwriting reputation of Stern and Marks, was built on the indestructible foundation of a single hit.

In 1894 Stern and Marks also wrote and published a second ballad, "His Last Thoughts Were of You," and in 1895, "No One Ever Loved More than I." Then came a second hit

JOSEPH W. STERN

of the formidable dimensions of their first song, a sentimental ballad which also had its origin in an actual occurrence. While sitting in a New York restaurant, Stern and Marks happened to notice a dapper patron at a nearby table who was insulting the waitress. She burst into tears, exclaiming, "My mother was a lady," adding that the man surely would not have dared to insult her if her brother Jack had been present. Marks' imagination was sparked by this episode and that very day he completed a set of verses describing the incident. The dramatic climax of his lyric, however, was his own invention: the patron turns out to be Jack's lifelong friend, and in remorse offers to marry the waitress. "My Mother Was a Lady" was published in 1895, introduced that year at Tony Pastor's Music Hall by Meyer Cohen, and later performed in vaudeville with sensational success by Lottie Gilson. Millions of copies of sheet music were sold and the phrase "my mother was a lady" became a popular slang expression of the day.

"The Little Lost Child" and "My Mother Was a Lady" were the two outstanding successes of Stern and Marks as songwriters. (As publishers, however, they issued many other important sentimental ballads of that era.) Among their lesser efforts were two ballads popularized by Lottie Gilson, "Games We Used to Play" and "I Don't Blame You,

Tom." Other ballads by Stern and Marks included "Teacher and the Boy," "The Old Postmaster," and "Don't Wear Your Heart on Your Sleeve."

After the turn of the century, Stern devoted himself primarily to publishing. He went into complete retirement in 1920. He died at his home in Brightwater, Long Island, on March 31, 1934. Just before his death he was planning a return to the publishing business.

ABOUT:
Geller, James Jacob. Famous Songs; Marks, Edward B. They All Sang.

John Stromberg *1853-1902*

JOHN ("HONEY") STROMBERG, noted as the composer of Weber and Fields extravaganzas produced at the Music Hall in New York in the closing years of the nineteenth century, was born in 1853. He received his musical instruction from private teachers and served an apprenticeship as an arranger for the publishing house of Witmark. In 1895 he published a song to his own lyrics entitled "My Best Girl's a Corker," which brought him to the attention of Weber and Fields. At that time they were planning to produce and star in extravaganza-burlesques in their own theatre, and they engaged Stromberg as both composer and music director. The first of these Weber and Fields productions was *The Art of Maryland,* which opened on September 5, 1896. During the next half dozen years Stromberg wrote the scores for all the Weber and Fields extravaganzas, including *The Geezer* (1896), *The Glad Hand* (1897), *The Pousse-Café* (1897), *Hurly-Burly* (1898), *Helter-Skelter* (1899), *Whirl-i-gig* (1899), *Fiddle-dee-dee* (1900), *Hoity-Toity* (1901), and *Twirly-Whirly* (1902). Many of Stromberg's songs from these varied productions, most of them to lyrics by Edgar Smith, became very popular. "Dinah" (or "Kiss Me Honey Do") was introduced by Peter F. Dailey in *Hurly-Burly.* "When Chloe Sings a Song" was the vehicle for the stunning debut of Lillian Russell at the Music Hall in *Whirl-i-gig.* "Say You Love Me, Sue" also came from *Whirl-i-gig;* "Ma Blushin' Rosie," "Come Back My Honey Boy," and "I'm a Respectable Working Girl"

JOHN STROMBERG

from *Fiddle-dee-dee;* "De Pullman Porters' Ball" from *Hoity-Toity;* "Tell Us Pretty Ladies" from *Pousse-Café.* What is probably his greatest song hit of all—and the last he was destined to write—was "Come Down, Ma Evenin' Star" (lyrics by Robert B. Smith), which Lillian Russell made famous in *Twirly-Whirly.*

Stromberg wrote the music for only four numbers for this last-named production: He was working on the score when he was found dead in his New York apartment in July 1902, apparently a suicide. The manuscript of "Come Down, Ma Evenin' Star" was found in his pocket. When Lillian Russell introduced the song at the première of *Twirly-Whirly,* she broke down and wept and could not continue. Since then this song has been the one with which she is always identified.

Jule Styne 1905-

JULE STYNE was born in London on December 31, 1905. His passion for the theatre revealed itself early. He was only three when he became so enthralled by Harry Lauder that he ran up to the stage and joined the famous Scot in a duet. Styne's family came to the United States when he was eight, settling in Chicago, where he received comprehensive piano training. As a child he displayed his talent in successful performances

with the Detroit and Chicago symphony orchestras. When he was thirteen he received a scholarship for the Chicago Musical College, where he specialized in the piano but also received instruction in music theory.

After reaching maturity, Styne decided to concentrate on popular music. He made vocal arrangements for and played the piano in several jazz bands before forming an ensemble of his own in 1931. He not only directed the group but also did all their orchestrations and played the piano. Through most of the 1930's the band was heard in leading hotels and night clubs.

Styne then went to Hollywood to write background music and make vocal arrangements for several motion pictures. He also served as a vocal coach for Twentieth Century-Fox, working with such stars as Shirley Temple and Alice Faye. Several of his songs during this period were interpolated into various films. The best were to lyrics by Frank Loesser: "Since You" in *Sailors on Leave;* "Conchita, Marquita, Lolita" in *Priorities on Parade;* and "I Don't Want to Walk Without You" in *Sweater Girl.*

In 1942 Styne met Sammy Cahn, a young lyricist who had already achieved some repute in New York. They decided to collaborate and one of their first efforts proved a resounding success, "I've Heard That Song Before," written in 1943 and first sung by Frank Sinatra in a motion picture short, *Youth on Parade,* propagandizing racial tolerance. A year afterward they had another pre-eminent success in "I'll Walk Alone," which was first heard in the picture *Follow the Boys* and which became one of the outstanding ballads of World War II. Their leading songs during the next three years included the following: "It's Been a Long, Long Time"; "Poor Little Rhode Island," adopted by Rhode Island as the official state song; "Let It Snow, Let It Snow"; "The Things We Did Last Summer"; "Saturday Night Is the Loneliest Night in the Week"; "There Goes That Song Again" from the film *Carolina Blues;* "What Makes the Sun Set" and "I Begged Her" from *Anchors Aweigh;* "Love Me" from *Stork Club;* "I'm Glad I Waited for You" from *Tars and Spars;* "Five Minutes More" from *Sweetheart of Sigma Chi;* "I Love an Old-Fashioned Song" and "You're the Cause of It All" from *The Kid from Brooklyn;* "I've Never Forgotten" from the *Earl Carroll Sketch Book;* "I Got a Gal I Love" and "What Am I Gonna Do About You?" from *Ladies' Man;* "It's the Same Old Dream," "I Believe," and "Time after Time" from *It Happened in Brooklyn.*

In 1944 Styne and Cahn were offered a contract to write songs for a Broadway musical, *Glad to See You,* a show which expired during its Boston tryout. When the songwriters finally made their bow on Broadway, their debut proved impressive indeed; the production was *High Button Shoes,* starring Phil Silvers and Nanette Fabray, which began a run of more than seven hundred performances on October 9, 1947. The principal musical numbers were "Papa, Won't You Dance with Me?" and "I Still Get Jealous." In 1949 (this time with Leo Robin as his lyricist) Styne wrote the songs for *Gentlemen Prefer Blondes,* the Broadway musical comedy adaptation of the Anita Loos novel and play. *Gentlemen Prefer Blondes* also enjoyed a run of more than seven hundred performances following its opening on December 8, 1949. In it Carol Channing achieved stardom with such winning Styne numbers as "Diamonds Are a Girl's Best Friend" and "I'm Just a Little Girl from Little Rock."

Two lesser Broadway musicals followed: the revue *Two on the Aisle* (1951) starring Bert Lahr, and the musical comedy *Hazel Flagg* (1953), which included "How Do You Speak to an Angel?" (lyrics by Bob Hilliard). In 1954 Styne contributed three songs to the Broadway production of *Peter Pan* starring Mary Martin. Then, on November 29, 1956, he scored decisively for a third time on Broadway with the musical comedy *Bells Are Ringing,* which starred Judy Holliday in her first Broadway musical appearance. Three ballads from the Styne score joined the hits of that year: "Just in Time," "Long Before I Knew You," and "The Party's Over," all of them with lyrics by Betty Comden and Adolph Green. The highly successful motion picture adaptation, produced by Arthur Freed, also starred Judy Holliday.

In 1958 several of Styne's songs were heard in *Say Darling,* a Broadway comedy built around the events and episodes leading to the production of *The Pajama Game,* the musical comedy by Adler and Ross. In 1959 Styne wrote the music (to lyrics by Stephen

JULE STYNE

Sondheim) for another smash Broadway hit, *Gypsy,* an adaptation of Gypsy Rose Lee's autobiography, starring Ethel Merman, which opened on May 21, 1959. Ethel Merman's surefire delivery helped make three of the songs standouts: "Everything's Coming Up Roses," "Together," and "You'll Never Get Away from Me."

Do Re Mi, opening on December 27, 1960, brought Phil Silvers back to the musical comedy stage after an absence of a decade. The book by Garson Kanin concerned the invasion of the flourishing jukebox business by a group of gamblers headed by a small-time conniver. With lyrics by Betty Comden and Adolph Green, Styne provided two fetching numbers: "Cry Like the Wind," and a 1961 hit tune, "Make Someone Happy."

Do Re Mi was followed in the late fall of 1961 by *Subways Are for Sleeping,* co-starring Carol Lawrence and Sydney Chaplin. It was based on a book by Edmund G. Love, adapted by Betty Comden and Adolph Green, who also provided the lyrics.

While working within the Broadway theatre, Styne did not desert motion pictures. His most significant songs for the screen after 1947 were: "It's Magic" and "Run, Run, Run" from *Romance on the High Seas;* "Every Day I Love You a Little Bit More" from *Two Guys from Texas;* and "Give

Me a Song with a Beautiful Melody," "Fiddle-dee-dee," and the title number from *It's a Great Feeling*, all to lyrics by Sammy Cahn. In 1954 Styne and Cahn received the Academy Award for the title song from *Three Coins in the Fountain*.

The twenty-fifth anniversary of Styne's career in show business was commemorated on August 10, 1959, with the following paragraph in the *Congressional Record*: "The lives of Americans throughout our land as well as the lives of people throughout the corners of the world have been enriched by the artistry and genius of Jule Styne. As an American, he has brought great credit to his country—the United States of America. It is, therefore, fitting and proper for his fellow Americans to pay tribute to Jule Styne on the occasion of his twenty-fifth anniversary in show business. His accomplishments have been great—the position he holds in the hearts and minds of his fellow Americans is just as great."

Jule Styne has been a producer of several Broadway plays and musicals as well as of television "specials." He has written music for three ballets, *Wallflower, Side Show*, and *Cops and Robbers*.

ABOUT:
Green, Stanley. The World of Musical Comedy.

James Thornton *1861-1938*

JAMES THORNTON was born in Liverpool, England, on December 5, 1861. When he was eight, his family came to the United States, settling in Boston, where he attended the Elliott School. He soon abandoned his education to earn a living. At seventeen he worked as a night watchman in a Boston printing plant; in this occupation he was able to do a considerable amount of reading, an activity in which he was both guided and encouraged by Henry Wadsworth Longfellow.

Thornton's professional career in popular music began in Boston when he found employment as a singing waiter. Soon thereafter he found engagements in New York City, principally at Allen's Bal Mabille café on Bleecker Street. While holding this job he wrote his first song, "Remember Poor Mother at Home," which he sold for $2.50.

With John L. Sullivan, the famous pugilist, as his drinking companion, he made the rounds of cafés and saloons on and near the Lower East Side, playing the piano and singing his songs for Sullivan's delectation.

For many years Thornton toured the vaudeville circuit as a partner of Charles B. Lawlor, the composer of "The Sidewalks of New York." In this act Thornton appeared dressed in clerical garb, rendering a humorous monologue in mock seriousness. He also sang some of his own songs, a favorite at the time being "The Irish Jubilee," for which he wrote the lyrics in 1890 to Lawlor's music.

Thornton's first song hit came in 1892 with "My Sweetheart's the Man in the Moon." His wife, one evening, had implored him to come home after his performance on the stage instead of visiting neighborhood saloons. When he refused, she asked him lightly if she was still his sweetheart. He replied lightly, "My sweetheart's the man in the moon." The phrase appealed to him, and the next morning he used it as the basis of a song lyric for which he wrote his own music. Much of the early success of this song was due to the effective rendition given it by his wife in leading theatres and cafés.

From that time Thornton wrote both lyrics and music for his songs. In 1893 he produced "The Streets of Cairo," inspired by a hootchy-kootchy dancer at the Chicago World's Fair. A year later came a sentimental ballad, "She May Have Seen Better Days." In 1896 he boasted three solid hits in "On the Benches in the Park," "Don't Give Up the Old Love for the New," and "It Don't Seem Like the Same Old Smile," a song which won first prize in a contest sponsored by the New York *World*. In 1897 he published "There's a Little Star Shining for You."

Thornton's most famous song was "When You Were Sweet Sixteen," published in 1898. Like "My Sweetheart's the Man in the Moon" this song is said to have been stimulated by a casual remark to the composer's wife. Asked by her if he did not love her any longer, Thornton replied: "I love you like I did when you were sweet sixteen."

Thornton sold "When You Were Sweet Sixteen" for a pittance to two different publishers. When Witmark's publication proved a bonanza, the house was sued by Stern and

Marks, who were able to prove that they had previously purchased the song for fifteen dollars. A settlement was reached whereby Witmark paid Stern and Marks five thousand dollars. "When You Were Sweet Sixteen" has never lost its popularity; to this day it is a favorite of barbershop quartets everywhere. In 1944 it was revived in the motion picture *The Great John L.*, starring Bing Crosby.

In 1900 Thornton wrote "The Bridge of Sighs"—the bridge being that which connects the criminal court and the Tombs prison in New York City. His last successful song, also a sentimental ballad, appeared three years later, "There's a Mother Waiting for You at Home Sweet Home."

Thornton wrote little after that, and nothing that achieved any measure of success. For some years he continued to make appearances in vaudeville. He was greatly embittered by the fact that the kind of songs he loved best and knew how to write best— the sentimental ballad—had seemed to lose popular favor. Thornton's last public appearance was as himself in the Jerome Kern-Oscar Hammerstein musical comedy *Sweet Adeline* in 1929. He died in New York City on July 27, 1938.

Harry Tierney 1895-

HARRY TIERNEY was born in Perth Amboy, New Jersey, on May 21, 1895. His was a musical background. His father played the trumpet in a symphony orchestra and his mother was a competent pianist. His mother gave him his first piano instruction and his uncle taught him composition and harmony. Tierney subsequently attended the Virgil Conservatory of Music in New York City. For a while he toured the country as a concert pianist. In 1915 he went to London, where he was employed as staff composer for a British publisher and where three of his popular songs were issued ("Just for Tonight," "Pass Along," and "King of the Maniac Band"). In London he also started to write music for the stage, producing scores for a musical comedy and a revue.

He returned to the United States in 1916. Convinced that his talent lay in popular music, he decided to embark on a career

ASCAP

HARRY TIERNEY

as a composer of songs. One of the first numbers he wrote at this time was "M-i-s-s-i-s-s-i-p-p-i" (lyrics by Bert Hanlon and Benny Ryan), which Frances White introduced successfully at the Ziegfeld *Midnight Frolics*. In 1917 Anna Held sang "It's a Cute Little Way of My Own" (lyrics by Alfred Bryan) in *Follow Me*, a score that also included two more Tierney interpolations. In 1918 "On Atlantic Beach" and "Honky Tonky Town" were introduced in *Everything* at the Hippodrome Theatre. For both of these songs, Joseph McCarthy was the lyricist; it was to McCarthy's lyrics that Tierney subsequently wrote some of his most successful numbers.

Tierney now found employment as a staff composer in Tin Pan Alley with the publishing firm of Jerome Remick. In 1919 and 1920 several of his songs were interpolated into Broadway productions: "My Baby's Arms" and "They're So Hard to Keep When They're Beautiful" in the Ziegfeld *Follies* and "A Wee Bit of Lace" and "Charming" in the George M. Cohan production *A Royal Vagabond*.

Tierney's first great achievement as the composer of a complete score for the Broadway theatre came on November 18, 1919, with *Irene*, one of the most successful musical comedies of the decade. *Irene* enjoyed the longest run of any Broadway musical up to that time (670 performances) and went on tour with seventeen road companies. For this delightful play with a Cinderella theme, Tierney created the most famous song of his entire career, the lovable waltz "Alice Blue Gown," with which the star, Edith Day, stopped the show nightly. Other fascinating numbers were "Castle of Dreams," for whose main melody Tierney went to Chopin's *Minute Waltz*, and the title song.

In 1920 Tierney went to England to help produce *Irene* for the London stage and to write the score for *Afgar*, a comic opera produced by Cochran. He was back in New York in 1922 with *Up She Goes*, a musical comedy adaptation of Frank Craven's farce *Too Many Cooks*, for which Tierney wrote "Lady Luck, Smile on Me," "Journey's End," and "Let's Kiss and Make Up." In 1923, Ziegfeld engaged Tierney to write the music for *Kid Boots*, in which Eddie Cantor was starred; here the main musical numbers included "If Your Heart's in the Game" and "Someone Loves You After All" (lyrics by McCarthy). In 1923 and 1924 Tierney contributed songs to the Ziegfeld *Follies*, and in 1927 he wrote the complete score for still another Ziegfeld triumph, *Rio Rita*, the show with which Ziegfeld opened the palatial theatre bearing his name. The title number of this musical (lyrics by McCarthy) became one of the hit songs of the year.

Tierney's next musical, *Cross My Heart* (1928), was a box office failure. He went to Hollywood to help adapt *Rio Rita* for the screen, and between 1929 and 1931 wrote the music for *Dixiana* and *Half Shot at Sunrise*. Hard luck now dogged his steps relentlessly. For more than a year he devoted himself to writing the music for an operetta, *Omar Khayyam*, which never reached the stage. A second operetta, *Beau Brummel*, opened and closed in St. Louis in 1933.

In 1939-1940, Tierney assisted in adapting his Broadway stage triumph, *Irene*, for the screen. Since then he has completed the score for a ballet, *Prelude to a Holiday in Hong Kong*.

Dimitri Tiomkin *1899-*

DIMITRI TIOMKIN was born in St. Petersburg, Russia, on May 10, 1899. His father was a physician, assistant to the renowned German biochemist Paul Ehrlich; his mother was a music teacher and pianist. As a boy Dimitri's interests were divided among mathematics, the stage, and music. But it was for the last that he showed the most pronounced talent, and it was finally decided that he be given comprehensive musical training. He attended the St. Petersburg Conservatory, where his teachers included Alexander Glazunov in composition and Felix Blumenfeld in piano. While pursuing these studies he made numerous appearances in Russia as a child prodigy pianist, often as soloist with major orchestras. In 1921 he went to Berlin to complete his music study with Egon Petri, Ferruccio Busoni, and Hugo Leichtentritt.

In 1922 he continued his career as a concert pianist with performances throughout Germany, including important appearances with the Berlin Philharmonic. One year later he decided to make a specialty of modern music. For the next few years he gave provocative concerts of contemporary music, introducing in Germany and France several important works that were dedicated to him. In 1925 he made his first tour of the United States. During his subsequent appearances in the United States he remained a champion of modern music in general, and American music in particular. In 1928 he received special permission from the French government to give performances at the Paris Opéra; on this occasion he presented the French première of George Gershwin's Concerto in F.

During his American visit in 1925 he met and married Albertina Rasch, the famous dancer and choreographer. At this time, too, he met such giants of American popular music as George Gershwin, Jerome Kern, and Richard Rodgers, who stimulated his interest in writing popular music.

In 1930 Albertina Rasch was engaged by MGM to help produce several screen musicals. While in Hollywood with her, Tiomkin was given a contract to provide the score for *The Rogue Song*, in which Lawrence Tibbett was starred. Tiomkin also created the musical setting for three motion pictures starring Ramon Navarro and for *Resurrection*.

Following this initial contact with films, Tiomkin returned to New York, where he resumed his career as a concert pianist. But he was also writing popular music, some of which was heard in Broadway productions put on by Ziegfeld and the Shuberts. He even tried his hand at producing, but his Broadway play (Montague Glass's *Keeping Expenses Down*) survived only three weeks.

He returned to Hollywood in 1933 to write the background music for *Alice in Wonderland*. This time he planted his roots permanently in Hollywood soil. He became one of the most prolific and successful composers of background music and popular songs for motion pictures, having written scores for over 120 screen plays. Between 1939 and 1961 he was nominated for Academy Awards for his musical contributions to the following important films: *The Corsican Brothers, The Moon and Sixpence, Mr. Smith Goes to Washington, High Noon, Champion, The High and the Mighty, Friendly Persuasion, Giant, Wild Is the Wind, The Old Man and the Sea, Young Land,* and *The Alamo*. He has won Academy Awards four times: for the scoring of *High Noon* in 1952, *The High and the Mighty* in 1954, and *The Old Man and the Sea* in 1958; and for the song "Do Not Forsake Me" (lyrics by Ned Washington) from *High Noon* in 1952.

Several other Tiomkin songs have been hits. These include the title songs of *The High and the Mighty* and *Friendly Persuasion* (lyrics by Paul Francis Webster); the title songs of *The Long Night* and *The Happy Times* (lyrics by Washington); "Strange Are the Ways of Love" from *Young Land;* "Green Leaves of Summer" and "Ballad of the Alamo" from *The Alamo;* "They Call It Love" and "The Legend of Navarone" from *The Guns of Navarone.* "Friendly Persuasion" was honored as the best song of 1956 in a national survey of radio and television editors. "Strange Are the Ways of Love" and "Green Leaves of Summer" were nominated for Academy Awards in 1960 and 1961, respectively. In 1960 Tiomkin also wrote the score for the successful motion picture *The Sundowners*.

Tiomkin has been the recipient of numerous other awards besides those of the Motion Picture Academy. They include three Golden Globe Awards, an Award of Merit from the National Association for American

DIMITRI TIOMKIN

Composers and Conductors for significant contributions to American music, and a special plaque from the French Society of Authors, Composers, and Editors for high achievement in music.

During World War II Tiomkin worked with the Signal Corps as music director, adviser, and consultant. In this position he scored music for many training and orientation films, including *Negro Soldiers in World War II, War Comes to America, The Battle of Britain,* and *The Battle of China.* For this service he was the recipient of several ribbons and citations.

In the spring of 1960 Tiomkin was named Chevalier in the French Legion of Honor.

ABOUT:
Tiomkin, Dimitri. Please Don't Hate Me. Cue, March 23, 1957; Overture, March 1949.

Egbert Van Alstyne *1882-1951*

EGBERT ANSON VAN ALSTYNE was born in Chicago on March 5, 1882. A musical prodigy, he played the organ in the Methodist Sunday School in Marengo, Illinois, when he was only seven. A scholarship brought him to the Chicago Musical College; his academic education took place in Chicago's public schools and at Cornell College in Iowa. His schooling completed, he toured

ASCAP
EGBERT VAN ALSTYNE

the West as pianist for and director of various stage shows. After that he appeared in vaudeville in an act that included Harry H. Williams.

In 1900 he went to New York with Harry Williams. For two years he worked as staff pianist for a publishing house in Tin Pan Alley. He also began to devote himself seriously to the writing of songs, with Williams as his lyricist. They had their first success in 1903 with "Navajo," one of the earliest commercial songs to exploit Indian names; this was a hit when introduced on Broadway in *Nancy Brown* by Marie Cahill. They wrote two more Indian songs: "Cheyenne" in 1906 and "San Antonio" in 1907. But before that, in 1905, they had produced one of the greatest song hits of the decade, "In the Shade of the Old Apple Tree," of which several million copies of sheet music were sold.

Among other songs written between 1904 and 1911 were a Negro comedy number, "Back, Back, Back to Baltimore"; "Won't You Come Over to My House?"; "There Never Was a Girl Like You"; "What's the Matter with Father?"; "I'm Afraid to Go Home in the Dark" (a phrase supposedly quoted by O. Henry just before his death); "The Tale the Church Bells Tolled"; "It Looks Like a Big Night Tonight"; "Good Night, Ladies"; "When I Was Twenty-one

and You Were Sweet Sixteen"; and "Oh, That Navajo Rag."

Van Alstyne and Williams provided songs for two Broadway musicals. The first was *A Broken Doll*, starring Alice York, in 1909; the other was *Girlies*, with Ernest Truex and Maude Raymond, in 1910.

In 1912 Van Alstyne wrote "That Old Girl of Mine" to lyrics by Earle C. Jones. After that he worked mainly with the lyricist Gus Kahn. Their first important songs were "Sunshine and Roses" in 1913 and "Memories" two years later. Subsequent hits included the following: "Pretty Baby" (the melody written collaboratively with Tony Jackson); "Your Eyes Have Told Me So" (written collaboratively with Walter Blaufuss), which was popularized by Grace La Rue in vaudeville and in 1936 revived in the motion picture *Sing Me a Love Song;* "Sailin' Away on the Henry Clay"; "On the Road to Home Sweet Home"; "Little Old Church in the Valley"; "Old Pal"; "Kentucky's a Way of Saying Good Morning." He wrote "Drifting and Dreaming" to Haven Gillespie's lyrics and "When I Was a Dreamer" to lyrics by Little and Lewis.

Van Alstyne lived the last years of his life in Chicago, where his mother (then in her eighties) enjoyed a successful career as "Aunt Em" on a weekly radio program. Van Alstyne died in Chicago on July 9, 1951.

Jimmy Van Heusen *1913-*

JAMES VAN HEUSEN was born Edward Chester Babcock in Syracuse, New York, on January 26, 1913, the son of a building contractor. His mother (the former Ida May Foster) is believed to be descended from Stephen Foster. Van Heusen began writing songs while he was still attending Central High School in Syracuse; he was in charge of a regular radio program over a small local station and often presented his own numbers. It was during this period that he assumed the name of James Van Heusen, taking his last name from a collar advertisement. But music was relegated to the background as he pursued his academic education at Cazenovia Seminary and Syracuse University.

At Syracuse University he met Jerry Arlen, younger brother of the composer Harold Arlen. Upon Harold Arlen's invitation, Van Heusen went to New York to write songs for the Cotton Club, the Harlem night club. He held this assignment only a few months. After that Van Heusen worked as an operator of a freight elevator, while trying to market his music in Tin Pan Alley. He managed to sell one of his songs to Santly Brothers, "There's a House in Harlem for Sale."

For about four years Van Heusen worked as staff pianist for several publishing houses in Tin Pan Alley. As an employee of Remick he met Jimmy Dorsey in 1938, and to Dorsey's lyrics he wrote "It's the Dreamer in Me," a modest success. On the strength of this number he was given a two-year songwriting contract by Remick at a salary of $250 a week. Under this arrangement, and with Eddie De Lange as his lyricist, Van Heusen created several noteworthy numbers, among them "So Help Me," "Oh! You Crazy Moon," "Deep in a Dream," and "Heaven Can Wait."

In 1939 Van Heusen and De Lange wrote all the songs for *Swingin' the Dream*, a Broadway musical in which Shakespeare's *A Midsummer Night's Dream* was presented in a jazz version set in New Orleans in 1895. The show was a failure, but one of its songs, "Darn That Dream," did well commercially. This number and a second one—"I Thought About You" (lyrics by Johnny Mercer)— were Van Heusen's first successful attempts at writing swing music as opposed to ballads and sentimental pieces.

Early in 1940 Jimmy Van Heusen wrote the music for Billy Rose's aquacade at the New York World's Fair. During that year he published no fewer than sixty songs, many of them heard repeatedly on the radio. Once three Van Heusen songs were on the Hit Parade in a single week: "Shake Down the Stars," the title song of the motion picture *All This and Heaven Too* (lyrics to both by De Lange), and "Polka Dots and Moonbeams" (lyrics by Johnny Burke). Van Heusen's outstanding hit song of the year, however, was "Imagination" (lyrics by Burke). A year later Van Heusen and Burke enjoyed success again with "It's Always You."

Having established a permanent working arrangement with Burke, Van Heusen arrived in Hollywood in 1940 to write three songs for *Love Thy Neighbor*, a film in which Fred Allen, Jack Benny, and Mary Martin were

JIMMY VAN HEUSEN

starred. At this time, Van Heusen and Burke attracted the interest of Bing Crosby, who, also in 1940, asked them to supply the songs for *The Road to Zanzibar*, a Bing Crosby-Bob Hope-Dorothy Lamour picture. The association of Crosby as star and Van Heusen as composer proved unusually creative; with Burke or Sammy Cahn as lyricist, Van Heusen provided songs for almost twenty Crosby productions, including several of the most popular in the Crosby-Hope-Lamour "Road" series.

Among Van Heusen's best songs for these Crosby films were "Moonlight Becomes You," "Constantly," and "Ain't Got a Dime to My Name" for *The Road to Morocco;* "Sunday, Monday, or Always," and "If You Please" for *Dixie;* the title song, "Day After Forever," and "Swinging on a Star" for *Going My Way* (the last an Academy Award winner in 1944) ; "Personality," "Put It There, Pal," and "Would You?" for *The Road to Utopia;* "Aren't You Glad You're You?" for *The Bells of St. Mary's;* "As Long as I'm Dreaming," "Smile Right Back at the Sun," and "Country Style" for *Welcome Stranger;* "But Beautiful" and "You Don't Have to Know the Language" for *The Road to Rio;* "Once and for Always," "When Is Sometime?" and "Busy Doing Nothing" for *A Connecticut Yankee;* "You're in Love with Someone" and the title song for *Top o' the Morning;* "Sunshine Cake" and "Sure Thing" for *Riding High;* "Life Is So Peculiar" and "High on the List" for *Mister Music;* "Cela M'est Égal" and "The Magic Window" for *Little Boy Lost;* "You Can Bounce Right Back" for *Anything Goes;* the title number and "I Couldn't Care Less" for *Say One for Me.*

But the songwriting activity of Van Heusen and Burke was not confined exclusively to Bing Crosby's pictures. They wrote "Got the Moon in My Pocket" for *My Favorite Spy;* "Suddenly It's Spring" for *Lady in the Dark;* "It Could Happen to You" for *And the Angels Sing;* "Like Someone in Love" for *Belle of the Yukon;* "That Little Dream Got Nowhere" for *Cross My Heart;* and the title song and "So Would I" for *My Heart Goes Crazy.*

Van Heusen and Johnny Burke have also worked together on songs for the Broadway stage. In 1946 they wrote "Just My Luck" and "You May Not Love Me," among other numbers, for *Nellie Bly,* and in 1953 they created the score for *Carnival in Flanders.*

The other lyricist with whom Van Heusen has worked with a high degree of success is Sammy Cahn, with whom he achieved two Academy Awards: "All the Way" from *The Joker Is Wild* in 1957 and "High Hopes" from *A Hole in the Head* in 1959. "The Second Time Around" from *High Time* was nominated for an Academy Award in 1961. These are some of the other outstanding screen songs by Van Heusen and Cahn: the title songs of *The Tender Trap, They Came to Cordura, Paris Holiday, The Earth Is Mine, The Night of the Quarter Moon,* and *Pardners;* "Love Is a Career" from *Career;* "To Love and Be Loved" from *Some Came Running;* and "Incurably Romantic" and "Specialization" from *Let's Make Love.* They also wrote "Come Fly with Me," "Only the Lonely," and "Come Dance with Me," as well as the score for *Ocean's 11,* starring Frank Sinatra.

In 1955 Van Heusen and Cahn wrote the songs for *Our Town,* a television adaptation, with music, of the Thornton Wilder play. The score yielded two solid hits in "Impatient Years" and "Love and Marriage," the latter winning the annual "Emmy" Television Award as the best musical contribution. In 1960 they wrote the songs for a television musical comedy starring Bob Hope, *Potomac Madness.*

Since 1948 Van Heusen has been active as a publisher of music, first with Burvan Incorporated, then with Burke-Van Heusen Publishing Company and Maraville Music Corporation, and finally with Famous Music.

Albert Von Tilzer *1878-1956*

ALBERT VON TILZER was born Albert Gumm in Indianapolis, Indiana, on March 29, 1878. He received his academic training in the elementary schools of Indianapolis. Abandoning his education at the high school level, he went to work in his father's shoe store. Then, having had some lessons in harmony, and having learned to play the piano by ear, he found a job as a music director of a vaudeville troupe. In 1899 he worked for the Chicago branch of the publishing firm of Shapiro, Bernstein and Von Tilzer, which his brother (Harry Von Tilzer) had recently joined. By this time he had assumed the name Von Tilzer, which his brother had concocted for himself. Soon after the turn of the century, Albert Von Tilzer went to New York to work as a shoe salesman in a Brooklyn department store. Meanwhile, in 1900, he had published his first piece of music, *The Absent-Minded Beggar Waltz,* for piano. In 1903 his brother's publishing house issued his song "That's What the Daisy Said," for which he wrote lyrics as well as the music.

In 1903 Albert Von Tilzer formed the publishing house of York Music Company, which henceforth issued his songs. "Teasing" (lyrics by Cecil Mack) was introduced in 1904, and in 1905, "The Moon Has His Eyes on You" (lyrics by Billy Johnson) and "A Picnic for Two" (lyrics by Arthur J. Lamb).

With "Honey Boy," a tribute to the minstrel George ("Honey Boy") Evans published in 1907, Albert Von Tilzer initiated a successful partnership with the lyricist Jack Norworth. They created three substantial song hits in 1908: "Good Evening, Caroline," "Smarty," and most important of all, a song that is still remembered and inevitably associated with our national pastime, "Take Me Out to the Ball Game."

After 1908 Von Tilzer worked productively with several other lyricists, especially with Lew Brown. Their first songs were "I'm the Lonesomest Gal in Town," "Ken-

ALBERT VON TILZER

tucky Sue," and "Please Don't Take My Lovin' Man Away," all published in 1912. Between then and 1921 their most important songs were "I May Be Gone for a Long, Long Time," an outstanding ballad of World War I, introduced by Grace La Rue in *Hitchy-Koo;* "Au Revoir, but Not Good-Bye, Soldier Boy," still another World War I favorite; "Oh, By Jingo!"; "Chili Bean"; "I Used to Love You but It's All Over Now"; and "Dapper Dan."

During this period Von Tilzer wrote the following leading song hits with other lyricists: "Carrie" and "Put Your Arms Around Me, Honey" (lyrics by Junie McCree); "Waters of Venice" and "I'll Be With You in Apple Blossom Time" (lyrics by Neville Fleeson); "Oh, How She Could Yacki, Hacki, Wicki, Wacki, Woo" (lyrics by Stanley Murphy and Charles McCarron) with which Eddie Cantor made his momentous New York stage debut in a Ziegfeld revue in 1917; "They're All Sweeties" (lyrics by Andrew B. Sterling).

Albert Von Tilzer also wrote the scores for several Broadway productions. The most successful were *Honey Girl* in 1920 and *The Gingham Girl* in 1922. For the latter, which had a Broadway run of more than a year, Von Tilzer wrote "As Long as I Have You" (lyrics by Neville Fleeson).

While pursuing his successful career as a Tin Pan Alley composer and publisher, Albert Von Tilzer was also for many years a headliner on the Orpheum vaudeville circuit. In 1930 he settled in Hollywood where, for a brief period, he worked for motion pictures before going into retirement. He died in Los Angeles on October 1, 1956.

Harry Von Tilzer *1872-1946*

HARRY VON TILZER was born Harry Gumm in Detroit, Michigan, on July 8, 1872. He was one of five children; his brother was Albert Von Tilzer. During Harry's childhood, his family moved to Indianapolis, where his father acquired a shoe store. Above the store, in a loft, a theatrical stock company gave regular performances; and Harry soon learned to love show business by watching these shows. He attended the city theatres whenever he could afford the price of admission. Badly smitten by a passion for the theatre, he would haunt the lobbies of hotels to watch for visiting stage stars.

At fourteen he ran away from home to join the Cole Brothers Circus. A year later he worked for a traveling repertory theatre, filling juvenile parts, playing piano, and writing songs for its productions. It was on this occasion that he abandoned his family name for "Von Tilzer"; "Tilzer" was his mother's maiden name, and "Von" was affixed to lend distinction to his assumed name.

For a while Von Tilzer performed with a burlesque company throughout the Midwest. When this troupe reached Chicago, he met the popular vaudeville star Lottie Gilson, who took an interest in him. Miss Gilson urged him to devote himself seriously to songwriting and to go to New York to advance his career. In 1892 Von Tilzer arrived in New York by working as groom of a trainload of horses. With only $1.65 in his pocket, he rented a furnished room near the Brooklyn Bridge and found a job as a pianist and entertainer in a saloon at fifteen dollars a week. For a while he left New York to perform with a traveling medicine show; then, he returned to work again as a saloon performer, and later as a vaudeville entertainer in a popular Dutch act with George Sidney.

ASCAP

HARRY VON TILZER

Meanwhile he wrote songs—hundreds of songs, none of which he could publish. Tony Pastor sang a few in his Music Hall, and several other entertainers bought some outright for two dollars each.

Finally a song of his was published, and it proved a fabulous success. It was "My Old New Hampshire Home," with lyrics by Andrew B. Sterling. Von Tilzer sold it outright for fifteen dollars to a small print shop owned by William C. Dunn, who issued it in 1898. To the amazement of all concerned, the song caught on, was performed by vaudeville entertainers throughout the country, and sold more than two million copies. In 1899 three more Von Tilzer songs were published: "I'd Leave My Happy Home for You" (lyrics by Will A. Heelan); and, to lyrics by Sterling, "I Wonder If She's Waiting" and "Where the Sweet Magnolias Grow."

The fantastic success of "My Old New Hampshire Home" induced Maurice Shapiro, the publisher, to make the young composer a partner in his firm, which was renamed Shapiro, Bernstein and Von Tilzer. It did not take Shapiro long to profit by this new arrangement. In 1900 Von Tilzer wrote, to lyrics by Arthur J. Lamb, one of the most successful sentimental ballads of that era, "A Bird in a Gilded Cage," whose sheet music sale surpassed the two million mark. When

Lamb first showed Von Tilzer his lyrics, the composer insisted that he could not write the music for it unless the verses made it explicit that the girl in the song was the rich man's wife and not his mistress.

In 1900 Von Tilzer also wrote "When Harvest Days Are Over" (lyrics by Howard Graham), and, in 1901, "Down Where the Cotton Blossoms Grow" (lyrics by Sterling). In 1902 Von Tilzer abandoned his publishing partnership with Shapiro and Bernstein to form the Harry Von Tilzer Music Company. He proceeded to write a succession of formidable hits that put his new organization on a solid financial footing. One of these songs was "Down Where the Wurzburger Flows" (lyrics by Vincent P. Bryan), in 1902. This song was at first intended as a drinking number for a Broadway musical. When it was dropped from that production, Nora Bayes introduced it at the Orpheum Theatre in Brooklyn to such acclaim that it became a staple of her vaudeville act; in fact, she was often identified as "the Wurzburger Girl."

A success of equal dimensions was achieved in 1902 with "The Mansion of Aching Hearts" (lyrics by Arthur J. Lamb). This became one of the best loved and most frequently sung ballads of the early 1900's. As a boy busker, Irving Berlin often sang it on the Bowery.

There was still a third outstanding Von Tilzer hit song in 1902, "On a Sunday Afternoon" (lyrics by Sterling). The inspiration for it came to the composer one Sunday at the beach. As he lay stretched out lazily on the sand, the line "they work hard on Monday, but one day that's fun day" entered his mind, and he brought this idea for a song to his lyricist, Sterling, who took and developed it.

Extraordinarily prolific, Von Tilzer wrote and published several other songs in 1902: "Down on the Farm" (lyrics by Raymond A. Browne); "Jennie Lee" (lyrics by Lamb); "When Kate and I Were Comin' Thru the Rye" (lyrics by Sterling); "Please Go 'Way and Let Me Sleep" (lyrics by the composer); and "Pardon Me, My Dear Alphonse" and "In the Sweet Bye and Bye" to Bryan's lyrics.

The dominating position Von Tilzer achieved in his dual capacity as composer and publisher was maintained in the following decades. He remained one of the most active composers in Tin Pan Alley for the next twenty years, and by the same token one of its most successful publishers. In 1905 he wrote still another phenomenal song hit, the ballad "Wait 'Til the Sun Shines, Nellie" (lyrics by Sterling). Some say the idea for this song came to the composer from a news item about a family disaster; others maintain that Von Tilzer overheard the phrase "Wait till the sun shines, Nellie" while standing outside his hotel. In any event, he gave Sterling the idea for the ballad, and it turned out to be one of the smash song triumphs of the decade. Von Tilzer's own daughter, then appearing on the vaudeville stage under the name of Winona Winter, was the first to popularize it; but it was not long before many of vaudeville's great singing stars began to include the song in their acts.

As a creator of ballads Von Tilzer remained in the front rank of his profession. These are some of the most important that were written between 1905 and 1920: "Where the Morning Glories Twine Around the Door" (lyrics by Sterling); "Don't Take Me Home" (lyrics by Bryan); "I Want a Girl, Just Like the Girl That Married Dear Old Dad" (lyrics by William Dillon); "And the Green Grass Grew All Around" (lyrics by William Jerome); "In the Evening by the Moonlight, Dear Louise" (lyrics by Sterling); "Last Night Was the End of the World" (lyrics by Sterling); "All Alone" (lyrics by Dillon); "On the Old Fall River Line" (lyrics by Jerome and Sterling); "A Little Bunch of Shamrocks" (lyrics by Jerome and Sterling); "Goodbye, Boys" (lyrics by Sterling and Dillon); "You'll Always Be the Same Sweet Girl" (lyrics by Sterling); "Close to My Heart" (lyrics by Sterling); "That Old Irish Mother of Mine" (lyrics by Jerome); and "I Lost the Best Pal That I Had" (lyrics by Dick Thomas).

But Von Tilzer was adept at styles other than the sentimental ballad. He created some of the era's most effective Negro songs— "Alexander, Don't You Love Your Baby No More?" and "What You Goin' to Do When the Rent Comes 'Round?" to Sterling's lyrics. In various other styles were songs like "Take Me Back to New York Town" (lyrics by Sterling); "I Love, I Love, I Love My Wife, but Oh You Kid" (lyrics by Jimmy Lucas); "The Cubanola Glide" (lyrics

by Bryan); "Under the Yum-Yum Tree" (lyrics by Sterling); "All Aboard for Blanket Bay" (lyrics by Sterling); and "They Always Pick on Me" (lyrics by Stanley Murphy).

Von Tilzer also contributed unwittingly but significantly to the jargon of popular music, for it is to him that the industry owes its designation as "Tin Pan Alley." In the early 1900's, Von Tilzer kept an upright piano at his publishing firm. He would stuff pieces of paper between its strings to create a tinny kind of sound to which he was partial. Monroe Rosenfeld, a journalist and lyricist, was in Von Tilzer's office one day, and he heard the composer play on that instrument. Its tinny sounds suggested the title for a series of articles on popular music that Rosenfeld was preparing—"Tin Pan Alley."

Von Tilzer wrote songs for several Broadway musicals (none of them successful) including *The Fisher Maiden* (1903), starring Al Shean and Edna Bronson, and *The Kissing Girl* (1910).

The last years of Von Tilzer's life were spent in retirement at the Hotel Woodward, New York; he died there on January 10, 1946.

ABOUT:
Down Beat, April 4, 1952.

Fats Waller 1904-1943

THOMAS ("FATS") WALLER was born in New York City on May 21, 1904. His father, a clergyman at the Abyssinian Baptist Church, hoped that his son would follow in his footsteps. But from boyhood on Thomas was drawn to music. He played the organ in his father's church, and at fifteen won first prize in an amateur contest for pianists. After graduating from De Witt Clinton High School, he served as organist for a Harlem theatre where he worked with the Negro singer Florence Mills. By the time he was sixteen he was employed regularly as a pianist in night clubs. He was only seventeen when he pressed his first records and made his first piano rolls, and at nineteen he initiated his first radio broadcasts. From 1924 on he toured the vaudeville circuit, played in jazz orchestras, performed on the organ in motion picture theatres, and served as accompanist for several blues singers including Bessie Smith. He was one of the first mu-

FATS WALLER

sicians to perform jazz on the pipe and Hammond organs, and he distinguished himself as a jazz pianist in small and large combinations that made many outstanding recordings. His first tour of Europe took place in 1932. In 1938 he performed in theatres in London, Glasgow, and Scandinavia.

His first published song appeared in 1925 —"Squeeze Me" (lyrics by Clarence Williams). Most of his songs were written to lyrics by Andy Razaf, who also collaborated with him at times on the melodies. In 1929 he wrote "My Father, in Your Hands," the extremely popular "Honeysuckle Rose," "Blue Turning Gray over You," and "Zonky." One of Waller's hit songs of this period, "I've Got a Feelin' I'm Fallin'" (1929), was written in collaboration with Harry Link to lyrics by Billy Rose.

In the late 1920's Waller also contributed hit songs to the Broadway stage. With J. C. Johnson as collaborator, he wrote the score for *Keep Shufflin'*, a Negro revue produced in 1928; its most popular number was "Willow Tree." Probably the most famous song Waller ever wrote—"Ain't Misbehavin'" (written in collaboration with Harry Brooks to lyrics by Razaf)—was heard in another Broadway Negro revue, *Hot Chocolates*, in 1929. That score boasted a second important Waller song, "What Did I Do to Be So Black and Blue?"

Waller's most important songs during the 1930's were "Keepin' out of Mischief Now," "Doin' What I Please," "If It Ain't Love," and "Ain'tcha Glad?" In addition to these songs, Waller created several compositions for piano solo; the best were *Minor Drag*, *Handful of Keys*, *Viper's Drag*, and *London Suite*.

In 1943 Waller wrote his last Broadway musical comedy score, *Early to Bed*. He died on December 15, 1943, in Kansas City, Missouri, on the Sante Fe Chief en route from Los Angeles to New York.

ABOUT:
Band Leaders, May 1944; Record Changer, December 1950.

Harry Warren *1893-*

HARRY WARREN was born in Brooklyn, New York, on December 24, 1893, one of eleven children. His father was a bootmaker. Unusually musical from childhood on, Harry sang in the church choir and taught himself to play several instruments, including the accordion. He attended public and Catholic schools in Brooklyn. When he was fifteen he left school to make his own way in the world. His first job was as a drummer with the John Victor brass band. After that he worked with various carnival shows touring the Eastern states; as stagehand for a vaudeville theatre in Brooklyn; and as property man at the Vitagraph studios in Flatbush, then producing silent films. At the film studios he was a jack-of-many-trades, working as a movie extra, assistant director, pianist providing off-stage mood music, and in other capacities on the lot.

After serving in the Navy during World War I, Warren worked as a pianist at a night club in Sheepshead Bay, Brooklyn. During this period he started to write songs. His first effort, "I Learned to Love You When I Learned My A-B-C's," was never published. But it was good enough to gain him a job as staff pianist and song plugger for the music publishing house of Stark and Cowan. "Rose of the Rio Grande" (lyrics by Edgar Leslie), Warren's first published song, appeared in 1922 and was a modest success. Soon afterwards he wrote "I Love My Baby and My

Baby Loves Me" (lyrics by Bud Green) and "Where Do You Worka John?" (lyrics by Mort Weinberg and Charles Marks).

Warren's major songs began to appear between 1927 and 1930, beginning with "Away Down South in Heaven" (lyrics by Green), and continuing with "Nagasaki" (lyrics by Mort Dixon), "Where the Shy Little Violets Grow" (lyrics by Gus Kahn), and "Absence Makes the Heart Grow Fonder for Somebody Else" (lyrics by Sam M. Lewis and Joe Young). In 1930, Warren began to achieve recognition in the Broadway musical theatre. Two hits were heard in the revue *Sweet and Low:* "Cheerful Little Earful" and "Would You Like to Take a Walk?" (lyrics by Mort Dixon and Billy Rose). His score for an Ed Wynn extravaganza, *The Laugh Parade* (1931), included the first of his standards, "You're My Everything," as well as "The Torch Song" and "Ooh That Kiss" (lyrics by Dixon and Young). *Billy Rose's Crazy Quilt* (1931) boasted still another all-time Warren favorite, "I Found a Million Dollar Baby in a Five-and-Ten Cent Store" (lyrics by Dixon and Rose). In 1931, Warren also created an important independent song, "By the River Sainte Marie" (lyrics by Edgar Leslie).

But his most significant work has been done in Hollywood for motion pictures. Through the years, he has occupied a high position among composers for the screen. He went to the motion picture capital in 1929 and was first represented by "Cryin' for the Carolines" and "Have a Little Faith in Me" (lyrics by Lewis and Young) in *Spring Is Here.* Soon after that, working mainly with Al Dubin, Warren produced the following hits in Hollywood: "We're in the Money," "Shadow Waltz," and "I've Got to Sing a Torch Song" for *The Gold Diggers of 1933;* "You're Getting to Be a Habit with Me," "Young and Healthy," "Shuffle Off to Buffalo," and the title song for *Forty-second Street;* "Three's a Crowd" for *The Crooner;* "Shanghai Lil" for *Footlight Parade;* "Boulevard of Broken Dreams" for *Moulin Rouge;* "Keep Young and Beautiful" for *Roman Scandals* starring Eddie Cantor; the title number of *Wonder Bar,* which starred Al Jolson; "I'll String Along with You" and "Fair and Warmer" for *Twenty Million Sweethearts;* and "I Only Have Eyes for You" for *Dames.*

HARRY WARREN

Warren received his first Academy Award in 1935 for "Lullaby of Broadway" (lyrics by Dubin) from *The Gold Diggers of Broadway.* That year was a particularly productive one for Warren, yielding "About a Quarter to Nine," "The Little Things You Used to Do" and "She's a Latin from Manhattan" *(Go Into Your Dance);* "You Let Me Down" and "Where Am I?" *(Stars over Broadway);* and "Lulu's Back in Town" *(Broadway Gondolier).*

Warren again received the Academy Award in 1943 for "You'll Never Know" (lyrics by Mack Gordon) from *Hello, Frisco, Hello;* and in 1946 for "On the Atchison, Topeka, and the Santa Fe" (lyrics by Johnny Mercer) from *The Harvey Girls.*

In addition, Warren has produced other hits of major importance for more than fifty motion pictures since 1935. These are perhaps the best: "I'll Sing You a Thousand Love Songs" *(Cain and Mabel);* "Summer Night" *(Sing Me a Love Song);* "September in the Rain" *(Melody for Two);* "Remember Me?" and "Am I in Love?" *(Mr. Deeds Takes to the Air);* "Plenty of Money and You" *(Gold Diggers of 1937);* and "I Know Now" *(The Singing Marine).* The lyrics to all these songs were by Al Dubin.

To Johnny Mercer's lyrics, Warren wrote "You Must Have Been a Beautiful Baby" and "Jeepers Creepers" for *Hard to Get;* and

"It's a Great Big World," for *The Harvey Girls.* To Mack Gordon's lyrics, he wrote "I Know Why and So Do You," "It Happened in Sun Valley," and "Chattanooga Choo Choo" for *Sun Valley Serenade;* "Serenade in Blue" and "At Last" for *Orchestra Wives;* the title song for *Down Argentine Way;* "I Had the Craziest Dream" for *Springtime in the Rockies;* "My Heart Tells Me" for *Sweet Rosie O'Grady;* "There'll Never Be Another You" for *Iceland;* and "The More I See You" and "I Wish I Knew" for *The Diamond Horseshoe.*

With other lyricists Warren wrote: "This Heart of Mine" (Arthur Freed) for *The Ziegfeld Follies;* "The Stanley Steamer" (Ralph Blane) for *Summer Holiday;* "My One and Only" and "Highland Fling" (Ira Gershwin) for *The Barclays of Broadway,* starring Fred Astaire and Ginger Rogers; "You Wonderful You" and "Friendly Star" (Jack Brooks and Saul Chapin) for *Summer Stock;* "That's Amore" (Brooks) for *The Caddy;* "A Love Affair to Remember" (Harold Adamson) for *An Affair to Remember;* and the title song of *Separate Tables* (Adamson). With Adamson, Warren also wrote "The Legend of Wyatt Earp," the theme music for the popular weekly television program.

Kurt Weill *1900-1950*

KURT WEILL was born in Dessau, Germany, on March 2, 1900. In the Weill household music occupied a respected place. Kurt's father was a synagogue cantor; his mother, an excellent amateur pianist. At an early age Kurt was given lessons in piano and composition by Albert Bing. He continued his music education in 1918 at the Berlin Hochschule under Humperdinck and Krasselt, and studied with Ferruccio Busoni from 1921 to 1924. Before becoming Busoni's student, Weill had worked in Dessau as an opera coach and as a conductor with the Leudenscheid Opera.

At first Weill's compositions employed the advanced techniques and iconoclastic approaches of the German avant-garde school. He completed a symphony in 1921 (long considered lost, but rediscovered in 1958). Various orchestral works, performed at leading European festivals between 1924 and 1926, brought him to a leading position among the younger German composers of his time.

But he was soon infected with the new spirit sweeping through the German theatre, which was bringing to the musical stage vital contemporary problems, racy modern subjects, and social satire. He was already beginning to think of opera in terms of entertainment for the masses—with contemporary, realistic, or satiric texts, and with music leaning heavily on popular styles. He began to feel that composers had too long occupied an ivory tower which isolated them completely from their audiences. When he discussed this matter with Busoni, the master inquired: "Do you want to become a Verdi of the poor?" Weill replied: "Is that so bad?"

In 1924 Weill wrote his first opera, *The Protagonist,* his text a one-act melodrama by Georg Kaiser. It was produced in Dresden in 1926. Here Weill made a tentative effort to write in a popular style, using jazz techniques in his rhythms and melodies. This opera was so successful that the Berlin State Opera commissioned him to write a new work, *The Royal Palace* (text by Ivan Goll) produced in 1927. Motion picture sequences, projected on a screen, were used in presenting this experimental play, and drama was often combined with pantomime. The score demonstrated Weill's increasing interest in American jazz. In 1927 he also wrote *Mahagonny,* a one-act *Singspiel* or song-play. The text, by Bertolt Brecht, consisted merely of a succession of lyrics and choruses.

Jazz was now becoming so basic to Weill's writing that one German critic did not hesitate to describe the one-act *Mahagonny* as a "jazz opera." Actually Weill was evolving a new kind of theatrical form which he designated as a "song-play." It dispensed with recitatives, arias, and other features of formal opera, and leaned heavily on the popular song "Mahagonny," wrote H. W. Heinsheimer "was a turning point in Weill's career as a composer. He had achieved in this work a new simplicity, a new skill and sureness, that was to sweep away the last vestiges of high browism implanted in him by Busoni. His music was now subject to the law of the theatre, and he was groping for a style that would be absolutely original and native to the theatre."

Weill himself said at the time: "I want to reach the real people, a more representative public than any opera house attracts. I write for today. I don't care about writing for posterity." Thus he became a leading spokesman for a new cultural movement then dominating German life: *Zeitkunst* (contemporary art) and *Gebrauchsmusik* (functional music).

In 1928, after writing the music for a satire by Georg Kaiser, *The Czar Has Himself Photographed*, Weill went on to create a modern opera whose impact was cataclysmic. With Brecht as his librettist, he completed *The Three-Penny Opera (Die Dreigroschenoper)*, a modern adaptation of John Gay's famous eighteenth-century ballad opera, *The Beggar's Opera*. Bringing to Gay's text his own leftist social viewpoints and his bent for satire, Brecht produced a text that was bitter, sardonic, brutal—a cynical commentary on crime and corruption in the Germany of the late 1920's. Weill's music was a brilliant fusion of the classic and the popular. It began with a blues and ended with a mock chorale. It included a shimmy, a canon in fox-trot tempo, popular tunes, ballads, airs, ensemble numbers, and choruses. Each musical episode was calculated to point up a character or situation; each was basic to the story.

First performed in Berlin on August 31, 1928, *The Three-Penny Opera* proved a sensation with few parallels in the German theatre. In one year it was performed over four thousand times in about one hundred twenty theatres. G. W. Pabst, one of Germany's outstanding movie directors, adapted it successfully for the screen. It was soon presented in virtually every European capital. On April 13, 1933, it was presented in New York; there, strange to say, it was a dismal failure. Since then it has been adapted for motion pictures several times and has often been revived in many countries. On March 10, 1954, it returned to New York in an off-Broadway production. (The text and lyrics were modernized by Marc Blitzstein, but Weill's music was left intact). It ran for about seven years to achieve one of the longest runs in the history of the American theatre, and went on a national tour. Its principal song, "Mack the Knife" (or "Moritat"), has twice become a leading song hit. In 1955-1956 it was issued in about

Blackstone Studios

KURT WEILL

twenty different recorded versions, including one in Dixieland style, and was frequently presented on the "Hit Parade." Issued again in a Bobby Darin recording in 1959, it sold over one million discs.

In the first German production the starring role of Jenny was played by Lotte Lenya Blamauer, whom Weill married in 1928. She was again the star of *The Three-Penny Opera* in its New York revival in 1954.

By 1930 Weill had become one of the most successful and controversial composers in Germany. Now he and Brecht expanded their one-act *Singspiel, Mahagonny,* into a three-act production entitled *The Rise and Fall of Mahagonny.* The plot concerns the efforts of three escaped criminals to found in an American desert a new society in which man's basest instincts will be catered to. In this opera, Weill's music was not merely "popular" but often in a Tin Pan Alley style—for instance, the song that became a smash hit in Germany, "Alabama Song" (English title and lyrics in the original German production).

Weill wrote several more operas, the last of which was *The Silver Lake* (book by Georg Kaiser), which opened on February 18, 1933. One day later the Reichstag was set aflame in Berlin. Recognizing the handwriting on the wall, Weill did not wait to see how his new opera would fare, but packed his bags and escaped with his wife to Paris.

In Paris, and later in London, Weill was involved in several unsuccessful musical productions. In 1935 he was invited to the United States by the celebrated director Max Reinhardt to write the music for *The Eternal Road,* an elaborate pageant of Jewish history by Franz Werfel which Reinhardt was producing in New York. Weill arrived in New York in the fall of 1935 for what proved to be permanent residence; in 1943 he became an American citizen.

Weill's bow in the American theatre, however, did not take place with *The Eternal Road,* which suffered many delays. His first American production was *Johnny Johnson,* a "musical fable" of World War I by Paul Green, which was presented on Broadway on November 19, 1936. *The Eternal Road* followed in 1937. For *Johnny Johnson* Weill created a breezy score filled with American idioms: Tin Pan Alley songs—"To Love You and To Leave You" and "Oh, Heart of Mine"; satirical songs—"They All Take Up Psychiatry"; and cowboy tunes and sentimental ballads. For *The Eternal Road,* on the other hand, he wrote music of an exalted, deeply reverent, at times even spiritual character. Two scores so contrasting in style, mood, and atmosphere immediately pointed up Weill's versatility and flexibility in adapting his musical style to the demands of his plays.

Though neither of these two productions was particularly successful, Weill immediately found himself in great demand. He went out to Hollywood where he provided scores for several motion pictures including *Blockade* and *You and Me.* He also contributed the background music for *Railroads on Parade,* a spectacle at the New York World's Fair.

With *Knickerbocker Holiday,* which came to Broadway on October 19, 1938, Weill became solidly established as a composer for the musical stage. This production, for which Maxwell Anderson wrote his first musical comedy text, was set in New Amsterdam in 1647. Walter Huston starred as Peter Stuyvesant. For Huston, Weill wrote what is probably the leading song success of his entire career, "September Song" (lyrics by Maxwell Anderson). The story is told that when Weill first heard that Huston would appear in *Knickerbocker Holiday* he wired the actor to find out the range of his voice. Huston replied succinctly: "No range. No voice."

Later on, when Huston appeared on a coast-to-coast radio broadcast, he informed Weill he would sing a song expressly to demonstrate to the composer his capabilities in that direction. When Weill heard Huston's rasping, nasal, husky voice he decided to write a song with a special mood and special progressions suitable for this kind of "singing"; and the number he wrote was "September Song."

A success of even greater dimensions was achieved with *Lady in the Dark,* which opened on January 23, 1941. The text, by Moss Hart, followed the heroine (portrayed by Gertrude Lawrence in a most remarkable performance) through her psychoanalytic treatment and her dream life. Weill's score was one of the most sensitive and expressive he had thus far written for the American stage. The theme song, "My Ship," with its unorthodox intervallic structure, had a haunting quality uniquely suited to the dream sequences. "The Princess of Pure Delight," "Saga of Jenny" and "Oh, Fabulous One, in Your Ivory Tower" were also noteworthy. A patter song made up of the names of Russian composers and entitled "Tchaikovsky" helped to raise Danny Kaye to Broadway stardom. (The lyrics for *Lady in the Dark* were all by Ira Gershwin.)

One Touch of Venus (1943) starred Mary Martin in a musical comedy based on the S. J. Perelman and Ogden Nash adaptation of F. Anstey's *The Tinted Venus.* Nash wrote the lyrics. "How Much Do I Love You?" "Speak Low," and "That's Him" were among its main musical numbers. In *Firebrand of Florence* (1945) the authors—Edwin Justus Mayer as librettist, and Ira Gershwin as lyricist—tried unsuccessfully to translate into musical comedy terms Mayer's amusing Broadway comedy about Benvenuto Cellini; this production was one of Weill's few box office failures.

Firebrand of Florence was Weill's last musical comedy. From this point on he was to compose for musical plays scores which would be so integral to the over-all production and arise so naturally and inevitably from the text that the plays would often assume the dimensions of opera. But before his first attempt he went to Hollywood to write a score, to Ira Gershwin's lyrics, for the motion picture *Where Do We Go from Here?*

Weill's first Broadway musical play, as distinguished from musical comedy, was *Street Scene* (January 9, 1947). Aptly described by its authors as a "folk play with music," *Street Scene* was an adaptation of Elmer Rice's realistic Pulitzer Prize-winning play of 1929. Rice himself wrote the text for the musical, and Langston Hughes supplied the lyrics. So remarkably did Weill's music succeed in heightening and emphasizing the passions and frustrations of this tragedy set in a New York City tenement slum that Rosamond Gilder wrote: "Kurt Weill turned *Street Scene* into a symphony of the city with its strands of love and yearning and violence woven into the pattern of daily drudgery. His music reflects the hot night, the chatter and gossiping housewives, the sound of children at play, the ebb and flow of anonymous existence." In his wonderfully unified and integrated score, several songs were especially poignant, notably "Lonely House," "A Boy Like You," and "We'll All Go Away Together."

Street Scene was introduced in Germany by the Duesseldorf Opera in the winter of 1955; and on April 2, 1959, it entered the repertory of the New York City Opera. On the latter occasion Howard Taubman said in the New York *Times:* "It is an American opera, if you emphasize the adjective more than the noun. For it is a congeries of musical idioms. It has some genuine operatic writing, in the sense that the music furnishes the emotional core of a scene, but it also has numbers that belong in a fast Broadway musical comedy or an old-fashioned operetta. The main point is that all these musical devices contribute to effective theatre."

Love Life (1948) was an interesting experiment as a text. The story by Alan Jay Lerner (who also wrote the lyrics) carries a married couple through a century and a half, from 1791 to 1948. During that period neither the hero nor the heroine ages; but their marriage does—it grows, withers, and dies. This musical play did not always have conviction, and it was not successful, but it deserves to be remembered for its score, which included one of Weill's most famous popular songs, "Green-Up Time."

For *Lost in the Stars* (October 30, 1949) Kurt Weill created another score of ambitious proportions. Described as a "musical tragedy," this was an adaptation by Maxwell

Anderson of Alan Paton's moving novel of South Africa, *Cry, the Beloved Country.* The play, like the novel, was rich in human value—deep in its compassion, eloquent in its plea for racial tolerance, touching in its pathos, noble in its promises of a better world. Weill's choral music provided a constantly moving commentary on the action; his songs, with lyrics by Maxwell Anderson, often had the dramatic impact and emotional thrust of art songs or operatic arias. Among the best choral numbers were "Cry, the Beloved Country" and "Bird of Passage"; the leading solo numbers included "Lost in the Stars," "O Tixo, Tixo," and "Trouble Man." *Lost in the Stars* was presented by the New York City Opera Company as part of its permanent repertory on April 11, 1958.

In another vein was a one-act American folk opera, *Down in the Valley,* first performed at Indiana University on July 15, 1948. The text was by Arnold Sundgaard. In his score Weill made effective use of five American folk songs: "Down in the Valley," "The Lonesome Dove," "The Little Black Train," "Hop Up, My Ladies," and "Sourwood Mountain."

Kurt Weill died in New York City on April 3, 1950. In a tribute in the New York *Herald Tribune,* Virgil Thomson wrote: "Nothing he touched came out banal. Everything he wrote became in one way or another historic. He was probably the most original single workman in the whole musical theatre, internationally considered, during the last quarter of a century. . . . He was an architect, a master of musico-dramatic design, whose structures, built for function and solidity, constitute a repertory of models that have not only served well their original purpose but also had wide influence on composers as examples of procedure."

In 1961 one of Weill's old songs was revived on a record by Andy Williams and achieved extraordinary success. It was "The Bilbao Song," written in 1929 with lyrics by Brecht for an unsuccessful opera, *Happy End.*

ABOUT:
Paris, Leonard Allen. Men and Melodies.
High Fidelity, May 1957; International Musician, April 1950; Music Journal, March 1955; Musical America, April 1950; Music and Letters, July 1958; Theatre Arts, December 1950; Tomorrow, March 1948.

Percy Wenrich *1887-1952*

PERCY WENRICH was born in Joplin, Missouri on January 23, 1887. He was the son of the town postmaster. His mother, an amateur pianist, gave him piano and organ lessons when he was still a boy. It was not long before he began to write melodies, for which his father provided lyrics; these songs were featured at local political rallies and conventions. At twenty-one Wenrich entered the Chicago Musical College for training as a serious musician. But he continued his efforts in popular music. He succeeded in having two songs published by a Chicago firm: "Ashy Africa" and "Just Because I'm from Missouri." Both titles were suggested to him by the senior member of that publishing firm—Frank Buck, who later became famous as a producer of travel and adventure films on Africa.

For a while, Wenrich worked as a song plugger in a Milwaukee department store. While holding this position, he had another song published—"Under a Tropical Moon" (lyrics by C. R. McDonald). Soon afterwards he went to New York where, in 1908, he wrote and published two more hit songs, "Rainbow" (lyrics by Alfred Bryan) and "Up in a Balloon" (lyrics by Ren Shields). One year later, a song which is still a favorite with many, "Put On Your Old Gray Bonnet"

(lyrics by Stanley Murphy), appeared. Two other extremely popular songs which keep his name alive are "Moonlight Bay" (lyrics by Edward Madden), written in 1912, and "When You Wore a Tulip" (lyrics by Jack Mahoney), written in 1914.

The following are some of Wenrich's other successful songs: "Silver Bell" (lyrics by Madden); "She Took Mother's Advice" (lyrics by Murphy); "Sweet Cider Time" (lyrics by Joseph McCarthy); and "Where Do We Go from Here?" (lyrics by Howard Johnson), a World War I tune about the draft.

Wenrich also wrote scores for several Broadway musical comedies. These plays included *Crinoline Girl* (1914), *The Right Girl* (1921), *Castles in the Air* (1926), and *Who Cares?* (1930).

For fifteen years Wenrich toured the vaudeville circuit with his wife, Dolly Connolly. Then he retired from performing and composing. He died in New York City on March 17, 1952.

ABOUT:
Musical Courier, April 1952.

Charles A. White *1830-1892*

CHARLES A. WHITE was born in Boston, Massachusetts, in 1830. In his boyhood he demonstrated an unusual love for music. Unable to purchase a violin, he made one of his own out of a cigar box and taught himself to play tunes on it. As a young man he became a member of the faculty at the naval school in Newport, but left teaching to form the publishing house of White-Smith with W. Frank Smith and John F. Perry. Only after he had helped establish this organization on a sound basis did he turn to songwriting (both lyrics and music). One of his first published songs, however, was issued in 1868 by another firm—Oliver Ditson. It was "The Widow in the Cottage by the Seashore." Two years later he became his own publisher with "Come, Birdie," his first success. This was followed by some other hit songs among which were the Negro dialect number "I'se Gwine Back to Dixie," the waltz ballad "When the Leaves Begin to Turn" and "A Bird from o'er the Sea." The song triumph of his career was "Marguerite,"

ASCAP

PERCY WENRICH

published in 1883. He improvised the melody on his violin before the title or lyrics were conceived. One day he took his manuscript to Denman Thompson, then appearing at the Old Boston Theatre in *The Old Homestead*. White hummed the tune, and Thompson, impressed, decided to interpolate it into his play. Published soon after its first performance on the stage, it went on to become one of the most famous of American popular songs. For over a generation there was hardly a vocalist of popular music anywhere in America in whose repertory this song did not hold a prominent place; nor were there many living rooms which did not possess a copy of the sheet music.

After "Marguerite," White's most important songs included "The President Cleveland March," "My Love's a Rose," and an early exercise in nonsense lyrics, "Oo-le-mena." These appeared between 1884 and 1887. White was also the composer of several well-loved ballads, the best of these being "When 'Tis Moonlight," "Come Silver Moon," "Beyond the Clouds," "Birds in Dreamland Sleep," and "Thou Art an Angel."

Charles A. White died in Boston in 1892.

Richard A. Whiting *1891-1938*

R ICHARD A. WHITING was born in Peoria, Illinois, on November 12, 1891. His parents were musical. His mother had been trained as a pianist, and his father (a real estate dealer) was a competent performer on several instruments. Except for some lessons in harmony in his boyhood, Richard had no formal instruction in music, but taught himself to play the piano. While attending Harvard Military School, in Los Angeles, he devoted his spare time to making music and writing songs. Eventually he was able to sell three songs to Remick for fifty dollars each, and to get a position as office manager with that firm (then established in Detroit). Whiting supplemented his income by playing piano with a Hawaiian orchestra in a Detroit hotel.

In 1914, with Charles L. Cooke, Whiting wrote "I Wonder Where My Lovin' Man Has Gone" (lyrics by Earle C. Jones). The following year his first hit, "It's Tulip Time in Holland" (lyrics by Dave Radford) was issued by Remick. Since Whiting's great

ambition at the time was to own a Steinway grand piano, he felt he had made a highly favorable deal by selling this song outright for a grand piano. But it turned out to be an injudicious transaction, for the song sold over a million and a half copies in a few months.

In 1916 Whiting wrote and published two more hits, both to Ray Egan's lyrics: "And They Called It Dixieland" and "Mammy's Little Coal Black Rose." This time his earnings from the two songs, on a royalty basis, brought him almost thirty thousand dollars.

From 1917, for about a decade, Whiting continued to compose some of Tin Pan Alley's leading songs: "Where the Black-Eyed Susans Grow" (lyrics by Radford), which was introduced in the Al Jolson extravaganza *Robinson Crusoe, Jr.;* "Some Sunday Morning" (lyrics by Gus Kahn and Ray Egan); "Where the Morning Glories Grow" (lyrics by Kahn and Egan); "Till We Meet Again" (lyrics by Egan), one of the most celebrated ballads of World War I, which has sold about twelve million copies of sheet music; "Japanese Sandman," "When Shall We Meet Again?" and "Sleepy Time Gal" (lyrics by Egan), the last composed in collaboration with Ange Lorenzo and Joseph R. Alden; "Ain't We Got Fun?" (lyrics by the composer); "Ukulele Lady" (lyrics by Kahn); "Horses" (lyrics by Byron Gay); "Honey" (lyrics by Haven Gillespie and Seymour Simons), revived in 1945 in the motion picture *Her Highness and the Bellboy;* "She's Funny That Way," written with Neil Moret and revived in 1946 in the motion picture *The Postman Always Rings Twice.*

During this period of intensive activity in Tin Pan Alley, Whiting was also producing scores for the Broadway stage. The first was *Toot-Sweet* in 1919. That year he was engaged by George White to write the songs for the first edition of the *Scandals. Free for All*, in 1931, and *Take a Chance*, in 1932, proved Whiting's greatest Broadway stage successes. For the latter production (which starred Ethel Merman) Whiting wrote two of his standards, "Eadie Was a Lady" and "You're an Old Smoothie" (lyrics by Buddy De Sylva).

Notable as his achievements had been in Tin Pan Alley and on Broadway, it was in Hollywood that Whiting created his greatest

RICHARD A. WHITING

songs and earned his most resounding triumphs as a composer. His first assignment in the motion picture capital, in 1929, was *Innocents of Paris,* in which Maurice Chevalier made his American film debut singing "Louise" (lyrics by Leo Robin). During the next decade Whiting's songs were heard in almost thirty films, and some of them were the best songs of his career: "True Blue Lou" (lyrics by Robin and Sam Coslow) heard in *Dance of Life;* "My Sweeter than Sweet" (lyrics by George Marion, Jr.) in *Sweetie;* "Beyond the Blue Horizon" and "Give Me a Moment, Please" (lyrics by Robin), composed in collaboration with W. Franke Harling for *Monte Carlo;* "My Future Just Passed" (lyrics by Marion) heard in *Safety in Numbers;* "My Ideal" (lyrics by Robin), composed in collaboration with Newell Chase for Chevalier in *Playboy of Paris;* the title song (lyrics by Robin) of another Chevalier film, *One Hour with You;* "On the Good Ship Lollipop" (lyrics by Sidney Clare) for Shirley Temple in *Bright Eyes;* "When Did You Leave Heaven?" (lyrics by Walter Bullock) heard in *Sing, Baby, Sing;* "I Can't Escape from You" (lyrics by Robin) in *Rhythm on the Range;* "Too Marvelous for Words" (lyrics by Johnny Mercer) in *Ready, Willing and Able;* and "Have You Got Any Castles, Baby?" (lyrics by Mercer) in *Varsity Show.*

Whiting's last song success for motion pictures was "I've Got a Heart Full of Music" (lyrics by Johnny Mercer), which Dick Powell sang in *The Cowboy from Brooklyn.* Whiting died of a heart attack in Beverly Hills on February 10, 1938. After his death his daughter Margaret became one of America's leading singers of popular music. She made her debut on Johnny Mercer's NBC radio program in 1940, singing her father's "Too Marvelous for Words." Another daughter, Barbara, has also become successful as a singer and actress.

Meredith Willson 1902-

MEREDITH WILLSON was born in Mason City, Iowa, on May 18, 1902. His parents were musical. While attending Mason City High School he learned to play the flute and piccolo. In 1919 he went to New York where he continued his study of the flute with Georges Barrère at the Institute of Musical Art. From 1921 to 1923 he was a flutist with John Philip Sousa's band, with which he toured the United States, Mexico, and Cuba. Next he worked for a year in the Hugo Riesenfeld orchestra of the Rialto Theatre in New York. From 1924 to 1929 he was a flutist with the New York Philharmonic Orchestra and the New York Chamber Music Society.

In 1929 Willson moved to San Francisco to become music director of radio station KFRC. In 1932 he became music director of the Western Division of NBC, with headquarters in San Francisco, supervising and directing broadcasts of musical programs. On occasion he appeared as a guest conductor of orchestras such as the Seattle Symphony. the San Francisco Symphony, and the Los Angeles Philharmonic. In 1937 he settled in Los Angeles, retaining his position with NBC. Among the many programs he directed was the Maxwell House "Good News" program. At that time he was described as "one of the most genuinely versatile maestros in the country," the conductor and composer of "every conceivable type of musical composition—symphonic works, popular dance tunes, semiclassical melodies, as well as minstrel and novelty numbers."

An avocation during these years was writing symphonic music. One of Willson's orchestral works, *Parade Fantastique,* was presented in New York in 1924. Among his more important serious works in the 1930's were two symphonies. The first, *San Francisco,* was performed by the San Francisco Symphony, under the composer's direction, in 1936. The second, *The Missions of California,* was first performed by the Los Angeles Philharmonic, with Albert Coates conducting, in 1940.

He became active as a composer of music for the screen in 1940 with a score for Charlie Chaplin's *The Great Dictator.* A year later he wrote the score for Samuel Goldwyn's *The Little Foxes.* In 1942 he enlisted in the United States Army, where he was put in charge of the music division of the Armed Forces Radio Service. After the war he returned to his radio work, starring in many coast-to-coast broadcasts as a conductor, composer, commentator, and homespun philosopher.

His career as a composer of popular songs was established solidly in 1941 with "You and I," for which he wrote both lyrics and music. It retained first place on the "Hit Parade" for nineteen weeks and was adapted into several classical transcriptions; one, for strings, was written by Eddy Brown. Willson's later song hits included "Iowa," "Two in Love," "I See the Moon," and "May the Good Lord Bless and Keep You." The last of these was written in 1950 for the Sunday night radio program "The Big Show," starring Tallulah Bankhead, of which Willson was music director. Within a four-month period it sold more than half a million copies of sheet music. During the Korean War this song and "I See the Moon" were among the selections most frequently requested by G.I.'s.

Willson's debut as composer for the Broadway stage was made with one of the outstanding musical comedy successes of the late 1950's, *The Music Man,* for which he wrote music, text, and lyrics. It opened in New York on December 19, 1957, after which it received the New York Drama Critics Circle Award as the best play of the season, the Antoinette Perry (Toni) Award for the best musical, and several other honors. Walter Kerr of the New York *Herald Tribune* described it as "easily the brightest, breeziest, most winning new musical to come along since *My Fair Lady* enchanted us all." Set in River

MEREDITH WILLSON

City, Iowa, the musical describes the efforts of a swindling music man, played exuberantly by Robert Preston, who travels from town to town selling the idea of a boys' band, and then absconding with the money entrusted to him for the purchase of instruments and uniforms. He falls in love with the local librarian and he himself becomes infected with the rage for music making which seizes the town. Willson's charming score included a resounding hit, "Seventy-six Trombones," and several other winning items, including "Goodnight, My Someone," "Till There Was You," and "Lida Rose."

During its long run on Broadway (1376 performances) *The Music Man* grossed well over ten million dollars. A national company, starting in Los Angeles in August 1958, went on tour for several years. Warner Brothers paid more than a million dollars for the screen rights.

Meredith Willson's second Broadway musical (book by Richard Morris) was *The Unsinkable Molly Brown,* starring Tammy Grimes. This was described as a "rousing, true-to-life saga of a beautiful rugged gal who rose from chambermaid to society queen in the colorful turbulent era of the Colorado silver strike during the fabulous 1870's." It opened on Broadway on November 3, 1960. The score included at least one number in the catchy style of "Seventy-six Trombones"—"I

Ain't Down Yet." Other winning songs included "Dolce Far Niente" and "Are You
Sure?"

Willson is the author of several humorous
books, all with eccentric titles: *And There I
Stood with My Piccolo*; *Who Did What to
Fedalia*; *Eggs I Have Laid*; and *But He
Doesn't Know the Territory*. In 1957 he was
nominated "Showman of the Year" by the
Broadway Historical Society, and in 1958
was given the State of Texas Award as "the
outstanding person in the musical entertainment world."

ABOUT:
Musical Courier, May 1, 1947; Time, May 14,
1951.

Septimus Winner *1827-1902*

SEPTIMUS WINNER was born in Philadelphia, Pennsylvania, on May 11, 1827.
After studying violin he opened a music store
in Philadelphia in 1847, and at the same time
gave lessons in violin, guitar, and banjo. He
subsequently became one of the most active
and prominent figures in the musical life of
his city. He was a pioneer in bringing good
music to the masses; the author of over two
hundred instruction books for twenty-three
instruments (including a famous one for
banjo); arranger for violin and piano of
several thousand compositions; founder of the
Philadelphia Music Society; and contributor
of articles on music to *Graham's Magazine*,
of which Edgar Allan Poe was the editor.

A composer of more than a hundred
songs (many of which he issued under the
pen name of Alice Hawthorne, and for which
he wrote lyrics as well as music), he achieved
his first success in 1854 with the sentimental
ballad "What Is Home Without a Mother?"
One year later he sold outright for five dollars his most famous ballad, "Listen to the
Mocking Bird" (described on the cover as
"a sentimental Ethiopian ballad"). Over
the years, "Listen to the Mocking Bird" sold
more than twenty million copies of sheet
music.

During the Civil War he wrote some war
songs; but none of these was particularly suc-
cessful. One was "Yes, I Would the Cruel
War Were Over," a reply to the ballad
"Weeping Sad and Lonely, or When This
Cruel War Is Over" by Charles Carroll
Sawyer and Henry Tucker. Another of Win-

Courtesy of The New York Public Library, Music Division
SEPTIMUS WINNER

ner's war songs was "Give Us Back Our Old
Commander: Little Mac, the People's Pride."
Here he gave voice to the popular sentiment
for the return of General McClellan. Winner's
song was considered so subversive that he
was arrested and, for a brief period, confined
to prison. During the presidential campaign
of General Grant, however, the song reap-
peared with altered lyrics as one of Grant's
campaign songs.

During the war, Winner also wrote the
still famous nonsense lyric "Oh Where, Oh
Where, Has My Little Dog Gone?" to the
melody of the German folk song "Lauter-
bach."

Winner's best songs after 1865 included
the sentimental ballad "Whispering Hope,"
the jingle "Ten Little Injuns," "Ellie Rhee,"
and "Abraham's Daughter."

He died in Philadelphia on November 22,
1902.

ABOUT:
Claghorn, H. E. The Mocking Bird: The Life
and Diary of Its Author; Jones, F. O. Handbook of
American Music and Musicians.
Music Journal, January 1958.

Jacques Wolfe *1896-*

JACQUES WOLFE'S art songs, in the
style of the Negro spiritual, have enjoyed
such popularity both in and out of the concert
hall that they are often included in our

JACQUES WOLFE

popular song literature. He was born in Botoshan, Rumania, on April 29, 1896. His family came to the United States when he was a child, settling in New York. Jacques later attended the Institute of Musical Art, studying piano with James Friskin. He graduated from the Institute in 1915. During World War I he was a clarinetist in the 50th Infantry Band. While in uniform he was transferred to a musical unit in North Carolina where he became so fascinated by Negro songs that he began to make a comprehensive study of them and to do a considerable amount of research in this field. After the war, Wolfe made numerous appearances on the concert stage, sometimes as a piano virtuoso, on other occasions as an accompanist. He subsequently taught music in a New York City high school.

Wolfe first achieved fame as a composer of songs in 1928 with the publication of two numbers that are still considered his best and his most famous. One was "De Glory Road," and the other "Short'nin' Bread," with lyrics by Clement Wood. It is probable that the latter is a transcription rather than an original melody, since several Negro composers have been credited with writing it; one is Reese d'Pree, who is said to have composed the melody in 1905. Nevertheless, it is through Wolfe that the song has become indispensable to the song repertory of American baritones.

Other successful songs in a Negro style were "Gwine to Hebb'n," and "Hallelujah

Rhythm," both "remarkable," as John Tasker Howard has written, "for their authentic . . . flavor."

Among Wolfe's other songs are "Betsy's Boy," "The Hand-Organ Man," and "Sailormen" as well as songs of a more serious character such as "Prairie Waters by Night" and "Lost," based on poems by Carl Sandburg. Wolfe has also written choral and piano music together with music for the Broadway play *John Henry*, in which Paul Robeson starred in 1939.

Since 1947 Wolfe has devoted himself to creative photography and has had numerous exhibitions in museums and art galleries in the South. However, he is still involved in music. An opera, *The Trysting Tree* (libretto by Irving Rowan), was presented in Miami on November 6, 1957.

Harry M. Woods *1896-*

HARRY M. WOODS was born in North Chelmsford, Massachusetts, on November 4, 1896. His mother, a concert singer who continued to perform publicly until her eightieth year, soon introduced him to music. He immediately demonstrated unusual aptitude. Although born with a deformed left hand, he managed to learn to play the piano. While attending Harvard College, he supported himself by giving piano recitals and singing in church choirs. After graduating from Harvard he settled as a farmer on Cape Cod. During World War I, as a member of the armed forces, he started to write songs; but for several years after the war composing was only a hobby, incidental to his farming career.

Among his earliest published songs were "I'm Going South," written in 1923 in collaboration with Abner Silver, and "Paddlin' Madeleine Home," which he wrote to his own lyrics in 1925. In 1926 he wrote his first major song hit, "When the Red, Red Robin Comes Bob, Bob, Bobbin' Along," again to his own lyrics. This song was made famous by Al Jolson, who incorporated it into his repertory. This song success made Woods consider songwriting as a career. Without losing his interest in farming or his fascination with the sea, and still preferring the secluded settings of New England to the market places of New York City, he now directed his main energies to writing popular songs. The most important were: "I'm Looking Over a Four-Leaf Clover," "Just Like a Butterfly That's Caught in the Rain," and "River, Stay 'Way from My Door" (lyrics by Mort Dixon), the last song introduced by Jimmy Savo in the Broadway revue *Mum's the Word* (1931) and used as one of his favorite routines; "Here Comes the Sun" (lyrics by Arthur Freed), introduced in a *March of Time* picture in 1930; "The Man from the South," written with Rube Bloom; "When the Moon Comes Over the Mountain" (lyrics by Howard Johnson), written in 1931 and later adopted as Kate Smith's theme song; "We Just Couldn't Say Goodbye," to his own lyrics; "A Little Street Where Old Friends Meet" (lyrics by Gus Kahn); and "Try a Little Tenderness," written in collaboration with Reginald Connelly and Jimmy Campbell.

In 1929 two of his songs were heard in *A Vagabond Lover*, a motion picture starring Rudy Vallee; one of these was "A Little Kiss Each Morning" (lyrics by the composer). In 1934 Woods went to London where he remained several years, writing songs for Gaumont-British film productions, including *Jack Ahoy, Evergreen* (starring Jessie Matthews), and *It's Love Again*.

Since World War II, Woods has been living in retirement in Glendale, Arizona.

Henry Clay Work *1832-1884*

HENRY CLAY WORK, a composer of Civil War songs, was born in Middletown, Connecticut, on October 1, 1832. He was the son of an Abolitionist who made his home a station on the "underground railway" and who was thus instrumental in the escape of several thousand slaves. Henry Work himself was a dedicated Abolitionist and Union supporter.

Work, trained as a printer, became a specialist in setting music type. In music he was self-taught. At twenty-three he went to Chicago; working as a printer, he began to write songs—lyrics and music. Before long the first of his efforts, "We Are Coming, Sister Mary," was published in Chicago. A decade after its publication, this song was successfully performed by the Ed Christy Minstrels.

Courtesy of The New York Public Library,
Joseph Muller Collection, Music Division

HENRY CLAY WORK

In 1862 Work wrote the first of his important songs—"Kingdom Coming," in which his lyrics, in Negro dialect, were set to a robust melody. This song is still popular. A part of it was used effectively in 1944 in the Judy Garland motion picture *Meet Me in St. Louis;* the entire song had been performed in the Jerome Kern Broadway musical *Good Morning, Dearie* (1921).

The Civil War inspired him to write war songs. In 1862 he published a delightful comedy tune, "Grafted into the Army." This was followed in 1863 by "Babylon Is Fallen." When Lee invaded Pennsylvania, Work wrote "The Song of a Thousand Years," and when it seemed that the cause of the Union was in grave danger he composed "God Save the Nation."

The greatest of his war songs, and the one by which he will always be remembered, was written during the closing months of the Civil War. In 1865, inspired by General Sherman's march to the sea, he wrote "Marching Through Georgia," a song which has become a classic in the literature of American patriotic ballads. Its melody was also appropriated by Princeton University for a football song.

Several other songs written during the war years deserve mention. In 1864 he wrote "Wake Nicodemus," which became a minstrel show favorite after the war. A sentimental ballad, "Come Home, Father," expressed his passionate convictions about Prohibition. First introduced in Timothy Shay Arthur's stage melodrama *Ten Nights in a Barroom*, the song became a favorite at Temperance meetings.

After the war, Work proved a talented creator of sentimental ballads. The most popular were "The Lost Letter," "The Ship That Never Returned," and the greatest commercial success of his entire career, "Grandfather's Clock." The last, published in 1876, was introduced in New Haven by Sam Lucas, and went on to sell almost a million copies of sheet music.

Henry Clay Work died in Hartford, Connecticut, on June 8, 1884.

ABOUT:
Thompson, David. Songs That My Mother Used to Sing.
Notes, March-June, 1953.

Vincent Youmans *1898-1946*

VINCENT MILLIE YOUMANS was born on September 27, 1898, in New York City. His father was the prosperous owner of several hat stores. When he was still a baby, the Youmans family moved to a spacious home in Westchester, New York. Vincent was only four when he started to take piano lessons. Though he demonstrated a marked gift for music, his parents wanted him to specialize in the sciences, with engineering as a possible career. Youmans attended private schools in Westchester (Trinity School in Mamaroneck and Heathcote Hall in Rye) before entering the Sheffield Scientific School at Yale. He never graduated. Having decided soon after entering the school that he had no interest in engineering, he left in 1916 and found a job as a clerk in a brokerage firm on Wall Street.

During World War I Youmans enlisted in the Navy, where his assignment was to prepare musical shows for naval personnel. He often wrote music for these shows, and one of his pieces impressed John Philip Sousa, who frequently included it in his band concerts. This number proved to be so popular that other military and naval bands took it over and soon there was hardly a serviceman in the States who was not familiar with the

ASCAP

VINCENT YOUMANS

melody. A decade later Youmans adapted the same melody to new lyrics; as "Hallelujah," it became a hit song in *Hit the Deck*.

When the war ended Youmans decided upon a career in popular music. "Who's Who with You" was the first of his songs heard in a Broadway musical—*From Broadway to Piccadilly* (1918). In 1920 he published "The Country Cousin," a song inspired by a motion picture with that title. Youmans now attracted the attention of Max Dreyfus, head of the publishing house of Harms, who engaged him as a staff pianist and song plugger. During this period Youmans also worked with Victor Herbert, helping the veteran composer rehearse singers for Herbert musicals and revues. In describing the value of this musical experience, Youmans once said, "I got something in less than a year that money couldn't buy."

Vincent Youmans wrote his first complete score for the Broadway stage in collaboration with Paul Lannin. The show was the successful *Two Little Girls in Blue* (May 3, 1922). This was also the first Broadway musical for which Ira Gershwin wrote all the lyrics, though at this time he was still using the pseudonym Arthur Francis. The two hit songs in this production were the title number and "Oh Me, Oh My, Oh You." In his book *Lyrics on Several Occasions*, Ira Gershwin confesses that the title "Oh Me, Oh My, Oh

You" was merely a functional dummy at first, used to illustrate the rhythm and accent of the melody's opening bar until Gershwin could find an appropriate lyric. "Nevertheless, Youmans insisted that he was crazy about that particular title—which was fine with me, because I couldn't think of anything else—and the song turned out to be the most popular in the show."

On February 7, 1923, *Wildflower* opened at the Casino Theatre in New York. This operetta, with book and lyrics by Otto Harbach and Oscar Hammerstein II and music by Youmans and Herbert Stothart, had the longest run that any Youmans musical achieved—586 performances. Two of its songs, the title number and "Bambalina," are still favorites.

Later in 1923 Youmans and Stothart had a second musical on Broadway: *Mary Jane McKane,* a minor effort whose day on the boards was brief. One of its best songs was a waltz, "My Boy and I." But this melody did not become famous until over a year later, when it was adapted to new lyrics and used as the title number of *No, No, Nanette.*

No, No, Nanette was one of Youmans' best musical comedies. Although it did not enjoy as long a Broadway run as *Wildflower,* its over-all production history makes it Youmans' greatest triumph. It tried out briefly in Chicago in 1924, then opened in London on March 11, 1925, to begin a run of 665 performances. Finally, on September 16, 1925, it arrived on Broadway and remained a year. It also went on tour with seventeen companies to Europe, South America, China, New Zealand, and the Philippines.

No, No, Nanette (book by Otto Harbach and Frank Mandel, and lyrics by Harbach and Irving Caesar) had as its central character a wealthy publisher of Bibles whose irresistible urge to help young girls leads him into a helpless involvement with three charming young ladies. The score, by Youmans, had three outstanding songs: the title number, whose melody was a carry-over from *Mary Jane McKane;* "Tea for Two," one of the composer's most memorable songs; and "I Want to Be Happy."

Youmans' last great stage success was *Hit the Deck,* which opened on Broadway on April 25, 1927. This was a musical comedy adaptation by Herbert Fields of the successful Broadway comedy *Shore Leave.* It was

for this production that Vincent Youmans rewrote his old World War I song as the exciting sailors' chorus "Hallelujah" (lyrics by Leo Robin and Clifford Grey). The second hit song, "Sometimes I'm Happy," also came out of Youmans' trunk. Youmans had originally written the melody for *Mary Jane McKane,* but had removed it before the musical reached New York. Two years later he adapted the melody to new lyrics by Irving Caesar. Retitled "Sometimes I'm Happy," it was intended for a musical called *A Night Out.* But *A Night Out* never reached New York. Youmans finally interpolated the song into *Hit the Deck. (Hit the Deck* enjoyed a successful revival at Jones Beach on Long Island during the summer of 1960.)

Although Youmans also wrote scores for many musicals that were failures, some of these shows boasted a number of excellent Youmans songs, and these hits have survived as standards even when the plays in which they originated have been forgotten. Those particularly noteworthy are "I Know That You Know" (lyrics by Anne Caldwell) from *Oh, Please* (1926); the title song, "More than You Know," and "Without a Song" (lyrics by William Rose and Edward Eliscu) from *Great Day* (1929); the title song and "Drums in My Heart" (lyrics by Edward Heyman) from *Through the Years* (1932). Still another Youmans classic, "Time on My Hands" (lyrics by Harold Adamson and Mack Gordon), had been intended for *Smiles* (1930), but was removed when the star of that show, Marilyn Miller, objected to singing it. It was issued as an independent number. "Rise 'n' Shine," in the style of a Revivalist hymn, and "So Do I," both to lyrics by Buddy De Sylva, were interpolated into the musical comedy *Take a Chance* (1932), whose basic score was composed by Nacio Herb Brown.

One box office failure deserves special attention because of the unusually high quality of its text and score. This was *Rainbow* (November 21, 1928), a romantic musical play with book by Laurence Stallings and Oscar Hammerstein II. The musical was far ahead of its time in integrating book and music, projecting atmosphere, delineating character, and creating dramatic impact. As this writer has noted, "Here was a romantic play almost in the folk style later made popular by Rodgers and Hammerstein. Had *Rainbow* come in the 1940's it would surely have enjoyed a far greater audience response than it received in 1928, when it could not survive a single month." Some of the critics, however, recognized its value. Howard Barnes described it as a play with "absorbing melodramatic overtones which burst through the thin veil of a graceful score and pretty dances." Robert Littell found it to be "wonderfully good and also brand new . . . gorgeously different in its high spots." Some of Youmans' choral numbers and dance episodes carried conviction as simulations of authentic American folk music; the best vocal numbers were "The Bride That Dressed in White" and "I Want a Man" (lyrics by Hammerstein).

In 1932 Youmans went to Hollywood to write an important score for the first of the Fred Astaire-Ginger Rogers song-and-dance screen triumphs, *Flying Down to Rio*. Its most important numbers were the title song, "Carioca," "Music Makes Me," and "Orchids in the Moonlight" (lyrics by Gus Kahn and Edward Eliscu).

Late in 1933 Youmans succumbed to tuberculosis and was confined in a sanitarium in Colorado. The long rest caused him to reevaluate his career as a musician. Fired with a new ambition to write serious music— a symphony, perhaps an opera—he began to study music when he left the sanitarium for a rest period in New Orleans, and started to sketch some ideas for a major musical composition.

He never realized these hopes. Late in 1943 he felt well enough to return to the theatre. He envisioned a new kind of production that would feature classic and modern ballet, serious music, elaborate costuming and stagecraft, and the use of puppets. When Doris Duke stood ready to finance this venture, he set out to make his production one of the most lavish and artistically ambitious yet seen on the popular Broadway stage. Called *The Vincent Youmans Ballet Revue*, it opened in Baltimore on January 27, 1944, then went on to Boston for a short run. In Boston it suddenly collapsed, and never reached Broadway.

Again Youmans' health began to deteriorate. In 1945 he entered Doctors Hospital in New York, and a year later he was back in a Colorado sanitarium. He died there on April 5, 1946. His body was brought back to New York. At his funeral services, held at St. Thomas' Episcopal Church, the organist played "Through the Years" in his memory.

ABOUT:
Gershwin, Ira. Lyrics on Several Occasions; Paris, Leonard Allen. Men and Melodies.
Musical America, April 25, 1946; Variety, July 31, 1940; Variety, January 6, 1960.

Victor Young *1900-1956*

VICTOR YOUNG, the son of an opera singer, was born in Chicago, Illinois, on August 8, 1900. When he was ten he was taken to Warsaw, Poland, to live with his grandparents. There he attended the Warsaw Conservatory, studying violin with Isidor Lotto, and received the Diploma of Merit. After additional violin study with private teachers, he made his concert debut with the Warsaw Philharmonic. Next he toured Europe, appearing in recitals and as guest performer with major orchestras.

At the outbreak of World War I he returned to Chicago, where he made a successful American concert debut. For a while he lived in Los Angeles, working as concertmaster of a motion picture theatre. Then he moved back to Chicago and was concertmaster of the Central Park Theatre; a violinist and arranger with Ted Fiorito's orchestra; and a supervisor of vaudeville productions. In the late 1920's he began a long and active career in radio, and in 1931 went to New York to expand his activities in this field. He had already begun to write songs. "Sweet Sue" in 1928 (lyrics by Will Harris) and "Can't You Understand?" in 1929 (lyrics by Jack Osterman) were moderately successful. In 1933 one of his songs, "Sweet Madness" (lyrics by Ned Washington), was heard in the film *Murder at the Vanities*.

In 1935 he returned to Los Angeles, where he remained for the rest of his life. He formed his own orchestra, which played at Grauman's Theatre, gave radio performances, and accompanied recording stars. Before long, Young became associated with the motion picture industry. In 1935, with Joe Young, he wrote "A Hundred Years from Today" (lyrics by Washington) for *Straight Is the Way*. He scored the music for over three hundred motion pictures; the most significant were *For Whom the Bell Tolls, The Big Clock, Golden Earrings, Love Letters, Samson and Delilah,* and *The Greatest Show on Earth.*

Some outstanding songs by Young were based on the scores or background music that he wrote for films. The best were "I Live Again Because I'm in Love Again" from *All Women Have Secrets;* "Born to Love" *(I Wanted Wings);* "Stella by Starlight" *(The Uninvited);* "My Foolish Heart" (title song); "Loveliness" *(Lucky Stiff);* "The Heavy Bomber Song" *(The Wild Blue Yonder);* and the title number and "Be a Jumping Jack" from *The Greatest Show on Earth.* These were written to lyrics by Ned Washington. He also wrote, to lyrics by Frank Loesser, "Does the Moon Shine Through the Tall Trees?" from *Northwest Mounted Police;* to lyrics by Edward Heyman, the title number from *The Searching Wind* and "You've Changed" from *The Fabulous Senorita;* and, to lyrics by Jay Livingston and Ray Evans, the title numbers from *Golden Earrings* and *Samson and Delilah.*

The last score by Young was for the Michael Todd production *Around the World in Eighty Days,* whose title song (lyrics by Washington) became one of the leading hit songs of 1956.

Victor Young died of a heart attack in Palm Springs, California, on November 10, 1956. Young had been working on a score for a musical comedy based on the life of Mark Twain. He completed only half of the score, and Ferde Grofé was called in to take up where Young had left off.

A CHRONOLOGICAL LIST OF
POPULAR AMERICAN COMPOSERS

William Billings   1746-1800
John Hill Hewitt   1801-1890
Henry Russell   1812-1900
Dan Emmett   1815-1904
George Frederick Root   1820-1895
Stephen Foster   1826-1864
Septimus Winner   1827-1902
Charles A. White   1830-1892
Henry Clay Work   1832-1884
H. P. Danks   1834-1903
Will S. Hays   1837-1907
David Braham   1838-1905
Theodore Metz   1848-1936
Percy Gaunt   1852-1896
John Stromberg   1853-1902
James A. Bland   1854-1911
John Philip Sousa   1854-1932
William J. Scanlan   1856-1898
Paul Dresser   1857-1906
Gustave A. Kerker   1857-1923
Chauncey Olcott   1858-1932
Ludwig Englander   1859-1914
Reginald De Koven   1859-1920
Victor Herbert   1859-1924
Ivan Caryll   1861-1921
James Thornton   1861-1938
Robert A. King   1862-1932
Carrie Jacobs Bond   1862-1946
Gustav Luders   1865-1913
Charles K. Harris   1867-1930
Joseph E. Howard   1867-1961
Scott Joplin   1868-1919
Kerry Mills   1869-1948
Joseph W. Stern   1870-1934
A. Baldwin Sloane   1872-1926
Ben Harney   1872-1938
Harry Von Tilzer   1872-1946
Theodore F. Morse   1873-1924
W. C. Handy   1873-1958
Oley Speaks   1874-1948
Fred Fisher   1875-1942
Manuel Klein   1876-1919
Karl Hośchna   1877-1911
Ernest R. Ball   1878-1927
George M. Cohan   1878-1942
Edwin Franko Goldman   1878-1956
Jean Schwartz   1878-1956

Albert Von Tilzer   1878-1956
Gus Edwards   1879-1945
Chris Smith   1879-1949
Raymond Hubbell   1879-1954
Rudolf Friml   1879-
Lewis F. Muir dates unknown; flourished
    1904-1912
Ted Snyder   1881-1965
Egbert Van Alstyne   1882-1951
Victor Jacobi   1883-1921
Dave Stamper   1883-1963
George W. Meyer   1884-1959
Jerome Kern   1885-1945
Jimmy Monaco   1885-1945
Shelton Brooks   1886-
Louis Hirsch   1887-1924
Sigmund Romberg   1887-1951
Percy Wenrich   1887-1952
Anatole Friedland   1888-1938
Harry Archer   1888-1960
Irving Berlin   1888-
Max Steiner   1888-
Felix Arndt   1889-1918
Victor Schertzinger   1890-1941
Con Conrad   1891-1938
Richard A. Whiting   1891-1938
Fred Ahlert   1892-1953
Harry Carroll   1892-1962
Ferde Grofé   1892-
David W. Guion   1892-
Walter Donaldson   1893-1947
Milton Ager   1893-
Cole Porter   1893-1964
Harry Warren   1893-
Isham Jones   1894-1956
Joseph Meyer   1894-
Jimmy McHugh   1895-
Harry Ruby   1895-
Harry Tierney   1895-1965
Nacio Herb Brown   1896-1964
Jay Gorney   1896-
Ray Henderson   1896-
Jacques Wolfe   1896-
Harry M. Woods   1896-
J. Fred Coots   1897-
George Gershwin   1898-1937
Vincent Youmans   1898-1946
Billy Hill   1899-1940

Hoagy Carmichael   1899-
Duke Ellington   1899-
Dimitri Tiomkin   1899-
Kurt Weill   1900-1950
Peter De Rose   1900-1953
Victor Young   1900-1956
Arthur Schwartz   1900-
Ralph Rainger   1901-1942
Alfred Newman   1901-
Louis Alter   1902-
Sammy Fain   1902-
Richard Rodgers   1902-
Meredith Willson   1902-
Vernon Duke   1903-
Fats Waller   1904-1943
Frederick Loewe   1904-
Harry Revel   1905-1958
Harold Arlen   1905-

Jule Styne   1905-
Leroy Anderson   1908-
Johnny Green   1908-
Harold Rome   1908-
Raymond Scott   1909-
Frank Loesser   1910-
David Rose   1910-
Burton Lane   1912-
Morton Gould   1913-
Jimmy Van Heusen   1913-
Hugh Martin   1914-
Jay Livingston   1915-
Leonard Bernstein   1918-
Albert Hague   1920-
Richard Adler   1921-
Bob Merrill   1921-
Jerry Bock   1928-
André Previn   1929-

INDEX OF SONGS AND OTHER COMPOSITIONS

Only songs and other compositions mentioned in the text are included in the index. In the case of works written by more than one composer, only those composers are noted who are subjects of biographies in this book.

Titles of songs are enclosed in quotation marks. Titles of all other works are in italics.